ANGLICAN
ESSENTIALS

ANGLICAN ESSENTIALS

RECLAIMING FAITH
WITHIN THE
ANGLICAN CHURCH OF CANADA

George Egerton, editor

Anglican Book Centre
Toronto, Canada

1995
Anglican Book Centre
600 Jarvis Street
Toronto, Ontario
Canada M4Y 2J6

The publication of this book has been assisted by a grant from the Anglican Foundation.

Canadian Cataloguing in Publication Data

Main entry under title:

Anglican essentials : reclaiming faith within the Anglican Church of Canada

Proceedings of Essentials 94, a conference hld in Montreal, Quebec, June 16–21, 1994.
ISBN 1-55126-095-6

1. Anglican Church of Canada – Congresses.
2. Church renewal – Anglican Church of Canada – Congresses.
I. Egerton, George W., 1942–   .

BX5614.A54 1995   283'.71   C95-930241-7

CONTENTS

SECTION IV: OUTREACH

SECTION V: ADVANCE

Dedicated to the life and ministry of

Bishop Desmond Hunt

(1918-1993)

At least to his friends, Des was quite frank about the secret of his success—his wife, Naomi. Early in his ministry he lost to polio his ordained twin brother, the Rev. Maunsel Hunt, who died as a young man while Rector of Lakefield, Ontario. His brother Dr. Leslie Hunt was the distinguished principal of Wycliffe College, and his brother Aubrey was an ordained Baptist minister with a reputation for keeping his Anglican brothers honest! The family was brought up in the Church of the Messiah on Avenue Road in Toronto. Desmond was serving as Rector there in 1980 when he was elected as a suffragan bishop of Toronto. Brought up under the influential ministry of Ramsey Armitage, that parish, and the Hunt family, have made a tremendous contribution to the Canadian church.

Desmond was a very popular speaker and preacher, who won enormous respect for Anglicanism beyond its denominational boundaries. He spearheaded evangelism in the Anglican Church with both his organizational skills and his own gifts as an evangelist. He was contagiously enthusiastic about the faith and had what seemed an inexhaustible supply of jokes and anecdotes that allowed people to relax while hearing the gospel.

In the non-Anglican Christian community, he was an unapologetic champion of our Anglican heritage; in the Anglican community he refused to let Anglicans take themselves too seriously.

He was a very strategic thinker with loving and natural leadership, always knowing whom to suggest for every job that needed to be done. A great preacher and a very sensitive pastor, he was overseeing the development and articulation of evangelical teaching, biblical ministry, and Christian essentials long before he was elected bishop in 1980. Although he died in July 1993, by his life and ministry he was one of the architects of the Essentials 94 conference.

SPEAKING THE TRUTH IN LOVE

THE MOST REV. MICHAEL G. PEERS,
PRIMATE OF ALL CANADA

This is only the second time I have been asked to write a preface for a Canadian publication, and both have been in many places highly critical of the church in which I live and work. In the first case, the criticism was directed at the House of Bishops, a body of which I am the senior active member and president. In this case, criticism is directed at the Anglican Church of Canada more generally, but the same principle applies.

Why, the reader might ask, does the Primate get into these situations?

To answer that question I want to refer to words from the Epistle to the Ephesians, which the Archbishop of Canterbury quoted in his exposition of that text at the Essentials 94 conference. Indeed, they are the only words he quoted twice. In Ephesians 4:15, we read the great phrase "speaking the truth in love." Those words have always been very important to me and especially when I reflect on what is essential in the life of the church and of her members.

Sometimes people use those words as if "in love" were an adverbial modifier describing the way we should speak, a kind of theological version of the words of the song, "putting it my way, but nicely." But years ago one of the great teachers of the Canadian church, Bishop William Coleman, taught me that the words "in love" belong with "truth," not with "speaking." The truth-in-love is one concept, a whole entity, and it is what we are called to speak. If either part is weak, then the whole is weak. Loving words that are not true are not loving. True words spoken unlovingly are not true. Proclaiming the gospel must be "speaking the truth-in-love."

Like Jacob at Peniel, and like many of the authors included in this volume, I wrestle with issues of knowing the true purposes of God in our time, and I believe that I perceive those purposes when I hear that authentic ring of "truth-in-love."

And it is because I hear a love for the church, even in critical words about her, that I can accept and encourage, even if not always agree with, criticisms of her. The most critical of writers are so because they love the church and would wish her "without spot or wrinkle or any such thing." Even the voice that, at worship in the Essentials 94 conference, compared our church to a prostitute must presumably have done so out of some concern and affection.

When I profess our faith, and my faith, in the "one holy, catholic and apostolic church," I speak the truth, the truth-in-love, and so do the writers of these papers. However frustrated I may become on occasion, I believe in the church and I love the church, our church. I even do what some others seem to find harder, I even like the church.

And so for the good of our beloved church, this mysterious body which is, in the words of a previous Archbishop of Canterbury, "in for the long haul," I commend this work and express my gratitude to God for it.

HEARING THE TRUTH IN CHRIST

GEORGE EGERTON

The essays in this volume represent the efforts of Anglicans drawn from all parts of Canada who have thought deeply about the church they love and who have cooperated in planning and participating in Essentials 94, a conference held in Montreal, June 16–21, 1994, to celebrate our Christian faith and discern God's will for our church amidst the challenges and opportunities of our times. Some seven hundred registrants attended the conference, listening to a series of speakers present the central themes of previously circulated papers, and communicating their responses and advice in small-group discussions that followed the addresses. The conference was also privileged to hear a powerful and prophetic address by the Most Reverend George Carey, Archbishop of Canterbury, which forms a fitting epilogue to this volume.

Essentials 94 brought together several Anglican groups that, on first glance, seem an unlikely partnership. The principal cooperating bodies were the Prayer Book Society of Canada, devoted to the liturgy of the Book of Common Prayer and a catholic spirituality; Anglican Renewal Ministries, known for emphasis on charismatic spirituality; and Barnabas Anglican Ministries, marked by a commitment to evangelism and a reformational spirituality. The conjunction of catholics, charismatics, and evangelicals marks a new and historic moment in the history of Canadian Anglicanism. This conjunction also embodies a timely spiritual and theological synergy, where a joy in recognizing our unity in essentials far transcends distinctives that have proven divisive in the past. Indeed, recent years have witnessed growing cooperation between members of the Essentials partnership and significant overlap in both leadership and constituencies. Several regional coalitions have been formed (they preceded and sustained the collaboration of 1994), and a national Essentials committee will continue our cooperation in shared purposes.

Those who have come together in this venture share a common concern over the crisis facing our church—a crisis where the statistics of membership, participation, and finances but signify a deeper malaise of faith, mission, and morale. The easy temptation is to indict the leadership, programmes, and policies that have attended the coming of this crisis. This has not been the animus of those who have cooperated in Essentials 94 and in the production of this volume. We are cognizant of the tremendously difficult challenges that all the Canadian churches have faced in responding to the cultural shiftings of the last decades, which have seen the birthing of a post-Christian, postmodern Canada. We know also that we have all failed at times in our efforts to discern and fulfil Christ's mandate to his church. It is our prayer and hope to speak positively and prophetically and to shun hurtful criticism.

In wishing to speak as faithful Anglicans, honouring the best in the tradition and wisdom of our communion, we sense equally that our voice has not been adequately articulated, nor heard, in the counsels of our church. The themes addressed in this volume's essays, and delineated in the appended Montreal Declaration of Anglican Essentials, mark an overdue step in reclaiming a rightful voice for traditional, orthodox Anglicanism in the Canadian church. They represent, in part, an appeal to remember our theological heritage and honour those who have shaped our spiritual foundations. Without conscious effort to keep this heritage alive, we will continue to lose identity and unity in face of the ever-shifting agenda and lobbies of cultural "progress."

At the same time, we have no desire to retreat to a past golden age of Anglican myth. The themes presented in this volume endeavour to bring the wisdom of biblical Christianity, as received in Anglican tradition, to enlighten our present path, to guide our way into a new century and millennium, and to lead us on our journey to the Heavenly City. It is our hope that the wisdom here offered will prove both truthful and enduring—not because of any superior insight the authors would claim, but because we seek to discern principles and precepts that have their origins in God's revealed truth and in his incarnate Word. If there is one "essential" that unites the diverse contributors to this volume, it is the affirmation that the church is to be subject to the Lordship of Christ; the church is not itself the arbiter of good and evil and truth. From this foundation it follows that we will seek to discern God's will in light of his covenants and commandments, the life and teachings of Christ, and the whole of the scriptural record communicated faithfully to us. This is a recipe neither for dogmatism nor triumphalism; it is a call, rather, to humility and obedience before a transcendent God of justice and love. It is a call, also, to use our best learning and insight, nurtured by the Spirit of truth, and mindful of a faithful tradition, to address the new challenges and dilemmas that confront us in our place and time.

The essays are written by authors who have specialized competence to address their subjects; their intended readership, however, is not primarily other specialists but rather a popular lay and clerical readership, within the Anglican communion and beyond. Indeed, most of the subjects here addressed span the principal Christian denominations, as the theological divisions between the orthodox and the progressives within denominations now hold more significance than the classic distinctives that originally generated and demarcated the denominations.

The essayists address a wide span of difficult subjects. Whatever their strengths and failings, they are not lacking in courage as they tackle contemporary issues in Christology, sexuality, gender, spirituality, liturgy, ministry, missiology, ecclesiology, and personal and social ethics. It is perhaps paradoxical that many of the orthodox and traditional Anglican themes here presented by the authors sound radical and controversial in the contemporary postmodern context of pluralism.

Indeed, the terms "postmodern" and "pluralism" provide concepts that will increasingly engage theologians and church people deeply, as Western cultures leave the so-called "modern" age behind. Much attention has recently been focused on various postmodern thinkers who, it is claimed, have "deconstructed" the legacy of Enlightenment rationalism and the certainties of scientific methodology, arguing that these reflect but socially constructed forms of understanding, with no convincing claim to privilege over other forms and other voices. While Christians might be tempted to applaud the humbling of dogmatic liberalism—the dominant ideological paradigm of modernity—there is little we will find for comfort in the confused moral compass of postmodernism, and there is even much we might wish to reaffirm in the central themes of liberal tradition, which Christianity itself did much to nurture.

Whether the churches will find the pluralism of postmodern cultures hospitable or hostile to Christian faith is a question addressed in several of the essays—not, as the reader will see, with total agreement. In any event, the churches will likely have little control over the cultural matrix in which they will exist in the foreseeable future; they can and must, however, guard the authenticity of their own faith and witness. And it is to this vital responsibility that the following essays offer their contributions as they seek to voice the gospel of Christ and its good news for all peoples; pre-modern, modern, or postmodern, we are all equidistant from eternity and in need of God's saving love.

Both the Archbishop of Canterbury and the Canadian Primate offer wise words on the call by the author of Ephesians to "speak the truth in love." This Epistle spoke to a church "tossed to and fro and blown about by every wind of doctrine," and admonished Christians not to live like the Gentiles, "darkened in their understanding, alienated from the life of God because of their ignorance and hardness of heart ... greedy to practice every kind of impurity." Rather, the church was reminded that it had heard about Christ, and been taught in Christ, "as truth is in Jesus." Let us equally open our hearts and minds to hearing the truth in Christ, and "speak the truth to our neighbors, for we are members of one another" (4:14-25).

Another wise mentor, Richard Baxter (1615-1691), provided a precept that has been in the minds of many of our authors and stands as good counsel for those who would seek to discern "essentials":

> In essentials, unity
> In non-essentials, liberty
> In all things, charity.[1]

As we strive to reclaim faith and renew hope, all will be futile if we forget that love is the cardinal virtue in "living up to our calling."

Finally, it is a pleasure to express gratitude to the Anglican Foundation for a generous grant that has aided publication of this volume, and to members of the editorial committee who have assisted and guided the editorial process: George Cummings, Don Erickson, Ron Dart, Donald Lewis, Jim Packer, Archie and Barbara Pell, and Harry Robinson. Manya Egerton served as a shrewd reader and editorial assistant, while Ruth Samarin advised on the design of the cover.

ENDNOTES

1. From the Latin: *In necessariis unitas, in non-necessariis libertas, in utrisque caritas.* Baxter borrowed this precept from the Lutheran, Rupertus Meldinius. N. H. Keeble and Geoffrey F. Nuttall, eds., *Calendar of the Correspondence of Richard Baxter, Volume I, 1638–1660* (Oxford: Clarendon Press, 1991), p. 226. Both Baxter and Meldinius would have been familiar with St. Augustine's *In veritate, unitas; In dubiis, libertas; In omnibus, caritas (De Civitate Dei,* Book 15, chapter 15).

RECONNAISSANCE

1

CANADIAN ANGLICANISM AT THE END OF THE TWENTIETH CENTURY
CRISIS AND PROSPECTS

GEORGE EGERTON

The decline in service attendance and group membership that began in Canada around 1950 for Protestants and 1965 for Roman Catholics is continuing in the 1990s. Exceptions to the pattern are minor — few groups are being spared. What's more, the situation is not being turned around by baby boomers, new Canadians, or efforts to reach the unchurched. Beyond numerical involvement, relatively few Canadians give evidence of being profoundly influenced by any organized faith. But it's not just that growing numbers of people are ignoring religious groups and their messages. The proportion who express confidence in religious leaders has dropped markedly in the past decade. Of considerable importance, what to date has been a serious numerical decline problem will expand into nothing less than a full-scale crisis for most religious groups within the next 25 years. The United and Anglican Churches will be among those that may well be almost decimated.

—Reginald W. Bibby, *Unknown Gods: the Ongoing Story of Religion in Canada,* 1993, p. 1.

I think Bibby is being pejorative because he's trying to shock people.

—Rev. Helen Patterson, Communications Committee Chair, Diocese of New Westminster. *Vancouver Sun,* September 10, 1993. p, B 3

INTRODUCTION: THE REALITY OF CRISIS

For over three decades Christian churches have been advised by an array of theologians, sociologists, demographers, statisticians, pollsters, and journalists that they are facing crises of membership, participation, belief, social standing, and cultural relevance. Reginald Bibby's prediction that the United and Anglican Churches in Canada "may well be almost decimated" within twenty-five years is the most recent, and comprehensive, sociological study of ecclesiastical crisis and impending demise.

In contrast to this we hear from other authorities that levels of religious affiliation, belief, and behaviour have cyclical patterns and that any recent declines will likely be reversed in the longer-term operation of the cycle. National and diocesan officials have assured us, at least until recently, that the declines have levelled off, and that indices of commitment suggest hope, if only for denominational survival. Some analysts have argued that "conservative" churches have been expanding amidst the general religious decline. As well, "church growth" experts tell us religious organizations that embrace appropriate programs and techniques can flourish, even in hard times. And there are the intermittent findings of popular magazines and writers whose studies of Canadian values and behaviour report high levels of interest and engagement in widely varying forms of "spirituality." *Maclean's* (April 12, 1993) can assure us that "God is alive" and "Canada is a nation of believers."

What are we to make of this? Are the churches — and specifically the Anglican Church of Canada — facing radical crisis? If so, can we understand the nature of the crisis and the causes which have generated it? Can we discern the likely consequences of continuing crisis? What would it mean for Canadian society were its "mainline" or "oldline" churches to experience Bibby's predicted decimation and demise; would anybody notice in twenty-five years? Can we do anything effective to address the crisis; or are the causes and conditions largely beyond our control? What should those who identify themselves as "orthodox," "evangelical," "conservative," or "traditional" be thinking and doing if they love their church and wish to be faithful to the Christian gospel?

In attempting to address the crises and prospects of our church, let us confess our share in the bewilderment and confusion that is wide spread in our church. Who can pretend to speak with confidence about the vast shiftings of religion in modern, and now "postmodern," cultures, or specifically about the churches in contemporary Canada, when so little of their recent history has received scholarly attention? At the same time, the scope of the present crisis calls for faithful analysis and discourse, not least because no one else is going to do it for us, and the nostrums that have guided our church in its recent past have proven to be both spiritually impoverishing and sociologically ineffective. The analysis which follows is written from the personal perspective of: an evangelical Christian, of (I hope) generous but intentional orthodoxy; an Anglican, by choice, who loves his church, its traditions, beauty, wisdom, diversity, and catholicity; a historian who values the perspective that historical analysis can contribute to the understanding of contemporary challenges; a participant/observer over many years at most levels of our denomination, in parish and diocesan service and with General Synod and its national committees.

Does the Anglican Church of Canada (ACC) face a crisis of the scale predicted by Bibby? Maybe not "decimation"; but it strikes me as plausible that, as sociological and demographic evidence suggests, there will be a severe decline in membership, participation, and resources when the aging generation now attending church passes on, and a generation with much lower participation and commitment ratings takes its place. Without a major change in trends from 1990 to 2015, Bibby's twenty-five-year projections of Anglican membership (720,000 down to 500,000), and weekly attendance (220,000 down to 100,000), seem well-founded (Bibby, table 4.4, p. 104). As this happens, the ACC as a denomination and an institution will have to manage radical retrenchment of budget, staff, programmes, mission, facilities, and services at every level. Indeed, we already see the painful realities of financial stress and necessary retrenchment in several dioceses, and in national financial planning, staffing, and programming. It is possible, God forbid, that after decades of understandable reluctance to acknowledge and address demographic decline, the ACC might experience institutional implosion in face of unmanageable imperatives of retrenchment. Another form of radical crisis could well be generated by theological conflict and schism over controversial issues. The cacophony of conflicting opinions expressed regularly in the *Anglican Journal* on core elements of faith and practice — most dramatically, but by no means exclusively, on issues of human sexuality — signifies divisions and confusion of an unprecedented scale in our church and threatens discord and schism. The combination of demographic decline, financial retrenchment, and theological discord seems likely to confront the ACC with severe challenges to its episcopal unity and synodical procedures.

THE ENDING OF CHRISTENDOM: THE CRISIS OF THE CHURCHES

The crisis facing the ACC is at once part of a general crisis facing traditional religion in modernized cultures, a crisis with multiform causes and aspects, and a crisis with elements specific to Canadian religion and Anglicanism. What follows is an attempt to survey briefly the salient themes of this crisis.

Since the pioneering work of Max Weber and Emile Durkheim, sociologists have attempted to describe and explain the decline of traditional religion attending the processes of industrialization and cultural modernization. Although there is much debate and controversy associated with the so-called "secularization thesis," its central themes, as presented by such contemporary sociologists as Brian Wilson in Britain, Peter Berger in America, and Reg Bibby in Canada, offer helpful understanding of the present religious malaise. The theory argues that the process of industrialization in societies is attended by radical change and decline in traditional religious values, behaviour, and institutions. The regularities and rationalization demanded by urban industrial life and its technologies are seen as destructive of the mystical, transcendent, supernatural elements of pre-modern consciousness, replacing them with the rationalist, "this-worldly," humanist, and materialist consciousness of the "industrial worldview." Such secularization of consciousness dovetailed with the spread of the ideas of the scientific revolution and the Enlightenment, fostering the secular ideologies of liberalism and, later, socialism. The secularization of consciousness and ideology, in turn, was accompanied by a contraction of the social functions of traditional religious institutions, as churches lost territory to secular institutions (for example, in education and health care), becoming specialized and marginalized in an increasingly instrumental society. Religion is removed from the public domain; no longer does it serve to integrate society around a core of shared and sustained values, nor does religion continue to serve as a principal source of legitimation for political institutions. Legitimation and integration in pluralist societies are sought elsewhere — mainly in ideology and nationalism.

In modern, secular, pluralist societies, then, churches play a marginal and diminishing role, as religion is largely privatized within vestigial subcultures of the faithful. In public, religion finds itself disestablished, peripheralized, and forced to compete for the attention of a largely indifferent population whose interests seem caught by the seductions, entertainments, and values of more powerful rivals in pluralist cultures of consumption. Specialized and privatized, religion loses out on the personal level as well, as indices of knowledge, belief, experience, and practice related to faith show marked decline over time, while churches and believers tend to construct and consume their faith in eclectic and fragmented fashion.

Although British North America turned away from the Church of England's tradition of establishment, for nearly the first hundred years of the Canadian Confederation an informal religious establishment prevailed, with the BNA giving constitutional protection to certain religious rights in provincial education, while Catholic and Protestant cultural hegemonies maintained themselves in the respective French- and English-speaking provinces. Religion thrived as the nineteenth century gave way to the twentieth. The churches followed the waves of settlers and the growth of towns and cities across the Canadian West, and missionary activity was directed to conversion of aboriginal peoples. Nationally, the informal Christian establishment served to legitimate government institutions through civic liturgies and ceremonies; religious values informed Canadian jurisprudence; and the churches provided support for the Canadian government and its allies in two world wars. While the operations and dislocations of Canadian capitalism inspired a critical and prophetic response in the form of the Social Gospel movement of the early twentieth century, Canadian Anglicanism remained largely conservative in its politics, and remedial rather than radical in its social mission, reflecting the concentration of Anglicans in the upper regions of Canada's "vertical mosaic."

The post–World War II years represented a seemingly golden era of religious revival for the Canadian churches, as membership figures rose to new heights, the burgeoning new suburbs supported major programmes of church construction, and the post-war baby boom filled out the ranks of Sunday schools. Canadian Christendom remained intact as political elites and the public continued to look to the churches for ultimate values at the levels of personal morality, community standards, and national purpose in an era that had seen the victory over pagan Nazism quickly replaced by the Cold War challenge of atheistic communism. The ACC flourished institutionally in this milieu, as church leadership focused congenially on opportunities for growth, while expanding diocesan and national bureaucracies undertook new administrative and planning functions.

What went largely unrecognized through the 1950s was the demographic reality that, despite the dramatic growth in church membership and attendance, such expansion failed to keep pace with the growth of Canada's post-war population. Indeed, the war effort's attendant acceleration of industrialization, modernization, and urbanization fuelled the social dynamics of secularization in the 1950s. By the mid-1960s, just as the crest of the "boomers" had begun to wane in the Sunday schools, and immigration patterns were eroding the "WASP" hegemony, Canadian Christendom itself was confronted with a dramatic, rapid, and radical process of "disestablishment," in the context of social, cultural, and political secularization.

The history of this fundamental Canadian cultural shifting remains to date largely unexamined with regard to its genesis, development, and consequences. Preoccupied with other interests, historians have largely left this part of contemporary history to the ministrations of sociologists and theologians. Here we can only suggest an outline of salient causes and features of the ending of Canadian Christendom:

- the secularization of consciousness accelerated by industrial modernization;
- the growth of arts and entertainment industries, their use of mass media distribution, especially television, as competitors with religion for popular attention;
- the successes of Keynesian capitalism and the state in fuelling unprecedented economic growth, and in promoting consumerism, materialism, and social welfare;
- the ideological conquests of liberal pluralism in English-speaking Canada, signalled by Trudeau's jurisprudence and the entrenchment of the Charter of Rights and Freedoms in the patriated constitution of 1982;
- the dramatic secularization of Quebec during the "Quiet Revolution" of the 1960s, and the displacement of Catholicism by nationalist ideology.

It is this cultural matrix that has generated crisis for Canadian mainline Protestant and Catholic churches. While sectarian Protestants had never embraced Christendom, the principal churches of Canadian Christendom — Roman Catholic, United, Anglican, and Presbyterian — have been confused, humiliated, and traumatized by their cultural and ideological disestablishment and the experience of social peripheralization. While the displacement of Christendom encompasses a long-term historical phenomenon in Western cultures, the Canadian, and particularly the Quebec, process has been particularly rapid and demoralizing, perhaps in some measure due to the relative innocence and insularity of Canadian churches and theology compared with American, British, and European experience. The retrenchment of Canadian Anglicanism has also been powerfully affected by the post-war decline of British cultural influence and the cultural ascent of America.

AFTER CHRISTENDOM: PATTERNS OF CHURCH RESPONSE

The problematic status of the churches in modern cultures, which formed a major theme in theological studies by the mid-twentieth century, entered popular discourse in the 1960s when such best-sellers as Bishop John Robinson's *Honest* *to God (*1963) and Harvey Cox's *The Secular City* (1965) stirred controversy and interest in radical theology. In Canada, journalist Pierre Berton's best-seller *The Comfortable Pew* (1965) sparked impassioned debate of the teachings and mission of the Protestant churches. Concurrently, Roman Catholicism initiated a comprehensive study and renewal of its theology, liturgy, and mission with the convocation of the Second Vatican Council (1962–65), while, on a much smaller scale, world Anglicanism addressed the "new frontiers" of its mission at the Anglican Congress convened in Toronto, 1963.

Since the controversies of the 1960s, the Canadian churches have been attempting, with varying degrees of intentionality, confusion, resistance, and urgency, to comprehend their shifting status and develop appropriate responses. The history of this complex process — the theological disputes, doctrinal divisions, and political struggles over programmes, budgets, and leadership — awaits the attention of future scholars. Again, we are reliant mainly on sociologists, journalists, and theologians in attempting to discern the theological patterns marking responses to the contemporary crisis of the churches, and the trends of church policies and strategies which reflect and inform these theological patterns.

Sociologists like Peter Berger have identified two principal responses by churches to the challenge of modernity and secularization:

1. a liberal strategy of accepting and legitimating "progressive" values and practices in secular culture, while revising, de-mythologizing, or abandoning traditional doctrines in a search for renewed relevance;

2. a conservative strategy of reaffirming orthodox doctrines and traditional practices, while resisting accommodation of secular values and maintaining an identity and witness distinct from the dominant culture.

This dyad is, admittedly, reductionist of the complexity and variety of possible relationships between "Christ and Culture," but the distinction seems both fundamental and helpful as we search for understanding and direction. Each of these strategies has powerful attractions and liabilities, theological and sociological, as shown in the counsels offered by respective apologists and critics.

The predominant strategy of the "Christendom churches" has been to articulate the moral framework of their respective cultures, aspiring to serve as "the conscience of the nation," while legitimating national institutions and political ideals. So long as the churches' ideals and membership permeated culture and politics, this was a viable strategy — despite some anguish when it came to such hard cases as accommodating national wars and imperialism, or dealing with the economic inequities of capitalism. However, with the present disestablishment and dissolution of Christendom, when neither the churches' membership nor ideals permeate culture or politics, the identity and mission of the Christendom churches become increasingly problematic. The general response of mainline Protestantism in this new cultural matrix, again necessarily in reductionist terms, has been twofold:

1. to present a prophetic, radical theological critique of capitalism's injustices, domestic and international — embracing the Bible's "preferential option for the poor" through redistributive economic action and entitlement for aboriginal peoples, liberation theology's indictment of First World imperialism, and environmentalism's crusade to defend the earth's bio- and eco-systems against the depredations of exploitive development;

2. to modernize religious moral teaching in the personal domain of family, gender, and sexual relations — embracing feminism's critique of patriarchy, and liberal pluralism's jurisprudence of individual rights and freedom of choice in sexual behaviour.

The theologians and apologists of this "progressive" strategy have found a responsive forum for their agenda in leading theological colleges, in national church bureaucracies, and in the various organs of the World Council of Churches. Progressive theologians have buttressed their agenda by reference to biblical imperatives of love, peace, and justice. The injustices, cruelties, and international exploitations of modernized capitalist economies have not been hard to identify and castigate, especially when only a vestigial remnant of corporate leadership has remained active in the churches; support for the environmentalist cause from a stewardship perspective on God's created order counters some opposition from both corporate and labour sectors, but engagement on this issue has become less controversial in light of growing cultural and political support for environmental protection.

Critics of the progressive theological agenda have identified the following problems and lacunae:

- the immanence of theologies which are informed by such secular ideologies as liberalism, marxism, and feminism, and the consequent loss of transcendence;

- the denial of doctrine and loss of religious distinctiveness in issue-directed political engagement;

- the loss of identity and continuity resulting from denial of tradition and commitment to "presentism";

- the neglect of pastoral and priestly religious functions — preaching, liturgy, worship, sacraments, spiritual disciplines, counselling — in favour of political activism;

- the violation of biblical and traditional teaching on family life and sexual morality entailed in accommodating liberal permissiveness on such issues as divorce, abortion, pre- and extra-marital sexual expression, and homosexual behaviour;

- the theological division, confusion, and polarization of church membership in face of rapid, radical change, and the consequent alienation and loss of membership;

- the disinterest in the institutional survival of the church.

In contrast with the liberal Protestant and liberationist Catholic agendas, the conservative and neo-orthodox response to the crisis of the churches in modernity has come from the Papacy, the "non-Christendom" Protestant churches, and the growing evangelical and charismatic movements within the former Christendom churches, along with their burgeoning Third World adherents. Here we can but allude to the salient themes of conservative theological and strategic responses:

- the reassertion of Papal authority for Catholics in the wake of the discourse and pronouncements generated by Vatican II in such encyclicals as *Humanae Vitae* (1968); the defence of traditional Catholicism through such movements and organizations as Opus Dei; the Papal affirmation of the social mission of the church in struggles for economic justice and human rights, while restating traditional doctrine on such issues as the priesthood, divorce, abortion, birth control, sexual morality, gender roles, and homosexual behaviour — encoded now in the new *Catechism of the Catholic Church* (1992, U. S. English translation, 1994) and the Papal encyclical, *Veritatis Splendor* (1993);

- the resurgence of evangelical Protestantism, nationally in interdenominational alliances, and internationally in the World Evangelical Fellowship, with the renewal of theology and mission signified by the International Congress on World Evangelization (Lausanne, 1974), and the publication of the *Lausanne Covenant* (1975) and the *Willowbank Report: Christ and Culture* (1978), which reaffirmed Reformational Protestant themes on the authority of Scripture and traditional teaching on personal morality, while inviting greater cultural and social engagement as part of a renewed international mission of evangelization;

- the development of the charismatic movement beyond classic Pentecostalism, first in American Episcopal and Catholic circles in the 1960s, but spreading powerfully, internationally and denominationally, in its emphasis on spiritual renewal and expression;

- the counter-modernist, ecumenical critique and repudiation of immanentalist theologies and their rationalist, relativist, subjectivist, universalist, and humanist presuppositions, manifested in the Hartford Appeal for Theological Affirmation (1975);

- the generation in the 1970s of a body of "church growth" theory, spreading out from Fuller Theological Seminary to be developed and applied, in the main, by conservative Protestant churches;

- the emergence of a "new religious right" in American politics in the 1970s and 1980s, dedicated to traditional Christian personal and family values and neoconservative economics, and skilful in exploiting the medium of television;

- the renewal of evangelical Anglican theology and mission heralded in Britain by the Keele '67 Congress with its *National Evangelical Anglican Congress*

Statement (1967), and *Guidelines: Anglican Evangelicals Face the Future* (1967), followed by the Nottingham Congress of 1977; in Canada by the Barnabas Anglican Ministries' Declaration, 1990; and in America by the Baltimore Declaration, 1991.

CRISIS AND RESPONSE IN THE ANGLICAN CHURCH OF CANADA

In an address to the 1983 General Synod, as a member of its Long Range Planning Committee, I referred to the ACC's commissioning of Pierre Berton to undertake a critical study of Canadian churches some twenty years earlier, and the resulting publication of *The Comfortable Pew* in 1965. Berton's book had provoked fundamental questioning about the beliefs, purposes, programmes, and traditions of the churches. Espousing many of the themes propounded by the radical popular theologians — especially John Robinson — and prescribing new strategies for churches wishing to regain relevance in modern conditions, Berton's critique was taken deeply to heart by Anglicans across Canada. I suggested to Synod that it would be a fascinating exercise to study the degree to which Berton's recommended agenda had been fulfilled in the changing programmes and policies of the ACC in the following decades. Alas, no one took up my suggestion; but I have little reason eleven years later to revise my 1983 assessment that the dominant drift of Anglican change through recent decades has been in the direction championed by Berton and the "progressive" popular theologians. Placed in the larger context sketched above, the Anglican course has generally entailed a liberal strategy of embracing "progressive" values and practices in secular culture, while revising or abandoning traditional doctrines in a search for renewed relevance.

What have been the more significant themes, events, and changes in Canadian Anglicanism over the last decades? Again, without comprehensive historical treatment of the ACC through this period, we can but outline salient features:

- the stimulus to critical thinking, theological discourse, and planning given by the Anglican World Congress which met in Toronto (1963), and the dramatic self-questioning that followed publication of Berton's *The Comfortable Pew* (1965);

- adoption and implementation of the Price Waterhouse recommendations for restructuring and enhancing the national church bureaucracy in the late 1960s;

- engagement in ecumenical dialogue and negotiation of a basis for union with the United Church of Canada, which failed to achieve Anglican acceptance in 1975;

- increasing theological and political engagement in issues of peace and justice, including relations with native peoples;

- the widely-respected international role of Primate Edward Scott in the 1970s and 1980s within the World Council of Churches, particularly in promoting justice for Third World peoples and dismantling apartheid in South Africa;

- liberalization of Anglican canon law and teaching on divorce and abortion;
- democratization of church polity with enhanced role of laity in synodical government, and retrenchment of Episcopal authority and leadership;
- ordination of women to the priesthood (1977);
- liturgical experimentation, revision, and controversy leading to production of the *Book of Alternative Services* (1985);
- liberalization and radicalization of ecumenical theological curricula with incorporation of liberationist, feminist, and creation theological paradigms, including affirmation of native spirituality and other faiths;
- major decline in Anglican census affiliation, membership, and attendance statistics after mid-1960s, with relative stabilization of attendance by 1980s;
- emergence of orthodox Anglican opposition to liberal theology, heretical teachings, and radical innovation;
- Anglican conservative theological renewal centred in Wycliffe and Regent Colleges;
- resurgence of Anglican evangelicalism, encouraged by the Barnabas Anglican Ministries and its Declaration and Statement of Faith;
- Anglican spiritual and charismatic renewal, supported by Anglican Renewal Ministries;
- defence of classic liturgy and traditional faith, directed by the Prayer Book Society of Canada;
- increasing theological polarization within the Anglican communion;
- coalition-building among orthodox Anglicans, calling for theological and spiritual renewal, culminating in the Essentials 94 convergence of Anglican evangelicals, charismatics, and catholics.

PROSPECTS FOR THE ANGLICAN CHURCH OF CANADA

The theologies and praxis of liberalism and progressives have not brought renewed mission or cultural relevance to Canadian mainline churches. As institutions they at best remain in a survival/maintenance mode and at worst face Bibby's predicted demise. Bibby's studies demonstrate the low levels of Christian faith, knowledge, practice, and participation in Canada; data specific to Anglicanism offer little encouragement. Further accommodations of cultural liberalism, as in the powerful pressures now mobilized to legitimate homosexual behaviour and same-sex unions, will result in deepening theological division, polarization, and probable schism. As with our sister denomination, the United Church, many will leave, or separate to form dissident congregations. The result, God forbid, would leave the ACC mortally wounded and ill-equipped to face a new century.

The more radical theologians, such as Douglas Hall (*The Future of the Church:*

Where Are We Headed?, 1989), are willing to concede the demise of the institutional church, its utter disestablishment, and liberation from dogma — to serve God and humanity, in solidarity and suffering, witnessing to God's inclusive love and universal redemption. The call for religionless Christianity, faith without dogma, and a church without institution, strikes this historian as sociologically naive. Bibby, by contrast, seems equally to strain credibility in the potential he sees in the institutional church to reverse its decline. His prescriptions tell us that those churches that revise their agenda to (1) address Canadians' fascination with mystery and the supernatural, and their continued belief in "the gods," (2) affirm personal meaning and hope, and (3) provide rich social and communal engagement, can flourish in the current cultural matrix — if only they learn from the American churches about packaging, selling, and delivering the product demanded in a de-regulated religious market. Bibby seems to me to underestimate the deep cultural appeal — and now entrenched constitutional status — of liberal pluralism, which functions as a new surrogate religious establishment in Canada, legitimating our governments, informing our jurisprudence, and guiding our schools. Equally, he is perhaps too impressed by the quantity of American religion, as compared with its content and quality. Nevertheless, Bibby has more to teach the churches than does the legacy of Berton and the radical theologians about the potential for religion — even true religion — in contemporary conditions.

CONCLUSION

In conclusion, I would commend two imperatives for Canadian Anglicanism in its present crisis: (1) to be true to the Lord of the church in reaffirming the essentials of a scripturally revealed faith that transcends time and culture and knows its reasons; and (2) to live and present this gospel, charismatically, evangelically, and sacramentally, in a culture which itself seems destined, as with all past cultures, to face crisis and transition.

In the course of some two hundred years liberal capitalism has propelled the dynamic forces of industrialization and created unprecedented wealth for about one third of the world's population; liberal pluralism has concurrently generated equally unprecedented human freedoms and rights, again for a fortunate fraction of the world's peoples. But the greeds of capitalism, including communist state-capitalism, have ravaged and polluted the riches of the created order; and the seductive freedoms of liberal individualism have been exploited to pollute the moral order. To use the Paradise analogue, we have devoured the forbidden fruit of the knowledge of good and evil; we have encoded the knowledge of good and evil and the right to choose in our constitutions. But in defying God in the quest for moral autonomy, we find ourselves alienated from the creator, at enmity with nature and each other, in gender wars, and driven from the garden with its Tree of Life, cursed with the pain of reproduction and careers.

Anglicans together with other Christians have come to understand and critique the evils of our economic order, locally and globally, and to work for peace, justice, and stewardship of the environment. In this we owe much to the leadership of liberals, Christian activists, and progressive theologians grounded in the biblical vision of God's kingdom. The liberal/progressive critique, however, has often been selective, ignoring the pollutions of our moral order. In focusing externally on social injustices, liberal/progressives tend to forget or deny the classic Christian teaching that what defiles a person is what comes out of the unredeemed human heart — "evil intentions, murder, adultery, fornication, theft, false witness, slander" (Matt. 15:10-20). The scale of violence, crime, sexual abuse and exploitation, family breakdown, and maltreatment of children and aged reported daily in our media testifies to the enduring truth of Christ's reading of the human heart and our need to transcend the illusions of liberalism in this area.

If the churches of Christendom have been disestablished and humiliated, the proud towers of capitalism and liberalism, like communism, seem similarly vulnerable in face of the increasing human impoverishment and social pathologies generated in secular liberal cultures of consumption. So too, the ideological hegemony of liberalism in modernized capitalist states finds itself increasingly vulnerable in face of both the "deconstructions" of postmodern theorists, and the personal alienations and social distress of secular societies. The light of the gospel compels us to see our nakedness and alienation behind the fig leaves of culture and ideology; the cross of Christ and his resurrection offer the fruit of the Tree of Life to all who believe.

Canadian Anglicanism has a radical message of love, redemption, and hope for Canadians, their families, and their communities. Reaffirmation of Anglican essentials, in word and deed, not only signifies faithfulness to the Lord of the church, it also holds the greatest promise of regaining cultural relevance in a "postmodern" world — where the intellectual certainties of secular rationalism and the cultural illusions of liberal pluralism dissolve in face of the enduring anguish and needs of the human heart.

SUGGESTED READING

Peter Berger, *Against the World For the World: The Hartford Appeal and the Future of American Religion* (New York: Seabury Press, 1976).

Peter Berger, *The Heretical Imperative* (Garden City, N. Y.: Anchor/Doubleday, 1980).

Pierre Berton, *The Comfortable Pew* (Toronto: McClelland and Stewart, 1965).

Reginald W. Bibby, *Fragmented Gods* (Toronto: Irwin, 1987).

———, *Unknown Gods* (Toronto: Stoddart, 1993).

Philip Carrington, *The Anglican Church in Canada* (Toronto: Collins, 1963).

Philip Crowe, ed., *Keele '67: The National Evangelical Anglican Congress Statement* (London: Falcon Books, 1967).

David Edwards, with John Stott, *Essentials: A Liberal-Evangelical Dialogue* (London: Hodder & Stoughton, 1988).

John Webster Grant, *The Church in the Canadian Era* (Burlington, Ont.: G. R. Welch, 1988).

Douglas Hall, *The Future of the Church: Where Are We Headed?* (Toronto: United Church Publishing House, 1989).

William Kilbourne, ed., *The Restless Church: A Response to the Comfortable Pew* (Toronto: McClelland and Stewart, 1966).

Mark Noll, *A History of Christianity in the United States and Canada* (Grand Rapids, Mich.: Eerdmans, 1992).

E. Radner and G. Sumner, eds., *Reclaiming Faith: Essays on Orthodoxy in the Episcopal Church and the Baltimore Declaration* (Grand Rapids, Mich.: Eerdmans, 1993).

George Rawlyk, ed., *The Canadian Protestant Experience* (Burlington, Ont.: Welch, 1990).

Robert VanderVennen, ed., *Church and Canadian Culture* (Lanham, Md.: University Press of America, 1991).

SINGING THE LORD'S SONG IN POST-CHRISTIAN CANADA
A SERMON[1]

HARRY ROBINSON

In the happy and far off days of the sixties, we sang with great enthusiasm, "This land was made for you and me." To sing such a song now would precipitate another constitutional crisis. The words "our home and native land" are a contradiction of our new reality. The patriotism which once was, in the brave new world of multiculturalism, has been replaced by a sense of alienation. Living in our post-Christian country, Anglicans are made to feel as people without a home. There is a way in which this could be our greatest hope.

The process of alienation among us is never-ending. We have experienced a growing sense of alienation in this country that is hard to understand and even more difficult to control. Constitutionally, we were established as a country with two founding nations. The pattern has been for Anglo-Prostestants to think of themselves as the first nation; and then there is that other nation. This tension has now been heightened by the acknowledgement that there is already a first nation, which leaves Anglo-Prostestants, at best, in a contest for second place. And, given the statistics of post-war immigration, even this struggle has become a non-event. The Anglican Church, which once had the look of an established church, is now just another minority group.

We have found new ways of dividing and alienating one another. The Green movement testifies to the alienation between the people and the land. Our new gender awareness has alienated us from traditional family values. Membership in the church has forced us into the recognition that at best we are "resident aliens." The massive reorganization of the world economy has made us global citizens who belong everywhere and nowhere.

The media daily inform us of bloody, bitter, and continuing struggles in every quarter of the globe, struggles for a defined piece of geography that for particular historic, ethnic, or religious reasons is the homeland of one group of people and not of another. Germaine Greer with trenchant simplicity contends that there is no such "homeland":

> The only unchanging place where we really belong and all will be satisfied is heaven, and heaven cannot be brought about on earth. Failure to recognize the fact that earthly home is a fiction has given us the anguish of Palestine, and the internecine raging of the Balkans. The ideology of home primes

the bombs of the P.P.K. and the I.R.A. The rest of us can face the fact that our earthly journey is away from home. Exile being the human condition. No government subsidy can provide the chariot that will carry us home (*Manchester Guardian*, October 24, 1993).

A pious person might hesitate to say such a thing, but Germaine Greer does not have a reputation for being pious.

For the whole of its history, the church has been in possession of documents which state very clearly that we must never forget that we are aliens. "My father was a wandering Armenian"; or "Here on earth we have no continuing city ... we belong to Him who is outside the gate." It is nevertheless our continuing mandate to seek the welfare of the city, or indeed of the country, even if the city is Babylon, or the king is Nero.

Our absolute priority remains that, while seeking the welfare of the city, we are to seek first God's kingdom and his righteousness. When the church as an institution gets confused and is persuaded to seek first the welfare of the city, with the vague and undefined hope that this may bring in the kingdom, then it is certain that we will still have no continuing city; nor will we have a continuing church.

At this moment in history, the culture we belong to in post-Christian Canada has successfully excluded the church and its book, the Bible, from having any place in the public realm, for reasons both good and bad. Given this situation, it is not as easy to wholeheartedly seek the welfare of the city. So we have to work harder at seeking the welfare of the city, and yet have an unbroken commitment to seek first the kingdom.

You will have observed that when there are railways to build, cotton to pick, boats to row, cattle to herd, and canoes to paddle, the work goes better when we find a song to sing. We are able to take the dull but strenuous and often monotonous tasks that need to be done and find in the menial nature of that labour the glory of eternity. The necessity of an alienated people is to rediscover their song and to sing it with all their hearts.

Please look at the throbbing pain of Psalm 137 to discover, in its articulate and eloquent words, the reason why it becomes next to impossible to sing the Lord's song in a strange land or a lost world. It is Psalm 137 that frames the question,

How can we sing the Lord's song upon an alien soil?

It is a verse that conjures up the wonderful picture of Ruth, who stood in tears amidst the alien corn.

We cannot rip the question from context, for, in fact, we won't properly understand the question unless we see it within that wonderful lament, the anguished cry of the heart which begins,

By the waters of Babylon we sat down and wept at the memory of Zion.

They sat by the waters among the triumphs of the great Assyrian Empire. They were surrounded by splendid gates, richly adorned temples, palaces, towers, magnificent gardens, and a network of canals. It was a square city, encompassed by one hundred kilometers of wall that stood two hundred feet high and was pierced by one hundred gates of brass.

They were in the heart of a world and worldly city, amidst a deservedly arrogant people who were powerful, cruel, and wealthy. They wore pride as a chain about their necks and violence covered them as a garment (Ps. 73). A sleek, fat. and lusty people, sustained by the alcohol of a thousand lush vineyards. What a place to be! What a time to live! What a marvel to behold was this great city of the ancient world!

The magnificent city that had been built by the cruelty of the Assyrians took the heart out of the children of Israel and left them weeping that they were exiles, surrounded by and included among all the trophies of their captors. It was the memory of Zion — David's appointed capital, the hill on which the temple of the Lord had been built, a rock promontory in a sun-drenched and arid land — that brought tears to their eyes.

Harps hanging on the willows...

They had hung their harps on the trees. Music was no longer a part of their lives. This was for them no place for the sounds of music.

The throbbing pain of this Psalm is intensified when, having humiliated them in battle, driven them into exile, and exploited them as trophies of war, their captors demand that they sing the Lord's song. It was not to be a song of thanksgiving, a chorus of praise, or a reminder of the Lord's faithfulness; it was to be sung for no other reason than to entertain their captors. Humiliated, defeated, exiled, and taken in bondage from their promised land, the captives were now to sing of that land, speak of their Lord and be reminded of the history of their people with the very words they had been taught to rehearse as a form of entertainment.

How could we sing the song of the Lord upon alien soil? How could we sing Yahweh's hymns in a pagan country? How shall we sing the Lord's song in a strange land?

Jerusalem! The memory comes like the thrust of a spear into their broken hearts. For it was in that very city of Jerusalem that they had said with shameful complacency "peace! peace!" where there was no peace. Jerusalem evoked remembrance of the temple, the place the Lord our God had chosen as a dwelling for his Name. It was to Jerusalem that they had gone to celebrate. It was in Jerusalem that they had sung. It was there that they had reminded themselves and exhorted one another time and time again, "O come, let us sing unto the Lord, let us heartily rejoice in the Rock of our salvation." They had come and they had rejoiced. But now they were reminded with a searing poignancy of the meaning of the words that they had allowed to fade from their consciousness.

Moses had taught them the song. The song had told of blessing and cursing. The song had spoken of a people forged out of "no people." Their song spoke of a wife prostituting herself to a multitude of lovers. The song told of a slavery that had been broken, a covenant that had been given, a great wilderness trial that had miraculously been survived. The song told of a promised land flowing with milk and honey and it told that the promise had been fulfilled. The song brought back to memory a thousand things they had chosen to forget. The palliative of amnesia was now swept away. They remembered that Moses had taught the song and had said, "These are not just idle words for you — they are your life." It was their *life* to sing the song and to remember the words.

Moses had told them as he had taught them to sing, "If you ever forget the Lord your God, and follow other gods and worship and bow down to them, I testify ... that you will surely be destroyed." The clouds of their chosen amnesia rolled away. The honour of the name of the Lord their God retook possession of them — like lead in their bellies.

If I forget you, make my right hand wither.

The very hand which plucked the music of the song on the harp seemed to have withered. It could no longer play the music. The skill of the musician, in the hand of the musician, could no longer play music that was intended not for the praise of the Lord but for the entertainment of their captors.

May I never speak again.

In the same way the voice of the musician was silenced, the thought of Jerusalem flooded the singer's heart with the remembrance of the Lord's faithfulness and his own faithlessness. The words that had to be sung paralyzed the tongue that had to sing them. Jerusalem was meant to be the pinnacle of the greatest human joy. Guilt, failure, exile and alienation had silenced the song.

It is at this point that the Book of Common Prayer, with becoming modesty, ends Psalm 137, omitting the horror that follows. But the Psalm goes on and the Psalmist continues to explore the heart more deeply.

Remember O Lord:

The difficulty is that, while to remember is to heal, to remember is to wound, to open again the wound that will not heal. So often when you speak to someone about the love and forgiveness and faithfulness of the Lord, the cruel remembrance of things hidden, denied, and repressed comes welling up to the surface. The remembrance of Jerusalem is not just the pinnacle of joy. It is also the searing remembrance of violence, abuse, and victimization. As the captives sat by the waters of Babylon, they recalled scenes of brutal humiliation and betrayal. The Babylonian war machine could be expected, with cruel military efficiency, to move ruthlessly towards unconditional surrender. Unexpectedly, the ruthlessness of the enemy brought with it the howling cries of betrayal by those who were thought to be friends. The Edomites, our own people, followed the

Assyrian soldiers like a pack of jackals. Like looters after a fire or an earthquake, they compounded the horror by screaming for the destruction of the city, urging the soldiers to a holocaust, to reduce the city to rubble.

O daughter of Babylon.

You must know that retribution will most certainly come. You must know that terrible violence will be reciprocated to you in kind. The victims of your cruelty will in time see you as the victims of the same cruelty. You smashed our children's bodies against the rocks. Your children's bodies will be smashed against the rocks. At your hand we are the victims of betrayal, abuse, and violence; we are alienated, estranged, and exiled. We are paralyzed by the recollection of our own unfaithfulness, struck dumb by the remembrance of what we have lost. You, daughter of Babylon, have been the agent of God's judgement on us. The kingdom and the power and the glory does not belong to you. The judgement which you brought on us will be visited on you.

Now, do you still want to sing? I hope with this introduction to the question "How can we sing the Lord's song in a post-Christian Canada?" you will see immediately how wise and bold it is to pray as you begin the service of worship, "O Lord, open Thou our lips," and immediately to make the condition that only then will "our mouths show forth Thy praise." To recognize the depths of the difficulty of doing this we ask God to "make speed to save us," and "make haste to help us."

The church is now alienated from the culture of which it was formerly believed to have been a principal architect. Markus Bockmuehl has written:

> ... public sentiment in a number of countries (Canada included) has begun to favor the opinion that Christianity is now definitely discredited. The Church and especially the Roman Catholic Church is no longer even an equally valid minority, but has come to be portrayed as a sinister and oppressive institution which everyone loves to hate.
>
> Such anti-Christian public sentiment shows no signs of abating, and one wonders if Christians of all stripes have really begun to think seriously about how to assess their new position in society.[2]

In quoting this passage I only want to illustrate the reality of the alienation that exists, to help to understand the difficulty the church has in singing the Lord's song. The church is in the vice. It is commanded to seek the welfare of the culture that has dismissed it, and in so doing it suffers the abuse and victimization of an alienated people. The song it has to sing is only a form of entertainment in the culture in which it is captive.

When I talk about the church, I want it understood that I mean fifty to a hundred people gathering in a building that will hold four times that number. They usually have the wisdom, the commitment, and the loyalty that comes with age. They are sustained by their liturgy. They have learned the patience and the comfort of the Scriptures, the place and importance of the sacraments, and they are generous in giving back what has been given to them. But they also have a deep sense that this won't go on much longer. The foreboding which weighs so heavily upon them can be wonderfully expressed in the question "How long can we sing the Lord's song in a strange land?" A land upon whom God's judgement must fall.

This little congregation of people is not unfamiliar with the assurance, "Fear not little flock for it is the Father's good pleasure to give you the Kingdom." But they are also among those peripheralized by the culture in which they live and whose welfare they seek. They have to live with indictments made against the church, its traditions, its hierarchy, and its proselytizing. They watch the great hammer of enlightenment smash down on the Scriptures, the institution, and the cherished traditions of the church. They suffer the agony of the moral failure and confusion in the church. They watch the great doctrines of the church being trivialized.

That small congregation of the faithful has accepted the indictment made against them by the prevailing culture. They have been willing to learn a new language, to submit to new patterns of leadership, to seek the welfare of the great human enterprise, to accommodate the great triumphs of our culture, and to seek relevance by accommodation to contemporary ideologies. Then this little community, in captivity to the culture to which it belongs, has agreed not to sing the song as a public declaration, the song that emotionally they cannot sing, politically they must not sing, and that, with the passage of time, they have forgotten how to sing; except, of course, to entertain.

The hand that has lost its skill must learn again the music. The voice which was dumb must miraculously break into song.

It is important that the song be sung. Peter Kreeft tells the story of the Chinese emperor who ruled hundreds of cities by music, cities that could be ruled in no other way. The emperor wandered through the streets of the city in disguise, listening to the music, to the songs being sung. If the music was healthy, the emperor knew the souls of the people were healthy. If the music was diseased, the emperor sent his servants to find and cure the source of the disease. It looks like a wonderful model for a bishop's oversight of the parish! The bishop need only go around and listen to the song being sung and then send out his archdeacons and deans to bring healing so that the song may again be sung.

I suppose that all over this country there are such congregations struggling to sing the Lord's song. They are struggling to be relevant to, and in harmony with, the community to which they belong. They wonder among themselves whether they remember the words. They are in conflict about the appropriate tune. How it is to be sung we will have to rediscover. There is no option to the fact that it must be sung — to maintain the welfare of the country and establish the absolute priority of God's kingdom.

The primary reason to sing the song is still the same. The words of the song, as Moses said, must be taken to your heart. "They are not just idle words for you, they are your life, by them you will live...."

St. Paul picks up the word of Moses in Deuteronomy and puts it in a New Testament frame when he writes to the Romans about the song that is to be sung. "The word is very near you; it is in your mouth and in your heart; that is, the word of faith we are proclaiming: that if you confess with your mouth that Jesus is Lord and believe in your heart that God has raised him from the dead, you will be saved." "The Song" brings the option of life to the strange land that knows nothing but death and must face the judgement of God...

The church has a very specialized and essential task — in a thousand languages, through music that belongs to as many different cultures. "The song" is to be sung.

Therefore with angels and archangels, and all the company of heaven, with apostles, prophets and martyrs and saints of every generation, we are to invite the whole of creation and every creature under heaven to raise our voices and praise the Holy Name, singing "Holy, Holy, Holy, the Lord God of Hosts, Heaven and Earth are full of Thy Glory, Glory be to Thee, O Lord Most High."

"This is no idle song, and these are no idle words, they are your life." Our essential business is to sing the song, which will be heard both by the God who inhabits our praises and by the land he has given us to inhabit.

ENDNOTES

1. Delivered at St. George's, Place du Canada, Montreal, June 19, 1994, during the Essentials 94 conference.
2. In *Crux*, Vol. 28, no. 3 (Sept. 1992), p. 2.

CHAPTER

3

AFFIRMING THE TRUTH OF THE GOSPEL
ANGLICANS IN PLURALIST CANADA

DONALD POSTERSKI

INTRODUCTION
On New Year's Day, the blaring religion page headline in the *Toronto Star* declared a "Dire warning for Anglicans." To make the point, the article cited Archbishop Percy O'Driscoll from Western Ontario: "In the next 10-15 years, the largest group of the present Anglican Church will be dead.... At the end of two generations there will not be enough people to say there is an Anglican Church alive in this country."[1] The despondent bishop is so alarmed about the future of the church on earth that he didn't even cushion the prognosis with the hope of heaven.

In his latest assessment of the state of organized religion in Canada, sociologist Reginald Bibby spins a similar scenario. Noting that only 15 percent of Anglican members currently attend regularly and analyzing the generation attendance trends toward the year 2015, Bibby presents data which predict that Anglican attendance levels will tumble to less than one-half the present levels.[2]

Acknowledging that "many churches are having trouble dealing with change," a study in the Diocese of Toronto acknowledged that while the population had almost doubled, the average weekly attendance had declined 45 percent and envelope contributions were down 30 percent. Regrettably, although 34 percent of the churches in the diocese were showing increases and 13 percent were staying equal with 1960 levels, 53 percent of the churches were in a state of decline.[3]

Such findings converge to create "doomsday data" for the future of the Anglican Church. Clearly, clinging to the assumptions of the past will not be an adequate strategy to survive the pressured and pressing realities of the future.

THE PREVAILING CULTURAL CONSENSUS
In the past, the church was so powerful in the culture that the world had to come to grips with the church. Today, the reverse is the case. The culture is so powerful that the church is pressed to come to grips with the world. The balance of power has shifted.

Canadian Christendom Reigns No More
Into the 1960s, at least six out of ten Canadians attended church regularly. On any given Sunday, from Newfoundland to Vancouver Island, the majority of the population followed the gravitational pull of the culture and went to church.

Just three decades ago, there was social stigma projected towards those who stayed at home or scheduled their Sunday mornings with other activities. Today, approximately two   urch attenders, and it is the people who heau out to worsnip wno reei out ot step with the mainstream of society. Not only has the prerogative of cultural Christian privilege been relegated to the past, "sometimes it seems as if all the words and signs that make up our conceptual framework and provide us with our basic system of distinctions are dissolving before our eyes."[4]

For the first time in our country's history, churched Canadians stand alongside other minorities. Instead of having automatic access to political power brokers and being acknowledged as influential citizens, today's church leaders are readily ignored. Because active Christians so recently represented the majority in the culture, the courts and the media are often more concerned about protecting other minority groups and their rights than defending traditional Christian views. God's people are finding that living on the sidelines of society can be frustrating and sometimes intimidating. In times of reflection, God's people will do well to remember that when they held cultural power, they were not always ready to share it with those in the society who represented minority views.

Although there are those who long for the "old days" when reciting the Lord's Prayer was routine in Canada's public schools and the Bible was the sole sacred book in the country's courtrooms, those days are gone forever. As we journey towards the year 2000, "Nostalgia for Christendom is very understandable but it is futile."[5]

Secular Pluralism Rules the Day

When changing beliefs are the issue, societies act much like people. Just as people who alter their beliefs move from believing something to believing something else, cultures that move away from one set of assumptions that define how they believe and behave also embrace something else. In Canada's case, particularly in the past three decades, we have moved from a cultural consensus defined by Christian assumptions to those increasingly defined by secular pluralism.

The process of secularization, with its attendant erosion of significance for traditional religious values, symbols, and institutions, has operated in Canadian society for a very long time. This progressive shift from religious dominance towards secular control has not only demoted the social standing of our churches, it has also pushed God to the edges of people's lives. When translated into a cultural creed, secularism creates a world where God is unnecessary. Accordingly, the majority of Canadians construct their lives without any practical need for God's intervention or assistance. God may exist as a hypothesis for modern Canadians but his active role in the daily events of life is considered superfluous.

There are two qualifiers about secularism Canadian-style that merit clarification. Because our Christian roots are still embedded in present-day culture,

Canadian-style secularism is more a matter of practice than it is an articulated ideology. In other words, Canadians have not consciously voted God out of business by formally altering what they say they believe. Rather, they have practically pushed God to the outskirts of society and the margins of their personal lives by simply ignoring his will and ways.

The second qualifier about Canadian secularism is that it is still socially friendly towards religion. Canadians are not anti-Christian. There is very little religious animosity in the mainstream of our society. Those who contend that there is an anti-Christian conspiracy in the land are either subscribing to their own propaganda or behaving in ways that are culturally offensive. Certainly there are occasions where Christians are subject to reverse discrimination in the present milieu, but the exceptions should not be confused with the prevailing norms.

What is our understanding of pluralism in the current cultural equation? Briefly stated, the cultural code of Canadian pluralism is that many views about what to believe and how to behave are equally *permissible*. In the past, there was a cultural consensus that the tenets of Christianity embodied the one true way to *conceive life*. Even when people did not explicitly believe or obey the Christian way there was an understanding that it was "the right way." In pluralism, instead of one way to believe *and behave*, there are many ways to believe *and behave*. Multi-mindedness is the modern Canadian way. Beyond being a multicultural society, Canada is a multi-moral, multi-faith, multi–family structure, multi–gender role, and multi–sexual orientation culture.

Just as there are qualifiers for Canadian-style secularism, when we think about pluralism it will be crucial to distinguish between "ideological pluralism" and "cultural pluralism." When pluralism is accepted as an ideology, it becomes incompatible with biblical Christianity. As an ideology, pluralism subscribes to relativism. Truth is reduced to personal opinion and instead of everyone's ways of believing simply being "permissible," they become equally "valid." As missiologist Lesslie Newbigin observes: "It has become commonplace to say that we live in a pluralist society — not merely a society which is in fact plural in the variety of cultures, religions and lifestyles which it embraces, but pluralist in the sense that this plurality is celebrated as things to be approved and cherished."[6]

Cultural pluralism, however, stops short of becoming ideological pluralism. As a social structure for cradling diversity, cultural pluralism invites people who believe different things to live alongside each other. While making room for a plurality of cultures, religions, and lifestyles, it also leaves room for people to believe that truth exists as an external and knowable reality. For God's people, then, ideological pluralism is an enemy of the faith but because cultural pluralism makes room for a diversity of beliefs and behaviours in a society, it is a friend of the faith.

For those who are alarmed or subject to despair, it will be helpful to acknowledge that the current content of Canadian culture is increasingly like the circumstances God's people experienced in New Testament times. In those times the church flourished.

Christian Nostalgia Still Arouses Desires

The 1991 Statistics Canada portrayal of the present religious demographics of society is a striking reminder that our "Christian consensus past" is still connected to our "secular pluralism present" (see fig. 1).

Figure 1

Canadian Religious Affiliation

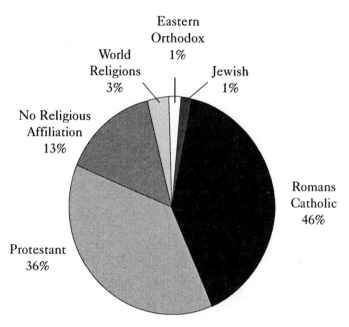

Source: Statistics Canada 1991
Graph: World Vision Canada

If the religious profile does nothing else, it clearly establishes that expectations for rites of passage will not cease. When 82 percent of Canadians continue to identify themselves as either Protestants or Catholics, we can safely conclude that the desire for the touch of the sacred on life's significant moments will also be present. And the adult expectations for the church's involvement is being passed on to the next generation. Even though fewer than 15 percent of today's senior teens involve themselves in regular church attendance, when it comes to wedding plans, 85 percent are expecting to walk down the aisle and exchange their vows in front of the church altar.[7]

Clergy and church decision makers have clear choices to make. They can either label the "rites of passage" people as "consumers," and deal with them accordingly, or they can envision them as people who have quiet yearnings for God and seek to link them to the church and the Christ they claim to believe in. Whatever the strategy, one certainty is that Canadians will continue to seek out the services of the church for the sacred rites and ceremonies related to birth, marriage, and funerals.

Regrettably there is also another predictable pattern. In its present form, the decline of the institutional church is inevitable. Even though the majority of Canadians continue to identify themselves as "religious somethings," they have detached themselves from the organized church. They are putting the agenda of their lives together without even pencilling in regular participation in church life.

The good news in the scenario is that in the inner spirit of Canadians a desire for the spiritual endures. Be it in the form of fragments of faith or an undefined acceptance of the supernatural, a baseline for belief remains. Douglas Coupland, an author in his early thirties, touched by the angst of his generation, may be overstating the case for the majority in society; but his portrayal still reveals an innate yearning for God that resides in the human spirit:

> Now here is my secret: I tell you with an openness of heart that I doubt I shall ever achieve again, so I pray that you are in a quiet room as you hear these words. My secret is that I need God — that I am sick and can no longer make it alone. I need God to help me give, because I no longer seem to be capable of giving; to help me be kind, as I no longer seem capable of kindness; to help me love, as I seem beyond being able to love.[8]

THE CHURCH IN THE CULTURE

Being nostalgic about the glories of the past is no match for the realities of the present. Whether Anglicans like it or not, we have to come to grips with the laws of life that prevail in pluralist Canada.

1. Surrender majoritarian mentalities

In former days, when the majority of Canadians attended church and the church had cultural power, there was a tendency to base the church's role in society on the operating premises of democracy. The assumption may not have been stated overtly, but in the perceptions of church leaders, "the majority rules" mindset prevailed. Accordingly, when politicians were drafting legislation that addressed a social concern or included a moral issue, it was simply assumed that church leaders could make an appointment with the cabinet minister in charge to communicate their perspectives. And, there was an understanding that their perspectives would be taken seriously. It was unthinkable that public officials would simply disregard the majority point of view. Not only was the Christian voice influential, it was considered to be both right and best.

In our "postmodern" age, the rules have changed. The church has been marginalized. Accessing political power is increasingly difficult. Sending denominational annual conference resolutions to Ottawa decrying the social state of affairs may be well intentioned, but it will have little impact. If the people of God are going to influence public life in the future, they will have to surrender majoritarian mentalities. In current nomenclature, they have to make a "paradigm shift." Instead of influencing from a base of power, God's people must learn to function as members of a minority group.

2. Give permission, take permission

We will find our way into a positive future if we can make room for the diverse views of life that have emerged during the past few decades. In some categories of life we are comfortable with diversity. We are relaxed with different economic theories, tastes in music, and choices on the theater and sports agendas. Matters of granting equality for multifaith truth claims, questions about what constitutes valid family structures, and unrestricted lifestyle alternatives leave many committed followers of Jesus unsettled.

Obviously, whether people are Christians or not, there are limits to what any culture can endorse. Behaviour that transgresses the criminal code is off limits for everyone. Stepping across socially accepted standards like advocating racism or the merits of child pornography are clearly outside the cultural boundaries.

But within these boundaries, in a pluralistic society, giving genuine permission to people to believe as they choose, and behave as they wish, is a social law of modern life. Stated in another way, pluralism demands that we accept people's right to believe and behave as they choose. Whether we agree with people's views and choices is not the issue. Neither are we asked to endorse or approve people's personal preferences. But in attitude and in practical ways that engender courtesy towards those who think and act differently, it is critical that God's people give other people permission.

Based on the assumption that sharing life in any society necessitates two-way traffic, permission givers also need to be permission takers. Giving permission to others gives them cultural room to be true to themselves. Taking permission allows God's people to be true to themselves. In the present cultural mood, there are greater pressures to give permission than there are to take permission. Individual followers of Jesus and denominational decision makers will only be able to obey Christ if they are prepared to counter carefully some aspects of the current culture and ground their convictions in established biblical norms.

For those who are feeling reticent about giving other people permission to believe and behave as they choose, they will be helped by reflecting on the question, "How does God treat people?" The realization that God does not force himself on people and gives all of his creation honest choices will encourage all of us to treat people as God treats them.

3. Shift from an "either/or" to a "both/and" mindset

Until very recently, most Canadians simply assumed that the tenets of Christianity were true. There were no wide-scale debates about the obvious. God existed, Jesus died to save people from their sins, the Bible was an authority for beliefs and practices, and life after death was a promise that God would keep. Accordingly, views of life that were framed within the Christian paradigm were "right," and those that conflicted with God's ways were "wrong." Until we edged into the 1960s, even those who disagreed with the consensus were relatively quiet.

One consequence was that it was natural to compute life in "either/or" categories. Whatever fit inside the Christian frame was deemed "right" and whatever fell outside the Christian way was understood to be "wrong." Even though Protestantism itself was diversified across a liberal-conservative spectrum, agreed-upon Christian boundaries still gave credence to a black-and-white world.

The emergence of a society based on pluralistic premises brings with it another set of operating assumptions. Instead of starting with an "either/or" mindset, the modern way is to perceive life with a "both/and" mentality. In other words, "My view is the only view" attitudes are out — and "all views are equally valid" views are in. Instead of one way of thinking, believing, and behaving, pluralism acknowledges and affirms many ways of thinking, believing, and behaving. Admittedly, as a nation, we are struggling with the "both/and" paradigm, but our social future is conditional on making it work.

There are examples of progress. In a number of places across the country, multifaith chaplains at correctional institutions and universities have gone through similar phases. Although there were variations of Jewish, Islamic, and Buddhist presence in the partnerships, a Christian majority and dominance prevailed. Often the tensions revolved around shared prayer, the expression of which proceeded through several stages.

Stage one meant that simply because Christians made up the majority, when it came time to pray together, the references to Jesus dominated.

Stage two was often triggered by a Jewish or Islamic voice expressing dissent and feeling offended by the Christian dominance. The resolve was to attempt to pray inclusively without offending any of the traditions of the world religions present in the group.

Stage three was also precipitated by dissatisfaction. Inclusive praying led to innocuous and unsatisfactory praying. The response of mature chaplains has often been to continue to express their faith through prayer but to do so by praying in a manner that is consistent with their particular beliefs. By giving each other permission to pray without reservation they are both true to themselves while respecting each other. The chaplains are also affirming another law of life in a pluralistic society — in order to retain privilege one must be prepared to give privilege.

4. Self define, take a stand

Chaplains at universities and in our correctional institutions who function within multifaith coalitions simply remind us that religious pluralism in Canada is a fact of life. The shared and sometimes controlled context of their mission demands that they deal with their religious diversity.

Looking more broadly at Canadian society, we see that religious pluralism is a subset of cultural pluralism. And it is within cultural pluralism that the church frames its existence. Because Canada's cultural pluralism is dominated by secular assumptions, many of God's people conclude that Canadian-style pluralism is an enemy of the church and the faith. They feel bewildered by the disarray of increasing diversity. Sometimes their confidence in their own faith is threatened. They intuitively feel that "given all the possibilities offered by pluralism, how can any of us have confidence in our own version of truth?"[9]

But, as previously acknowledged, it will be a mistake for the church to envision pluralism as an enemy. Rather, pluralism is a friend of the church. It is a friend because in its essence, cultural pluralism is simply a social structure for cradling diversity. Consequently, as well as making room for people from other faiths and other worldviews, Canadian pluralism also reserves a place for committed Christians. Pluralism allows Christians to stand alongside others who believe and behave in different ways. It provides social structures for coexisting with diversity.

The scope of this chapter does not permit an extensive treatment of the problems of present day pluralism, but one area needs to be addressed. Coexistence with diversity is not a mandate for tolerance.

> Why do we who live in the modern world think tolerance is valuable in and of itself, even though it's impossible to live with consistently? The answer is that tolerance is a value that conforms nicely to the world we live in. Having pretty much decided that truth is not attainable, we have made tolerance of a plurality of truths a virtue.[10]

But what are the consequences of tolerance? Put simply, tolerance trivializes people. Instead of stating, "I will take you seriously," tolerance says, "I will put up with you." Rather than calling a society to pursue the best, tolerance pulls life down to the lowest common denominator. Instead of developing convictions of conscience in people, tolerance moves a society step by step towards a convictionless culture. If we wish to become a more mature pluralistic society, it will be critical for Canadians to move beyond tolerance. And the church can have a strategic role to play in helping Canadians embrace a finer future.

The church's future role will be multidimensional; but surely it must include being a clear voice among the other cultural voices. A voice that is distinctive. A voice that has the ring of truth. A voice that articulates the ways of God and the teachings of Christ.

It will be a great mistake for the Anglican Church to abandon its prerogative in pluralism to *self-define and take a stand.* Whether the cultural issues relate to new birth technologies, doctor-assisted suicides, homosexuality, racism, environmental concerns, violence issues, the purpose of the cross for salvation, the sanctity of marriage, justice for the poor, or the consequences of sin, the church's mandate is to defend the truth. The summons is to be a definitive alternative for God in the pluralism parade. This is not to imply that discerning the mind of

Christ is straightforward or that the church will speak with one united voice; but it is to call the church to Christian distinctiveness.

This call to "self define and take a stand" will only gain a hearing in pluralist Canada if, while being a clear voice, it also affirms the rights of others to hold and follow other worldviews. To be listened to in contemporary Canada, the people of God will need to be infused with both conviction and compassion in attitude and practice.

Embracing both conviction and compassion will be critical. Conviction without compassion leads to triumphalism and harsh judgement. Compassion without conviction leads to compromise and accommodation. Carving out convictions preserves the people of God as the people of God. Extending compassion to others protects the convictions of others. Conviction joined with compassion leads to both integrity and empathy. In the present milieu, conviction and compassion expressed together will help make the gospel both plausible and desirable.

ESSENTIALS FOR EFFECTIVE CHURCHES

When kept in perspective, the prevailing cultural spirit represented in pluralist Canada should not tumble Anglicans into despair. In the current cultural climate, there are predictable ways for churches to be effective. The recent World Vision Canada research project, designed to answer the question, "What are the characteristics of effective churches?", identified four ministry cornerstones on which to cultivate healthy church life. The findings are cited in the book *Where's a Good Church?*[11]

1. Orthodoxy — in touch with truth

The first cornerstone is "orthodoxy" — to be in touch with truth. Rather than being an invitation to launch into a series of sermons on the doctrinal distinctives of a particular denomination, orthodoxy is a call to affirm the essentials of the faith. As a cornerstone, orthodoxy means that people want to go to church and have their confidence in the historic basics of faith affirmed. They want to hear again that God does exist, the Scriptures are reliable, and the resurrection of Christ did happen in history. Particularly for laity, orthodoxy represents an unspoken desire for stability within a postmodern world which is open to negotiation and uncertainty. People who attend church are much more concerned with answers than with the process by which the clergy arrived at those answers, or what "alternative" explanations may exist. The data is conclusive. A scaled down gospel will not give the church a strong future.

In these times so influenced by relativism — a predictable consequence of cultural pluralism — orthodoxy is particularly important. And because the Anglican Church is not a confessional church, standing firm on the historic basics of the faith is especially crucial. An Anglican priest for twenty-five years, Reverend Colven from England amplifies the point: "The Anglican Church has always been a kind of amorphous thing.... It's never had a theological stance of its own that could be defined clearly."[12]

Churches that affirm faith, rather than applauding doubt and parading ambiguity, will find a starting point to pursue a strong future.

2. Community — in touch with people's needs

People who are active participants in Canadian church life are looking for a place to belong. Although very few Canadians will openly admit their desires, "most people come to a local church looking for community." Too often, we neglect their aspirations and "put them on a committee" instead.[13]

People who make a commitment to a church not only want to be involved, they have expectations that their involvement will meet some of their personal needs, as well as affirm their self-worth. In terms of reaping the benefits of community, they are also anxious that the faith needs of their family members are met. In fact, as children edge their way into adolescence, parents are often ready to deny their personal preferences and switch churches if the needs of their teenagers are more likely to be satisfied elsewhere. One pattern is clear, effective churches are first meeting the needs and expectations of the people who are present in the pews before focusing their energies on outreach ministries.

The clergy leader has a critical role to ensure that the congregation provides a sense of belonging and identity, both for those who are in the more secure position of having been raised in their tradition, as well as for those switchers who have crossed denominational lines in order to find a more meaningful expression of faith. Effective churches are in touch with people's needs as they intentionally create community.

Figure 2

Personal Importance of "Belonging"

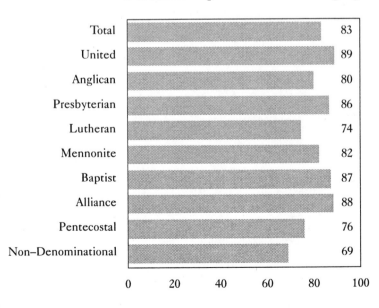

3. Relevance — in touch with the times

As a ministry cornerstone, relevance requires that Sunday worship be connected to the realities of the age and the circumstances of people's everyday lives. There is a desire to be open about tough issues, to relate the gospel to current concerns, and to present the teachings of the church in a way that has relevance to daily living. Clergy who are in touch with the perceptions of the laity will realize that there is more interest in personal concerns than there is in some of the broader social issues normally associated with being socially relevant. In other words, the primary interest of people revolves more around applying faith principles to issues like ethics in the workplace, family conflict resolution, and employee-employer relations, than around concerns like apartheid or racism, international armament controls, or the complexities connected to new birth technologies. Obviously, addressing both the personal and the broader issues will be important.

There is also a strong perception among lay members that many clergy live their lives in an artificial or insulated environment and are not well equipped to help their parishioners live out their daily lives. Regardless of clergy limits, 84 percent of those Christians surveyed still agreed with the statement that "a church is not worth attending unless it provides practical guidance for expressing one's faith in the world during the week."[14]

Figure 3

Importance of Excellent Preaching when Choosing a New Church

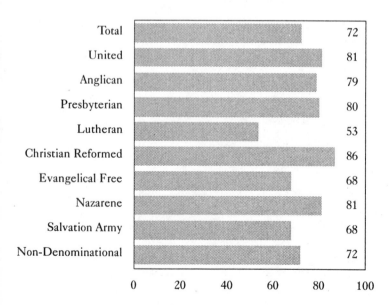

Total	72
United	81
Anglican	79
Presbyterian	80
Lutheran	53
Christian Reformed	86
Evangelical Free	68
Nazarene	81
Salvation Army	68
Non-Denominational	72

0   20   40   60   80   100

In the study, when we asked, "If you were planning to switch to another church, which characteristics would be important to you?", the first and highest priority was "preaching" (72 percent). And in the case of Anglicans it was also the most important (79 percent; see fig. 3). Anglicans who downplay the importance of preaching will make a serious miscalculation. Reliance on liturgy and worship that is solely sacramental will be short-sighted.

Preaching is the place for the clergy to demonstrate their commitment to both orthodoxy and relevance. Affirming the fundamentals of the faith throughout the Christian year will give people a sense of security and stability. Applying the tenets of faith to the issues of the age and the increasing complexities of modern life will lift people's spiritual confidence and help them serve God.

4. Outreach — in touch with the needs of others

Although effective churches are highly responsive to the needs of the people who are already present in their pews, they are also concerned about the needs of others outside the community of faith. A total of 59 percent of the respondents felt their churches should have a balanced commitment both to the needs of the congregation and the needs of the community. In addition, 14 percent favored an external focus, while 27 percent thought attention should be given to internal priorities. The majority of effective churches and their leaders have a sense of mission and a commitment to extend Christ's cause and his message beyond their sanctuary into the community.

Especially in today's world, where words are so frequently viewed with skepticism, outreach is best understood as a response to people's "whole person needs." The task of the church, then, is to express the gospel as both words and deeds in local communities and cooperatively around the world. When God's good news is conceived as both words and deeds, the gospel takes on both personal and social implications. Accordingly, Jesus' words to "Come unto me" invite a response to live in a personal relationship with Christ. Sequentially, faith conceived as deeds mandates a social response. Accordingly, authentic faith compels a commitment to compassionate ministries, an unrelenting pursuit of justice on behalf of the poor and powerless, and specific responses to the tangible needs of people.

Distinguishing between outreach and church growth is also important. Despite the emphasis on numerical growth among some clergy and some denominations, members are rather unimpressed with church growth tactics. Only 7 percent of lay members believe that placing explicit emphasis on numerical growth in their local congregation will be effective. More often, numerical growth will result from an effective ministry mix represented in the "four cornerstones," if this mix takes care to remain compatible with denominational ethos and style (see fig. 4).

Using trend analysis, Reginald Bibby projects that "by around 2015, conservative Protestants will have more congregational members than any mainline group. Perhaps of much greater significance, beyond membership, on any given

Sunday, there will be three conservatives in the pews for every mainline Protestant!"[15] Churches that settle for a maintenance approach to ministry will die a slow and certain death. Those churches that find Anglican ways to motivate their people into mission will have a future.

Clergy have an important and often difficult role to play in integrating the factors that create effective churches. But difficult or not, as church decision makers intentionally design and pursue ministries that include the four cornerstones of orthodoxy, relevance, community, and outreach, churches will reach toward the New Testament criteria, and they will also experience effectiveness (Acts 2:37-47).

CRITICAL DIRECTIONS FOR EFFECTIVE CHURCHES

"Efficiency is doing things right; effectiveness is doing right things."[16] When the lens is lowered on Anglicans, and the assumptions of the past are contrasted with the realities of the present, "doing right things" suggests several ministry priorities.

1. Shift a measure of ministry resources from the institutional to the individual

In English Canada, the Anglican Church was in many ways a creation of culture. In the historical frame of Canadian national development, the Anglican Church was a by-product of English settlers bringing their religion with them. In the early days, the Anglican Church was both protected and nourished by the state.

Figure 4

Ministry Mix for Effective Churches

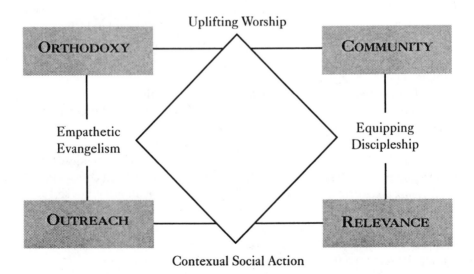

Uplifting Worship

ORTHODOXY

COMMUNITY

Empathetic
Evangelism

Equipping
Discipleship

OUTREACH

RELEVANCE

Contexual Social Action

Until three decades ago, along with other mainline churches, Anglicans were like magnets at the centre of society. Together, they were at the institutional heart of the culture and people were drawn naturally towards them. In post-Christian Canada, Anglicans in particular will only find a viable future by being re-nourished and re-created. Instead of being a consequence of culture, they will have to be carved out of the current culture. They will have to be intentionally redesigned. Anglicans will have to operate according to the cultural and social realities that smaller "sects" and minorities have faced all the way along.

Part of the redesign will involve shifting a measure of ministry resources from the institutional to the individual. Retaining and enhancing institutional church life will continue to be important; the age of organized religion is not over. However, hinging hope on institutional ministry alone — that is, ministry contained inside church buildings — will be a fatal calculation.

An enhanced future will emerge, as resources and vision for ministry are focused more on individuals. The scenario is clear. The majority of Canadians have stopped attending church regularly and that overall pattern is unlikely to change. But people who attend church regularly also enter the world regularly. They live in neighborhoods, attend schools, labour in workplaces, participate in communities, and spend their leisure hours in the world. The strategy is obvious. As Anglicans who go to church are better equipped and supported to live and talk the life of faith in the world, the cause of Christ and the mission of the church has promise.

In the 1990s, people are turning to each other rather than to institutions. People are not looking for organizations to join; they are looking for people to share their lives with. The world is an increasingly messy and confused place. Those who are able to find their way coherently through the mazes of modern life are noticed. People who demonstrate even a measure of poise in the midst of crises are intriguing. Individuals who are known as Christians and also live with conviction and compassion are respected. Those who are generous with their time and money send signals that others are important to them. People who express the stability of faith in an unstable world are in natural positions to bring the role of Christ in their lives into their conversations. Those who have a vital personal faith are the people to "offer reasons for the hope that is within them" (1 Pet. 3:15).

Churches with a desire for mission will refocus their priorities to equip and support those in their congregations who have the social temperament and spiritual desire to represent Christ in their Monday-to-Saturday worlds. They will then begin to notice that the personal dynamics of people connected to people will draw new members to their communities of faith.

2. Balance ministry initiatives between the internal and the external

There is no substitute for faith communities that worship authentically, accept outsiders while creating community, and connect the teachings of the gospel with the realities of life. Welcoming new people and involving them is what we should be doing.

For churches situated in expanding population suburbs with young families, or even where there is a cluster of retirement havens, the possibility of "doing church well" the old way will still produce positive results. Young families and retirees often bring themselves to church. But these favorable circumstances are not the reality for most churches. The majority of churches will be better advised to balance their ministry initiatives between the internal and the external. Specifically, the preferred strategy will be to minister to people who are in the pews while at the same time extending mission to those who live within reach of the people who attend church.

Excessive words have already been used to challenge today's churches and their leaders to convert from "maintenance mode" to "mission mode." There are numerous ways to motivate a church into mission. The two following approaches merit attention.

Affirming a variety of ministry interests is one way to encourage "mission mindedness." The common denominator is to provide a supportive environment within the church for regular participants who have spiritual concern for people and problems outside the church. Encouraging these people to take initiative and pursue their ministries beyond the church building and outside the regular church program will be fruitful.

In practice this means that members of the parish who are troubled about social injustices will be prayed for and affirmed. Those who believe that personal evangelism is an indispensable part of the Christian life will be given training and encouragement. Members of the congregation who ache for street youth, have compassion for the physically hungry, the unemployed, and the victims of substance abuse will all be raised up as ministers of both Christ and the church. The leadership perspective will emphasize that "all God's people have gifts for ministry" and in God's design for life, somewhere in the scheme of things, "everyone is a contributor."

Another productive way to spend the resources of the church in a balanced ministry is to respond to the needs of families inside the church while offering family-centred ministries to the community around the church. Many church youth groups work with para-church groups like Young Life and Inter-Varsity Christian Fellowship, thereby combining nurture and outreach.

Debates about what constitutes a family swirl around us, together with the diversification of family structures; but the family remains, and will remain, the basic building block of Canadian life. Young people aspire to get married and expect to stay married. The vast majority of older Canadians are hinging their hopes for a positive life on the prospects of living in healthy families. Accordingly, for the church, ministry to the family is the widest door back into the culture.

The baseline for ministry to families starts with Canadians' unrelenting desire for the church to administer rites of passage. Birth ceremonies, marriages, and funerals are hooked to the family. Churches that augment a sensitive response to the demand for rites of passage with ministries such as pre-marital counselling (not necessarily done by the clergy), conflict-resolution forums, parenting principles for teenagers, counselling expertise or referrals, seniors' abuse counselling, and opportunities for marriage renewal ceremonies, will be going down the right road. Equally, churches that can offer vibrant youth ministries will touch the nerve centres and cherished values of concerned parents both inside and outside the church.

3. Treasure and transcend tradition — through innovation

Anglicans treasure tradition. They extol the long-standing richness of the Prayer Book, genuinely appreciate the ceremonial, and seldom think that "casual" is an improvement over "formal." The saints relish their enduring memories of the days when there were three services to accommodate the masses who attended faithfully. And even though life has changed radically around them, many "true Anglicans" can be counted on to resist change.

Loren Mead of the Alban Institute adds further light to Anglican dynamics by observing that "under the Christendom paradigm, churches have structured themselves for uniformity and permanence.... We badly need innovators.... We must encourage innovation to find some new paths and get models of innovation widely known...."[17]

Because Anglicans in Canada are often bonded to both tradition and Christendom, and because innovation will be a necessary ingredient in the future, wise decision makers will both treasure and transcend tradition. They will inherently value and respect the old while deliberately experimenting with the new. They will understand that "established congregations must find ways to validate the cultural needs of the older generation while not forgetting that the future of their congregation depends on the younger generation."[18] For example, they will compute that differing styles of worship will be important, particularly in congregations that have reached a plateau or are experiencing decline. But if there is a possibility to do so, instead of just scrapping the Book of Common Prayer (BCP), people will be given the option of alternative liturgies that offer both the BCP and the Book of Alternative Services (BAS). But accommodating the differences between the BCP and the BAS will only be a beginning.

4. Leadership is indispensable

One of the clear conclusions that both the research data and wide-spread observations confirm is that the future of the church is dependent on competent leadership. Obviously, people's leadership style is linked to personality and temperament, but in today's world, some leadership styles are definitely more desirable than others (see fig.5).

Leadership that is destined to fail in contemporary circumstances will tend to disregard pastoral concerns and exploit people to get jobs done, rely on positional authority, and overemphasize the priority of numerical growth.

In the *Where's a Good Church?* research, the image of the effective church leader that emerged is "one who is focused on equipping others to develop their gifts; who seeks consensus but is not afraid to take risks; who meets people's needs rather than counting people as numbers; and who is ready to share authority."[19] A crucial factor in providing competent leadership is the ability to build group consensus around a shared vision. Combining the skills of group process with personal conviction about God's direction through the work of the Holy Spirit is particularly important.

Another key result area for church leadership in this age will be the ability to manage organizational change — to hang on to the old while pursuing the new. Wise leaders will not abandon the "Anglican way" but neither will they be caught in the trap of cloning churches within the constraints of the past.

Figure 5

Preferred Leadership Styles

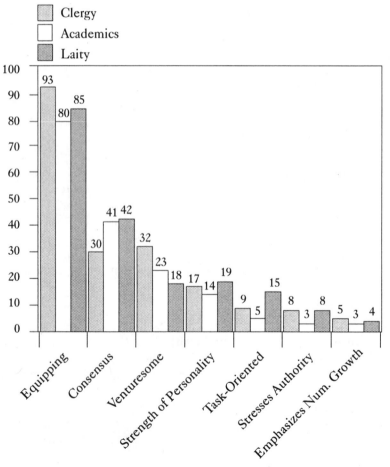

Effective leaders in the future will increasingly contextualize the vision and function of their churches. They will understand and address the prevailing *culture*. They will know that the post-Christian culture of the 1990s is socially stronger than the church and they will make adjustments for that fact. They will take time to look with fresh eyes at the *community* that frames their parish. They will alter programme patterns and ministry initiatives in response to the community needs around them. They will understand the strengths and weaknesses of their *denomintation*. They will build on the strengths of Anglicanism and seek to compensate for the weaknesses. And they will be students of their *congregation*. Competent and effective leaders will respect the history of their parishes, affirm the gifts of members and participants, and seek to help write the next chapter of faithful service for God and that local situation. And in the back of their minds, clergy and lay leaders will intuitively know that the future of Canadian Anglicanism will depend mainly upon the capacity of local churches in local parishes to find the way into a fruitful future.

CONCLUSION

As we make our way toward the year 2000, the truth of the gospel remains intact. However, in Canada, God's truth has to be intentionally reaffirmed. It has to be authenticated in the present tense. In the past, the assumptions of the gospel were taken for granted. In our pluralistic and postmodern society, the gospel has to merit the choice of being both plausible and believable.

In his book *The End of the Modern World*, Romano Guardini observes, "Christianity will once again need to prove itself deliberately as a faith which is not self-evident; it will be forced to distinguish itself more sharply from a dominant non-Christian ethos."[20]

Today's church faces numerous challenges. In our pluralistic society, living the faith so that it is the "preferred choice" of Canadians is the most pressing reality.

SUGGESTED READING

Jack O. Balswick and Judith K. Balswick, *The Family: A Christian Perspective* (Grand Rapids: Baker Book House, 1991).
Reginald Bibby, *Unknown Gods* (Toronto: Stoddart, 1993).
David J. Bosch, *Transforming Mission* (New York: Orbis Books, 1991).
Stephen Carter, *The Culture of Disbelief* (New York: Basic Books, 1993).
Howard Hanchey, *Church Growth and the Power of Evangelism* (Cambridge, Mass.: Cowley Publications, 1990).
George G. Hunter, *How To Reach Secular People* (Nashville: Abingdon Press, 1992).
Loren Mead, *The Once and Future Church* (Washington D.C.: Alban Institute, 1991).
Lesslie Newbigin, *Foolishness to the Greeks* (Grand Rapids: Eerdmans, 1986).
Donald C. Posterski, *Reinventing Evangelism* (Downers Grove: InterVarsity Press, 1989).
Donald C. Posterski and Irwin Barker, *Where's a Good Church?* (Winfield, B.C.: Wood Lake Books, 1993).

ENDNOTES

1. "Dire Warning to Anglicans," *Toronto Star* (Jan. 1, 1994).

2. Reginald Bibby, *Unknown Gods* (Toronto: Stoddart, 1993), pp. 5, 104.

3. "Most Churches in Diocese in State of Decline, Study Finds," *The Anglican*, Diocese of Toronto, p. 1.

4. Leszek Kolakowski, *Modernity on Endless Trial* (Chicago: University of Chicago Press, 1990), p. 70.

5. Lesslie Newbigin, *Truth to Tell: The Gospel as Public Truth* (Grand Rapids: Eerdmans, 1991), p. 61.

6. Lesslie Newbigin, *The Gospel in a Pluralist Society* (Grand Rapids: Zondervan, 1989), p. 1.

7. Reginald Bibby and Donald Posterski, *Teen Trends* (Toronto: Stoddart, 1992), p. 50.

8. Douglas Coupland, *Life After God* (New York: Pocket Books, 1994), p. 359.

9. S. D. Gaede, *When Tolerance Is No Virtue* (Downers Grove: InterVarsity Press, 1993), p. 27.

10. Gaede, *When Tolerance Is No Virtue*, p. 27.

11. Donald Posterski and Irwin Barker, *Where's a Good Church?* (Winfield, B.C.: Wood Lake Books, 1993).

12. Bill Schiller, "Women Priests Trigger Mass Church Defections," *Toronto Star* (March 5, 1994).

13. Kennon L. Callahan, *Twelve Keys to an Effective Church: Strategic Planning for Mission* (San Francisco: HarperCollins, 1983), p. xiii.

14. Posterski and Barker, *Where's a Good Church?*, p. 38.

15. Bibby, *Unknown Gods*, p. 105.

16. Leith Anderson, *A Church for the 21st Century* (Minneapolis: Bethany House Publishers, 1992), p. 16.

17. Loren Mead, *The Once and Future Church* (New York: The Alban Institute, 1991), p. 73.

18. William Easum, *Dancing with Dinosaurs* (Nashville: Abingdon Press, 1993), p. 89.

19. Posterski and Barker, *Where's a Good Church?*, p. 173.

20. Cited in Newbigin, *Truth to Tell*, p. 65.

Anglicanism Today
The Path to Renewal

GRANT LeMARQUAND, ALISTER E. McGRATH,
JAMES I. PACKER, AND JOHN PAUL WESTIN

By every criterion that we normally use to judge institutions, the Anglican Church in Canada is in grave decline. It is shrinking in numbers and influence, and sinking into obscurity as a social institution. Our preoccupations are with maintenance and ventures in adjustment to secular fashion, rather than with mission, evangelism, discipling the faithful, and challenging sin. Our public style is low-key, timid, and concessive; what we stand for, and what we stand against, are often hard to discern. "The place for the ship is in the sea," said D. L. Moody long ago, "but God help the ship if the sea gets into it." He was speaking of the relation of the church to the world, and were he back with us now we fear he would point to Canada's Anglican Church as illustrating what he meant.

Does it have to be like this? Must the decline continue? Is it entirely due to factors beyond our control? Is there a path of renewal that might be taken? In sub-Saharan Africa, where a renewal movement among Anglicans has been in progress for more than fifty years, Anglican Christianity flourishes and, despite terrible upheavals, the church grows steadily. Is that vitality and growth just a local cultural freak, or could it be that Canadian Anglicans, like those in Britain, the United States, and Australasia, who face similar decline, are actually missing something? That is the question we are to explore.

What is Anglicanism?

We begin at the beginning. What is Anglicanism? How should we define it?

Historically and humanly, Anglicanism was an accident. It resulted from the anti-Papalism of one Tudor monarch, plus the free hand given to church leaders by the ruling nobility under another (a teenager), plus the quest of a third for a nationalist traditionalism with catholic order that former Papalists could accept. Within Elizabeth's Church of England, however, a characteristic ethos, style, and outlook soon developed, and Anglicanism was set on the rails upon which, essentially, it still runs. Eventually it followed the flag and spread worldwide. Today there are some seventy million Anglicans, of whom a little over 1 percent are Canadian.

If, now, we define Anglicanism genetically, we shall describe it as a form of churchly existence, spread from England, that has two characteristic features: first, the linking of congregations in geographical dioceses of Constantinian type,[1] managed by bishops in the historic succession; and second, the shaping of worship by a Prayer Book that derives in some way from the English Prayer Books of the sixteenth century. Whatever emerges within this frame is then Anglican in at least one sense.

But if we go deeper and define Anglicanism substantively, by reference to its own key documents and stated purposes over four and a half centuries since Henry VIII, what we find is a clear-cut churchly ideal, which we can formulate as follows:

Anglicanism — ideal Anglicanism, that is, as thus defined — is a biblically controlled trinitarian, incarnational, liturgical, sacramental, rational, pastorally committed, and community-oriented version of mainstream Western Christianity. Its reformational face-lift did not mar its authenticity as mere Christianity, Christianity without additions or subtractions, a true and pure expression of the historic catholic faith, but rather restored it. As proof of this, Anglicanism offers its worldwide array of Prayer Books, which use revised versions of ancient worship forms correlated with the Patristic creeds and with Anglicanism's own doctrinal and disciplinary supplement, the Thirty-Nine Articles of Religion. The Anglican goal everywhere is to blend old and new, ecumenical and indigenous, yesterday's biblical insights and today's, in a way that, while it may seem eccentric to some who might be thought eccentric themselves, brings all the wisdom and vitality of the Christian heritage to all its adherents and unites them in truly worthy worship. Dignity, energy, and enterprise in Christ, for the making and nurturing of Christians, the Christianizing of communities, and thereby the glory of God, are intended to be the hallmarks of the Anglican lifestyle. The aim, we may say — somewhat shamefacedly, for it is so rarely achieved — is a Christianity of highest quality, everywhere in the world.

The ideal Anglican ethos, as the documents portray it, can be specified by conjoining seven words. It is *catholic* in the theological sense of ever seeking to embrace the fullness of the faith and not fall victim to any sectarian narrowing of it. It is *protestant* in the theological sense of rejecting medieval distortions of apostolic Christianity. It is *reformed* in the theological sense of endorsing from Scripture the Augustinianism of Luther and Calvin, according to which salvation is by grace alone through faith alone for the glory of God alone, and spiritual formation rests on the three "R's" of the gospel: ruin, redemption, and regeneration. It is *evangelical* in the theological sense of centring its thought-life on Christ and his salvation as everyone's need, and in conceiving the church as the fellowship of the faithful who are alive in Christ. It is *disciplined* in piety, inculcating (1) faith in Christ and his cross for forgiveness; (2) repentance from sin, self-humbling, and the pursuit of righteousness; (3) love to the Father and the Son through the Spirit; (4) daily Bible reading; and (5) the verbalizing of praise and petition in a passionate rhetoric of the heart, as modelled in the Psalms, in Augustine and others of the Fathers, and in the Prayer Book itself. It is *rational* in outlook, refusing no question about the content of the faith and its relation to other forms of thought, ever striving to show the reasonableness of Christian belief, and habitually choosing the discipline of debate over that of the big stick when erratic views arise in Anglican ranks. And it is *moral* in mindset, stressing that the law from which, as a system of salvation, Christians are freed, nonetheless binds them in its character as God's family code for those who have become his children.

The Anglican perspective can be further specified, in two ways. First, Anglicanism is *ecumenical*, in the sense of desiring to associate with and learn from other traditions in Christendom, declining to make the claim or act the role of present self-sufficiency, and remaining open to discover that, as John Robinson the Pilgrim Father put it, "God hath yet more light and truth to break forth from his holy word." To be sure, the local politics of Anglicanism, notably England's long-standing hostility to dissenters and early Anglo-Catholic negativism towards the Free Churches, sometimes obscured this ecumenical posture, but all major Anglican theologians have maintained it, and when in this century Anglicans took the lead, as they did, in the emerging ecumenical movement, they were simply being true to their tradition and to themselves. So are all Anglicans who from time to time worship and fraternize with other denominations to see what of value can be learned from them. That is the true Anglican way.

Second, Anglicanism is *institutional*, because of the way it understands its mission under God to communities. Churches that limit their concern to nurturing their own membership and augmenting it by evangelism often detach themselves from the larger life of the civic communities to which they belong, but Anglicans have never been willing to so limit themselves. Maintaining the sanctity of what is called the secular as well as what is called the sacred order of things, Anglicanism has always been concerned that community life be lived Christianly at all points. As Anglican churches organize themselves to welcome and include all who will come, so they see themselves called to fulfil a prophetic ministry to the larger society around, as well as a directly pastoral ministry to their own adherents. Anglican churches seek to be a force for God's kingdom in every sphere, and see the upholding of human dignity and public justice, no less than the furthering of education, community health, and appropriate support for the needy and underprivileged, as belonging to their mission. The breadth and complexity of this wider outworking of neighbour love, on top of the church's own primary calling regularly to gather for worship and learning, calls for fulltime salaried agents (both ordained and lay), human and financial structures, and buildings of many kinds. Responsible sponsoring of cross-cultural mission also requires organization. No apology, therefore, is needed for the fact that wherever Anglicanism goes it becomes institutional — is, in fact, institutionalized. If the institution becomes static and immobile, as has seemed to happen in Canada (it is, for instance, disturbingly rare to hear of an Anglican Church–plant in this land), there is indeed cause for concern; but Anglican institutionalism as such is a necessity, and we should not imagine that there is anything intrinsically improper about it.

ANGLICANISM IN CANADA

Anglicanism in Canada has declined, and is declining still. Why? Leaving divine factors out of account, and speaking strictly on the human level, we affirm that two things have been mainly responsible. One is the external pressure under which the church has been placed by contemporary culture's abandonment of its former Christian rootage; the other is the internal uncertainty and division that has resulted from contemporary developments in theology. The two are linked, for both have resulted from the anti-Christian thrust of the so-called European Enlightenment over the past two centuries. But they call for separate discussion.

Look first, then, at current Canadian culture. Note, to start with, how completely all the institutions that mould national opinion — schools, universities, press, television, radio, the arts, theatre, cinema — have detached themselves from any overt endorsement of Christianity. Note, too, how completely Canada has abandoned the axiom of what historians call the Christendom era, that Christian faith is the cement of society. The sacred and the secular have now been divorced, with sad loss to both church and state. We are now officially a multicultural patchwork, which means a multifaith aggregate, and Christianity in Canada has been put on the same footing as, for instance, Sikhism and Islam — protected, yes, but no longer actively approved, and thus effectively demoted. Modern Canada holds the ring for all religions as private opinions but does not claim to be a Christian country, as it would have done until quite recently.

Nor is that all. Note next the main features of our culture as it is today: its technological triumphalism; its materialism; its consumerism; and its egoistic ethical relativism, which says in effect that different behaviour patterns suit different people and anything goes provided it does not really harm anyone else — a sure formula, we think, for further erosion of moral character and further growth of sophisticated corruption and dishonesty as the years go by. And note, finally, how the secularizing of our society has produced alienation from the churches. According to a recent poll,[2] more than three-quarters of Canadians believe in some sort of God, but less than a quarter of them have any link with a church. Those figures tell the story. Churches have become irrelevant in Canadian eyes, and are marginalized accordingly. No church, therefore, that is not prepared to roll up its sleeves and start evangelizing from scratch on the basis that modern secular Canada is pagan can hope to have a future. In England, where the story is similar, the Anglican Church is beginning to adjust to this fact, and it is urgently necessary for the Anglican Church of Canada to do the same.

The external pressures on the church, then, are great and ominous enough in their own right. But the internal pressures, which have grown out of theology, are to our mind greater and more ominous than the external pressures. Within the framework of Anglican institutional order, liturgical precision, and formal acknowledgment of the sufficiency of Scripture, a new theological method has emerged and become dominant, one that makes a variety of views inevitable and incurable. The views that result however have one thing in common: sitting loose to the historic faith, they all offer revisionist versions of defined Anglican beliefs. This is where most of the perplexities and confusions come from, as we shall now see.

Older Anglicans embraced the classic Christian theological method that is implicit in the Fathers and medievals and explicit in the magisterial Reformers and the major writers of all schools of thought till the last century. This method follows from the recorded teaching of Jesus and his apostles and especially from their use of the Jewish Scriptures, the Christian Old Testament.[3] Assuming the incompetence of unaided reason to discover what we need to know about God and ourselves, the method affirms the reality of revelation in the sense of God showing and telling the saving truth about our sin, his grace, and the way of life. It sees the Holy Scriptures — the two Testaments — together, from one standpoint a responsive witness to and interpretation of God's revelation in history, and from another, the form and channel through which God's revealed truth reaches us. Thus it recognizes the Bible as the written Word of God — a coherent, life-giving unity, authoritative as a guide to the belief and behaviour that will glorify our triune Creator and Redeemer. When fully stated, this view celebrates Jesus Christ as the focal centre of the biblical message, and the Holy Spirit as its producer, authenticator and interpreter to our darkened minds and hearts. The Christian experience has ever been that the Spirit, who gives applicatory understanding of Scripture, gives with it a sense of the divine presence as the source of the light we are receiving, so that we commune with God in responding to what Scripture shows us.

Where do tradition and reason fit into this view of how Scripture makes us wise? Tradition, which means the transmitted thought and experience of those who were in Christ before us, has not a magisterial but a ministerial role in guiding our quest for the true and full meaning of what we read: the text itself must finally yield up its own meaning through theological exegesis and synthesis, and in so doing it will become the judge of the tradition that sought to state that meaning and actually helped us to see it. (Thus, for instance, exegesis confirms the Chalcedonian tradition that Jesus Christ is one person, fully human and fully divine, but corrects the tradition from Rome's fourth Lateran Council, that transubstantiation is the truth behind Jesus' words, "this is my body.") Tradition is insightful but not infallible. As for reason, it is to be exercised at full stretch in grasping and applying what the Holy Spirit through exegesis is showing, for the interpreting of this world as God's world, for the confirming of the faith as truth in every sense of that word, for the sanctifying of secular studies by relating them to the knowledge of God, and for the shaping of our lives in God's service.

The conjunction of the Word, the Spirit, and the teachable mind as the principle of all true knowledge of God is basic to this method, and so is the assumption that at bottom there is only one message conveyed in the Bible — only one coherent way, that is, of thinking together all the various items of truth that the Scriptures contain. This has to be so, because Holy Scripture is God-given, is in fact God preaching and teaching here and now, and it is not conceivable that God contradicts himself. And in the great ecumenical tradition of theology — Eastern and Western, Protestant and Roman Catholic and Orthodox — that has blossomed under the tutelage of this method for almost two thousand years, the coherence of the Scriptures has in fact been displayed time and time again. It can be shown, we think, that the common modern allegations of substantive inconsistency between the teachings of different Bible writers are all based on misreadings of texts, just as the common modern dismissals of biblical instruction as such are based on an unwillingness to let the Word of God correct current cultural and personal prejudices.

That last remark takes us to the heart of the new method that nowadays challenges the old, and does so from a position of dominance in the older mainline Western Protestant establishment. It recategorizes Scripture as an intellectually, morally, and culturally flawed human witness to God, which mediates God's message to us only as we sieve its contents through epistemological and ontological paradigms stemming from secular culture. In the late nineteenth century, the favourite paradigm was evolutionary, viewing Jesus as the model religious man, God-taught and God-filled, who leads us beyond the primitive and barbaric outlook of much of the Bible. It was often said in those days that we must criticize the Bible by Christ. However, this paradigm, which reflected an optimistic confidence that the world order itself was evolving under God from one degree of excellence to another, was thoroughly exploded by two world wars and the renewing of real global barbarism that came in with them, and a new paradigm had to be sought. The currently preferred paradigm is that God, being finite and limited in what he can do, is labouring, unsuccessfully so far, to establish his will of love and liberty throughout this world, and calls on us to help him: an agenda that clearly grows out of our secular concern for human rights in a world order that is felt, with reason, to be largely out of control. Within Protestantism (and much of Western Roman Catholicism too) the various kinds of liberation theologies are examples of this paradigm in action. And such paradigm change is likely to go on as long as theologians seek to baptize into Christ Western society's changing philosophies and hail as prophetic and profound all attempts to reconstruct the faith so that it matches the world's dreams and serves the world's goals. Built on the axiom that everyone should rely on his or her personal judgement as to how much of biblical teaching one should take seriously and how far any of it should be held to express God's own thoughts, this modern method guarantees a plurality of beliefs and purposes in the church, and makes it impossible to prove any theological affirmation either right or wrong. But when everything is thus disputable, theology becomes a confused noise, Christians are at cross purposes with one another, there is no united witness to the gospel of salvation from sin, and the church grinds to a halt. This seems to be the deepest root of the malaise of today's Anglican Church of Canada.

Many Canadian Anglicans of all schools of thought feel anxious about the church, and no wonder. The appropriateness of anxiety is plain from what has been said. Falling numbers, decreasing revenues, inability to hold on to baptized young people, discontent with the bureaucracy, and overall evangelistic impotence are clear signs that the church is in trouble, and aspects of its inner life raise serious questions about the possibility of recovery. Of the American Methodist Church the following was recently written:

> The sense is that most designated leaders ... lack either the knowledge, the fortitude, the skill or the will to bring about renewal in the church as a whole. Hedged around by committees, overwhelmed by extensive burdens, holding political debts and dues of some sort, perhaps unsure of the boundaries of their power and authority, most leaders have little time left to devote to thinking through renewal of the church.... Seminaries are perceived, at heart, as being out of touch with the church ... seminaries fail to nurture seminarians in a deep way in the gospel and the faith of the church ... and they often reflect theological convictions and values which are incompatible with the convictions of the church....

Pressure groups sponsor within the church

> a radical theological and political agenda which ends up excluding or ostracizing those who hold to the classic Trinitarian faith of the church [and] fosters a climate of intimidation, silence, fear, and indoctrination, which its creators generally fail to perceive.... Finally there is ... the simple fear that the church has lost its way spiritually. The church, it is believed, is not centred on God; it is not rooted and anchored in the life, death, and resurrection of Jesus Christ; it does not live by the power of the Holy Spirit.... In short the church as a corporate entity has wandered once more off its appointed course.[4]

Had the author been writing about the Anglican Church of Canada, he would hardly have needed to change a word. Our decline, and our need, correspond most unhappily to the picture this author paints.

TOWARDS RECOVERY

What would be the path of recovery? What would renewal of the Anglican Church of Canada involve?

The first step in addressing this question must be to agree on what the church, as the body and bride of Christ, is called to be, and then what constitutes renewal of it. At present, most Anglicans profess to be for renewal, but are vague as to what it is. Nor is this really surprising, for the word as used in this century has acquired many facets of meaning. The liturgical renewal, the biblical renewal, the theological renewal, the lay renewal, the small-group renewal, and the charismatic renewal, are only some of the self-styled renewal movements that have passed before us. A global concept of renewal is not easily formed when so many movements, each with its own limited agenda, claim the name. Yet it is clear that any adequate notion of church renewal must incorporate all these elements, plus something vital that those with roots in the evangelical heritage would add — namely, that if renewal movements are to be more than great clouds of dust raised by frenzied human activity they must have at their heart a divine visitation of the kind that since the eighteenth century has been recognized as the root of revival.[5] Such a visitation is an outpouring of the Holy Spirit that brings a deepened awareness of the near presence of the holy God who is also the God of grace, and leads to a deepened sense of sin, a profounder repentance, a more joyful and appreciative grasp of the reality of forgiveness, a more ardent worship, new life, new power, and new hope, all mediated through the ministry of the living Lord Jesus Christ.

Revival, then, in the older evangelical sense, is the inner reality of renewal; and renewal across the board, quickening and restoring all aspects of the church's life, will involve all the elements mentioned above. It is in essence a gift from God, but one that will only be found through being sought, and sought for the sake not of renewal itself but of the honouring and glorifying our Lord, the church's heavenly bridegroom. As knowing Jesus Christ by faith is salvation here and now, and knowing him by sight will be heaven's eternal glory, so coming to know him better and to love and adore him more while on earth is the heart of renewal experience, and it is this supremely that we are to seek. The quest for renewal will require of us thought and action, self-scrutiny and change, confession of need and of failure, honesty and humility, prayer and dependence on God at a deeper level than in the past. That we need it is clear; that we should talk, think, work, and pray for it is surely clear too.

And there is a negative corollary: we must abandon the alluring but lethal policy of scaling Christianity down, de-supernaturalizing it and so pulling it out of shape in order to give it credibility in the eyes of its "cultured despisers," to use Schleiermacher's term, by reflecting back to them their own secular philosophical norms. The sustained embrace of this policy by some has boomeranged on the church itself, bringing us near to, if not actually into, a state of internal schism, as the opponents of what we may call internal secularization of the faith square off against those who are committed to this process. The authentic Christian way has never been to edit and shrink down the gospel to make it reinforce current secularity; to do that would be, not rescuing the perishing, but sinking the lifeboat. The true path, rather, is that which Christians in the early centuries took, namely, to point up the antitheses between the world's thought and God's truth, to diagnose the world as being in darkness and in misery by reason of the darkness, and to commend Christianity as God's redemptive remedy for our intellectual and moral bankruptcy. There will be no renewal where this path is not followed.

What is needed, first and foremost, is an in-depth retrieval of our heritage. This could bring about the deep-level recovery of identity that we very urgently need. The Anglican Church in the modern West is out of touch with historic and global Anglicanism to a far greater extent than it realizes, and it is here that our cure must begin. So our first item of business needs to be returning in penitent trust to Christ himself, and immersing ourselves afresh in the Bible, in the time-honoured teachings of the creeds, the Fathers, and the classical Anglican writers, and in the classical disciplines of the Christian life itself. The renewal of the church must start with the renewal of Christians, and this is where, humanly speaking, the renewal of Christians will start, if indeed it is ever going to start at all. There needs to be a recovery of *orthodoxy* — that is, faith in the work of the supernatural triune God who is Lord of creation, of providence, and of grace — and with it a restored *orthopraxy* — that is, total conversion to our Lord and Saviour Jesus Christ, and a devoted practice of Christian holiness and active, loving outreach as the basic form of our discipleship to him.

According to the teaching of the New Testament, which Anglicans have in the past tenaciously upheld as the true account of reality, Jesus of Nazareth, the rural rabbi from Galilee, was the Son and Word of God through whom, as the Father's agent, the entire cosmos was made and is now upheld in being. In his incarnate life, which began with his virginal conception, he died to atone for our sins; then he rose and ascended to the place of cosmic dominion; and now from his throne he mediates God's pardon and power to us sinners for our transformation into his likeness. The church militant worldwide, with the church triumphant in heaven, is his body, the extension of his resurrection, and an organism of his ongoing life whereby through the Holy Spirit he reproduces in his people his own worship and service of the Father, and his own ministering love for those he calls his siblings in the Father's family. This Christ, and this church, are for real, as we say, and in the total Christian view of the way things are, this Christ and this church stand centre stage.

Central to the new grip on these things that we must establish should be a fresh focus on the truth of the Trinity, so that we learn to live our lives as what our baptism proclaimed them to be — a matter of relating to the Father, to the Son, and to the Holy Spirit. When our lives are not intentionally structured in terms of this tri-personal relationship, orthodoxy becomes barren intellectualism, and orthopraxy degenerates into Jesus-olatry or, in some circles, spirit-obsessed charismania, with the Father forgotten in both cases. But when the Christian gospel is understood biblically, as a declaration of what the Father, the Son, and the Holy Spirit do together for our salvation, and when the Christian life is understood biblically — as the acknowledging of a relationship with each of the three Persons distinctly and a practice of cooperation with and adoration of each, no less than of the three in their unity — not only does orthodoxy become true doxology and orthopraxy become true devotion, something else happens too. There is convergence. Word-centred evangelicals, sacrament-centred traditionalists, and fellowship-centred charismatics — the Christ-centred, the Father-centred, and the Spirit-centred, as they appear to those outside — find themselves drawing together, as each group discerns more and more of what it holds most dear appearing in the lives of the others. Each group also discerns that more and more of what the others hold most dear belongs to the true reality of spiritual life in a trinitarian frame and is there for them too. Thus, by a process of what might be called domestic ecumenism, fragmented insights and values coalesce in a fullness of trinitarian faith and life that none of the groups had on its own; and live orthodoxy regains credibility as the viewpoint that can lead the Anglican Church beyond rationalistic and relativistic revisionism, to clarity and vitality in worship, work, and witness.

"In the end," wrote the Methodist author quoted above, "the renewal of the church involves this simple but manifold immersion in the life of the Triune God mediated in the canonical life of the church. This is how the church was birthed in the first place; this is how it has been sustained through the ages; and this is how it is renewed when it goes astray."[6] Exactly so.

Should God visit us to bring about the kind of renewal we are describing, there would be many significant consequences. The new-found clarity and vitality would overflow in many directions, and the necessary concern for making contemporary application of the faith would be informed by the unchanging realities of God and godliness in a way that has not been seen for many years. Evangelism, which is currently a problematic concept in many quarters, would be clearly seen as a matter of introducing others to Jesus Christ; one beggar telling another where to find bread, as it has sometimes been put. Theological colleges would not see it as their priority to be laboratories for theological experiment, but rather to be schools garnering proven spiritual and pastoral wisdom, undergirded with scholarship and focused on our neopagan population with sociological realism. Congregations would embrace cheerfully, as a requirement both of Scripture and of our times, the calling to be different from the secular world, to live as Christ's church, expressing the reality of his indwelling presence, and so to be God's counter-culture in an era of drift away from the faith. Christian families would similarly learn to rejoice, parents and children together, in being different from those around them for Jesus Christ's sake. And practical Samaritanship would abound, as individuals and groups took action to relieve human needs on their own doorsteps, and addressed the social and political causes of those needs.

Let us resolve to talk, think, work, and pray for renewal. This is the way forward, and there appears to be no other. We look forward to the time when the Anglican Church will once more be able to say with the psalmist: "I will not die but live, and will proclaim what the Lord has done" (Ps. 118:17). May that day come soon.

SUGGESTED READING

The Truth Shall Make You Free: The Lambeth Conference 1988 (London: Anglican Consultative Council, 1988).

Alister E. McGrath, *The Renewal of Anglicanism* (Harrisburg, Pa.: Morehouse Publishing, 1993).

Stephen Neill, *Anglicanism* (Harmondsworth: Penguin Books, 1958; 4th ed., Oxford: Oxford University Press, 1977).

Ephraim Radner and George R. Sumner, eds., *Reclaiming Faith: Essays on Orthodoxy in the Episcopal Church* (Grand Rapids: Eerdmans, 1993).

Stephen Sykes and John S. Booty, eds., *The Study of Anglicanism* (Philadelphia: Fortress Press, 1988).

David Watson, *I Believe in the Church* (London: Hodder & Stoughton, 1979).

ENDNOTES

1. When Christianity became the most favoured religion in Constantine's Roman empire, bishops, who had previously been chief pastors of single local churches, were given oversight of all the churches in areas that were often large. As a result, episcopal oversight of particular congregations became increasingly remote.

2. Reported in *Maclean's*, April 12, 1993, pp. 32–50.

3. For some Anglican analysis of this, see, for instance, John W. Wenham, *Christ and the Bible* (Downers Grove, Ill.: IVP, 1973); "Christ's View of Scripture" in *Inerrancy*, ed. Norman L. Geisler (Grand Rapids: Zondervan, 1979), pp. 1–36; and J. I. Packer, *"Fundamentalism" and the Word of God* (London: IVP, 1958), pp. 54–64.

4. William J. Abraham, "The Renewal of the Church: A Short Essay on its Nature and Significance" (unpublished paper), pp. 11–14.

5. Jonathan Edwards was the classic eighteenth-century theologian of divine visitations. See J. I. Packer, *A Quest for Godliness* (Wheaton, Ill.: Crossway, 1990), pp. 309–27.

6. Abraham, "The Renewal of the Church," p. 21.

SECTION II
TRUTH

5

ON TRACK WITH THE WORD
THE AUTHORITY OF THE BIBLE TODAY

PETER MASON

Christians call their book of sacred writings the Holy Bible. My first experience of the Bible's "holiness" took place in a high school English literature class. We were required to study selected portions of Scripture as literature, and one day the teacher discovered that I had inadvertently placed another book on my copy of holy writ. "Get that book off the Bible!" he roared; "I thought you were going to be a minister." What made the scene as incongruous as it was tense was the well-known fact that this particular teacher had no Christian affiliation, nor did he ever attend church. I can only surmise that some vestigial remnant of superstition lingered in his approach to the Bible; I know he succeeded in transferring some of it to me for several years to come.

There must be more substantial reasons for taking the Bible seriously than tradition, superstition, or nostalgic sentiment. However, many people, including serious Christians, struggle to understand just why the Bible deserves a unique and authoritative status as they formulate their religious beliefs and spiritual values.

How can a collection of ancient stories, poems, letters, and speeches be true or relevant today? Do science and modern thinking make the Bible obsolete? Can I turn to the familiar words of Jesus for spiritual comfort, and safely ignore his harder sayings about obedience and judgement? Besides, whose interpretation of the Bible is correct when so many different and contradictory voices are being heard, even among scholars and church leaders?

It is important to recognize where we ourselves are and begin there even though others are at different starting points. Some are veteran, convinced Christians. They are as comfortable in the world of the Bible as in the 1990s. Others are more tentative in their faith, having discovered new meaning and hope in the good news of Christ, while still unsure of many of its implications and perhaps not certain where to turn for appropriate answers. Some are seekers; they have been attracted to the story of Jesus and need that special word of assurance that Jesus' story is as true as it is compelling. And among others are the skeptics — men and women who for a multitude of reasons are moving away from faith rather than towards it. And, perhaps most significantly, there are those who are experiencing second thoughts as new and difficult issues emerge, challenging their previously unquestioned assumptions. What, for example, does the Bible really say and mean about homosexuality? Is the traditional, "biblical" teaching still correct, or should it be revised?

Wherever we are in our understanding of the role of Scripture in the life of individuals and the church, it is safe to say that most of us seek deeper insight and assurance in this critical issue. Indeed, when we think about it we shall likely realize that most of our faith as Christians is based upon the contents of the Bible. Is the Bible true, is it understandable, is it practical for contemporary living? These are the sorts of questions I am addressing in this chapter. Many of them are my own questions; I suspect they are yours too.

GETTING STARTED

It is a universal human instinct to wonder about our origins and destinies. From the initial question of a pre-school child — "Mommy, where did I come from?" — to the imaginative theories and painstaking calculations of the astrophysicist, all of us are more than a little curious about the beginnings of life.

From time immemorial, people have conjectured that the existence of the cosmos and the life of each piece and person in it owed its being to a creator, a super-person or principle that transcended everything and everyone in it. This argument for the existence of God, known by the philosophers as the cosmological argument, appears in virtually every religious tradition and school of thought, although not with unanimous approval or existence. The Psalmist put it like this:

> The heavens are telling the glory of God;
> and the firmament proclaims his handiwork.
> (Psalm 19:1)

This argument from design may or may not convince you of the existence of God. But if it awakens in you, as it does in me, a deep instinctive hunch that, after all, there must be something more, then we need to move to another even more crucial question: if there is a God, is it likely that this infinitely powerful creator would choose to communicate or reveal himself to his creation?

Let me illustrate. Imagine a woman and a man who are thrilled to become parents. After months of keen anticipation they finally welcome the new baby with joy and excitement. Within moments of the birth, however, they inexplicably decide to confine their infant to a mechanical, impersonal environment, in which all of the baby's physical needs — food, warmth, bathing — are managed by a system of high-tech robots. Not a word is ever spoken, not a hug is shared, as the little one grows into a young child. The only consolation is that eventually other orphan children join the first, and while they learn to cooperate and enjoy each other, they forever sense the frustration of not knowing their parents. For their part, the parents too are missing the fulfilment that the act and process of creation was supposed to provide.

I cannot imagine God creating this universe of breathtaking beauty and warmth and grandeur, then withholding his own divine presence from those very beings who seem so willing and able to love him in return. As Professor Eugene Fairweather once remarked, "Why did God create us? Because he wanted friends." So we are here, not fully understanding the story of our beginnings, yet sensing that those beginnings are more than coincidence or accident.

REVELATION AND INSPIRATION

Christians therefore are people with a story. It is a story that grows out of the conviction that a creator-God would also be a revealer-God, and in some sense the story is more God's than ours. In fact, we easily speak of the Bible as the Word of God, that is, the story told by God so that we might discover who we are and, more important, who he is. The formal title of this process of communication is *revelation*: God discloses his nature and purposes to humankind in ways that they can grasp. It should be noted in passing that the use of the word *story* does not imply fantasy, fiction, or unimportance; it simply means that the vehicle of God's self-revelation is first through the events of history and then through the recalling, retelling, and recording of those decisive, saving events.

What are the origins of this story? Where did it come from? Obviously it comes to us most directly in the pages of the Bible. But while the Bible is the most immediate and authoritative source of God's story, it is not our only source. Several other religions possess their own writings, some of which support and parallel the biblical account of creation; other ancient documents from the Jewish world supply information about Old Testament characters and events, and such historians as Josephus and Tacitus confirm the existence and significance of Jesus of Nazareth in the New Testament period. Archaeological discoveries and research add to our knowledge of life in biblical times and further substantiate the accuracy of the Bible's record.

Nevertheless, in the final analysis it is the Bible itself which provides the fullest and most complete account of the story of God's action in creating, guiding, and eventually saving humankind from self-destruction. The key question, however, is whether we can say that the Bible itself, as well as the story it contains, functions as an extension of God's self-revelation. In other words, is the Bible "inspired"? Inspiration means that the authors of the biblical texts, and consequently the texts themselves, were controlled and produced under the influence of God the Holy Spirit. Certain well-known biblical texts declare this very point themselves: in 2 Peter, people are moved by the Holy Spirit to speak from God, while in 2 Timothy, it is the texts themselves that are inspired (literally "breathed out") by God and are therefore foundational for faith and obedience. Technically, of course, these particular New Testament passages must refer to the earlier writings of the Old Testament, although in certain places we find New Testament texts implying their own authority. So, for example, at the end of the fourth Gospel, John declares that his words have been written so that readers might believe in Jesus and thereby receive eternal life (John 20:31).

We cannot treat the Bible as inspired, however, simply because it claims to be so. It cannot be used to prove what it already assumes. Otherwise we should have to regard other religions' scriptures, which make an identical claim, in a similar way. It is necessary, therefore, to examine the question of biblical interpretation in a broader light.

Along the way, several different approaches to the Bible have developed. Space does not permit a thorough review of the history of biblical interpretation, but we should at least note that at different times in history Christians have regarded the Bible in a variety of ways. In the first few centuries, the church held the Bible in high regard and formulated creeds and doctrines with constant reference and appeal to what was found in Scripture. Somewhat later the church began using the Bible allegorically, seeing special meanings encoded in the parables, images, and stories that went beyond the plain meaning of the text. The reformers of the sixteenth century called the church back to the plain, literal meaning of the text, with enormous and far-reaching success. Later centuries saw the rise of a new kind of biblical study and interpretation that often seemed more critical and skeptical than what previous generations of Christians had experienced. The consequences of this two-century controversy have left the church still polarized, with some radically critical scholars on the one side seemingly unable to articulate a clear attractive gospel for the church, and individuals on the other side longing for a safe, irrefutable faith built unquestioningly on the Bible. In the estimate of the latter, the Bible has become "holy, gold-leafed," immune to serious critical examination.

Many Christians have indeed found faith in the God of the Bible, bringing them new hope and purpose for their lives. Their experience of God's love and mercy prompts them to return again and again to the pages of the Bible. Is there another way to reach the same conclusion that the Bible is the Word of God, God's inspired instrument of his own revelation?

THE BIBLE AND HISTORY

While Christians may eventually decide that the Bible is more than a record of certain historical events, they insist that it is not less than history, or at least not outside the realm of history. Not all of the Bible can be described as history, of course; the opening chapters of Genesis and the book of the Revelation, for instance, express their meanings in different ways. But when we encounter the entire sweep of the Jewish-Christian story, it is evident that this story has a profoundly historical dimension to it.

Like any other history, the narrative of the Bible contains major and minor climaxes which stand out and give shape to the story. They are well known to most of us but it may be helpful to review them briefly at this point. While in one sense they are hardly a climax, the opening themes of the Bible are fundamental and crucial. There we are introduced to the whole notion of creation, creation by a powerful, good, and moral God. The first persons owe their existence to God in a special and direct way and are drawn into a covenantal relationship with God. This covenant is soon broken and the consequences of this "fall from grace" include separation from God, suffering, hostility, violence, and death.

God renews the covenant repeatedly and with the call of Abraham and Sarah links the covenant to a specially chosen people and a specially designated land. Thus is born the concept of Israel and the struggle of the people to remain faithful to God while inhabiting the land they inherited by divine promise.

Early in the story the Israelites leave the land in search of food in Egypt. Their escape and deliverance from slavery, under the leadership of Moses, is another climactic moment. As they return to the land of promise, they receive and develop a system of moral and ritual law to govern their behaviour and worship. Long chapters of their story are occupied with the challenge to be faithful to God in the face of competing tribes and false gods. Internal jealousies and ambitions plague the Israelites' society, eventually leading to civil war and then capture and expulsion into exile by neighbouring empires.

Still God does not abandon his people, and before long a new generation of faithful Israelites returns to the land of promise to restore worship, order, and peace. Gradually a new vision of the future emerges. Articulated by prophets, it focuses on God creating a new order, a new kingdom born out of suffering — suffering of none other than the chosen, anointed servant of God himself. This messianic servant will bring fresh light not only to the people of Israel but to the nations — the Gentiles — as well.

This hoped-for saving person eventually appears in the person of Jesus as the story moves in a new and surprising direction. His roots are firmly in Judaism and he never abandons the ancient people of Israel. But their response to him includes a complex mixture of acceptance and rejection, devotion and hostility. Eventually Jesus is captured, tried, found guilty of blasphemy, and sentenced to death. But his death on the cross leads, not to his extermination and oblivion, but to an astonishing new beginning; for in three days he is alive again, and in no time his disillusioned followers have rallied and are newly deputized to go into all the world with a powerful story of God's saving action and a clarion call to follow this resurrected Jesus. The implications of a life of discipleship include participation in a new community, the church; a mandate to work for the renewal of creation and society towards the pattern of God's heavenly kingdom; and, ultimately, the fulfilment of God's original and eternal purposes in a new and final age to come. In that consummated state "God himself will be with them; he will wipe away every tear from their eyes, and death shall be no more, neither shall there be mourning nor crying nor pain any more" (Rev. 21:3,4).

This, in a nutshell, is the Christian story, a story that is deeply inspiring, passionately compelling, and most important, profoundly true. If it is not true — and by that I mean true within history — then the rest of its attractiveness is bogus and nullified. Above all, this criterion of historical truthfulness must apply to the resurrection of Jesus. Few will deny the initial difficulty of fitting the resurrection of Jesus into the framework of history. For one thing, resurrection is completely foreign to our own experience of reality: dead people do not come back to life. That impossibility was as evident for Jesus' contemporaries as it is for us today. Furthermore, while the process of Jesus' resurrection begins in a space-time setting (a first-century Jerusalem tomb), it immediately moves outside these verifiable parameters and into the realm of external or eternal supernatural forces that are beyond our approach. Yet while these and other questions raise initial difficulties for thoughtful inquirers, they are far from insurmount-able and indeed diminish in their significance as we grow more confident that Jesus was, in fact, raised from the grave.

Space does not permit a thorough investigation of the evidence for Jesus' resurrection; others have thoroughly examined the various elements of the case for resurrection, and the reader is referred to such well-known teachers as John Stott or Alan Richardson.[1] It is their conclusion and its implications that concern us here.

To put it bluntly, if Jesus was raised from the dead, so what? Why is it so important for twentieth-century women and men? From the very beginning, the resurrection of Jesus has been seen to lead to four critical conclusions. First, the resurrection of Jesus gives powerful evidence for the reality of God and his involvement with his creation. The disciples could not resuscitate the corpse of Jesus; they could only embalm and bury it. All of Jesus' own energy and vitality was exhausted; only the will and power of the transcendent God could raise him up.

Second, the resurrection makes sense out of Jesus' otherwise tragic and im-moral death. Jesus identified his mission and purpose with the suffering servant of the Old Testament prophets, who would give his life for others as an atoning sacrifice for sin. The resurrection is God's vindication of that sacrificial offering and its effectiveness in accomplishing that for which it was intended.

Third, the resurrection becomes a sign and foretaste of human destiny. So the Apostle Paul, for instance, links Jesus' resurrection with ours: "He who raised the Lord Jesus will raise us also with Jesus and bring us with you into his pres-ence..."(2 Cor 4:14; see also 1 Thess. 4:14).

Fourth, and for our purposes here, most important, the resurrection of Jesus confirms and validates his identity and role in God's purposes to reveal himself to his creation and to save it. No one makes this point more clearly than Paul in Romans 1. The apostle writes of the unique presence of human and divine na-tures in the person of Jesus: "He was descended from David according to the flesh and designated Son of God in power according to the Spirit of holiness *by his resurrection from the dead,* Jesus Christ our Lord" (Rom.1:3,4; emphasis added). Previously, at his baptism and then on the Mount of Transfiguration, the voice of God had heralded the identity and authority of Jesus: "This is my beloved Son; listen to him" (Mark 9:7). Now, in the resurrection, there can be no doubt; this man Jesus, in his words and actions, contains and conveys the supreme and unique voice and authority of the infinite, personal creator-God of the universe. What Jesus does and says originates in the mind and expresses the will of God, possessing such authority that to reject any or all parts of it leaves one danger-ously at risk of offending and denying the very God who gave us life and then called us into friendship with himself.

JESUS AND THE AUTHORITY OF THE BIBLE

If the authority of Jesus governs and guides us in spiritual and moral matters generally, his authority certainly is crucial with regard to the Bible. (We should remember that it was the Hebrew Scriptures, our Old Testament, which constituted Jesus' Bible; we shall consider the authority of the New Testament separately.) It is difficult to find a chapter in the Gospels that does not record Jesus quoting from the Bible approvingly or referring to it indirectly. Over and over he called it the Word of God and constantly appealed to it to prove his point or to invoke the supreme divine authority.

Not surprisingly, Jesus interpreted the Bible in light of his own identity. Early in his public ministry, for example, he attended worship in the synagogue, where he was invited to read the Scripture lesson. The passage was a predictive one, announcing the Spirit of the Lord upon the speaker. No sooner had he finished reading than he declared, "Today this scripture has been fulfilled in your hearing" (Luke 4:21). On another occasion, he engaged in a debate with a Samaritan woman about the origin and identity of the messiah. When she spoke hopefully about the eventual coming of the messiah, he unhesitatingly announced, "I who speak to you am he" (John 4:1–26).

Furthermore, when the situation warranted it, Jesus challenged and corrected distorted interpretations of Scripture and reprimanded those who promoted them. Among his chief targets were the Pharisees, or spiritual rulers of the Jews who prided themselves on their biblical knowledge, yet twisted the texts to suit their own advantage (John 5:36–40).

What, however, of the New Testament — those writings which themselves contain the story of Jesus and therefore followed his ministry, and thus over which he had no direct control or input? Central to Jesus' strategy were his disciples, particularly the twelve apostles. These he recruited, taught, commissioned, and sent out with his own authority to preach, to teach, to baptize, and to heal. Their ministry was as much an extension of his as his was of the Father's. "Whoever receives you receives me, and whoever receives me receives him who sent me" (Matt. 10:40).

In the upper room with his disciples at the last supper, Jesus countered their anxiety about the future in which he would no longer be physically present for them. Their conversation is found in John 14–16, and parts of it need to be carefully considered here. In the face of his impending departure, Jesus promises to send the Holy Spirit to comfort and strengthen them. Then he spells out exactly how the Spirit will provide that encouragement: "The Counsellor, the Holy Spirit, whom the Father will send in my name, he will teach you all things, and bring to your remembrance all that I have said to you" (John 14:26).

In other words, Jesus will continue to be present to the extent that people remember, believe, and obey the promises, directions, and exhortations that Jesus gave while he was active on earth.

Then a little later in that same intense conversation, Jesus returns to the role of the Spirit in ensuring the accurate and authoritative survival of his words:

> I have yet many things to say to you, but you cannot bear them now. When the Spirit of truth comes, he will guide you into all the truth; for he will not speak on his own authority, but whatever he hears he will speak, and he will

declare to you the things that are to come. He will glorify me, for he will take what is mine and declare it to you. All that the Father has is mine; therefore I said that he will take what is mine and declare it to you (John 16:12–15).

Clearly Jesus expected that his words, which possessed unique authority when he initially spoke them, would be accurately and even supernaturally recorded and preserved for future generations who would seek as intimate a relationship with him as that enjoyed by the first-century apostolic band.

We can therefore see how our four Gospels have become definitive instruments of revelation in God's plan. Can the same be said for the rest of the New Testament? I believe the answer is "yes," for two reasons. First, the Gospels and Epistles were both written in roughly the same period, with some (though not a great deal of) overlapping of authorship. Second, the majority of the Epistles were written by Paul of Tarsus, who forcefully claimed, and received, apostolic status and authority on the grounds of Jesus' appearance to him on the Damascus road (1 Cor. 9:1; 15:3–11; Gal.1:1; 2:6–9). There is an illuminating comment in the second Epistle of Peter (3:15–16), in which Paul's writings are said to contain "the wisdom that God gave him," writings that ignorant and unstable people distort "as they do the other scriptures."

Statements such as these constitute the beginnings of a two-centuries-long debate about which writings would be accorded canonical or authoritative status within the early church. While the debate was long and sometimes divisive, at the end of the day the twenty-seven books that ultimately were accepted into the canon achieved that recognition, not arbitrarily, but because they possessed an internal consistency and clearly originated from within the first-century apostolic band. The early church did not so much confer its authority upon these writings as recognize their inherent authority, derived from their God-givenness.

So at last we can join with the Apostle Paul in proclaiming that indeed "all scripture is inspired by God" — that is, breathed out by God — and therefore is profitable for every sort of spiritual use and purpose (2 Tim. 3:16).

IMPLICATIONS, APPLICATIONS, AND COMPLICATIONS

The history of biblical understanding and interpretation is long and complex. At this point we can only flag a small number of issues that grow out of our conviction that the Bible is God's inspired Word, the chief instrument of his self-disclosure or revelation.

The first and, to my mind, the most important of these issues has to do with interpreting or understanding the meaning of the biblical text. The technical words associated with this issue include *exegesis*, that is, deciding what the text said or meant to its human author and original readers, and *hermeneutics*, which means interpreting and understanding the Bible's meanings for our own day and situation, taking account of our own assumptions and biases.[2] Christians who hold a particularly "high" view of Scripture as God's Word need to set the example of using the Bible responsibly. We shall want to take the plain, unadorned meaning of the text; pay attention to the literary genre of individual texts; make every effort to factor in our own cultural and personal biases and limitations; and assume a high degree of internal consistency within the whole range of Scripture, despite the vastness and diversity of its individual parts.

A second concern is what I call proportion. Within the entirety of Scripture we find certain ambiguous, controversial texts. Some of these have led to doctrinal, ecclesiastical, and ethical differences between serious Christians. Perhaps because of our fallenness and consequent insecurity, we are inclined to fasten onto these problems at the expense of a sense of the overall clarity and therefore trustworthiness of Scripture. As an antidote we need more contact with a wider range of Christian individuals and church bodies with whom we find unity and fellowship centring around a shared confidence in the Bible as God's Word.

Thirdly, we are challenged to search for convergence, for a clearer understanding of the relationship between Scripture, human reason, and experience, and of the role of the church and its tradition in understanding and interpreting the Bible. Some interpreters would suggest we have three equal authorities — Scripture, tradition, and reason — much like a three-legged stool. But this nicely balanced theory fails to recognize that final authority rests only in Jesus Christ, who is encountered primarily in Scripture and secondarily in the lives of his people, past or present. We indeed use our God-given reason to the best of our ability but we recognize its finiteness and fallibility and therefore submit to God's Word at those crucial points where our logical conclusions seem at variance with it. Furthermore, we humbly test our individual understandings and interpretations of Scripture with the insights of the wider community, the church, drawing upon the wisdom of scholars, commentators, wise and godly mentors, and all those whose Christian experience qualifies them to help us discern God's truth and God's will.

A final and possibly most difficult challenge has to do with *submission*. It is not simply a matter of individual Christians yielding their personal attitudes and agendas to the directives of God's Word. Rather, it is the call to the whole church, and indeed to humankind in its entirety, to bring every thought, every value, every decision, every action into conformity with the will of God as it is disclosed in Scripture. Our age is characterized by a consumer mentality in which individuals are encouraged to identify their own needs and goods, and then find "meaningful" ways to actualize them. Some may find fulfilment in religion, others in political action, still others in the retreat into privatism. But this is a far cry from the biblical vocation to make Jesus Christ known, trusted, obeyed, and glorified by each and every human being who owes his or her very existence to the one great God of the universe and to whom accountability will ultimately still be given by one and all.

Today more than ever, individual Christians, and every church congregation, diocese, and denomination, must recapture confidence in the truthfulness, reliability, and power of Scripture, to save, renew, and prepare women and men for life in God's kingdom, now and in the age to come.

SUGGESTED READING

Alan Richardson, *History, Sacred and Profane* (London: SCM Press Ltd., 1964).

John R. W. Stott, *The Contemporary Christian* (Downers Grove: InterVarsity Press, 1992).

Tony Thiselton, "Understanding God's Word Today," in *Obeying Christ in a Changing World,* Vol. 1, ed. John Stott (London: Foundation Books, 1977).

ENDNOTES

1. John R. W. Stott, *The Contemporary Christian* (Downers Grove: InterVarsity Press, 1992), pp. 78 ff, and Alan Richardson, *History, Sacred and Profane* (London: SCM Press Ltd., 1964), pp. 184 ff.

2. For a good discussion of the subject of biblical interpretation or hermeneutics, see Tony Thiselton, "Understanding God's Word Today," in *Obeying Christ in a Changing World,* Vol. 1, ed. John Stott (London: Foundation Books, 1977).

CHAPTER

6

WHO WAS JESUS?
RE-ENVISIONING THE HISTORICAL JESUS
AND THE VISION OF GOD'S PEOPLE

EDITH HUMPHREY

THE QUEST AND THE FAITHFUL INQUIRER:
AT CROSS PURPOSES?

I recently found, buried in my file-folder on the quest for the historical Jesus, a 1991–1992 catalogue from Polebridge Press, a California-based press heavily influenced by Robert Funk and others associated with the "Jesus Seminar" of the Westar Institute. "The Jesus Seminar" has recently become known in popular as well as scholarly circles, mainly because of the publication at the end of 1993 of a book entitled *The Five Gospels.*[1] This book was discussed widely in newspapers across North America and evoked strong reaction from many quarters. *The Five Gospels* is only one of a number of pieces that have made public the findings of the Jesus Seminar, a seminar in which the authenticity of Jesus' sayings was voted upon by scholars who used mutually acceptable literary criteria. Their votes were registered through the use of various coloured balls — red for probably authentic, pink for possibly authentic, grey for possibly not authentic, and black for likely unauthentic. It is clear that for several members of the seminar, their deliberations are no in-house scholarly game but are intended to attract the attention of the general public. Dominique Crossan and Burton Mack, for example, have published popular versions of their most recent scholarly works,[2] and Robert Funk has gone on record speaking about the importance of communication with the public at large. The catalogue from Polebridge in my file is in accord with this goal. It advertises a new journal, *The Fourth R,* in a manner that is both informative of the Press's purpose, and helpful in showing how we, as those concerned for orthodoxy within an Anglican perspective, might be viewed. Here is its text, in part:

The Fourth R
An Advocate for Religious Literacy

Separation of church and state is not a license to remain piously ignorant. Religion is the fourth R.

Religious literacy is essential to:
understanding world conflicts
bringing religious matters into perspective
reducing bigotry and intolerance

liberating oneself from evangelical bullies
understanding culture and freedom

The Fourth R provides important information for making intelligent choices in a free society.

The Fourth R addresses the following questions:
Who was Jesus?
The year 2000: Is the world really coming to an end?
Where is fundamentalism leading us?
What must faithful Christians believe today?
Do ecclesiastical translations of the Bible really work?
What books belong to the Bible?
What secular stories do Americans live by?[3]

This lively advertisement is probably not aiming to be inflammatory, although it may strike some that way because it targets certain groups. Rather, the text is being true to the increasingly heard plea in postmodern discussion that scholars not assume a false "disinterested" stance of neutrality, but show their hand when they write. Moreover, it is correct in its assumptions that questions about the Bible and about Jesus are not simply of academic interest in our day. Just a glance through both popular and scholarly religious catalogues for the last few years will confirm that the issue "Who was Jesus?" is of ongoing concern. Here are some titles for 1994 from just one press, Trinity Press International: Leif E. Vaage, *Galilean Upstarts: Jesus' First Followers According to Q*; Marcus J. Borg, *Jesus in Contemporary Scholarship*; James H. Charlesworth and Walter P. Weaver, eds., *Images of Jesus Today*; Willi Marxsen, *Jesus and the Church*; Bernard Cooke, *God's Beloved: Jesus' Experience of the Transcendent.*

In our own country we could cite the Canadian Society of Biblical Literature's (CSBS) "Historical Jesus Seminar," which began in June 1993 in Ottawa and continued to June 1994 in Calgary. The public and scholarly interest shown in this discussion, as well as the diversity of opinions expressed there, indicate how much work is being done in this area. One Scandinavian scholar, Halvor Moxnes, made explicit his concern for the public interest in Jesus research that he has noted. I was struck, however, by the embarrassment which met a question asked by one non-scholar in the crowd. This man was obviously working from inside the Christian tradition and was trying to grapple with the possible implications of Dead Sea Scrolls findings for our understanding of Jesus. The awkwardness with which he was treated by the members of the society came, it seemed to me, from a sense of dissonance in the rarefied atmosphere of the conference rather than from the confusion he displayed. Despite the efforts of advocates for religious literacy, there was a distance between the questioner's concerns — How does this affect faith? How does this affect the church? — and the intricate discussions of the seminar. This is not to say that members of the seminar never displayed personal engagement with the issues — individual pain of a particularly vocal feminist was both heard and discussed — but the issues faced by the questioner I mentioned were not so easily heard by the seminar members. There was a distinct gap between his concerns and the cut-and-thrust of scholarly debate or the ideological plea for feminist scholarship. My awareness of that gap has been mirrored by other scholars who continue to ask, What is the relationship between the academy and the church? Between the academy and society at large?

Well, then, what difference does religious literacy in the matter of the historical Jesus make for those who are seeking to maintain a faithful perspective? The quest, or rather, quests for the historical Jesus have gone on now for more than 100 years and are complex. From the point of view of some in the church, scholarly discussions and reconstructions of the historical Jesus are abstruse and unapproachable, hence of no use. We might cite the response of such a thinker as C. S. Lewis who was, of course, not a New Testament specialist, but an academic well respected for his work in Middle English literature and well known for his popular Christian writings. The attitude of Lewis towards the quest for the historical Jesus in his own day was firmly negative. In fact, he implies in his well-known *Screwtape Letters* that New Testament scholars' attempts to reconstruct a historical figure of Jesus is a task directed by the devil:

> In the last generation [explains "Screwtape"] we promoted the construction of such a "historical Jesus" on liberal and humanitarian lines; we are now putting forward a new "historical Jesus" on Marxian, catastrophic and revolutionary lines. The advantages of these constructions, which we intend to change every thirty years or so, are manifold. In the first place they all tend to direct men's devotion to something which does not exist, for each "historical Jesus" is unhistorical.[4]

Lewis's discomfiture is clearly due to the manner in which the quests had proceeded up to his time. As N. T. Wright suggests, "presumably, he didn't like the portraits [of Jesus] that had been produced to date. And who can blame him?"[5] Of course, some of the issues have changed from Lewis's time, and the quest has continued in different directions since the forties. Be that as it may, the gap between the academy and those of the general public who identify themselves as part of the church of God is still there and seems to be mutually created. The awkwardness that I observed at the CSBS meetings in dealing with a layperson is seemingly matched by disinterest or even hostility when faithful readers who are not specialists in New Testament studies hear about the newest developments in scholarly Jesus research. In a way, this is to be expected. What difference does a heated discussion of the development of Q communities mean to someone who has no idea of what kind of document Q[6] was supposed to be? What should a Christian think when informed by a newspaper review of the latest book that Jesus probably never uttered the words of institution at the Last Supper and that, in fact, two-thirds of his words were "ghost-written"?

First it needs to be stated clearly that neither knee-jerk antagonism nor uninformed lack of interest are good enough. The former response has been seen in extreme forms in the book-burning of *The Five Gospels* by some overzealous fundamentalists in the southern states, or even by the attempted bombing (!) of property belonging to Jane Schaberg, a scholar who has been under fire from conservative Roman Catholics for her view that Jesus was one of the large ranks of illegitimate children. Most of us can probably identify better with a second possible response, one of disinterest. There is, it seems, a continuing pietism in the churches that plays off the Christ of faith against the Jesus of history, and that looks to inner individualistic experience as the measure of faith: "You ask me how I know he lives? He lives within my heart!" Here I think we need to admit that there is a danger of abandoning the utterly essential emphasis upon history in the Judaeo-Christian story. Our faith looks *back* to the actions of God through Abraham, Sarah, and Moses, and to God's supremely important activity in the historic figure of Jesus of Nazareth; our faith does not look, in the first place at least, *in* to a demonstration of inner peace or a "Christ" experience. Often it is difficult to realize how profoundly our thinking has been influenced by the individualism fostered in Enlightenment thought, brought to a new peak in our own time in the sixties, seventies, and eighties. We read the prophetic words about "circumcision of the heart" and "the law written on the tablets of the heart" correctly as indicative of the difference between the Old and New Covenants, but incorrectly as indicative of an autonomous faith, unattached from community, and unhampered by logic or argument.

We need, then, to recapture a sense of what it means to have a Christian mind on such subjects as the historical Jesus. A sober evaluation of the various sketches of Jesus will neither dismiss them as unimportant, nor fear them as essentially subversive of faith, unless our view is that faith should "believe although it is absurd."[7] One of the great distinctions between Christianity and the Gnostic movement, which was to become a threat to the church beginning in about the second century, was that Christianity maintained the goodness of creation and the importance of activities in that creation (i.e., historical events). If we say "Lord, Lord," but do not anchor that title to the Jesus who preached, taught, died, and appeared after his resurrection in first-century Palestine, then we are not understanding what "Lord" really means. The incarnation is not simply a theological formulation but an indication of the human nature of Jesus, and a guideline as to how he is to be viewed. That God became human should in itself be a sign to us that historical questions and answers are important.

But why should there be any historical questions? Can we not simply read the Bible and see immediately what happened and why it did? Why do we need historical inquiry? In fact, none of us "just read the Bible" and get our theological or historical understanding directly from it. After all, a true appreciation of the New Testament will recognize that God has bequeathed to the church four separate Gospels, not a gospel harmony. When we bring these Gospels together, we make decisions about how to do this, or we rely on others who have done this for us: we engage in creating a picture, one coherent account. Careful consideration of Jesus must acknowledge the existence of four theological presentations of his life, mission, and role. These four Gospels are not sheer *curriculae vitae* unadorned by interpretation, nor sheer mythology devoid of an interest in history. The Gospels are a curious and bracing mixture of theology and history, and the differences between each should be explored rather than minimized or collapsed together. We need then to recover a faith that is robust enough to consider Jesus research carefully rather than rage at it or dismiss it. We need also to remember two points that are often forgotten: history is bound up with our faith, not irrelevant to it; and the Bible is a rich, multifaceted resource for our understanding of God and God's embodied Word, the Lord Jesus.

In our frank and open reading of Jesus research, however, let us not naively surrender to the irresponsible claim to neutrality that some experts have made. Let there be no mistake: all historical presentations are interpretations of the events. There is no such thing as "neutral" history, despite the bold declarations of dustjackets and the press that "Christian faith will be shaken by these facts." Indeed, the various questers for Jesus have not been motivated by scholarly or antiquarian concern alone. In their research of Jesus and the early church, few scholars begin by viewing the New Testament as an interesting text to be searched for vestiges of history. Rather, it is quite common — and this task is easier the more distant in time the scholar is — to see behind the quests the theological or existential concerns that have fuelled these and propelled them in one direction or another.

The sort of questions that can aid us in an assessment of scholarly pictures of Jesus would include:

1. What are the presuppositions of the scholar, and how have these coloured the questions asked and the resultant presentation of Jesus and the society in which he lived?

2. How many layers of hypotheses are necessary in order for the scholar to arrive at these conclusions?

3. Is the scholar dependent on the hypotheses of others as a basis for his/her work, and how certain are these preliminary arguments?

4. Does the picture of Jesus that emerges, or the picture of first-century society that is posited, sound uncomfortably like our own times? Are anachronistic concerns skewing the picture?

5. Is the quester skeptical about or open to the Gospels themselves providing data for the picture of Jesus and his world?

6. Are major issues begged routinely by the words, "of course" and "no one doubts"? If this seems the case, then it may be time to move beyond the popular presentations of the scholars (which often omit supporting arguments or complex hypotheses) to the more weighty volumes.

Obviously, not everyone in the Christian community has the leisure or concern to tease out these questions. However, all of us can be at least generally aware of the issues so that when "Jesus and History" finds its way into the newspapers, or when friends ask us what we think of the latest portrait, we have some idea of what is at stake. Nor is being in a believing community irrelevant — what I cannot do, someone else may be able to help me with.

THE QUEST: A MANY-HEADED MOVEMENT

There are several good presentations of scholarship on the historical Jesus which can be read (see Suggested Reading at the end of this chapter); but at this point, a brief caricature of the three (or, perhaps more accurately, three and one-half) quests may be helpful.

The First Quest — Liberal Lives of Jesus

In the nineteenth century, liberals such as Ernest Renan[8] and Johannes Weiss[9] adopted a "neutral" stance and, under the influence of Romanticism, stressed the biography of the life of Jesus. Along with other scholars who shared their perspective, they carried on the Enlightenment's interest in history and composed various lives of Jesus, in which the kingdom of God was seen as an ethical ideal, a symbol of personal fellowship with God, as exemplified in Jesus. The Gospel of Mark, now seen as the first through the new solution to the synoptic problem (H. J. Holtzmann), was the simplest expression of Jesus' mission and in it the internal ethical kingdom of God was central although somewhat obscured by theological overlay.

Pretty soon the death-knell to liberal lives of Jesus was sounded by the tiny but very influential book by Albert Schweitzer, *The Quest of the Historical Jesus* (1906).[10] Schweitzer argued that all the attempts to see Jesus as a liberal ethicist proclaiming a kingdom of brotherhood that could be enthusiastically adopted by his modern age were wrong-headed. Schweitzer was very shrewd in seeing through the agenda and presuppositions of his nineteenth-century predecessors and argued that their quest had tended to impose anachronistic individualism upon Jesus. What had been presenting itself as historical inquiry ended up placing Jesus in an ahistorical and universalizing *cul de sac*. Schweitzer also allowed the alien quality of Jesus and his culture to come forward. New scholarly interest in ancient apocalyptic writings influenced his thesis that Jesus was a Jewish apocalyptic prophet who predicted the end of the world but was of course mistaken. Jesus was to be best understood as a pure example of first-century Judaism; his teachings held little relevance for the early twentieth century despite the earnest attempts of past nineteenth-century liberal scholars.

The Second or "New" Quest

The response to Schweitzer came from theologians such as Rudolph Bultmann and Karl Barth, who insisted that the whole idea of the quest had been wrong-headed but that theology had a life independent of the discovery of the historical Jesus. Schweitzer's criticisms of the quest had not been radical enough, since Schweitzer had assumed that the Gospels could tell us at least something about the historical Jesus even if the liberal biographers had been too consumed by their own views to assess the evidence impartially. Bultmann and Barth led the way in moving decisively away from the pursuit of the Jesus of history. Form-criticism — that is, the search for early oral traditions of church narratives concerning Jesus — now became a primary goal of New Testament studies, and an interest in the faith of the early church which told these stories became the new focus. In the early part of the twentieth century, very little was said about the historical figure or the personality of Jesus; an understanding of Jesus was merely viewed as a prolegomenon, or introduction, to the real business of New Testament studies and theology.

However, the quest refused to lie down and stay dead. Maybe you couldn't get very far behind the Gospels in order to write a life of the historical Jesus, as Bultmann had insisted. Nevertheless, perhaps some of the actual words of Jesus had been preserved because of their value for the teaching of the church. Perhaps despite the Jewish apocalyptic aspect of the gospel's Jesus, we can find in some of Jesus' words a challenge for our own lives. Scholars who dealt with Jesus after Bultmann, then, concentrated on the *kerygma*, or proclamation of the word, as the aspect of the Gospels that spoke to them. A few writers, such as Bornkamm[11] and Dibelius[12] attempted to write about the figure of Jesus but it took until the 1950s for the spell to be broken by a former pupil of Bultmann's, Ernst Käsemann,[13] who insisted on attaching the Christ of faith to the Jesus of history. From this point the "New Quest" began in earnest. Where the liberals had hoped to get behind the fabulous and naive tales of the Gospels, back to the pure religion of Jesus himself, twentieth-century New Questers said that the centre of the Gospels was in the word, a word preached by an elusive historical Jesus, but a word that could still challenge today. The New Questers went on to discuss heatedly how to decide which sayings of Jesus are authentic; with these scholars we see a definite theological concern, a hope that critical study of the New Testament could still be a handmaid to the church. Jesus' words are emphasized in such studies, especially the personal, existential challenge of the parables.

The Third Quest — a Holistic Approach

A third and more recent movement, joined by such different scholars as E. P. Sanders,[14] Marcus Borg,[15] Geza Vermes,[16] and N. T. Wright,[17] has tended to emphasize the actions of Jesus and the proclamation of God's kingdom or rule as closely related to the Jewish community. Jesus is to be seen in his own particular society, and his words and actions are to be understood in that milieu. Most of these writers, while recognizing that much of Jesus' teaching was done in Galilee, far removed from the centre of Jewish cult (Jerusalem), insist that the Galileans were still "concerned about the essentials of the Jewish faith."[18] Against this backdrop, Jesus' proclamation of the kingdom, or the new rule of God, involved in some way the renewal of all Israel. Because these scholars come from very different backgrounds — Jewish, Anglican, agnostic, and so on — different answers are given to the riddle of Jesus' death and preaching. All of them, however, are unhappy with the New Questers' fixation upon the words of Jesus alone, and upon the conflicting criteria used to assess the authenticity of these words. Rather, the Third Quest scholars stress the overall picture: the Jewish milieu, the importance of the kingdom, Jesus' actions in the temple, and indeed the overall shape of the life, action, and words of Jesus, in so far as they can be reconstructed.

The New Quest, as Continued by Some "Untimely Born"

Arguing against the programme of the third quest is a group of scholars (Funk, Crossan, Mack, and others) who consider the apocalyptic and Jewish features of the Gospels to be an overlay, an embroidery. Working with a complex apparatus of dating various New Testament and extracanonical materials, they consider that the earliest layer of material discloses a peasant Jesus working in a thoroughly Hellenized milieu. Like the older New Questers, they emphasize Jesus' words, at least the ones they consider most likely to be authentic, and come out with a Jesus who looks rather like a Cynic philosopher.[19] Crossan believes that the radically egalitarian peasant-Jesus preached a kingdom immediately available to anyone, without mediator (including himself). The death of Jesus played no important part for the earliest Jesus movement, but a radical hand-to-mouth lifestyle, a reform of the Galilean villages, was the burden of Jesus' message. Using Crossan's own words, the Jesus who emerges is rather like a peasant hippy living in an Augustan yuppy age. But who would crucify such an innocuous philosopher?

STRUGGLING WITH THE SKETCHES AND THE SCRIPTURES

How, then, does the scholar or the informed nonspecialist who seeks to be faithful handle this diverse material? First, it seems that we, along with those who claim a postmodern stance, can learn some lessons from the past. There is something to be learned about interpretation and perspective: no one, in doing historical or theological work, needs to, or should, claim neutrality. We each work from a perspective and should recognize this as we come to the challenge of reading the New Testament and "reading" history. The danger is not our viewpoint but the unacknowledged smuggling of that viewpoint into a portrait of Jesus that we sketch or reformulate on our reading of the Scriptures. Nonetheless, we cannot be happy with a view that suggests that one person's vision of Jesus is just as fruitful or "faithful" — in the sense of a portrait's execution — as another's. The historical questions are not irrelevant, and the nature of the New Testament itself is such that it calls us to ask, "Who was — and is — Jesus?" rather than, idiosyncratically, "What does Jesus mean to me?" Nor is it good enough to throw up our hands at the multiplicity of scholarly pictures and say, "They all conflict — so much for historical research!" Rather, we can evaluate and appreciate each picture by asking questions about the presuppositions of the particular scholar concerning the emergence and reliability of the New Testament, her or his understanding of the milieu of Jesus, and the way in which various parts of the Gospels and Epistles are analyzed and related to each other.

We may be surprised to find ourselves challenged to rethink certain passages or certain ideas we have about Jesus and his life because of light shed upon them by the most unusual torches.

Despite the inroads made increasingly in North America by the re-emerging "New Quest" represented by Mack and Crossan, I am convinced that those portraits that try to evaluate the whole picture — actions and words of Jesus — within a Hellenized but still recognizably Jewish milieu are most helpful. The historical puzzle is set for us in that our pictures of Jesus are given to us in the form of Gospels. The Gospels are, again, not disinterested in history but certainly tell their stories from theological perspectives, from the perspectives of writers living within various expressions of the early Christian movement. The Gospels give us evidence not simply of their own concerns but also of how early Christian communities understood the life of Jesus; and we have other evidence as well (enriched by such finds as those at Qumran[20]) of the varied shapes that the Jewish community took prior to and during Jesus' time.

But how are we to move from our understanding of Judaism(s) and the early manifestations of the Christian movement to a historical portrait of Jesus? In the words of N. T. Wright, we can adopt a "pincer movement"[21] in trying to envisage Jesus — forwards from the picture of first-century Judaism, backwards from the Gospels. Simply on the historical data (see Sean Freyne[22] for this), this first-century milieu should be understood as fundamentally Jewish, even in rural Galilee, which, of course, had also been influenced by the dominant Hellenistic culture. While sociological studies of peasantry can be helpful to enrich our understanding, we must always remember that in the first century there was never a division of religious and political or economic matters; the peasantry may have been influenced by Greek culture but continued to see the ideal system as a theocratic one, with God as their Ruler. Jewish people of the village still saw as part of their heritage a unified people, a people joined together by the rule of God. In so far as the kingdom, or rule of God, was preached by Jesus, it would have been understood as referring not to individual or village reform but to God's action among God's people as a whole.

THE ONGOING CHALLENGE OF GOD'S RULE IN JESUS

It is against such a background that Jesus' remarkable statements and actions concerning the temple and the rule of God start to make sense. Jesus did not come proclaiming an internal kingdom of God (liberals, and sometimes evangelicals), nor announcing the end of the world, the physical order (Schweitzer), nor suggesting a radical individualistic lifestyle that would shake up the economic status quo of Palestine villages (Crossan *et al*). He came announcing a new beginning, a new era of God's rule through, and even, I would argue, in or as himself. And a beginning, of course, implies an end — or perhaps better, a conclusion — to the old. Even allowing for the shaping of anecdotes and sayings of Jesus from ongoing retelling in the church, the constant thrust of Jesus' words and actions point to his understanding of an imminent action of

God to judge Israel, and his own special place within that judgement. The parable of the tenants, the cursing of the fig tree, the weeping over Jerusalem at a point when most pilgrims would have sung songs of joy, the disturbance in the temple —all these demonstrate Jesus' prophetic call to repentance, and his message of judgement against a chosen but stubbornly wayward people. Israel as a nation had, not surprisingly, enacted the general stance of human rebellion against God rather than embraced her destiny to become a light to the world (Isa. 49:6, Mic. 4:1–4). The earthly ministry of Jesus, concentrated as it was in Galilee and Judea, called attention to the problem of Israel as a messenger *manqué*, and invited (implored at times) God's people to join in God's new way to reach and enlighten his creation.

And how did Jesus see his own role in all this? In the Gospels we find Jesus combining, in a unique way, apocalyptic Son of Man language (Dan. 7:8) with the language of the Servant (Isa. 42, and subsequent passages) who must face suffering:

> "Who do the crowds say that I am?" They answered, "John the Baptist; but others, Elijah; and still others, that one of the ancient prophets has arisen." He said to them, "But who do you say that I am?" Peter answered, "The Messiah of God." He sternly ordered and commanded them not to tell anyone, saying, "The Son of Man must undergo great suffering and be rejected by the elders, chief priests, and scribes, and be killed, and on the third day be raised" (Luke 9:18–21, NRSV).

Often we have read this language and viewed Jesus' actions as though they are, in the first place, about a universal truth, a means of individualistic salvation and enlightenment. We forget that Jesus' ministry was, in the first place, to Israel, and through that word to Israel, for the world. Jesus' joining of apocalyptic Son of Man language and prophetic Suffering Servant language is thoroughly tied to the Hebrew Scriptures and brings together two striking and emotive strands in Daniel and Isaiah. Through this interpretive strategy, Jesus indicated his own expectation and understanding of his death: *he* was to face the trial and suffering meant for Israel, a tribulation at the hand of the Romans but really sent from God. Such a death would issue in the long-awaited reversal of fortunes for God's own people: "Oh, that you would rend the heavens and come down" (Isa. 64:1). This reversal would be signalled by an apocalyptic event — by the resurrection of the one who had died. The reversal was to take a surprising shape, however, and bring about the reordering of God's people into a community that would include believing Gentiles as well as Jews, and those who had been the misfits and impious of society as well as the ceremonially pure. If Jesus enacted a parable against the temple and Jerusalem by overturning tables and creating a prophetic disturbance, he also spoke challenging but hopeful words which were turned against him in the trial: "Destroy this house, and I will build it up again in three days."

One of the difficulties in re-imaging the historical Jesus is that his hope is also his challenge. There was, and continues to be, an offence or surprise in his words and actions for every individual in every group: confusing to the zealots, disturbing to the Sadducean keepers of the status quo, libertine to the pietistic Pharisees, bizarre to the liberals, over-concerned with history to the New Questers, too intense and unmanageable to those who view him as cynic or yuppy in an Augustan age. And what about his challenge to us? Will we turn to Scripture simply to amass evidence for our own cherished system of faith, or will we allow the historical and living Jesus to both confirm and disturb that picture, enriching our traditions and challenging us where we are (unawares) more children of this age than children of the living God?

As we are Christ's ones, in the late twentieth century, how can we mirror the stance of Jesus? Jesus came to his own, a Jew amidst a first-century Jewish culture. This culture was replete with its own understandings, confusions, longings, disappointments, and even pluralism. He fulfilled the hopes and also cut across the dominant thinking of his time. The Son of Man must suffer before the triumph. Renewed Israel would include a vast household of Gentile and Jewish followers of Jesus the Messiah! Our own age displays, to the alert eye, its own understandings, confusions, longings, disappointments, and, of course, pluralism and syncretism. It is, above all, an age that celebrates "selfism," with popular songs and philosophy chorusing, "It's my life," and "And then a hero [i.e., oneself!] comes along." Jesus, the confirmor and disturber of Israel's dreams, speaks a word, through his people, to our own age, to this empty and tragic glorification of the self. To "It's my life," he responds, "Here's my life." To all tired minds and hearts that realize they aren't their own best friend, they are no hero, the gospel tells the story of the Hero, the One who was rejected, died, rose again, and still lives. How can we mirror Jesus' stance in his society as we encounter our own? How can we move beyond an intellectual re-envisioning of Jesus so that he will be seen in our lives, in our faithful communities? We can be aware of how people around us are thinking, aware of what they are saying about Jesus, aware of their longings, questions, hopes, and bankruptcies. Then we can speak a word of peace that was heard first almost two thousand years ago and continues to be current because it is living. In the postmodern climate, words that point to Jesus may at first only be heard as one option among many. We need not even enter into argument concerning their difference; for if we are echoing living words that points to the Word himself, they will have their own impact. "Who do the crowds say that I am? ... But who do you say I am?"

SUGGESTED READING

Marcus Borg, *Jesus: A New Vision* (San Fransisco: Harper and Row, 1987).
J. D. Crossan, *Jesus: A Revolutionary Biography* (San Fransisco: HarperCollins, 1994).
James D. G. Dunn, *Jesus, Paul and the Law* (London: SPCK, 1990).
C. F. D. Moule, *The Birth of the New Testament.*, 3rd ed. (San Francisco: Harper and Row, 1982).

E. P. Sanders, *Jesus and Judaism* (Philadelphia: Fortress, 1985).

Geza Vermes, *Jesus the Jew: A Historians Reading of the Gospels* (Philadelphia: Fortress, 1973).

N. T. Wright, *Who Was Jesus?* (Grand Rapids: Eerdmans, 1992); *Jesus and the Victory of God* (Minneapolis: Fortress, forthcoming).

ENDNOTES

1. Robert W. Funk and Roy W. Hoover, *The Five Gospels: A Search for the Authentic Words of Jesus* (New York: Polebridge/Macmillan, 1993).

2. Dominique Crossan's *Jesus: A Revolutionary Biography* (San Francisco: Harper, 1993) is a popularized version of the more intricate argument presented in his earlier *The Historical Jesus: The Life of a Mediterranean Peasant* (San Francisco: Harper, 1991). Burton L. Mack has presented his view of Jesus and the earliest Christian community in a popular format in *The Lost Gospel: the Book of Q and Christian Origins* (San Francisco: Harper, 1993) but is known in scholarly circles for such works as *A Myth of Innocence: Mark and Christian Origins* (Philadelphia: Fortress, 1988).

3. *Polebridge Press Catalog* (Sonoma, Calif.: Polebridge, 1991–92), p. 8.

4. C. S. Lewis, *Screwtape Letters* (originally Macmillan, 1943) in *The Best of C. S. Lewis* (Grand Rapids: Baker Book House, 1960), pp. 81–2.

5. N. T. Wright, *Who Was Jesus?* (Grand Rapids: Eerdmans, 1992), p. 93.

6. "Q" is the short form for the hypothetical document "Quelle" (German for "source") which is supposed to have been used by Matthew and Luke, along with the earlier Gospel of Mark, in the composition of their Gospels. Q thus forms an essential part of the two-documentary hypothesis (later refined into the four-documentary hypothesis) — the hypothesis accepted by the majority of scholars as the best explanation for the parallels and differences in the synoptic gospels of Matthew, Mark, and Luke. Q is meant to explain the points at which Matthew and Luke agree with each other in wording, when a similar passage does not appear in Mark's Gospel. Scholars describe Q as a sayings source, devoid of the overall narrative structure of Jesus' ministry, death, and resurrection, and think that it was similar in appearance to the Gospel of Thomas (a later second-century Gospel with Gnostic tendencies). Although probably the majority of Gospel critics treat the existence of Q as quasi-factual, some continue to emphasize the hypothetical nature of Q, and some even prefer to think of an oral source or tradition rather than an actual document. Recently, some writers have tried stressing Q as an important element in finding the earliest Christian community, and have even tried to divide Q into three (or more) different stages of writing, each corresponding to a different stage of development in the earliest groupings of Jesus' followers. The difficulties of building hypothetical communities upon a hypothetical source should be evident.

7. The classic phrase for this kind of thinking is *credo quia absurdum est*, first coined by the second-century father Tertullian, but surely not representative of the truly faithful view of the relationship between faith and thought. The stance of both Augustine and Anselm — *fides quaerens intellectum* (faith seeking understanding) — is more in line with Scripture and tradition.

8. Ernest Renan, *The Life of Jesus*, tr. C. E. Wilbour (London: Trübner, 1864).

9. Johannes Weiss, *Die Predigt Jesu vom Reiche Gottes* (Göttingen, 1892); Eng. tr., *Jesus' Proclamation of the Kingdom of God* (Philadelphia: Fortress, 1971).

10. Albert Schweitzer, *The Quest of the Historical Jesus* (Eng. tr., London: A and C Black, 1954).

11. Gunther Bornkamm, *Jesus of Nazareth* (Eng. tr., McLuskey and Robinson, London and New York, 1960).

12. Martin Dibelius, *Jesus* (Eng. tr., C. B. Hedrick and F. C. Grant, Philadelphia: Fortress, 1949).

13. Ernst Käsemann, "Blind Alleys in the 'Jesus of History' Controversy," *New Testament Questions of Today* (Philadelphia: Fortress, 1969), pp. 23–65.

14. E. P. Sanders, *Jesus and Judaism* (Philadelphia: Fortress, 1985).

15. Marcus Borg, *Conflict, Holiness and Politics in the Teachings of Jesus* (New York and Toronto: Mellen, 1984). See also his more popular *Jesus: A New Vision* (San Fransisco: Harper and Row, 1987).

16. Geza Vermes, *Jesus the Jew: A Historian's Reading of the Gospels* (Philadelphia: Fortress, 1973).

17. N. T. Wright, *Who Was Jesus?* and *Jesus and the Victory of God* (Minneapolis: Fortress, forthcoming).

18. Sean Freyne, *Jesus, Galilee and the Gospels* (Dublin: Gill and Macmillan, 1988), p. 200.

19. This school of philosophers took its lead from the founder Diogenes (fourth century BC). They were known for a simple lifestyle, and a disdain of prevailing mores, fashions, and worldviews.

20. The same word of caution concerning alarmist claims in the papers needs to be heeded in reports of the archaeological finds at the Dead Sea. Just as it is irresponsible for claims to be made that a particular reconstruction of Jesus contains facts that will "shatter the faith" of Christians, so is it a bully tactic to represent the Dead Sea Scrolls in this way. As far as the research which has been done to date is concerned, the scrolls tell us a great deal about one type of sectarian, or separatist, movement, likely a sub-group of the Essenes. Some of the symbols used in the scrolls have parallels in Christian writings but are not directly connected with the New Testament. Rather, both the Christian movement and the Essene movement (represented by the Qumran community) were responding to what they considered to be the faithlessness of God's community. Both groups recognized a problem, but their solutions, or responses to the problem, were quite different.

21. Wright, *Who Was Jesus?*, p. 95.

22. Freyne, *Jesus, Galilee and the Gospels*, p. 200.

Chapter 7

JESUS — GOD FOR US

JOHN WEBSTER

In Mark's Gospel we read how, early in Jesus' ministry, after the call of the first four disciples, Jesus went to Capernaum and "entered the synagogue and taught" (Mark 1:21). "And," Mark continues in his characteristically spare and unadorned prose,

> they were astounded at his teaching, for he taught them as one having authority, and not as the scribes. Just then there was in their synagogue a man with an unclean spirit, and he cried out, "What have you to do with us, Jesus of Nazareth? Have you come to destroy us? I know who you are, the Holy One of God." But Jesus rebuked him, saying, "Be silent, and come out of him!" And the unclean spirit, convulsing him and crying with a loud voice, came out of him. They were all amazed, and they kept on asking one another, "What is this? A new teaching — with authority! He commands even the unclean spirits, and they obey him." At once his fame began to spread throughout the surrounding region of Galilee (Mark 1:22-8).

Right at the beginning of the story of Jesus' public ministry, Mark throws his readers into a situation of crisis, in the literal sense of "judgement." What he narrates in this story and in the rest of his Gospel is not an encounter between relative good and relative evil but the absolute opposition between God and sin. And at the centre of the conflict stands Jesus, the "Holy One of God," against whom is ranged all that seeks to thwart God's goodness, holiness, and saving rule. Crucially, in this conflict Jesus is *victor*: with a word of command, he rebukes, expels, and does away with the pretended power of evil. His victory is almost effortless: as Mark presents the matter, it is unquestionably self-evident that Jesus is utterly and indefatigably "authoritative." He commands, they obey. And as the one possessed of this startling authority, he evokes wonder and worship. Those who witness the scene are "amazed," drawn into a "new" reality that exceeds everything they have experienced and expected. They "question," casting around for ways to make sense of what is real in a wholly new way. And as they do this, they are pressed to confess that Jesus' authority is such that he embodies a judgement that reorders human life in a way that can be accomplished only by God himself.

It is in stories like Mark's account of Jesus' first exorcism that Christian beliefs about Jesus' unity with God are rooted. The Christian doctrine of the incarnation has its rise not in speculative metaphysics but in something more primary: in the elemental disturbance of human life that the presence of Jesus of

Nazareth generates. Like all doctrine, the doctrine of the incarnation flows from amazement, a questioning about and confession of Jesus as a "lordly" reality, one who judges and renews our lives. And like all doctrine, the doctrine of the incarnation is an attempt to get some kind of conceptual purchase on these things, not by stating them better or in a more sophisticated way than they are stated in Scripture, but by pointing us back to the biblical story and saying, "Read, and be astonished."

Because of this, a compact summary of the doctrine of the incarnation might go something like this: Jesus of Nazareth is God in the world. Jesus' "flesh" — that is, his history, his actions, and his sufferings, his entire existence as this particular human person — is the place where God is. He, Jesus, and none other, is the embodiment of God. His humanity is God's humanity with us, among us, and for us. In and as Jesus, God rules in sovereign freedom and with saving love. For in and as Jesus, God takes upon himself our estrangement and guilt and condemnation, and finally and irrevocably makes an end of it, setting us free to be his people.

But what does it mean to say that God is and does these things "in and as Jesus"? Classical Christian orthodoxy answered that question by stating (in the Chalcedonian Definition of AD 451) that Jesus Christ is "one person" in whom "two natures" — human and divine — concur.[1] What is the force of this strange language? And is it possible to discern in it not only a radical statement of the confession of faith which the gospel evokes but also a radical call to the church today to renewed astonishment at the good news of God?

THE CENTRAL CHRISTIAN CONVICTION

To say that God is "God incarnate" is to say that God identifies himself as the particular human person Jesus of Nazareth. God identifies himself as this person, not simply with this person. God does not remain essentially external to Jesus, identifying with him the way we ourselves might identify with a person or cause without being that person or cause. Rather, God "becomes" Jesus, so that it is as this particular person that God is God. This is why the Chalcedonian Definition says that Jesus Christ is "truly God and truly human." Truly human, because Jesus is not God in human disguise. Jesus' "flesh" is not a temporary device, an expedient of which God made use for a certain purpose but later left behind. In Jesus, God is *enfleshed*, incarnate: truly divine, because Jesus is not simply a human person who has attained to a spiritual height that is quantitatively but not qualitatively different from that attainable by all other human persons. Nor is Jesus a human person who is essentially separate from God, but to whom God at some point enters into a deeper or fuller relation. Jesus is himself *as God*, and without God he is not himself. God *constitutes* Jesus in a wholly unique way.

All this means, then, that Jesus' flesh is the way in which God is God. And so Jesus is God among us. To think of Jesus properly is to think of him *as God*. And, no less important, to think of God is to think of him *as Jesus*. *Humanity* and *divinity* are not terms that stand for different parts of Jesus, as if he were some kind of composite figure assembled out of both human and divine components. The Christian tradition has on occasion tried to think of the incarnation in this way — seeing his divinity in his miracles or his resurrection, seeing his humanity in his human suffering, limitations, and death. But to follow truly the logic of the incarnation is to confess that the whole of Jesus is human and the whole of Jesus is divine. He suffers and dies *as God*; he rises from the dead as "this Jesus" (Acts 2:36). In the more abstract language of the Chalcedonian Definition, the human and divine "natures" of Jesus concur "without division, without separation" in the "one person and one subsistence." Less technically: look at Jesus and you see in this quite human person the word and work and ways of God himself; the Lord of all time present in this tiny fragment of one human person's living and dying.

Of course, none of this means that *God* and *Jesus* are simply interchangeable terms. For while the doctrine of the incarnation wants to set out the radical unity between Jesus and God, it is not a unity in which God simply collapses without residue into Jesus. The Chalcedonian Definition puts the point by saying that in Jesus, humanity and divinity come together "without confusion" and "without change": they do not mix together to make some third thing, nor does one transform into the other. Rather, as Chalcedon puts it with a touch of technical subtlety, "the distinction of the natures [is] in no way abolished because of the union, but rather the characteristic property of each nature [is] preserved." Put more concretely: God's "becoming" human is not the same as God ceasing to be God and instead being a human person. God's taking flesh in and as Jesus is the act of his utter sovereign freedom; he does not abandon his divinity in being among us as Jesus. And, from the other side, Jesus' divinity does not cancel out or annul his ordinary humanity. He remains Jesus, *this* person, knowable, particular, embodied. And it is *as* (not *despite*) this that he is God.

So far, so very technical! But it is crucial to appreciate that this rather convoluted and eclectic set of concepts and ideas that we call the doctrine of the incarnation is not a piece of obsolete metaphysical speculation, still less a somewhat bizarre psychological portrait of Jesus. On the contrary: it is a shorthand account of the story that Mark and the other evangelists narrate and that Paul and the other letter writers interpret. And what the doctrine does is set before us the central Christian conviction that Jesus is the ultimate expression of the first commandment: You shall have no other gods before me. He, Jesus, is God's great "I am who I am."

THE SUBSTANCE OF CONVERSION

What are the consequences of this? To what kind of confession of Jesus Christ does it press us? Three themes are of central significance here.

He, Jesus Christ, is basic for the Christian confession of faith. He is its beginning and its end, its sum and substance. This very simple, yet easily overlooked, point means that Christian faith is not arbitrary. Christian faith does not make up its confession as it goes along or attach itself to objects of its own choosing. It is not free to opt for Jesus Christ as if he were one of a number of possibilities competing for our allegiance, possibilities between which we ourselves must decide. He decides for us; he makes himself the object of our confession so that Christian faith is indissolubly tied to Jesus, forced into being by his living presence and therefore inescapably fixed to him. To say anything less would be to detract from his lordship, making him a kind of domestic deity whom we favour with our religious patronage. But: he *is* Lord, axiomatically real and true, *God* for us.

Moreover, it is he himself who is the object of Christian confession. Christians confess Jesus Christ and not simply some reality he symbolizes or to which he gives access. Jesus does not "stand for" some issue or commitment; he is not a pointer to, or sign, or example, of something we might also find in some other religious figure — commitment to justice, perhaps; an ethic of self-giving; a call to moral renewal. Rather, he is himself, and to confess Jesus Christ is to confess him, not to use him as a label for some commitment of our own devising. He is not a secondary reality, an illustration of some theme we regard as religiously or morally important. He *is* reality, and that to which he draws attention is simply himself. What makes the Christian confession "Christian," therefore, is the strictest adherence to Jesus as irreducibly himself, as absolute, final, not to be dissolved into some other cause or theme or conviction.

It is, of course, precisely as such that he is confessed as Lord. To confess that Jesus Christ is Lord is to confess that he is the centre around which all of our thinking about God and humanity is constructed. Even in his particularity as *this* person, Jesus is not simply just another fragment of the reality of the world. He is at one and the same time the one through whom all things are brought into being and through whom all things are restored and perfected. God's ways with his creation — in bringing it into being, in judging and redeeming it, and in finally bringing it to its perfection — are actual in him. For "in him all things in heaven and on earth were created, things visible and invisible, whether thrones or dominions or rulers or powers — all things have been created through him and for him" (Col. 1:16). And, because of this, Colossians continues, "He himself is before all things, and in him all things hold together" (verse 17). He embraces creation, but is not embraced by it; he relativizes all other realities, but is relativized by none; he is the Lord of all realities, but over him there is no Lord. As such a one — in, not despite, his humanity — we must say of him that he constitutes and makes effective God's plan "to gather up all things in him" (Eph. 1:10). And as such a one — again, in, not despite, his humanity — he is the one of whom we must say, "in him all the fullness of God was pleased to dwell" (Col. 1:19). The New Testament's fierce concentration on Jesus Christ as the core of the Christian confession commits us, therefore, to an equally firm refusal of any attempt to convert Christian faith into a religious or moral system in which Jesus has merely an honourable place in a larger reality. On the contrary, he "fills all in all" (Eph. 1:23).

He, Jesus Christ, is definitive for how Christians understand God. This, as we have seen, is one of the essential thrusts of the doctrine of the incarnation. Whatever Christians may say about God must be tested by the reality of Jesus. Worship of God, belief about God, and conduct before God are all given a distinctively Christian character by the way in which they allow themselves to be shaped by the gospel of Jesus Christ. Once again, the striking particularity of the New Testament is not to be overlooked. Knowledge of God and God's ways does not derive from reflection upon religious experience; in one sense, it does not begin with any "knowing" on our part. It is a given knowledge; and the place where it is given is in the story of Jesus, which we cannot improve upon or reduce to something more primary, but which we can at best only repeat. This is something of what we mean when we describe Jesus as the revelation of God. We do not mean that Jesus is some kind of sign pointing away from himself, revealing something that is in essence external to his person. Rather, we mean that Jesus is the point at which our thinking about God finds not only its beginning but its terminus: there is, literally, nowhere else to begin and nowhere else to go.

Once we find ourselves at this point, what we come to see of God is most simply described by saying: he is God *for us*. God is for us because in Jesus Christ he is the one who from all eternity wishes to be *with us*. God chooses to be with another reality, distinct from himself. He chooses not to be alone, but *God with, for* and *over* another. And this "other" is humanity. God chooses this: it is the exercise of his utter freedom to be God in his way. His being with us is not forced upon him but is the fulfilment of his eternal decision to be himself by being God for us. Put differently, God is the God who creates fellowship. Out of the abundance and overflow of his love, generosity, and goodness, he calls into being another reality and chooses that, alongside it, he will be God. His freedom is, therefore, not his freedom to remain aloof and alone, but his freedom lovingly to create, redeem, and sanctify that which he makes. It is fellowship-creating freedom. Crucially, it is in Jesus Christ that this God is made known to us. The "mystery of his will" (Eph. 1:9) — the truth of who God is and what God purposes — is "made known to us" because it is "set forth in Christ" (Eph. 1:9).

Moreover, God is God "for us" because in Jesus Christ God takes up our cause against sin and sets us free. Sin is the counter-movement to the grace of God; it is humanity's assertion of self-sufficiency, our consent to the deadly lie that we can live in isolation from God and remain truly human. Whether in the arrogance of self-assertion or in the hopelessness of self-recrimination, sin is the wicked and destructive rejection of fellowship with God as our life. But, however powerful a reality sin may be, for the New Testament it is entirely and effectively countered by the grace of God in the gospel. For God sets between us and our sins the one great fact: Jesus Christ. The New Testament is written around a conviction that in Jesus' human living and dying and in his being raised to new life, sin is dealt with, disarmed, stripped of its power, and cast to one side as an abolished reality. God's fellowship with his creation, his covenant commitment to be God with us, is not eradicated by humanity's wilful refusal to respond and humanity's reckless choosing of death and damnation. On the contrary, grace abounds and grace reigns "through Jesus Christ our Lord" (Rom. 5:20 f). Grace *abounds* because the goodness of God is limitless; sin can never set up a barrier against grace, for grace is always infinitely resourceful. And grace reigns because the goodness of God is effective, undefeated by human darkness. *Grace*, however, is a concept that stands in place of a name: Jesus, Emmanuel, God with us.

And, finally, God is "for us" because, in the power of his Holy Spirit, the risen Jesus Christ lives in fellowship with us. The Christian life is, in essence, fellowship with the risen Jesus. That fellowship is brought about by and sustained by the Holy Spirit, who is Jesus Christ himself reaching out into the world in the power of his victory, publicly declaring his triumph over sin and death, and establishing new life. In the power of the Holy Spirit, Jesus makes men and women new. In the power of the Holy Spirit, Jesus assembles the new people of God to hear the gospel and respond in praise. In the power of the Holy Spirit, Jesus sends the new people of God to witness to and serve the world. The Holy Spirit is Jesus Christ himself establishing and maintaining the bond of life between God and God's people. God, in Jesus Christ, shares his life with us. Here, too, God is for us — not simply holding on to his life as a possession, but sharing his life with us as a gift. God, in Christ, present in the Holy Spirit, is the one *in* whom we live, the one who lives *in* us.

God is "for us," then, as creator, redeemer, and giver of life, and it is in Jesus Christ that God is known to be such.

He, Jesus Christ, summons us to worship and confess him as the only true God. To be faced with the reality of Jesus Christ is to be summoned to decision. He is a disturbing, fundamentally unsettling reality. He calls into question; his presence exposes us to a judgement (a "showing of the truth") wholly unlike any human judgement because it is absolute and comprehensive. His presence to us is both his self-manifestation and his call to us — a call to live in the light of his reality, to become people for whom he is utterly and supremely real.

If this is so, then Jesus Christ is, once again, not one whom we are entitled to consider from a distance as one possibility for our lives, an option to which we are free to commit ourselves or not commit ourselves as we wish. He cannot be considered from a position of neutrality, at our leisure. To adopt such a stance towards him is to make him a matter about which we are competent to judge. But he is neither judged nor a matter for judgement; he is judge. And as judge he has competence and authority both to "tell the truth" about human life (the truth that it is created, redeemed, and glorified by the Lord of the covenant), and to issue a summons to that radical reorientation of human life we call "conversion."

"Conversion" is not primarily an experiential reality. That is to say, it is not best described in terms of the little drama of *what happens to me*, but in terms of *what faces me*: Jesus himself. He is not simply a trigger for a certain set of experiences (though, of course, experiences there will be); rather, he is a wholly absorbing, inexhaustibly sufficient, and glorious reality. To be "converted" is to be so taken up with and by that reality that it becomes supremely interesting, the centre out of which all things radiate. And, by consequence, to be converted is to exist in faith — to abandon the whole project of self-sufficiency, to let God be God, our God, and to live in the light of his inexpressible gift of himself.

Because conversion dislodges us from the centre in this way, opening to us the possibility of a life from and for the presence of God in Jesus Christ, converted life is "ecstatic." Converted life, the life of faith, has its centre not in itself but in him. It is, therefore, life "in Christ": "It is no longer I who live, but it is Christ who lives in me" (Gal. 2:20). The primary moments in converted life are therefore activities that insistently pull us away from absorption in ourselves. Worship is such an activity. Christian worship is not essentially a matter of community (though it is the primary reason for the assembly of the people of God), nor essentially a matter of texts (though Anglicans are committed to some kind of textual ordering of common prayer). Worship is the unfettered praise of the converted as they find themselves in the presence of the risen Jesus. In worship, God in Jesus Christ acts first, gathering us before him, speaking his word to us, evoking and giving voice to our praise. Our acts are secondary, responsive, wholly taken up with celebrating who Jesus Christ is and what he does as the impulse of our common life. Confession, in a similar way, is a primary mode of the Christian's "ecstatic" life in Christ. The language of confession is language arrested by and held captive to Jesus Christ. Whether in the most primitive form ("Jesus Christ is Lord"), or in the weighty propositions of Chalcedon or Augsburg or Barmen (or even the Thirty-Nine Articles), confession is, at heart, faith's struggle to say: this is who he, Jesus Christ, is. Confession responds with words, halting or fluent, to the insistent, demanding, and entirely unmanageable gift of the living presence of Jesus Christ. The task of confession is thus not primarily to define or to defend, still less to foreclose discussion by demanding assent. Confessions *point;* they indicate a reality beyond themselves as the decisive object with which faith has to do. Confession is, therefore, a counter-movement to idolatry and ideology, preventing us from assimilating Jesus Christ to our own interpretations of him, and forcing us instead to attend to him.

All of this may seem to take us quite far from the doctrine of the incarnation. But in fact what it shows is that "doctrine" is not a free-standing intellectual statement, an isolated theological proposal existing in another sphere from that of the life of faith. Doctrine has its place as one of a larger set of responses to the good news of Jesus Christ. Doctrines function within the church's life of convertedness, serving to set before the people of God in as focused a way as possible what — who — it is that compels them to repentance and renewal. For Christians, that compulsion is finally and irrevocably identified with a particular set of historical events and relations, at the controlling centre of which is the man Jesus, in whom, and as whom, God remakes the world.

INCARNATIONAL ORTHODOXY

If what has been said so far has any truth to it, then Christology is the article by which the church stands or falls. The health of the people of God is bound up with the vitality of their confession of Jesus Christ. If they stand in a disordered relation to that confession, neglecting it, treating it with skepticism, or simply letting it be crowded out by other concerns, then the church of Jesus Christ will find itself crisis-ridden about its own identity. In short, it will begin to wonder what it is.

From this vantage point, it would, of course, be a relatively simple matter to look at the life of the contemporary church, and of our own denomination in particular, and find it wanting. It would be easy enough to demonstrate the thinness of at least some strands of Anglicanism today, and to issue appropriate rhetorical rebukes. But to do so would be to miss the point, for two reasons. First, Christian beliefs about the incarnation need to be presented as gospel, not as threat. That is to say, the best "apology" for such convictions is the attempt to describe them, lovingly and winningly, letting their inherent persuasiveness emerge of its own accord. There is no need to press them upon the church with anxious or strident polemic. The good news of the gospel of Christ is not a weapon with which to attack; it is an invitation to delight in and celebrate the lavish goodness of God. Second, and more important, those who are self-consciously "orthodox" have no mandate to regard the doctrine of the incarnation as something which they may possess. "Orthodoxy" in Christology, as in any other matter, is not a static or finished product; it is not the kind of truth that can be held captive by a few propositions to which assent must be given. Orthodoxy is valuable not merely because it enables us to "settle" issues but because it enables us to be faced and critically interrogated by what lies at its heart: the gospel. And the gospel cannot be managed; it cannot become a religious or theological object that we can believe ourselves to have within our grasp. Recovering orthodoxy is quite different from recovering the kind of bitter traditionalism that confuses one rendering of the gospel with the gospel itself. Orthodoxy is about keeping before the people of God the permanent challenge of the reality of Jesus Christ; its primary function is to focus the imagination of the people of God in such a way that he is recognized, acknowledged, confessed, worshipped, and served.

"It is enough for us," said Calvin, preaching on Ephesians 1:19–23,

> to have Jesus Christ alone to make our recourse to; ... just as it was the Father's will to lift him on high in order that all should look to him, so also we may have our eyes fastened upon him and apply our whole minds to him in such a way that we may have no other way or preparation, nor to swerve one way or another, but when we are once brought into the right way, keep on continually towards our aim until we are fully come to perfection. That it may please him to grant this grace, not only to us, but also to all people....[2]

To confess that Jesus Christ is *God for us* is to do just that — to focus, "fasten," ourselves upon him, to have recourse to him, to move unswervingly towards him because he has already moved towards us and, above all, to look to him for grace. Such, I believe, is what is involved in "incarnational orthodoxy": a summons to us and to the whole church to astonishment at the gospel, repentance for our slowness to believe, and unfettered delight in the ever new goodness of God.

SUGGESTED READING

W. Kasper, *Jesus the Christ* (London: Burns & Oates, 1976).

J. Webster, *God is Here: Believing in the Incarnation Today* (Basingstoke, 1983).

R. Williams, "The Incarnation as the Basis of Dogma," in R. Morgan, ed., *The Religion of the Incarnation* (Bristol: Bristol Classical Press, 1989), pp. 85–98.

R. Williams and R. Bauckham, "Jesus — God with Us," in C. Baxter, ed., *Stepping Stones* (London, 1987), pp. 21–41.

ENDNOTES

1. The full text Chalcedonian Definition can be found in J. Stevenson, ed., *Creed, Councils and Controversies* (London: SPCK, 1966), pp. 334–7.

2. J. Calvin, *Sermons on Ephesians* (Edinburgh, 1972), pp. 125 f.

JESUS CHRIST, THE ONLY SAVIOUR

JAMES I. PACKER

"Praise, My Soul, the King of Heaven" and "Abide with Me" are the only hymns by Henry Francis Lyte that are sung much today. But he wrote other good ones, and one of them, using the same metre as "Praise, My Soul," starts like this:

> O how blest the congregation
> Who the gospel know and prize;
> Joyful tidings of salvation
> Brought by Jesus from the skies!
> He is near them,
> Knows their wants and hears their cries.
>
> In his name rejoicing ever,
> Walking in his light and love,
> And foretasting, in his favour,
> Something here of bliss above;
> Happy people!
> Who shall harm them? what shall move?
>
> In his righteousness exalted,
> On from strength to strength they go;
> By ten thousand ills assaulted,
> Yet preserved from every foe,
> On to glory
> Safe they speed through all below.

Lyte's formula of blessing for your congregation and mine is that we should know and prize the gospel of salvation, which was Jesus' central message, and with it know and prize Jesus and his love-gift of new life, new joy, new strength, and new security. Lyte is right! Whatever cultural shifts take place around us, whatever socio-political concerns claim our attention, whatever anxieties we may feel about the church as an institution, Jesus Christ crucified, risen, reigning, and now in the power of his atonement, calling, drawing, welcoming, pardoning, renewing, strengthening, preserving, and bringing joy, remains the heart of the Christian message, the focus of Christian worship, and the fountain of Christian life. Other things may change; this does not.

Thus it was from the beginning, as the New Testament shows. "Jesus is

Lord" (Rom. 10:9) was, by scholarly consensus, the first Christian confession of faith. Invoking and worshipping "our Lord and Saviour Jesus Christ" (2 Pet. 1:11; 2:20; 3:18) alongside the Father (his and ours) was the primary form of Christian devotion. Celebrating Jesus as "our God and Saviour" (Titus 2:13; 2 Pet. 1:1) was a basic focus of early Christian doctrinal teaching. "Believe in the Lord Jesus, and you will be saved" (Acts 16:31) was the original Christian message to the world. Reconciliation with God and pardon of sin through Christ's atoning death, adoption and new birth into God's family through regeneration in Christ and co-resurrection with Christ, life in the power of the Spirit of Christ, and hope of everlasting glory in the presence of Christ, were the staple themes of the apostolic explanation of what salvation means. "Christianity is Christ," the slogan beloved of so many preachers, sums it up most perfectly. When Lyte wrote, "O how blest the congregation / Who the gospel know and prize," it was of the gospel of salvation from sin and death through Jesus Christ that he was thinking — the gospel that finds us lost and broken and leaves us "ransomed, healed, restored, forgiven." Thus he anchored himself in the centre of the Christian mainstream, glorying in "the old, story / Of Jesus and his love." That is the place where today's Christians, with you and me among them, should be anchored also.

CHRISTOLOGY AND THEOLOGY

From the New Testament mindset that sees Christ at the centre of things grew mainstream Christian theology — that is, our understanding of God and his relation to everything everywhere that is not himself. The Christian consensus has always been that, as Scripture is the proper source from which theology should be derived, so Christology — that is, our knowledge of the person, place, and work of Christ — is the true hub around which the wheel of theology must revolve, and to which each of its spokes must be correctly fastened if the wheel is not to get bent out of shape. Take some examples.

Why do Christians hold that the one God is plural (tri-personal, to be exact), and that he is at once intolerably severe, terrifyingly perceptive, and infinitely gracious and good? Ultimately it is because they hold that Jesus, who prayed to the Father and promised the Spirit, and whose character was as described, was himself God.

Why are Christians sure, despite all the difficulties, that Scripture is God's own inspired and authoritative instruction? Ultimately it is because Jesus, the divine Son, always treated the Old Testament Scriptures as his Father's word, given to show him and his disciples his Father's way.

Why do Christians hold that personal relationships matter more than anything in this world, and that the truly human way to live is lovingly, constantly, unreservedly to give yourself away to God and others, and that anything less than this offends God? Ultimately it is because they hold that Jesus was as fully human as he was divine, and that as he taught these things, so he lived them, and that at the deepest level of personhood, his was the one perfect human life that the world has seen.

Why do Christians insist that God's forgiveness of sins is only ever possible on the basis of an atoning sacrifice? Ultimately it is because Jesus saw the making of atonement as the main purpose of his coming, and after three years as a preacher, went up to Jerusalem, deliberately courting death, in order that the Father's will in this matter might be done.

Why do Christians view their thousands of gatherings — congregations, as we call them — as not just a chain of clubs or interest groups, but as outcrops of a single organic entity called the church, within which they are brothers and sisters in one family of redeemed sinners, one "body" sharing a new supernatural life through common links with Christ their "head"? Ultimately it is because Jesus taught his disciples to see his Father as their Father, his death as their ransom-price, and himself as their way to the Father, and now as their bread of life and the vine in which, as branches, they must abide.

Why do Christians counter the world's endless speculations about the larger life of disembodied spirits by maintaining that full humanness requires embodiment, and hence look forward to physical resurrection? Ultimately it is because they are sure that Jesus rose bodily from the state of death and that his risen life is the model for ours.

And why do Christians cling to the hope of a cosmic triumph of divine justice and power when the world around them seems to be slipping, despite humanity's best efforts, into chaos at every level? Ultimately it is because they believe that God's risen Son reigns, really, if hiddenly, over all things, and is pledged to return in glory to judge and renew this world which he, with the Father and the Holy Spirit, first created.

These examples illustrate how historic Christianity conceives, defines, and explains itself in the Trinitarian, Christological, and Christocentric terms that are native to it. Christianity is what it is because Jesus of Nazareth was what he was, and every suggestion as to what Christianity should be today and tomorrow must be measured by Christ himself as its criterion. The fact that some versions of Christianity lose sight of this principle is a modern tragedy and a source of enormous confusion. We ourselves must try to avoid any such lapse.

UNIVERSITY AND UNIVERSALISM

A further principle of original Christianity was the universality of Jesus' claim on the human race, and of every person's need to know about, and respond to, the claim he makes and so to receive the gift of salvation that he gives. "All authority in heaven and on earth has been given to me," said the risen Jesus to his apostles, announcing his appointment as this world's proper king. "Therefore go and make disciples of all nations" (Matt. 28:18–19). Paul defined his ministry in terms of this universality: "We proclaim him [Jesus], admonishing and teaching everyone with all wisdom, so that we may present everyone perfect in Christ" (Col. 1:28). The great missionary movements of the early Christian centuries and the past two hundred years sought to implement the insights of Christ's universal claim and humankind's universal need. We should rejoice that in Asia, Africa, and Latin America, evangelism goes on apace today, with great fidelity to the New Testament and great fruitfulness among the common people, whatever may be happening in the modern and postmodern West. Soul-winning, church-planting outreach must always have pride of place in Christian strategy. For of all the tasks to which love of God and neighbour should lead us, disciple-making comes first.

Here, however, we find that something of an intellectual landslide has occurred in certain sections of the church. In place of a clear declaration of the universality of Christ's claim as Saviour, with salvation requiring faithful response, we find ourselves confronted with understandings of God's purpose for humanity, and of Christ's achievement on the cross, which produce either the dogmatic assertion that all human beings will finally attain eternal life or at least a confidence that sincere adherents of non-Christian faiths, and maybe others too, will be saved alongside Christian believers. Two identifiable new positions have emerged. *Pluralism*, championed by the universalist John Hick, is a restyled version of the old idea that all religions are climbing the same mountain and will meet at the top — in other words, that all religious persons are actually converging on the same goal, and all the key teachings of all the world's major religions actually direct their adherents on this convergent course.[1] *Inclusivism* is the idea, which takes many forms, that Christ does actually save persons who knew nothing of him but were serious and sincere in practising whatever their religion was. Each position makes the momentous claim that it does justice to the reality of God's love to humankind in a way that other positions do not. In a multi-ethnic, multi-religious society like today's Canada, these views generate no small bewilderment as to what we should hope, pray, and work for in evangelism, both at home and abroad.

Our present agenda is to try to dispel this bewilderment by offering some clarifications, and our first step to that end will be to analyse from Scripture the salvation that Jesus Christ the Saviour has wrought.

THE SAVIOUR AND THE SALVATION

It is hardly possible to overstress the magnitude of the intellectual achievement embodied in the New Testament. The New Testament, as we know, is a consensus collection of apostolic writings that were brought together after each had been separately produced as particular needs required. None of these twenty-seven books was written to be part of any such collection, or to back up any other items that are part of it, and all of them were produced within seventy years —indeed most , if not all, within forty years — of Jesus' resurrection when Christian theology might have been expected to be still in a rudimentary stage. But in fact they have within them a coherent body of thought that is fully homogenous in its substance and thrust, despite the independent individuality of each writer and the way in which all their thinking cuts across the dogmas of the Judaism out of which it came. The central place of Jesus Christ in creation, providence, the divine plan of salvation, the history of our race, and the coming universal judgement and new creation of the cosmos is the theme throughout, and amazingly there are no internal contradictions or loose ends.

This revolutionary consensus, involving as it does trinitarian and incarnational beliefs within a monotheistic frame — perhaps the hardest bit of thinking that the human mind has ever been asked to do — is so stunning that it is hard to doubt its supernatural origin. As from one standpoint the person, power, and performance of the Lord Jesus is its main focus, so from another standpoint all the books dilate in their different ways on the need and glory of the saving grace that he gives, thus furnishing a wealth of material to guide us in our enquiry.

Here, now, in a nutshell, are the basic lines of thought about Jesus Christ the Saviour to which the New Testament materials boil down.

1. Jesus Christ is the divine Word made flesh, the unique Son of God.

By being virginally conceived and born of Mary, with Joseph as his official father, the Son of God became a Jew of David's line while remaining as fully divine as he was in his pre-incarnate life. All that was involved in being fully human he acquired, though without ever becoming a sinner. His words, works, and personal life on earth displayed his divinity to those with eyes to see and ears to hear, and in so doing revealed the true nature and character of "God the Father Almighty." Through incarnation he added to his cosmic role as creator, upholder, and future renovator of all things, the further role of saving lost humankind. The church is currently emerging from two centuries of vacillation with regard to Jesus' personal deity; it is worth highlighting the fact that the first Christians had no doubt about it, and no reluctance to affirm it.[2]

2. Jesus Christ is our prophet, priest, and king, the one mediator between humankind and God.

The themes of Jesus as messenger from heaven, bringing news of God's saving mercy, as fulfiller of the priestly role of offering to God an atoning sacrifice for his people's sins, and as king now enthroned in the kingdom of God over all things and all people, pervade the entire New Testament. *Mediation*, which means bringing together alienated parties and establishing a firm basis for their future relationship, is the biblical term for the saving ministry that Christ in his triple office fulfils. "God our Saviour ... desires everyone to be saved and to come to the knowledge of the truth. For there is one God; there is also one mediator between God and humankind, Christ Jesus, himself human, who gave himself a ransom for all" (1 Tim. 2:3–4, NRSV).

The writer to the Hebrews develops the thought that as high priest, the incarnate Son is the mediator who deals with humans on behalf of God and with God on behalf of humans, and so brings and keeps them together. Before his passion the Son learned by experience to empathize with people under temptation, so that now he can minister to us in times of moral and spiritual need (Heb.

2:18; 4:15–5:3; 5:7–10). Following his passion, in which he "offered" to the Father "for all time one sacrifice for sins," and having "sat down at the right hand of God," "he is able to save completely those who come to God through him, because he ever lives to intercede for them" (10:12; 7:25; cf. Rom. 8:34). Through his two-sided ministry of intercession for us—based on his cross, and succour to us, based on his own temptation experience—he now communicates God's pardon and peace of conscience to believers, leads them in their worship, and shepherds them through life's vicissitudes to this heavenly home. This is the ongoing reality of his mediatorial ministry.

3. Jesus Christ is lover and lord of his people, and head of the body that is the church of God.

The New Testament views Jesus as having come to found a new community, and apostolic teaching is consistently church-centred. Christian "Lone-Rangerism" is really a contradiction in terms. Corporateness is fundamental to New Testament Christianity, which everywhere appears as a practice of personal devotion within a communal life that all are to share. Having been made "one new man" out of their distinct individualities (Eph. 2:15), "all one in Christ Jesus" (Gal. 3:28), believers must now relate to one another within the solidarity of their new identity. And where this communion of hearts is realized, wonderful things are found to happen. The church in Christ is supernaturalized by Christ; loving it, he animates and invigorates it, pouring out the Holy Spirit on it and leading those who make it up into a unique mode of interactive life in fellowship with his Father and himself on the one hand, and with fellow-believers, viewed as spiritual siblings, on the other. The power of united praise is experienced, and love and care overflow.

In Romans 12, 1 Corinthians 12, and Ephesians 4, Paul expresses this by using the organic image of the church as the body of Christ and each Christian, under Christ the head, as a unit within it — a distinct and individual unit, corresponding to the great variety of separate units (particular limbs, joints, muscles, nerves, and so on) in the human body. This image yields the particular implications that the church is one in its diversity, and diverse in its unity; that all the church's authentic worship, witness, and work is directed by Christ himself; that all service within the community is the ministry of Christ the head to his body through his body; that every-member ministry, with each believer contributing at Christ's behest to the health of the whole complex, is meant to be the rule within the body of Christ; and that some ability to contribute in this way (that is, some spiritual gift) is supplied by Christ the head to every Christian.

The headship of Christ is central to the thought that the body-image expresses in Ephesians 4:15 (see also 1:22; 5:23; Col. 1:18; 2:19). There has been debate as to whether, in the places cited, headship signifies Christ as the source of the body's life or as the authority over its functioning, which is what headship evidently signifies in 1 Corinthians 11:3. Perhaps the answer is both/and, rather than either/or; for certainly, the church's existence and spiritual energies do come from Christ, and submission to the lordship of the heavenly lover is set forth repeatedly in the New Testament as basic to the church's life.

Such, then, is Jesus the Saviour, according to the consistent witness of the New Testament and the sustained faith of the universal church across a wide range of contrasting milieux and cultures over nearly two thousand years. The self-sustaining and life-transforming power that these beliefs about Jesus have displayed from the first century to the present day needs to be explained, and the most rational explanation is that they are true, and have been proving themselves true through the Holy Spirit's application of them to human minds and hearts all the time. Of the confusions and diminutions of belief about Christ that have abounded in theological academia for more than a century, and are still being actively generated in some quarters, it need only be said that their *a priori* has always been some skepticism about the supernatural, and that without this prejudice to sustain them their arbitrariness and lack of inner cogency become apparent at once. Belief in the incarnation and the Trinity (the two belong together, for the doctrine of the Trinity is in the first instance just a clear spelling out of the divinity of Jesus Christ) is fully coherent and reasonable in a way that scaled-down revisionist Christologies simply are not. So we take it as a fixed point, and move on to further explore the salvation which, according to the New Testament, the Saviour bestows.

SALVATION ANALYZED

Salvation means, in broadest terms, deliverance from evil: rescue, that is, from a state of jeopardy and misery into one of safety and therefore of joy. God is revealed in the Old Testament as one who brings salvation from various evils, and in the New Testament, the gift of salvation is the focal centre of the gospel.

New Testament salvation is the divine gift, to persons who know themselves to be godless and guilty, of a new relationship of reconciliation with God the Creator through the mediatorial ministry of Jesus Christ the Saviour. In this relationship sinful human beings are no longer exposed to the prospect of God's wrath (judicial rejection and retribution) on judgement day, but are *justified* — that is, pardoned for the past, accepted in the present for the future, and guaranteed the eternal reward of the righteous, although in themselves they are sinners still. Justification by grace, on the basis of what Jesus did and suffered for us, is truly the last judgement so far as we are concerned; it is God the judge pronouncing here and now the verdict that determines how we shall spend eternity. Paul treats justification, "the gift of righteousness" as he calls it (Rom. 5:17), as the fundamental blessing that the gospel brings, and on which every other blessing rests (see Rom. 3:21–5:21; Gal. 2:15–3:29; Phil. 3:7–14). Linked specifically with justification is the gift of *adoption*, whereby the judge takes us into his family as his sons and heirs — "heirs of God and co-heirs with Christ" (Rom. 8:17). The gift is free, to sinners only; it cannot be earned on a basis of merit, only received on a basis of mercy. The receiving is by *faith*, which means the empty hands of the heart outstretched to embrace Jesus Christ as Saviour and Lord in the knowledge that he brings this salvation with him to make it ours. Faith involves *repentance*, a saying no to sin and self-centredness in order to say yes to the Christ who tells us to follow him, to take his yoke upon us and learn of him, and to serve him henceforth and forever. Such is salvation relationally, in its underlying dimensions.

And there is more to it than that. Those whose lives become a matter of faith and repentance in sustained exercise thereby show themselves to have been *regenerated*, or "born of the Spirit" (John 3:8, cf. 3-7); that is, they have been united by the Holy Spirit with Jesus Christ in his death and resurrection. The effect of this is that without losing their own personal identity they have become, in the most fundamental sense, new creatures in Christ, living with him a new life (2 Cor. 5:17; Gal. 6:15; see Rom. 6:1–14). The newness of the new life springs from the fact that the Son of God now reproduces and sustains in us at the motivational core of our being the same thrusting and controlling desire to love, honour, and glorify the Father that drove him throughout his life on earth (as it had driven him from all eternity, and drives him still, and will go on driving him in heaven for ever). With this desire, the Holy Spirit—Christ's emissary and deputy in this world—maintains residence within us to transform our character from being Adamic and Satanic to being Christlike, and to empower us for the obedience and usefulness that will please God. To have renounced deliberate sinning, and in steady purpose to have "crucified the sinful nature with its passions and desires" (Gal. 5:24), is what it means to be dead with Christ (Rom. 6:2–4,6; Gal. 2:20). To be driven by Christ's implanted desires while being changed by Christ's Spirit into Christ's moral image is what it means to be risen with Christ (Rom. 7:4–6). Thus the regenerate person is no longer ruled by the world, the flesh, and the devil, but is led by the Spirit through the biblical word into paths of enterprising and zealous obedience, and this constitutes *sanctification*, that is, heaven's glorification in the bud.

Salvation is a blessing of the kingdom of God, and like everything else in that kingdom it is both "now" and "not yet": *now* in beginnings and foretaste, *not yet* in completion and fullness. Hope of more grace and future glory, springing from faith that rejoices in present salvation and life in Christ, is therefore central to the Christ mindset (see Heb. 10:38–12:3). One day Jesus will have returned to consummate all God's purposes for this world; then the believers' character-change will be complete; they will have bodies to match that change, bodies through which they can perfectly express their Christlike longings; they will be part of a new world order in which sin and pain have no place; and they will endlessly enjoy the celestial vision of the Father and the Son, whom they love. This is a hope of glory indeed! The church is the fellowship of those who, having been saved from sin's penalty by justification, are now being saved from its power by sanctification and who look ahead to the day when they will be saved from sin's presence and perfected in holiness and joy through glorification. As Lyte's hymn put it: "On to glory / Safe" — saved! — "they speed through all below." Such, according to Scripture, is the full reality of the salvation that is mediated through Jesus Christ, our Saviour and our Lord.

A CHURCH YEAR SALVATION

A convenient way to analyse salvation further is provided by the church's liturgical year.

It is an Advent salvation. God painstakingly prepared the way over many centuries for the coming of Christ the Saviour to this world. He did this by means of promises, prophesies, and types that one way or another patterned out the rescue from sin and hell that Christ would achieve for his people when he appeared. Advent reminds us that we should understand salvation as the New Testament writers do, as the fulfilment of these foreshadowings. Also, as Advent looks ahead to Christ's return, it teaches us to hope for the completing of our salvation that his return will bring (Heb. 9:28).

It is a Christmas salvation. The incarnation of the Son of God, so Paul tells us, should be viewed as a step towards the cross (Phil. 2:5-8); but it has two further meanings in its own right. One is *identification.* The Son of God, by becoming human, came to know the human condition from the inside, as it were; his empathetic insight into our state and needs, gained through his experience of human living, is now as full as it could possibly be. The second meaning is *revelation.* As John says, "truth came through Jesus Christ. No one has ever seen God. It is God the only Son, who is close to the Father's heart, who has made him known" (John 1:17–18, NRSV; "made him known" carries the idea of "explained" or "expounded" him). Jesus himself said: "Anyone who has seen me has seen the Father" (John 14:9). Since God is Jesus-like, hearing and watching Jesus gives full knowledge of the divine character. Integral to salvation is the assurance that God knows us as we really are, and that we know God as he really is. The incarnation is foundational for that assurance.

It is a Good Friday salvation. Central to the New Testament, in the Gospels, Acts, Epistles, and Revelation alike, is the cross of Jesus, viewed as the atoning event through which our salvation was achieved. Paul is the great theologian of atonement, and his many-sided thought about the cross seems to be structured as follows. How does the cross save? By being a *blood sacrifice* (its sacrificial status is affirmed in Eph. 5:2; and "blood" in Rom. 3:25, 5:9, and Eph. 1:7 certainly means "life laid down in sacrificial death"). How did Christ's sacrifice save us? By *redeeming* us from the jeopardy of guilt and exposure to God's vindicatory wrath that we were in before (Gal. 3:13; 4:5; Eph. 1:7). How did Christ's sacrifice redeem us? By *reconciling* God to us and us to God, cancelling our sins (2 Cor. 5:18–21) and ending our mutual hostility (Rom. 5:10). How did Christ's sacrifice end God's enmity to us? By being a *propitiation* — that is, as the NIV margin on Romans 3:25 puts it, "one who would turn aside his wrath, taking away sin" (see also the margin on 1 John; 2:2; 4:10). How did Christ's sacrifice have this propitiatory effect? By being a *substitution* — that is, a vicarious enduring of the retributive judgement declared against us (the curse of the law, Gal. 3:13; the tally of our sins nailed to the cross to account for Christ's execution, Col. 2:14; cf. Matt. 27:37). Our justification "by [Christ's] blood" (Rom. 5:9), which, as we saw, is the foundational blessing in God's salvation package, is based not on judgement waived or suspended, but on justice actually done: it is *just* and *justified* justification, grounded on payment of the penalty by Christ in our place. He died for us, and now we go free. Salvation by substitution is the heart of the gospel message.

It is an Easter salvation. The bodily rising of Jesus into imperishable life, which showed forth his divinity (Rom. 1:4) and defeat of death (Acts 2:24), also guaranteed our forgiveness and justification by showing that our sins really had been dealt with (1 Cor. 15:17; cf. Rom. 4:25) and made certain our own resurrection into transformed bodily life when Christ returns (1 Cor. 15:16–21, 51–57; cf. Phil. 3:20–21). That will be our salvation completed.

It is an Ascension Day salvation. Jesus' journey from the tomb to the throne at the Father's right hand — that is, the place of executive rule — was like a two-flight air trip, with the forty days of the post-resurrection appearances as an extended stopover, and the ascension as the second flight, intended from the start (see John 20:17). Jesus' ascension is significant, not only because of the personal ascendancy and powerful intercession it betokened, but also because God the Father, in quickening us out of spiritual death (that is, separation from and unresponsiveness to himself), "raised us up with Christ and seated us with him in the heavenly realms in Christ Jesus" (Eph. 2:4–6). Christians may thus remain "on top," as we say, in relation to everything that happens, living as conquerors in the confidence that Lyte expressed in the final verse of the hymn with which we began:

> God will keep his own anointed,
> Nought shall harm them, none condemn;
> All their trials are appointed,
> All must work for good to them;
> All shall help them
> To their heavenly diadem.

This confidence is part of the reality of the Christian salvation.

It is a Pentecost salvation. Since other chapters in this volume deal with life in the Spirit, all we shall say about it here is that every Christian shares in the Pentecostal coming of the Paraclete to display Christ to us continually (see John 16:14) and to change us into his likeness as we gaze at his glory. "All of us, with unveiled faces, seeing the glory of the Lord as though reflected in a mirror, are being transformed into the same image from one degree of glory to another; for this comes from the Lord, the Spirit" (2 Cor. 3:18, NRSV). Here is the essence of present salvation — deliverance, that is, from the blinding and enslaving power of sin.

It is a Trinity salvation. Trinity Sunday points to the climactic New Testament truth that our salvation is, if I may so phrase it, a team job in which the Father, the Son, and the Holy Spirit work together. It is in this shared task that the divine tri-personhood is revealed; should the truth of the Trinity be denied, the apostolic gospel could not be stated. What God in grace does to save us sinners shows that *he* is *they*, essentially and eternally a society of mutual love engaged in enlarging the fellowship of that love by bringing us into it. Salvation means, in the final analysis, our unending personal fulfilment in adoring and pleasing the Father, the Son, and the Holy Spirit, as the divine Three lead the church ever deeper into the eternal enrichment that has been prepared for saved sinners to enjoy together. The triune God is love in the relational reality of the divine being, and is love to penitent believers in the further relational reality of the work of saving grace. Living in the life-transforming experience of God's sovereign salvation — trusting Christ, honouring the Father, and relying on the Holy Spirit — is this world's supreme good now, and the best is yet to be.

Jesus Christ is the only Saviour because it is through him alone that we find forgiveness and come to the Father and are re-created in love by the Holy Spirit, and are finally brought to the everlasting enrichment of the next world. "Thanks be to God for his indescribable gift!" (2 Cor. 9:15).

IMPLICATIONS

From what has been said it follows that any watering down, distorting, or obscuring of this gospel of salvation through Jesus Christ, any dismissal of it as untrustworthy fantasy, any distraction from contemplating and celebrating it as the centrepiece of worship, any suggestion that other faiths are adequate alternatives to it, and any attempt to fit it into a theological frame that is not incarnational or trinitarian or structured around the three "R's" of Christianity—namely, ruin, redemption, and regeneration—will weaken the church by corrupting its liturgy, its ministry, its message, and its mission. The sincerity with which non-Christian faiths are promoted in the world, and revisionist theologies are put forward in the church, is undoubted, but sincerity does not guarantee either truth or realism, and where the revelation of Christ the Redeemer, set forth in Scripture and embraced in the Creeds, the Articles, and the Solemn Declaration of 1893 (to look no further), is denied or imperfectly grasped, both truth and realism, and therefore both life and power, will be lacking. Experience in the present century has surely proved this up to the hilt.

What then should we say of *pluralism*, the relativistic notion that all theological clashes between religions can be transcended and that an ultimate oneness of worldwide religious outlooks can be demonstrated? Space forbids any extensive discussion of this idea, attractive in many ways as it is; but, speaking in general terms, three points seem to stand insuperably against it. First, the accounts of the religious ultimate (God), the human predicament (sin), and the nature and path of true life (salvation) that the world's religions offer are neither compatible nor convergent, but diverge radically. Second, all attempts to achieve an umbrella account of what they say on these three issues (the highest-common-factor quest in multifaith theology) have so far failed to produce anything substantial for which the exponents of the various world religions can settle, and the most careful analysis yields no likelihood of any greater success in the future. Third, New Testament theology is explicitly exclusivist. "I am the way and the truth and the life," said Jesus. "No one comes to the Father" — that is, no one comes to know God as Father, however strong they are on God's reality — "except through me" (John 14:6). "There is no other name under heaven given to men," preached Peter, "by which we" — who? Clearly in context, anybody and everybody — "must be saved" (Acts 4:12). "Must" implies that people both need to be saved and may be saved through Jesus: this is the universality of the Christian claim, of which we spoke at the outset, breaking surface once more. Pluralism, however, is categorically ruled out by such statements as these.

What should we say of *inclusivism*, the hopeful idea long embraced by Roman Catholicism and more recently by various Protestants also, that some, perhaps many, who did not encounter the Christian message in this world are nonetheless saved by Christ through a divinely induced disposition that is the equivalent of repentance and faith? Here again, full discussion is not possible in this chapter, but all who recognize the authority of the biblical revelation and the hazardous status of guesswork that goes beyond it will plead for reverent agnosticism at this point. We are not forbidden to hope for what Clark Pinnock calls "a wideness in God's mercy"[3] to at least some of those who do not hear the gospel, but the attempts that he and others have made to find in Scripture a doctrine of wideness in this sense cannot be regarded as a success, and this means that we are obligated in practice to evangelize on the basis that there is no salvation for anyone whom we encounter apart from faith in Christ. If we cannot be confident that there would have been any hope for us had we not learned of Christ and been brought to personal faith in him, we have no basis for holding out such hope in the case of anyone else, however strongly charity prompts us to want to do so. Inclusivist speculation about salvation for the unevangelized is thus necessarily unfruitful, and is likely to distract us from our present witnessing task.

What, finally, should we say of the Anglican Church of Canada? Why, simply what Lyte says, in a statement whose force we can now perhaps better appreciate than when we first took note of it:

> O how blest the congregation
> Who the gospel know and prize;
> Joyful tidings of salvation
> Brought by Jesus from the skies!
> He is near them,
> Knows their wants and hears their cries.

It is as such congregations multiply in the Anglican Church that there is hope for us, and not otherwise. Our future depends on how faithfully we maintain faith in, and fidelity to, Jesus Christ the only Saviour. The way is clear; the only question is whether we will walk in it. Lyte has indicated what is essential, and no more need now be said.

SUGGESTED READING

Stephen B. Clark, *Redeemer* (Leicester: IVP, 1986).
E. M. B. Green, *The Meaning of Salvation* (London: Hodder & Stoughton, 1965).
Robert Letham, *The Work of Christ* (Leicester: IVP, 1993).
John Murray, *Redemption Accomplished and Applied* (London: Banner of Truth, 1961).
Harold A. Netland, *Dissonant Voices: Religious Pluralism and the Question of Truth* (Grand Rapids: Eerdmans, 1991).
Lewis B. Smedes, *Union with Christ* (Grand Rapids: Eerdmans, 1983).
John Stott, *The Cross of Christ* (Leicester: IVP, 1986).

ENDNOTES

1. See John Hick, *God and the Universe of Faiths* (New York: St. Martin's Press, 1973); *God has Many Names* (Philadelphia: Westminster Press, 1982); *An Interpretation of Religion: Human Responses to the Transcendent* (New Haven: Yale University Press, 1989); J. Hick, ed., *The Myth of God Incarnate* (London: SCM Press, 1977); J. Hick and P. Knitter, eds., *The Myth of Christian Uniqueness* (Maryknoll N.Y.: Orbis, 1987). See also Harold A. Netland, *Dissonant Voices: Religious Pluralism and the Question of Truth* (Grand Rapids: Eerdmans, 1991).

2. On the incarnation as a fact, see John's Gospel, especially the prologue, 1:1–18; also the many references to Jesus' unique divine Sonship in the other Gospels (Matt. 3:17; 4:3, 5, 11–27; 14:33; 16:16; 17:5; 21:37; 27:54; 28:19; and parallels); also Paul's words in Rom. 1:4; 9:5, KJV, NASB, NIV, and NRSV; Col. 1:15–20; 2:9; also Heb. 1–2; 1 John 1; Rev. 1. On the virgin birth and Davidic identity, see the independent narratives and genealogies of Matt. 1; Luke 1–2, and 3:23–37; Rom. 1:3; Rev. 22:16. On the sinlessness of Jesus, see John 8:46; 2 Cor. 5:21; Heb. 4:15, and 7:26; 1 Pet. 2:22–23; 1 John 3:5. On Jesus as revealer of God, see John 1:18 and 14:9–11; 2 Cor. 4:4; Col. 1:15; Heb. 1:3–5. On the conjunction of the Son's cosmic and saving roles, see John 1:3-5; Col. 1:16-20; Heb. 1:31.

3. See Clark Pinnock, *A Wideness in God's Mercy* (Grand Rapids: Zondervan, 1992). See also John Sanders, *No Other Name: An Investigation into the Destiny of the Unevangelized* (Grand Rapids: Eerdmans, 1992).

SECTION III

LIFE

CHAPTER
9

BEING THE PEOPLE OF GOD
PRIORITIES AND STRATEGIES FOR TODAY'S CHURCH

ROBIN GUINNESS

INTRODUCTION

The purpose of this chapter is to focus on the Spirit-empowered community that God brought into existence through the life, death, and resurrection of Jesus Christ.

In the first century, the Apostle Peter wrote from Rome to the scattered community of Christians living in the northern part of Asia Minor (modern-day Turkey). He explained who and what God had called the community of his people to be: "You are a chosen race, a royal priesthood, a holy nation, God's own people, that you may declare the wonderful deeds of him who called you out of darkness into his marvellous light. Once you were no people but now you are God's people; once you had not received mercy, but now you have received mercy" (1 Pet. 2:9,10). In terms of identity this "people" transcends racial divisions and enmities; in terms of function this people is a priesthood, bringing men and women to God; in terms of character it is pure and holy; and in terms of purpose it is to declare in word and deed what God has done in and through Jesus Christ, who is the expression and demonstration of what God has done.

As Peter affirmed to these first-century Christians, the community of God's people is "called" by God: it is called into existence by him; it is called to a specific and clear-cut purpose by him; it is called by him to bear witness to Jesus Christ as Saviour and Lord; it is called to exhibit a certain character; it is called to embody a particular lifestyle; it is often called back by God to obedience and faith. It is from the fact of its calling that the community gets its name and significance: we are the *ecclesia* (Greek *ek* — "out," plus *kaleo* — "call"), the called-out ones. In the New Testament, the title *the church* refers both to the one, holy, catholic (universal), apostolic church militant here on earth, and also to the particular local expressions (often city-wide entities) of that one church.

What God calls his people from and to is clearly set forth in Scripture for each generation to understand and live out in the context of its own culture and historical situation.[1] Unless the church allows itself to be constantly reformed by Scripture it will fall far short of its calling. If the church holds onto the cultural form of a bygone age that has long ceased to be relevant and appropriate, it will fall far short of its God-given purpose. If the church adopts a contemporary cultural expression that distorts its God-given message and mandate, it will again fail in its divine calling. If the church today fails in word or deed to proclaim and live out the full message of the gospel of Jesus Christ as revealed in Holy Scripture in a way that effectively engages the critical issues and concerns of our own society, it will fail in its high and holy calling. As the 1989 Lausanne Congress on World Evangelization succinctly affirmed, God's purpose is for the whole church to take the whole gospel to the whole world.[2]

At various times during the last two thousand years the church has fallen into one of two equally disastrous but related tendencies. At times it has become blind to the Scriptures and simply failed to put itself humbly, trustingly, practically, and obediently under the authority of God's Word. At other times it has become deaf to the Spirit. It has failed to reflect on the cultural, social, educational, and intellectual realities in which it lived and failed to hear what the Spirit had been saying about how the gospel relates to these realities.

Part of the blindness and deafness of the church in past ages, as well as today, comes as a result of allowing reason, tradition, or experience to have an authority equal to that of Scripture. Jesus is quite clear in his teaching that the authority of God's Word always takes precedence over, and acts as a corrective to, any instruction or direction suggested from these lesser sources (Mark 7:1–14; 12:18–27). Similarly, the erroneous contention that Scripture is not the divine revelation of God's unchanging truth but rather a culturally conditioned entity, subject to human error and prejudice, leads the church into a blind alley that ends in oblivion.[3]

In order to look perceptively into God's Word, and to hear clearly what the Spirit is saying to the church today, this chapter will look at the origin of the church, the hallmarks of the New Testament church, and which priorities and strategies are important as we strive to be obedient to our calling to be the people of God today.

The Origin of the Church

Most Christians would affirm, quite rightly, that the church had its beginning on the day of Pentecost. This was some fifty days after the Jewish festival of Passover, which was the time when the crucifixion and the resurrection of Jesus had taken place. As the prophet Joel had foretold and as Jesus had promised immediately prior to his ascension, God poured out the gift of his Holy Spirit on the 120 disciples gathered in the upper room in Jerusalem. As a result, they began to speak in the diverse languages of the various nations represented at Passover to tell of the mighty works of God. This led into Peter's explanation as to what was happening. He gave a clear message concerning the death and resurrection of Jesus Christ as the fulfilment of Scripture and as the demonstration that God had made Jesus to be both Lord and Christ. In response to the call to repentance, about three thousand people were baptized so that they might receive forgiveness of sins and the gift of the Holy Spirit (Acts 2:14-38).

The church had been born. However, the church had been conceived many months — in fact about three years — prior to this date. The account of the church's birth is recorded in Acts 5, chapter 2, but the account of the church's conception is recorded in the Gospel of Mark, chapter 3. If the church is indeed the called-out ones, then it is logical to see the conception of the church in the first call of Jesus to his disciples. "He went up into the hills, and called to him those whom he desired, and they came to him. And he appointed twelve to be with him, and to be sent out to preach and to have authority to cast out demons" (Mark 3:13–15).

The origin of the church in terms of conception was the calling of the disciples by Jesus and the years of training with him. The implications of this are far-reaching. It means that *the church* is the company of those called by Jesus, living with Jesus, and witnessing to Jesus. This sets the model for all time. *The church* is a community, not an institution or an organization. *The church* is the people of God gathered around Jesus in worship and sent out by him as witnesses. As Bishop Lesslie Newbigin affirmed: "What he left behind was a fellowship, and he entrusted to it the task of being his representatives to the world."[4]

In the preface to the Acts of the Apostles, the author, Luke, states that in his previous book — the Gospel that bears his name — he has written of "all that Jesus began to do and to teach until the day that he was taken up" (Acts 1:2). The clear implication is that, in the second volume of his work, Luke would deal with all that Jesus continued to do and teach. The common thread and theme that ties these two books together is the action and teaching of Jesus. In the first book it is the action and teaching of Jesus in the days of his visible bodily presence; in the second book it is the action and teaching of his Spirit in the lives of his apostles and disciples. The essence of the unity of the church is not in its organization, structure, and hierarchy but in its relationship to Jesus to whom it bears witness; its relationship to God the Father, by whom it is called; and its relationship to the Holy Spirit, through whom it is empowered. We are a trinitarian people.

Changing the analogy from that of *conception and birth* to that of *root and fruit*, we could speak of the origin of the church in this way: the root structure of the church was created in the relationships, teaching, and modelling that took place as Jesus lived and worked among his disciples; the fruit of this was seen as this same company, empowered by the Holy Spirit, bore witness to the fact of Jesus' resurrection from the dead, demonstrating him to be both Lord and Christ (Acts 1:2).

The point of looking at the origin of the church in this way must by now be obvious: without conception there can be no birth; without root there can be no fruit. What God poured his Holy Spirit onto was a community of men and women centred on the person of Jesus; the coming of the Holy Spirit did not change the essential focus of the apostolic body brought into existence, formed and nurtured, trained and taught, by Jesus Christ. The coming of the Spirit enabled those who already knew him to become his witnesses. No amount of invoking the Spirit upon that which is not the church will enable it to become the church. Only when we see what the New Testament church is, eliminate from our version of the church that which is erroneous or superfluous and hold onto the essentials, only then — when we pray — will the fire of the Spirit fall from heaven. This brings us logically to the key question: What are the essential identifying features — the hallmarks — of the New Testament church?

THE HALLMARKS OF THE NEW TESTAMENT CHURCH

Every article of gold or silver is embossed with a hallmark, the true authentication of its genuine quality. In like manner there were certain characteristics of the New Testament church that were the hallmarks of the Spirit, testifying that this community was indeed the genuine article — a supernatural creation, and not merely a cunning counterfeit, the result of human organization and ingenuity. From the numerous references to the activity of the Holy Spirit in the Acts of the Apostles, it becomes clear that, until God poured out His Spirit, the disciples had neither the power nor the boldness, wisdom, or love to be who and what God had called them to be (Acts 2:4; 4:8,31; 5:3,9,32; 6:10, 55; 8:29; 10:44; 13:2).

The hallmarks of the New Testament church — all imprinted on the life of the church by the operation of God's holy and life-giving Spirit — can be examined in two parts: there were the obvious outward things, and there were the less obvious inner things.

THE MARKS OF THE CHURCH'S OUTWARD LIFE

In the course of delivering the Kerr lectures in Trinity College, Glasgow, in November 1952, Lesslie Newbigin posed the question, "How is Christ present to us today?" Reviewing the classical statements of reformed theology, he answered unhesitatingly: "He is present in the word and sacraments of the gospel." He then went on to make this pertinent statement: "No one, I think, would seriously wish to deny what these statements affirm. But it is a different matter when we go on to consider whether these statements convey the whole truth, and whether there is no place for other and distinct considerations in answering the question, 'How is Christ present to us today?'"[5]

Within five years of the crucifixion and resurrection of Jesus Christ, scores of Christian communities had come into existence. These flourished in the towns and villages that were the ancient landmarks on the trade routes and organizational arteries of the Roman Empire at the eastern extremities of the Mediterranean. If we had been casual observers in such places as Jerusalem, Antioch, or Philippi, we would have noticed at least four things about those who from earliest times came to be called Christians (Acts 11:26).

First, the New Testament Christians bore a *bold and incessant witness to Jesus Christ and his resurrection*. This living truth they shared dominated both public proclamation and private conversation. After Stephen, the first Christian martyr, died in Jerusalem, "those who were scattered because of the persecution that arose over Stephen travelled as far as Phoenicia and Cyprus and Antioch ... preaching the Lord Jesus" (Acts 11:19,20). When the Apostle Paul was in Athens, "he argued in the synagogue with the Jews and the devout persons, and in the market place every day with those who chanced to be there.... he preached Jesus and the resurrection"(Acts 17:17,18).

A few years ago I was in a car showroom on Rue St. Catherine in Montreal. In a conversation with the Jewish sales manager, I made this parting comment: "I really owe you so much and I want to say thank you." "What do you mean?" he queried. I explained, "I'm a Christian, and if it was not for your people and your culture into which Jesus came, I wouldn't even have a faith today." His immediate response was, "How can you Christians possibly expect anyone to believe that Jesus rose from the dead without even appearing to anyone?" I recounted to him the appearance of Jesus to Thomas in the upper room. He was so intrigued that he called in one of his salesmen, and I had the privilege of sharing with both of them how Jesus appeared to the two disciples on the road to Emmaus. To the best of my knowledge, neither man knew anything of those who claimed to have seen the risen Christ. We talked for over an hour.

Second, the New Testament Christians had a *vital life of prayer and worship.* The breaking of bread was obviously an integral part of this worship (Acts 2:42, 46). Accordingly, the Anglican Church affirms that the sacraments are "effectual signs of grace, and God's good will towards us, by the which he doth work invisibly in us, and doth not only quicken, but also strengthen and confirm our Faith in him."[6] The New Testament also witnesses to a dynamic and "untamed" element in the worship of the early church, sometimes within and sometimes not within the context of the Eucharist.

Pentecost itself not only grew out of an extended time of corporate prayer but began with a burst of prophetic utterance that was more of a worship event than it was a preaching event. The explanation as to what was happening in this Spirit-empowered extolling of the mighty works of God only followed the prophetic outburst itself. As God reveals himself in Spirit-anointed worship, those who preach in such a context have the privilege of opening the Scriptures and preaching Jesus to those who have already encountered the living God. This seems to have been something of the situation in Corinth to which the Apostle Paul refers when he writes: "But if all prophesy, and an unbeliever or outsider enters, he is convicted by all, he is called to account by all, the secrets of his heart are disclosed; and so, falling on his face, he will worship God and declare that God is really among you" (Acts 2:1–14; 1 Cor. 14:24).

The Anglican liturgy provides an excellent framework within which other edifying forms of worship can have their rightful place.[7] In the Sunday morning worship of the church of which I am a pastor, there is usually a time when we are led in three or four Scripture songs by our contemporary music group, followed by a time of extemporary prayer and praise from the congregation. Many times tears have run down my face as the Spirit of God moved deeply in my heart through a verse or phrase from one of the songs. My experience is by no means unique. God uses Spirit-anointed worship to draw men and women to himself. Such a time of open corporate prayer is in part a celebration of the numerous other smaller gatherings for prayer, and conveys the very essence of God's life-giving Spirit flowing through us.

A third characteristic of the outward life of the New Testament church was that it maintained *highly effective preaching and teaching*. Running through the entire New Testament is the consistent account of preaching that was good news indeed, centred on what God had done in Jesus Christ, bringing conviction of sin, sounding a call for repentance, offering God's gift of forgiveness of sins, and affirming the promise of God's holy and life-giving Spirit. Those who responded to the message gave themselves to the apostles' teaching (Acts 2:42). The disciples were but copying their Master in his highly effective preaching and teaching ministry. As on the day of Pentecost, the proclamation of the Word of God was "anointed" by God's Holy Spirit and immediately bore fruit in the lives of those who heard (Acts 8:4–6;10:44).

Few records afford greater insight into the nature of the apostolic ministry of preaching and teaching than that of Paul's address to the Ephesian elders gathered at the coastal city of Miletus to meet with the apostle as his ship made a brief passing visit to that port (Acts 20:17–38). Paul speaks here of "declaring anything that was profitable"; "teaching in public and from house to house"; "testifying of repentance to God and of faith in our Lord Jesus Christ"; "testifying to the gospel of the grace of God"; "preaching the kingdom"; "declaring to you the whole counsel of God"; and of not ceasing "night or day to admonish everyone ... with tears." As he left these pastors and teachers, he affirms: "I commend you to God and to the Word of His grace which is able to build you up." Twice in his address he implies that he was tempted to draw back from continuing to expound and apply the Word of God — a discipline so demanding spiritually, mentally, and emotionally — but he affirms, "I did not shrink from declaring [God's Word] to you."

Those to whom the apostles entrusted the immensely important task of bridging the gap between the apostolic and the post-apostolic age were similarly instructed to "preach the Word," and were warned of those who in the time to come "will not endure sound teaching, but having itching ears ... will accumulate for themselves teachers to suit their own likings and will turn away from listening to the truth and wander into myths" (2 Tim. 4:2–6). The Word of God as set forth in the Old and New Testament Scriptures is endowed by God with an utterly unique capacity, under the power of God's Holy Spirit, to set forth Jesus Christ and to bring women and men into a life-changing faith in him. Only God's Word can open blind eyes, convince stubborn minds, melt hard hearts, and bend proud wills. Churches that have given themselves to the regular, systematic, faithful, and practical exposition of God's Word have seen a harvest that is inexplicable outside the fact that God honours the Word of which he is author. Learning to preach and teach in this way is a lifelong task, which, sadly, has sometimes to begin only when theological college has been left behind.[8]

The fourth outward characteristic of New Testament believers was that they demonstrated *an extraordinary caring for people*. One of the dramatic contrasts between Jesus and the religious leaders of his day was between his profound care for people and their general indifference. The evangelists spoke of Jesus as "moved with compassion" (Matt. 9:36; 14:14; 15:32). This deep inner caring for people demonstrated itself outwardly in the way that he welcomed and had time for each individual who came to him. This was especially true in the case of those who were despised and rejected by the society of their day — such as the leper outside Capernaum, Mary of Magdalla, and Zacchaeus. This same caring for people that characterized the life of Jesus also marked the life of his early followers. The numerous "one another" injunctions in the Epistles show that person-to-person caring was expected to be a normal part of the Christian community. This caring was also expressed corporately. As a direct consequence of the initial policy of the Jerusalem Church "to hold all things in common," we are told that "there was not a needy person among them" (Acts 5:34). As part of the determination of that church to provide adequate daily distribution of food for widows irrespective of their ethnic background, seven men were set aside to supervise this ministry (Acts 6:1–7). The sacrificial nature of this love was demonstrated by Stephen, who in the moment of his martyrdom pleaded for the forgiveness of his murderers (Acts 7:60). Paul tells both the Christians at Ephesus and those at Colossae that it is "the love which they have for all the saints," which has come to his knowledge (Eph. 1:15; Col. 1:2). The writer to the Hebrews enjoins that brotherly love should continue, implying that this was already a mark of this Christian community (Heb. 13:1). Scattered through the letters to the young churches are innumerable injunctions to let the love of Christ shine through all their lives and relationships (1 John 3:11; Eph. 5:2; 1 Cor. 14:1).

In the days of his earthly ministry Jesus had said to his disciples, "By this shall all men know that you are my disciples that you have love for one another" (John 13:35). The genuine warmth and caring within the early Christian communities must have been an immensely significant factor, bringing men and women to turn to Jesus as the Way, the Truth, and the Life. When all that persons have known is the brokenness of their own families and the widespread indifference to people within their own culture, the discovery of the love of Christ shining through his people, imperfect though they may be, becomes something immensely attractive and almost too good to be true.

The Marks of the Church's Inner Life

Having looked at what a casual observer might have been aware of through interaction with Christians of the first century, we turn to some of the things that observers would have discovered had they become baptized and entered into the inner life of the Christian community. There were at least four characteristics that marked the inner life of first-century Christian communities.

Within the first-century Christian communities, there was *healing and transformation of lives*. On one level this healing was very public. In the ministry of Jesus, and to a lesser extent in the ministry of the apostles, people were set free from the ravages of disease and also from the bondage and oppression of evil spirits. These healings were the expression of Jesus' compassion and caring for people (Luke 7:13; Mark 6:34,56).

At the same time, both in the ministry of Jesus and in the ministry of the apostles, these healings and acts of deliverance were recognized as signs that God's kingdom had come in power (Matt. 12:28; Luke 10:9; Acts 14:3). Jesus certainly taught consistently that, with his coming, the kingdom of God had come to be present on earth, and with that came the confrontation with the kingdom of this world, the kingdom of darkness, that Jesus' coming instigated (Mark 1:15; John 12:31,32). Through Jesus' death on the cross, all the powers of darkness were vanquished, and this was demonstrated to be so by his resurrection from the dead. The early church moved out in bold expectation that Jesus would continue his work of healing and deliverance in and through them, and it was so (Acts 3:6; 16:16–18).

Though there was a public aspect to the healing, deliverance, and transformation of lives in the ministry of the early church, yet this was really the tip of the iceberg; nine-tenths lay hidden. This was the outward and visible sign of the inner transformation of lives: it was happening continually among those who met together in the name of Jesus. The apostle Paul reminded the believers at Corinth of the backgrounds from which some of them had come, "immoral ... idolaters ... adulterers ... homosexuals ... thieves ... greedy ... drunkards ... revilers ... robbers," and adds emphatically, "such were some of you. But you were washed ... sanctified ... justified in the name of our Lord Jesus Christ and in the Spirit of our God" (1 Cor. 6:9–11).

Transformation of sinful, self-centred lives is at the heart of God's work in the life of his people. Yet the healing and deliverance aspect of that work has come into new focus. This has been through the birth of the Pentecostal church at the beginning of the twentieth century and its subsequent phenomenal growth, and through the slow awakening of the wider church to the charismatic movement in the sixties, seventies and eighties; God is restoring something to his church. There are indications that at the end of the twentieth century this vital component of healing, deliverance, and transformation — never, of course, completely lost — is coming back. Many Anglican churches, in formal and informal ways, are rediscovering this joyful reality. The growth of the Vineyard Church across Canada, originating in the United States, is in part attributable to the slowness of the older churches to recognize this aspect of God's work.

The second thing that a new initiate into the Christian community of the first century would have discovered was *holy separateness in lifestyle*. One of the reasons the early church was so effective in penetrating the world was that the world was so ineffective in penetrating the church.

In writing to the Christians at Ephesus (and wherever else the letter was read), the Apostle Paul devoted the entire second half of the Epistle to spelling out in practical detail what it meant for these Christians to live Christianly in the midst of a pagan society. These chapters are replete with exhortations to develop Christian character and Christian relationships. Purity of life within the

Christian community was not an optional extra but a very high priority. The sudden death of the couple who thought that they could introduce corruption into the life of the church with impunity was not a lesson quickly lost on the church (Acts 5:1–11). The believers in the church at Corinth were explicitly instructed to expel members who continued to practice the morality of their old pagan lifestyle (1 Cor. 5:9–13). Churches that are beginning to develop a policy of pastoral discipline, difficult and painful though it is, are discovering the lost dimension of what it means to be the people of God. Not being conformed to this world is the necessary prerequisite for being transformed (Rom. 12:1,2).

The third thing that a new member of the Christian community would have discovered was the *practice of serious discipleship*.[9] This was a way of life and a way of learning that came directly from the kind of relationship that Jesus established with those whom he originally called to follow him. Discipleship was a common form of learning in the first century; John the Baptist trained disciples. Apprenticeship is a form of training somewhat familiar to us that comes closest to what discipleship provided.

Discipleship is a process of learning, usually built on the relationship between a senior partner and one or more junior partners. In this relationship the senior partner invests himself, his caring, his time, his experience, and his teaching, in those he is seeking to encourage, equip, and empower for ministry. This process continues over an extended period of time. Those who are "discipled" in this way in time begin to disciple others. The Apostle Paul, who discipled Timothy, was able to say to him, "What you have heard from me ... entrust to faithful men who will be able to teach others also" (Rom. 12:1,2). Here is a vision of discipleship that spans four generations. The growth potential is exponential, not merely linear. All those who are discipled are not only discipling junior partners but are training them to disciple yet others. Churches that give themselves to discipleship may feel at first that nothing is happening. On one level nothing happened in the first three and a half years of Jesus' ministry. The sowing may indeed seem futile to start with, but when the harvest begins to be reaped, we then recognize our past folly in wasting time with anything less than serious discipleship.

The fourth mark of the inner life of the early church was the *radical recognition that every member counted*. The church was understood as the body of Christ (Eph. 4:12–13; 1 Cor. 12,13,14; Rom. 12:4–8). The essence and vitality of a human body lies in its multiplicity of parts and organs, all functioning together in harmonious interdependence. This description of the church as the body of Christ was not merely an apt analogy, it was in fact an accurate representation of what God had created his church to be. Any organization became subservient to this fundamental reality: every individual believer had a unique and vital place in the community of God's people. The church was not an organization to which you belonged but a spiritual body of that you became a living part, uniquely gifted to manifest some rich facet of its life.

In subsequent centuries, unfortunate and unbiblical developments, such as that of giving undue significance to the distinction between clergy and laity, not only distorted our understanding of what the church is, but made it almost impossible for the church to function as originally intended.[10] In time, much of the church came to be run by salaried professionals. Of course there were great advantages to this arrangement; but there were also horrendous liabilities. The church in its gathered mode assumed a significance that let the importance of the church in its scattered mode be almost totally overlooked; the gifts and significance in ministry (whether in gathered or scattered mode) of nonsalaried members became tragically ignored; and the organization that at times almost seemed to have replaced the organism became obsessed with buildings, which consumed vast quantities of time, human energy, and financial resources.

PRIORITIES AND STRATEGIES OF IMPORTANCE TODAY

In the introduction to this chapter we promised to conclude with a look at priorities and strategies that are important as we strive to be obedient to our calling to be the people of God today. In the first place, and perhaps most important, we need to look at the four distinguishing marks of the outward life of the church and of the inward life of the church and build these into our local congregations. Beyond these vital steps I want to suggest ten additional priorities that I consider of the greatest importance today.

1. *Look to the Two Thirds World.* The church in Asia, Africa, and South America is growing phenomenally, while the church in the West is shrinking. We have a vast amount to learn from our brothers and sisters in such places as the Diocese of Singapore; through them God will rekindle our vision.[11]

2. *Establish "Vision, Purpose, Goals" for your church.* This will not get the work done. It may, however, lead us to stop doing certain things and start doing other things. A set of biblical and Spirit-inspired priorities and strategies for our church and our location could begin to make the dry bones live (Ezek. 37:1–14).

3. *Emphasize small groups.* Jesus spoke of the church in terms of "where two or three are gathered together in my name" (Acts 2:46; 5:42). As biological cells are the fundamental building blocks of the physical body, so nurture groups are indispensable to the body of Christ: every member needs to be part of one.[12]

4. *Redefine the functions of pastoral leadership.* If the primary place of ministry is in a person's neighbourhood, place of work, school, or recreational centre, it has serious implications for what takes place when God's people gather together. The primary work of the clergy is to encourage, enable, and equip the whole people of God to do the work of the ministry (Eph. 4:11–12). Serious retraining of clergy and lay leadership needs to take place.

5. *Develop transitional strategies.* There will almost certainly be several steps by which we get from where we are to where we would like to be. A church with

a highly conservative Sunday morning congregation may well have to run an alternative service where new patterns of worship can be freely developed.[13]

6. *Build faith-sharing teams.* However small a church is, it can get together three or four people (with a music component if possible) who will go off to share their faith at another church, a home meeting, a seniors' residence, or a high school. Whole churches have come into a revival of faith and purpose through such simple beginnings.

7. *Explore para-church partnerships.* God has brought into existence movements and organizations of extraordinary effectiveness and wisdom that are playing a crucial part in the work of the kingdom today. As we invite movements such as Navigators[14] and Pioneer Clubs[15] to work with us at the local level, hope and excitement about God's work are reborn.

8. *Pioneer in church-planting.* The most vital denominations in Canada are not closing down old congregations but opening up new ones. Why is this happening? Find out what these churches are doing. There is no reason why we should not be doing the same to the glory of God.[16]

9. *Get involved in world mission.* The church at Antioch sent out its own members in world mission (Acts 13:1–3). In addition to programmes offered by the national church, there are Anglican Mission Societies looking for workers, other missions willing to place Anglicans in Anglican contexts, and numerous opportunities to support teachers or business people from our parishes in secular employment overseas.[17]

10. *Take a second look at the Anglican Church of Canada.* Our church has to return to biblical priorities at the parish, diocesan, and national levels, or else sink into oblivion. "The fundamental issue is ... the obedience or the disobedience of the church to the authority of Scripture."[18] This will not happen by any master plan being handed down from "the top," but only through a whole host of ordinary women and men humbly, faithfully, and prayerfully grasping what God calls his church to be, and living it out courageously and obediently at whatever level he has called them to serve him.[19]

SUGGESTED READING

J. D. Douglas, ed., *Proclaim Christ Until He Comes*, the report of the International Congress on World Evangelisation (Lausanne II in Manila; World Wide Publications, 1990).

Michael Green, *Evangelism through the Local Church* (London: Hodder & Stoughton, 1991).

Alister McGrath, *The Renewal of Anglicanism* (London: Moorhouse, 1993).

Stephen Neill, *Anglicanism* (London: Penguin Books, 1958).

D. C. K. Watson, *I Believe in the Church* (London: Hodder & Stoughton, 1978).

C. Wright and C. Sugden, eds., *One Gospel—Many Clothes* (London: Evangelical Fellowship in the Anglican Communion and Regnum Books, 1990).

ENDNOTES

1. See Michael Green, *Evangelism through the Local Church*, pp. 79-108, for a study on the Church at Antioch. (London: Hodder & Stoughton, 1991).

2. See the report on the International Congress on World Evangelization (Lausanne II) held in Manilla: *Proclaim Christ Until He Comes*, edited by J. D. Douglas (World Wide Publications, 1990).

3. For a fuller treatment of this issue see John Stott, *Christ the Controversialist* (London: Tyndale, 1970).

4. Lesslie Newbigin, *The Household of God* (London: SCM Press, 1953), p. 50.

5. Newbigin, *The Household of God*, pp. 47, 48.

6. *The Book of Common Prayer 1959 Canada*, Articles Of Religion, XXV, p. 706.

7. See D. C. K. Watson, *I Believe in the Church* (London: Hodder & Stoughton 1978), pp. 179-198.

8. See Watson, *I Believe in the Church*, pp. 119–224.

9. Perhaps the most definitive work on discipleship was written in 1871 by A. B. Bruce, *The Training of the Twelve*. It is available today from Kregel publishers.

10. For one of the earliest critiques of this reality see the writings of Roland Allen, especially *The Spontaneous Expansion of the Church and the Causes which Hinder It*, written in the 1920s (Grand Rapids: Eerdmans, 1962).

11. For a fuller treatment of this subject see Alister E. McGrath, *The Renewal of Anglicanism* (London: Moorhouse, 1993). Also, *One Gospel — Many Clothes*, edited by C. Wright and C. Sugden (London: Evangelical Fellowship in the Anglican Communion and Regnum Books, 1990).

12. See Ralph W. Neighbour, *Where Do We Go from Here? A Guidebook for the Cell Group Church* (Houston, Texas: Touch Publications, 1990).

13. See Howard Hanchey, *Church Growth* (Cambridge, Mass.: Cowley Publications, 1990).

14. Navigators of Canada: P.O. Box 27070, London, ON, N5X 3X5.

15. Pioneer Clubs Canada Inc., P.O. Box 5477, Burlington, ON, L7R 4L2.

16. Arnell Motz, *Reclaiming A Nation* (Church Leadership Publications, 1990).

17. See *Challenging God's People In The Nineties (Barnabas Anglican Ministries)*, p. 8.

18. Evangelical Fellowship in the Anglican Communion, Canterbury Consultation 1993, *Summary Findings Report*, section D.

19. The Anglican Church of Canada has to be seen in the perspective of historic Anglicanism which is nowhere set out more clearly than in Bishop Stephen Neill, *Anglicanism* (London: Penguin Books, 1958).

10

BAPTISMAL MINISTRY
PARTNERSHIP, GENDER, AND INTEGRATION

ARCHIE AND BARBARA PELL

THEOLOGY OF MINISTRY

To explore the nature of Christian ministry in our contemporary Canadian society, we must first begin with the New Testament, the root of faith, of the church, and thus of our understanding of ministry. In New Testament times, the distinctions we too often employ, between "lay" ministry ("the members") and "ordained" ministry ("the minister"), were not to be found. There was, of course, a distinction between "apostles" — the eleven plus Matthias (Acts 1:26), plus Paul (Gal. 1:11–24 and 2:6–10) — and other members of the church. Otherwise it would appear that all Christians had ministries, each ministry appropriate to the gifts bestowed by the Spirit upon the individual.

1 Corinthians 12 presents us with a picture of the church as an organic whole, the Spirit-filled body of Christ. Early in the chapter Paul writes of the differing forms of service found within the Christian community and specifically identifies each as being a gift from the Holy Spirit (verses 4–11). He then describes the interdependence of these gifts, using the human body as an analogy for the Christian community. Some persons have one gift and others have more than one gift; some gifts are long-lasting and others are temporary. But all are needed for the health of the church and for its proper functioning in the world (verses 12–26). Then the chapter closes (verses 27–31) with two lists enumerating various spiritual gifts. The first uses personal terms to specify three ministerial functions: apostles, prophets, teachers. As H. J. Carpenter reminds us, these describe functions, not offices, within the church of Paul's day.[1] The second list speaks of other spiritual gifts in abstract terms: miracle-working, healing, helping others, providing guidance, ecstatic utterances. The chief difference between these two lists would appear to be that the former describes permanent gifts while the latter denotes "spontaneous and sporadic manifestations of the Spirit."[2] Paul's point is that all these gifts together represent a divine legacy showered upon the church.

To be the recipient of one or more of these gifts, and thus to be responsible for part of the ministry of the church, a person need only be a Christian. In the New Testament a Christian is a person who, receptive to the Spirit's gift of faith, can proclaim the simple creed "Jesus is Lord" (1 Cor. 12:3).[3] It is within this community, the body of Christ, that the Spirit pours out his riches for all to receive (1 Cor. 12:13). In this view, baptism is not a momentary experience or an empty ritual; it is the beginning of a lifelong period of service to and for Jesus Christ.

In baptism, then, a Christian becomes one of the people (*laos* in Greek) of God and thus a part of the body of which Christ is the head (Eph. 5:23). Now since Christ is Lord of the individual Christian's life and head of the corporate body of all Christians, there must be concrete manifestations of this fact that are apparent to all. Being baptized into "the truth of the gospel" (Gal. 2:14) means showing forth that truth in individual and corporate conduct. Spiritual gifts are the abilities that enable this to happen. Through the presence and operation of the Holy Spirit, all of life is touched by these gifts (Gal. 5:22–25). The gifts given to baptized believers are not limited to the spectacular and extraordinary; these gifts are equally for the ordinary, everyday living out of one's commitment to Christ as Lord. Spiritual gifts are not restricted to church-oriented activities; they are the abilities and guidance that empower all of life. All of a Christian's life is ministry.

The model for that life of ministry is Christ himself. From the resurrection onward, Christians found in Christ's teaching about ministry two key words that provide the outline for ministry: the verbs "to send" (*apostellein* in Greek) and "to serve" (*diakonein* in Greek).[4] To speak of the basis of ministry as being *sent* is to see ministry as a continuously widening series of concentric circles. At the centre stands Christ, the Son sent by God (John 3:17). The circle around Christ is made up of the apostles, those who were sent by him into the world just as he had been sent by the Father (John 20:21). In the next circle are found those men and women sent by the inner core of apostles on some particular task of ministry (Acts 15:27).

But as the number of concentric circles multiplies, the work of sending does not evolve from a totally divine doing (as in Mark 9:37) to a purely human activity. From the beginning, each new and expanding circle of ministry has been the work of the Holy Spirit. The original disciples understood their commissioning by Jesus to be the result of the gift of the Holy Spirit (John 20–22). Further, they recognized the commissioning of the next circle of ministers, the 108 believers present with the (once again) twelve apostles on the day of Pentecost, as being solely the work of the Spirit (Acts 2:4). Then as the church sent its members to ministries further and further afield, the commissioning of these ministers was by prayer, fasting, and the laying on of hands in obedience to the Spirit who is the true sender (Acts 13:2–3) and ongoing guide (Acts 16:6).

The idea of service, which was stressed by Jesus and the early Christians, finds its roots in the Old Testament. Here the Hebrew verb *abad* and the nouns derived from it indicate work both for others (Gen. 29:15) and for God (Num. 3:7–8). It is informative to note that, as J. A. Wharton points out, "the Hebrew word 'service,' when used to describe the service of Israel to God, is best rendered 'worship.'"[5] As with so many other ideas and practices from traditional Israelite religion, the idea of service was given much greater depth and breadth by the Son of God.

In a world and society where service was understood as the duty of the "lesser" to the "greater," Jesus proclaimed by word and by action a radically new understanding of service. He was the teacher and the twelve were the disciples: he was the greater and they were the lesser. Yet he spoke of his being greater in new terms: "I am among you as one who serves" (Luke 22:27). Along with his words, he showed them what this new view of service meant by washing the feet of his disciples and then challenging them to live this new life of service. Greatness means being a servant rather than striving for power or glory.

The Christian church in Acts and the Epistles took the idea and activity of service so seriously that *diakonas* (servant) became a term applied to all Christians. All Christians are ministers because all are called to serve. This service is seen as a communal ministry for the "common good" (1 Cor. 12:7) and extends beyond the Christian community to all people (Gal. 6:10). But to think of service only in terms of actions is too restrictive. There is also a *diakonia* of the word (Acts 6:4), and this combination of service by proclamation of the gospel and service by compassionate action becomes the evangelistic vehicle for the dramatic growth of the church (Acts 6:7).

As this two-fold view of Christian ministry is translated by the New Testament from the general to the specific, from the community of faith to the individual believer, three basic categories for personal living emerge: discipleship, evangelism, and lifestyle.

Personal ministry begins with discipleship. In the New Testament a disciple is a learner, a person called by a teacher to learn from him and to follow his teachings. Jesus selected a group of twelve men to gather around him for instruction. In the four Gospels they are called his disciples, a title applied only to those particular men until Acts 6:1, where the term is suddenly applied to all Christians. The mark of disciples is that they have been called by Christ (Rom. 1:17) through the preaching of the gospel message (Gal.1:6), and that they respond with confident trust (Acts 16:31) and a life of service to Christ (James 1:22–25).

Discipleship leads naturally to witness. First of all, Jesus spoke of himself as a witness to the truth of God (John 3:11,32). Then he instructed the disciples that they were to be public witnesses to the salvation he brought in his death and resurrection (Luke 24:44–48). The eleven apostles recognized the importance of being witnesses by adding Matthias to their number as a witness to the life and teaching of Jesus (Acts 1:21–26). However, being a witness was not just the prerogative of those specifically set aside as official missionaries of the church, as 1 Peter 3:15 demonstrates. There, in the middle of a letter exhorting average Christians to live a life of holy behaviour, Peter says, "Always be ready to make your defense to anyone who demands from you an accounting for the hope that is in you." Witnessing to Christ by one's words is the duty of every Christian.

Lifestyle is the congruence of faith and daily living in a form which draws thoughts, emotions, and actions together as a unity. Throughout the New Testament there is consistent teaching that the form of a person's life represents his or her response to the gospel. Jesus frequently emphasized the need for a holy lifestyle. For example, the Sermon on the Mount (Matt. 5–7) deals with a number of aspects of everyday living from family relations to charitable donations. Paul picked up this theme and kept it in the forefront of his teaching. He wrote to the Thessalonians to tell them "how you ought to live and to please God" (1 Thess. 4:1). He addressed the Corinthians on such matters as incest and personal relationships (1 Cor. 6) and reminded them that Christian living is "always carrying in the body the death of Jesus, so that the life of Jesus may also be made visible in our bodies" (2 Cor. 4:10). The power of the gospel is to become incarnate in every aspect of a believer's life.

In light of this New Testament view of ministry we wish to address three issues of ministry in the contemporary church. The last of these will be examined in the greatest detail, for we believe it to be the key issue for the ministry and survival of the church in the twenty-first century.

MALE AND FEMALE

Ministry, then, is a life of exercising the gifts (natural abilities and acquired skills) that the Holy Spirit bestows on each baptized follower of Jesus Christ. The gifts bestowed upon a particular individual are the Spirit's choice, in compliance with the divine plan of salvation. These two statements form a basic principle that has not always been accepted in its absolute fullness. Two decades ago our Canadian Anglican Church debated whether the principle was gender-free when applied to ordination. While there was a very vigorous debate about the ordination of women, there was not the same degree of opposition (or of intransigence) as has been the case in Anglican circles in England and Australia. In the end, our Canadian branch of Anglicanism decided that gifts for ordained ministry were to be recognized, celebrated, and utilized for men and women alike. That decision was carried to its logical conclusion with the consecration of Victoria Matthews as a bishop of the Diocese of Toronto in February of 1994.

We recognize that there are Canadian Anglicans who remain uneasy with and/or opposed to carrying the New Testament teaching on ministry to a genderless conclusion. Some of their objections are cultural, but often opposition centres on such passages as 1 Corinthians 11:2–16, 1 Corinthians 14:34–36, and 1 Timothy 2:8–15. In the first instance, Paul calls for the Corinthian women to wear headcoverings at worship services. But he does, at the same time, speak of women as praying and prophesying at these community gatherings, indicating an acceptance of their leadership roles through the exercise of two different spiritual gifts. In the second passage there is no such ambiguity — women are to be silent in church. And thirdly, Paul writes to Timothy that women are not to teach or have authority in the churches that look to Timothy as their leader. However, countering the limits placed on women in these passages are the references to women as leaders in several of Paul's letters. Priscilla appears in five passages and is referred to as a fellow worker by Paul (Rom.16:3), a term he usually uses for church leaders. Euodia and Synthyche have worked with Paul to advance the gospel (Phil. 4:2–4). Claudia is one in a list of otherwise male leaders who send greetings via Paul (2 Tim. 1:21; the Greek "brothers" is translated here as "brothers and sisters" in the New Revised Standard Version). These arguments and counter-arguments remind us of the arguments for and against infant baptism arising from Acts 16:33 — both sides can feel justified in their positions, but neither can claim absolute victory. The ambiguity about women and ministry in the above passages may well have cultural roots and/or be clouded by the reader's cultural assumptions.

It is when the discussion moves from precepts to principles that we believe the issue is decided. As was pointed out earlier, any and all forms of ministry for Jesus Christ are the results of baptism and the Holy Spirit's bounty. And while gifts for ministry are bestowed differently, baptism is the great Christian equalizer: "As many of you as were baptized into Christ have clothed yourselves with Christ. There is no longer Jew or Greek, there is no longer slave or free, there is no longer male and female; for all of you are one in Christ Jesus" (Gal. 3:27–28). Here is the principle, and it is an expression of grace. It is not by our own political or philosophical or cultural efforts but by the grace of our Saviour that we are united to Christ in baptism (Rom. 5:1-2). It is not by our efforts and ambition but by the grace of the Spirit that each baptized believer is given a talent, a service (1 Cor. 12:11). Similarly, as Paul wrote to the Galatians, it is not by accident of birth (race, gender, social/economic status), but by the grace of the Redeemer of the world that all are equal in the body of Christ. As we seek to identify gifts for ministry in ourselves and our fellow Christians, we are called to be ready for the serendipitous work of the Spirit, and not to close or open our eyes to the Spirit's surprises on the basis of a person's gender. That is how redeemed people are called to respond to God's redeeming grace.

LAY AND CLERGY

Second, there is the issue of the partnership of laity and clergy in ministry. This issue revolves around the respective functions of lay and ordained ministries. We focus on ministry in terms of function rather than office because that is what the description of ministry as *diakonia* is all about, stressing that a Christian's way of following Christ is by serving, by getting the Lord's work done without standing upon ceremony. Each and every ordinary Christian is called to be a servant of Christ wherever she or he lives and works. Further, each Christian must accept the full responsibility of this calling. That is the point of Jesus' parables of the talents (Matt. 25:14–30) and of the sheep and the goats (Matt. 25:3–46). The early Christians knew they were all servants and ambassadors of Jesus Christ. So wherever they went they sought to live in obedience to Christ, and they very naturally gossiped the gospel. When persecution struck and the early believers were scattered after the martyrdom of Stephen (Acts 8:4), this easy and natural life of ministry on the part of ordinary Christians led to the founding of churches in such cities as Rome and Ephesus long before any major church leader visited. A prerequisite for any form of ministry is that it be a natural part of the way a Christian lives.

A further prerequisite to discussing functions of ministry is to remember that it is not possible for a person to do everything at the same time, or even in one's lifetime. Every Christian has a particular calling and the gifts essential to that calling. But not every Christian can be expected to have the same calling and the same gifts (1 Cor. 12:27–30). There are some Christians who have been called to a lifelong ministry of marriage counselling and have been gifted with the ability and training to follow that vocation as a means of earning their living. At the same time there are some Christians who, at some point in their lives, may have spent time with a friend or neighbour whose marriage was in danger, helping that person understand the situation and deal constructively with it. But there are also many Christians who have done neither. Some are called to a permanent form of a particular ministry, others to a sporadic form of it, and others never called to it.

Ministry, then, consists of those acts of service in word and deed to which a Christian is continuously or occasionally called by God in the course of his or her lifetime. Ministerial functions vary so widely that it is impossible to catalogue these definitively in a limited space. Yet, if ministry is understood as the service of one's whole life, then the functions of lay ministry would include everything from one's occupation, to one's marriage and parenthood, to one's involvement in community affairs, to one's work within the structures of the church, to one's use of leisure time. Almost nothing that a person can do (exceptions must be allowed for such manifestations of the power of evil as murder, robbery, and pornography) is beyond being a ministerial function and thus beyond being a legitimate form of lay ministry.

It follows that while clergy and laity jointly share the whole ministry of the whole people of God, their functions differ (Rom. 12:3–8). Bishops, priests, and deacons are called to a specific ministry of word and sacrament within the structures of the church (Eph. 4:11–13). But they are not primarily called to be lawyers, carpenters, accountants, machinists, social workers, politicians, or computer programmers. The laity may be called to assume a fair share of the work and ministry within the church alongside the clergy, but they are not normally called to earn their livelihood within the church. To perform the whole ministry of Christ's "royal priesthood" (1 Pet. 3:9), clergy and laity are mutually interdependent. The laity are primarily called to be the whole people of God in "the world" where, by their lives, relationships, conversations, and lifestyles, they demonstrate the truth of the gospel and the presence of the risen Christ. Clergy are called to be aware of the issues, challenges, joys, and sorrows of life in "the world," but to work primarily in "the church" to teach the truth of the gospel and to administer the sacraments so that the laity are equipped, nurtured, and supported to be effective witnesses for Christ in all situations. And clergy and laity together are called to care for, pray for, and love each other as brothers and sisters in the family of God. In all this the Spirit provides the talents and power necessary to minister faithfully.

A WORLDVIEW FOR MINISTRY

Therefore, since the status of clergy and lay ministries is equal but the functions are different, it is important that these differences be defined and mutually supported. The clergy need to be given time and encouragement by the laity to develop their prayer and devotional lives, their spiritual discernment and leadership, and their teaching and preaching ministries in order "to equip the saints for the work of ministry, for building up the body of Christ" (Eph. 4:12). Similarly, the laity must recognize that it is a complex and difficult lifelong ministry to apply the Sunday precepts (taught by the clergy, one would hope) to their Monday-to-Saturday personal and professional lives.

Anglicanism, while having an extremely well-educated clergy, has too often demonstrated an anti-intellectualism with regard to the laity (in contrast to some other denominations with few seminaries but strong emphasis on adult "Sunday schools" and Christian post-secondary education). Confirmation at twelve years of age is often viewed as graduation from any need for further theological training or "worldview studies" (to develop a Christian perspective on one's life, work, and current social issues). We need the partnership of clergy and laity to help us integrate spirituality and lifestyle — spiritual precepts and secular practices. The world has become too complicated and fragmented for the clergy to supply theological applications for every professional problem ranging from the biologist's to the bus driver's. The only solution is lay people who are equipped and committed to translating their faith into the world.

Lay ministry in the world depends on a worldview that is incarnational and integrationist (rather than separationist or even transformationist). The integration of faith and life, the sacred and the secular, the holy in the daily, is particularly supported by (though not exclusive to) an Anglican theology. Two accessible, popular books outline the principles of a Christian perspective on our world: Arthur Holmes's *All Truth is God's Truth* and Harry Blamires's *The Christian Mind*.[6] We will base our outline of a Christian worldview on their precepts, which have both a biblical foundation and a historical validation in Anglican tradition.

An integrational worldview depends on a Christ-centred — as opposed to postmodern — concept of truth and knowledge in our lives and work. In John's Gospel, Jesus says, "I am the way and the truth and the life" (John 14:6), and Paul writes, "In [Christ] are hidden all the treasures of wisdom and knowledge" (Col. 2:3). In other words, all truth is God's truth, and in our daily living we must bear witness to the order and beauty that God has created, redeemed, and sustained. As Arthur Holmes reminds us, the development of Western culture was a product of a Judeo-Christian worldview; our arts, sciences, and political systems were born of a desire to seek and to reflect God's truth in our world. But modern humanity has lost this religious focus, and "truth" has become fragmented, relativistic, infinitely deconstructable, and ultimately unknowable.

Many of our most prestigious academic institutions — long considered the special domain of truth-seekers — were originally founded by the church and remember in their names and mottos that they once believed all knowledge comes from God. The words carved over the door to the main building of Victoria College of the University of Toronto are part of the passage from John 8:31–32: "If you continue in my word, you are truly my disciples; and you will know the truth, and the truth will make you free." There is no such thing as complete academic "objectivity," and even secular humanists agree that "value-free" and "education" are contradictory terms. But many secular academics believe that in the modern educational system there is no absolute truth; only the pursuit of truth is absolute. In that case, it is a pursuit without a goal and a journey without an end in which all the signposts are shifting and deceptive.

But if Christians reject the broad path of an ultimately meaningless quest for truth, we must equally avoid a narrow-minded and arrogant defensiveness towards the truth, as if we had invented it. If all truth is God's truth, the mind of God encompasses all of creation; it is much larger than the human mind can ever grasp. We still "see in a mirror, dimly" (1 Cor. 13:12), and we must not attempt — as do some political and moral evangelicals — to build frightened fences around our version of the truth, or put God in a little box. By common grace, God has revealed many truths to the secular world, and a Christian perspective can enable us to connect, analyze, and evaluate the pieces of information relevant to our lives and work — to discover where they are partial or limited and what their ultimate significance is. The pieces of the jigsaw puzzle will be the same for us as for the secular mind, but we should have a frame for it and glimpse the completed picture on the lid of the box. The Christian view of truth is not fragmented; truth has the same integrity, wholeness, and consistency as the mind of God. We may only know in part — but we can be assured that the parts are coherent.

Arthur Holmes defines the Christian perspective on truth as knowable, absolute, and unified: these are the characteristics of truth because they are the characteristics of God, the source of truth ("metaphysical objectivity"). Firstly, truth is knowable because God has created and sustains an orderly, intelligible, and purposeful universe, and humanity in his image. The existence of his natural and moral laws gives our quest for practical knowledge ultimate meaning (despite the denials of postmodern literature and existentialist philosophy) and ultimate value because, no matter how "secular" our jobs may appear, we are investigating God's revelation.

Secondly, truth is absolute because God is eternal and unchanging. This means there are moral precepts and ethical norms, as well as empirical facts, that we can discover and build on and measure our actions by. This is very reassuring in an age of moral relativism and situational ethics.

Finally, truth is unified in one trinitarian but interrelated, coherent, and personal God. Therefore, his world is not fragmented into subjective and objective, faith and reason, sacred and secular. In the mind of God, and therefore in our minds, there are connections between theory and practice, ethics and performance, faith and knowledge, and it is our responsibility to explore them. Therefore, the so-called "secular" knowledge and endeavours of a lay person's daily life have as much eternal significance and theological relevance as the ecclesiastical duties of the professional clergy.

Most important, since truth is of God and from God (John 14:6), it has a "personal" quality from his person that requires Christians to care about truth in a way our secular world no longer does ("epistemological subjectivity"). Since reason and faith are not incompatible, we can know what we believe, and believe what we know — we can be personally committed to the truth God reveals to us. A university student newspaper recently did a survey on whether it was legitimate to lie in certain circumstances when the end would seem to justify the means (for example, to keep a government in power or get into medical school). The majority of students (including those who identified themselves as religious) agreed that lying was justified, that truth was only pragmatic. As Christians we should care deeply that we might be governed by such people, or operated on by such doctors. We witness to the truth as we witness to God.

It is this combination of metaphysical objectivity and epistemological subjectivity that produces "the Christian mind." Harry Blamires points out that, generally, Christians have surrendered to secularism in their minds — we are not "thinking Christianly" about politics, social justice, economics, education, culture, or any of the secular spheres in which we live. Except for a narrow field of action — chiefly concerning personal morality — we accept an intellectual frame of reference and ethical criteria established by the secular world. That is, we are not only "in" the world but "of" it. But to think Christianly would mean a radically different orientation to life in the home, on the job, in the world: "to accept all things with the mind as related, directly or indirectly, to man's eternal destiny as the redeemed and chosen child of God" (p. 44). And "Christian thinking is the prerequisite of Christian action" (p. 43).

In addition to the concept of absolute and revealed truth (which we have just discussed), Blamires identifies five marks of the Christian mind that we can apply to our lives. First, the Christian mind has a supernatural orientation: an eternal perspective that believes life does not end in death, and mortal actions will be judged immortally. This mindset determines our views towards all issues dealing with death — war, capital punishment, euthanasia, suicide, life-prolonging medicine, and so forth — as well as those concerning suffering, disease, and human failures from divorce to crime. Second, the Christian also has an awareness of original sin, the human propensity towards evil (a most unfashionable concept in some contemporary church circles). Our chief sin is self-centred pride; the correcting virtue is obedience to God's will. This means that some secular "crimes" are less sinful than "a single meeting of the average parochial church council or a single vicarage garden-party"[10] (p. 93). Without condoning any evil, we must learn to discriminate between, for example, infractions of the legal code, which just supports a materialistic society, and the selfish exploitation of others, which nevertheless falls within social and legal respectability. We must also, however, offer a message of community and salvation to a sinful world.

Third, Blamires further points out that "the Christian mind has an attitude to authority which modern secularism cannot even understand, let alone tolerate" (p. 132). In an era in which authority in state, law, and education is rejected for the sake of individual self-realization, Christians must submit to the authority of God, his revelation in Scripture, his commandments (not suggestions), and his church when it speaks as "the institutional authority of a Body established by God" (p. 143). The danger is that Christians will try to submit his word or his church to the authority of the world and its latest intellectual or social fashion.

Fourth, "Christian thinking is incarnational" (p. 156). Therefore, it has a basic concern for the person as created and redeemed by God. It opposes the dehumanization of people by technology and materialism, and the mechanistic mindset that regards human beings primarily in relation to their jobs rather than their humanity. Finally, associated with this incarnational perspective is the sacramental view of life that celebrates, in the words of the Prayer Book, "all that is beautiful in creation and in the lives of people," the holy in the daily.

These are profound theological perspectives integrated into a complex human world, and Christians will not all agree on individual applications. The Christian mind does not produce automatic consensus or mindless conformity but informed discourse from a religious worldview. And our witness can change our world. "The truth will make you free" — but "having been set free from sin, [you] have become slaves of righteousness" (Rom. 6:18). A Christian worldview gives us the freedom from materialism and secularity, and the responsibility to witness to the world about God's truth. Bishop Desmond Hunt once said, "The world loves things and uses people. Christians love people and use things." Such a radical reorientation is characteristic of a Christian perspective on the world.

SUGGESTED READING

Oliver R. Barclay, *The Intellect And Beyond* (Grand Rapids: Zondervan, 1985).
William E. Diehl, *Thank God, It's Monday!* (Philadelphia: Fortress Press, 1982).
Richard J. Mouw, *Called To Holy Worldliness* (Philadelphia: Fortress Press, 1980).
Nelvin Vos, *Seven Days A Week: Faith in Action* (Philadelphia: Fortress Press, 1985).

ENDNOTES

1. H. J. Carpenter, "Minister, Ministry," *A Theological Work Book of the Bible*, ed. Alan Richardson (London: SCM Press Ltd., 1950), p. 147.
2. Philippe H. Menoud, "Church, Life and Organization of," *The Interpreter's Dictionary of the Bible*, ed. George Arthur Buttrick (Nashville: Abingdon Press, 1962), 1:624.
3. All scriptural quotations are from the New Revised Standard Version.
4. Massey H. Shepherd, Jr., "Ministry, Christian," *The Interpreter's Dictionary of the Bible*, 3:386.
5. James A. Wharton, "Theology and Ministry in the Hebrew Scriptures," *A Biblical Basis for Ministry*, ed. Earl H. Shelp and Ronald Sutherland (Philadelphia: Westminster Press, 1981), p. 37.
6. Arthur F. Holmes, *All Truth is God's Truth* (Grand Rapids: Eerdmans, 1977) and Harry Blamires, *The Christian Mind* (Ann Arbor: Servant, 1963).

Chapter 11

WORSHIP AND THE SPIRIT
A CATHOLIC, CHARISMATIC, AND EVANGELICAL GOSPEL

CHARLES ALEXANDER

THE GOD WE WORSHIP

"The chief end of man is to glorify God and to enjoy Him forever" (Scottish catechism). In the biblical stories of creation we realize that worship is at the heart of what might be described as "essential relationships." Such relationships are expressed (1) with God the Creator—in total dependence and submission; (2) with the community of Eden—whose focus and identity are not in itself, but in God; (3) with creation—in priestly acts of stewardship offering creation back to God; and (4) with oneself—as a result of prioritizing essential relationships. Here is a picture of awesome and joyous worship offered by a universal priesthood that does not yet sweat for the right to survive.

In the New Testament two words are commonly used to describe worship. One word is *latreia*. St. Paul uses the word to describe worship in terms of service (Rom. 12:1–2). The other word is *proskunaesis*. It is often used to denote a sense of awe in bowing down before the object of worship (Matt. 2:2). Both words are apt in describing worship before the fall and subsequently at the time of restoration.

God has no need to be worshipped and is not driven to create. He is totally complete in triune life. We, on the other hand, have a need to worship the focus and source of our life. It is in the worship of Almighty God that we discover who we are! True worship comes from the gifting of God the Father, made possible in God the Son, and effected in God the Spirit. As a gifted activity it is bestowed upon us by a transcendent God who continually reveals himself in acts of love. An understanding of God's transcendence is therefore necessary in order to appreciate the basis of Christian worship and also the character of a faith that is forged upon the anvil of God's self-revelation.[1]

Through revelation we realize that our God is unchangeable through time and culture (Heb. 13:8). However, when God changes with the variations of human needs, we have worship with "I" at the centre. This is a God to be manipulated to suit our own needs. True worship is less concerned with saying, "Lord, bless me," than it is to utter, "Bless the Lord."[2] At its best moments the renewal of worship expresses this great reversal.

HOW WE WORSHIP IS AN EXPRESSION OF WHO WE WORSHIP

How we worship says something about what we believe. The Holy Spirit is at the heart of authentic worship. "God is spirit, and those who worship him must worship in spirit and truth" (John 4:24). Renewed worship is the adoration of God in trinity of persons. In John 16, Jesus presents us with a picture that has God the Father as focus. The Spirit is seen to be the Spirit of truth (*alaetheia*, meaning "to unveil"). The Holy Spirit reveals Jesus ("the truth" of John 14:6), who in turn points to the Father (John 16:15; 12:49).

In addressing God we often use abstract symbols to honour the fact that God is ontologically transcendent and ineffable. (His immanence is often expressed in metaphor, which honours the variety of ways God acts). The word glory is therefore a symbol that reveals and conceals God at the same time (e.g., Ex. 33:11,18,20,23). God's nature cannot be circumscribed by words. God the Father is the "Father of Glory" (Eph. 1:17); the Son of God is the "brightness of his glory" (Heb. 1:3) and "possessed the glory of the Father before the world was" (John 17:5); so too the Spirit of God is the "Spirit of glory" (1 Pet. 4:14).[3]

Creation is the outcome of a benevolent decision of God (John 1:13). Gregory of Nyssa puts it this way: "God is true Being, for he is the only self-subsisting nature; on him all else depends for existence."[4] The language we use is therefore vital in worshipping the transcendent God who becomes immanent in acts of creation and revelation.

Being made in the image of God, humanity has an innate desire to worship. However, the desire to worship (Ps. 42:1) is no guarantee that its object is the triune God who is fully revealed in the historical Christ (John 14:9).[5] To participate in the mystery of trinitarian worship is to enter into charismatic dimensions of faith. Yet, having been raised to think in a rational tradition, Westerners tend to circumscribe the limits of what we do, or experience, by the parameters of our own imagination and intelligence.

It is this mindset that presents the greatest barrier to the mystery found in charismatic life. "The Greek noun *mustaerion* is derived from the verb *mneo*, which means 'to shut (the mouth)' and thus suggests being silent as in the presence of the inexpressible."[6] To come to God's temple is to be silent before him (Hab. 2:20). To seek him in quietude is to be charismatic. Maybe the silent spirituality of the desert fathers says something to Westerners who are more comfortable in offering to God the fruit of language and imagination!

An emphasis on sacramental life predominates in some Christian traditions. Without raising positions of contention, we may be assured that the sacraments remind us of the "seeking God" whom we serve. "And thus indeed I know, not that I have found him, but that I have been found by him. The sacraments assure us that he has found us, for in them he makes himself known."[7] In the great mystery of the Eucharist, we are ushered into the dimensions of a banquet celebrating life in the eternal now.

Samuel Shoemaker challenges conservatives of evangelical and charismatic bent to enter this mystery with both the heart and mind.[8] If experience and mind do not come together we are left with an impoverished understanding of the vital sychronicity of Word and Spirit. "Equally, prophecy and the word without worship and sacraments is in serious danger of becoming merely cerebral and moralistic."[9] In worship we are reminded that there is a humility required, not only of dependence upon, but of submission to, the Spirit.

With such an approach we are delivered from the ego-centricity that is characteristic of a worship based in nature that makes humanity indistinguishable from deity. Worship and theology cannot be separated; maybe this is why Anglicans enter into theological discussion more from the perspectives of liturgy than doctrinal apologetic.[10]

Words can be distorted so that they take on different symbolic meanings. So, it is possible to worship different gods using the same liturgy. It is a tactic employed by some feminist theologians who express a political need for church institutions. For example, "Rosemary Reuther says we need the Church because it's the global power it is; we need it across the world as a force for change." Donna Steichen warns us therefore that "full-blown feminism is not a transient fad but a rival belief system."[11]

As a social movement, feminism has made important progress, but the goals of many feminist theologians are questionable. The words we use in liturgy are very important. For this reason most Anglicans are subliminally orthodox. But changes in symbolic perceptions may easily produce a subliminal heresy that is prostrate before the altar of strange gods.

When we live our liturgy we are more concerned to focus on the God we worship than the "partyisms" which make for different expressions. Being evangelical, or catholic, or charismatic is much less important than the desire to worship alongside another "publican" who prays for salvic mercy. It is the redeemed publican who understands that essential meaning is found in the gifted grace to worship. This is worship, motivated by the Spirit through the Son and focused in the Father; this is worship that truly unites the body of Christ. Clearly, we have much to confess, and so worship and confession are inseparable.

WORSHIP AND TRANSFORMATION

In Isaiah, chapter 6, we are invited to catch a glimpse of the *Shekinah* glory that transformed the lifestyle and motivation of Judah's poetically powerful prophet. This extraordinarily descriptive encounter makes it clear to us that Isaiah, firstly, came to grips with the reality of his own sinful condition and, secondly, called out for mercy and forgiveness. The reason both conditions came into being is clearly stated: his eyes had seen the glory of the Lord! (Isa. 6:5–7). The New Testament often describes this transformed condition of salvation with the Greek word *sotaeria*. However, another word is also employed to describe the condition of salvation; it is the word *sozo*. This particular word is sometimes used interchangeably to describe both salvation and healing. For example, *sozo* is employed when the woman suffering from a haemorrhaging condition says to herself, "If I only touch the hem of his garment, I shall be made well." The same word is used when Jesus subsequently assures the woman that her faith has made her well (Matt. 9:21–22). In the examples of Isaiah and this woman, salvation and healing are seen to be synonymous; and transformation takes place through an encounter with the living God, the pioneer and perfecter of faith (Heb. 12:2).[12]

In Romans 12:1–2, St. Paul speaks of the process of conversion occurring through acts of spiritual worship. He reminds us that such transformation is gifted through the total sacrifice of our bodies to God. Secondly, he tells us that we are commanded to prove what is the acceptable and perfect will of God by a transformation of thinking. In Philippians 2:5, he points out that this mindset can be nothing less than the humble, obedient mind of Christ. Surely, when we, the people of God, are called to worship, we are challenged to a worship that demands nothing less than that required by Scripture.

WORSHIP AND CATHOLIC FAITH

Commitment to the worshipping community assures us that our worship is genuinely catholic. The salvation offered by Christ, who transcends the limits of time, implies that our faith is truly transferable. New Age influences in the church have left some with an individualistic faith connected to nothing but self-needs and personal perceptions of truth. Worship, with the catholic community, means that we experience the same resurrected Christ as did Paul on the road to Damascus, as did Palamas in the barren desert, as did Luther in his monastery closet, as did Cranmer in the fires of martyrdom, as did Wesley in his meeting room at Bristol. This catholic faith means that we worship with the redeemed community of all ages, and with the angels and archangels in the eternal Now. In our liturgy, the words of St. Paul or Thomas Cranmer express that *my* faith is that of the entire historic community (2 Pet. 1:20).

Only a catholic, transferable faith would motivate us to "contend for the faith which was once delivered to the saints" (Jude 1:3). Such a faith instils in us the yearning to worship God who longs to meet with us in our need.

WORSHIP AND CHARISMA

In worship, we are called not only to meet the God we adore but to appreciate his desire to meet with us. Pentecost enabled us to appreciate this mystery in a most profound way. One cannot deny the Holy Spirit's work in Old Testament times. What is different at Pentecost is that an entire community was gifted with charisms of extraordinary character.

On that astounding day, prophecy was fulfilled; an entire priesthood of believers was anointed with power (Joel 2:28–29; Luke 24:49). Pentecost connected the community of Jesus with that of Abraham (Gen. 12:1–3). As a community, Israel failed to live up to its universal commission. But, by creating a representative community from this community, Jesus, by the power of the Spirit, incarnated the promises and signs of the kingdom for all time and to all nations (Acts 1:8).

Some people thought the disciples were drunk. They just would not cease from telling the crowds about the wonderful works of God (Acts 2:11). Their enthusiasm was a bit embarrassing! How often are we embarrassed when there is a hint of spontaneity in parish worship? How often does it happen? What do we do to prevent it? Do we at least allow for such possibilities of worship when we think that someone may be embarrassed?

HUMILITY AND CHARISMA

The virtue of humility perhaps represents a strange starting point from which to approach the questions of charisms but, as Bishop Fison reminds us, humility is the essential mark of the self-effacing Spirit.[13] To worship in spirit and truth places us in a relationship of Creator-creature. Pentecost was not an event that spoke of the goodness of humanity but that of a giving God.[14] The event was a manifestation of the gifting of grace. Receiving the Holy Spirit motivated worshippers in an attitude of humility and gratitude.

Cognizant of God's ultimate unknowability, Eastern Fathers deliberated on the term *theosis*[15] as an expression of awe and humility. The term does not refer, as some believe, to a sense of being raised to God in a complete and indistinguishable union. In *theosis*, "we are made to participate in saving acts that are abruptly and absolutely divine."[16] "Theosis describes man's involvement in such a mighty act of God upon him that he is raised up to find the true centre of existence not in himself but in Holy God."[17]

As Christians we do not receive status in relation to others but graciously are raised to the status of adopted children of God (John 1:14). Worship in the Spirit is the only guarantee of the self-effacing quality of this relationship. "It is only as the community has its distinct centre in its worship that it can and will stand out from the world."[18] It is only as we worship in the Spirit that our creatureliness becomes apparent in relation to a holy and omnipotent Creator.

As the Holy Spirit points to Jesus (John 16:14), the Lord Christ points to the Father who calls us beyond our fallenness. Maybe the Eastern Fathers are right in speaking of the ultimate unknowability of God! Eternity will never be exhausted by our desire to know him. "If one knew the very nature of God, one would be God."[19] Union with God can never be accomplished by techniques of prayer. If this were so, then surely there would be no need for the incarnation. So when Jesus points to the Father he does not speak of union but of obedience and submission.

It is such an attitude of humility (as distinct from the self-centred emotionalism of cultivated "revivalism") that Jonathan Edwards cherished: whatever it means to be Spirit-filled surely means that the worshipper longs to be God-centred and to hunger and thirst after righteousness rather than to be satiated with self-congratulation.[20]

The Holy Spirit bestowed upon the waiting community a power to enable it in its universal mission. Worship and mission are intrinsically linked together. In signing the life of Christ, the Holy Spirit develops the characteristics of Jesus in the submissive worshipper. Both in worship and mission the people of God are called to reflect the transforming power of the gospel in the graces of the risen Christ (Gal. 5:22–23).

Speaking in tongues is the most misunderstood phenomenon of Pentecost. It is not the point of this chapter to expound a theology of glossolalia, but simply to connect a nonrational ability to speak in tongues with a particular need for humility. It requires a bending of pride for intelligent, cerebrally-directed people to submit to an experience that is not rationally directed. It represents a point of "letting go" that is replaced "by a willingness to allow God to act within us."[21]

There is no common emotional, psychological, intellectual, or educational profile for those who speak in tongues.[22] Under the right conditions of repentance and faith, tongues, as a gift, can be received or rejected by anyone. It bears no particular spiritual merit. Morton Kelsey describes it as a "supernatural gift of a foreign non-human language given at the time of the breakthrough of the Holy Spirit into an individual life."[23]

Glossolalia, common in most charismatic worship, seems to free up the ability to let other charisms flow. St. Paul did not want tongues to be denied in worship (1 Cor. 14:39); he simply wanted it to be regulated for the sake of order (1 Cor. 14:40). Obviously, gifts of a supernatural nature can lend themselves to serious abuse. Paul was prepared to risk such problems in order that the body of Christ be edified (1 Cor. 14:5,12).

One of the risks of subjective experience is that banality, arrogance, and trivia may dominate. For these and other reasons, charismatic renewal does not represent the "sum total of God's renewing activity."[24] It takes sensitive and strong leadership to bring all such activity under the mature demands of the Word.

CHARISMATA IN THE EARLY CHURCH

In order for charismatic life to emerge (under the guidance of elders), Pauline churches held to very simple structural principles: (1) Worship should have a liturgical form (from temple and synagogue roots); and (2) there was built into the formal structure possibilities for the spontaneous movement and charisms of the Spirit.

No doubt we would have known little about worship in the primitive church had it not been important for Paul to lay down some rules. He wanted the spontaneous movement of worship to be conducted decently and in order (1 Cor. 14:40). Obviously, in Corinth, charisms of prophesy, tongues, and interpretation were commonplace. Most certainly he did not want to abolish their use. According to Romans 12, the same might also be assumed for worship in the community at Rome. There seems to be no reason to doubt that, at least in all the Pauline churches, charismatic gifts were normally in use. In light of Paul's claim to apostleship, it might also seem doubtful that his churches worshipped in a radically different way than churches elsewhere.

This principle of liturgical form, coupled with spontaneous charisms of the

Spirit, subsequently gave way to increasing organization and form. Flexibility, which was characteristic of early Christian worship, eventually gave way to forms according to recognized canons.[25] Form, though no less Spirit-inspired by liturgists, consequently dominated the worship process so that all liturgical acts became more predictable and controlled.

Certainly, for the first two hundred years of the church's life, charisms of the Spirit were commonplace in ministry and worship.[26] Charismatic gifts and offices of ministry were coupled; Ignatius was recognized as a "prophet-bishop"; Irenaeus spoke naturally of such gifts as exorcism, tongues, and healing.[27] In the *Didache*, "we are left with the conclusion that, in addition to any administrative responsibilities they might have had, bishops and deacons were also teaching and delivering prophetic messages."[28]

Further into the second century, the Shepherd of Hermas urged that, when the church assembles for prayer, "a man, filled with the Spirit, should be allowed to prophesy."[29] In Justin Martyr's "Dialogue With Trypho," the apologist speaks of some receiving the spirit of counsel, strength, healing, foreknowledge, teaching and fear.[30]

After demonstrating that charismatic gifts were normally accepted in the church through the second century, Ronald Kydd[31] concludes that they ceased to be part of day to day experience by about AD 260. The crucial time was the early part of the third century.[32] In the West, and to a lesser extent in the East, charismatic gifts appeared only sporadically. Evidence is cited in the experience of people like Francis of Assisi and Martin Luther; of people in the Wesleyan Revival, the Holiness movement, the Pentecostal movement, and the Ruanda Revival; and, further into this century, of mainline Christians in the "charismatic movement."

CHARISMATA AND THE ANGLICAN CHURCH OF CANADA

Anglicans have never professed a doctrine of dispensationalism, but do we behave as if we believed such a doctrine? The late David Watson used to say, "The job of a preacher is to answer to the praises of God's people." In special ways, during the last thirty years, manifestations of the Spirit have prompted such an apologetic in ordinary Anglican churches.

Clearly, the Holy Spirit is present whenever sincere people meet to lift up the name of the Lord Jesus. But what a joy it is when the preacher has to explain to puzzled minds how God has been present in acts of salvation, healing, and edification. The principle of coupling form with spontaneity undoubtedly elicits such questions.

CHARISMATIC CHARACTER AND INFLUENCE

Professor David Reed records figures suggesting that charismatics represent about 21 percent of Christianity globally.[33] In Canada, about 30 percent of Anglican parishes have been affected by the charismatic movement. At least half of the charismatics surveyed tithe from 7 to 15 percent of net income. They have a comparatively high level of involvement and leadership; are not roamers, but are loyal and committed members; have a deep desire to witness for Christ; and possess a heart for social aspects of the gospel.[34] John Chrisostom once said, "We shall not find Christ at the altar in Church, unless we are finding him in the homeless outside."[35] David Reed asserts that charismatics claim to have a normative Christian experience that tends to be "confessional, not arguable; more relational than rational" and "belongs more to the scattered church than to academia."[36]

Charismatics strongly agree that "Spirit-filled" worship has enormous potential for evangelism. However, in no way does their desire for expressive worship diminish their hunger to hear good biblical preaching. Although they tend towards the conservative end of the spectrum, about 65 percent of those surveyed preferred the Book of Alternative Services (BAS), not for its doctrine, but for the freedom it offers in the engagement of praise and ministry.[37] For example, in my own parish, charismatic liturgy is regularly practised at a Sunday service that uses the BAS. However, the order of Word-Sacrament is reversed to facilitate the perception that teachers and students have "met with God" before they go to classes.

Although shared experiences and ideas tend to fade over time, for most charismatics ritual is the best vehicle to sustain ideas and experiences. Charismatic worship expresses a "truth of the gospel" (John 14:12) in that the Holy Spirit inspires worship and meets the worshippers at the level of their need. It is usually a joyous experience, filled with praise, charisms, and music of a folk style that invites engagement. Some churches use a wide variety of styles in music, but most find that classical forms do not lend themselves easily to the engagement that is found in folk-style music. Such music usually draws its lyrics from Scripture but may lose the poetic majesty that is rigidly applied to tested hymns of the church.

PERSONAL EXAMPLES OF CHARISMS IN WORSHIP

It has been my personal joy to explain charisms of God's powerful presence many, many times. To give a few examples:

1. During intercessions, a lady in a church in British Columbia received prayer for healing of breast cancer. The next day, she excitedly returned to the church to say that her specialist had examined her and reported that the lump had completely disappeared.

2. A man in Calgary had Hodgkinson's disease. During the administration of the chalice, a prayer that the blood of Christ would bring healing had immediate effects. After three years of negative tests the man was told he was free of the disease.

3. A man in Madras asked me for prayers of blessing for his family. God revealed to me that the man was playing games with his Christian life and was abusive to his family. An interpreter checked this out and reported that the

man agreed on both counts. As a result, instead of receiving a simple bless-ing, the man repented and accepted Jesus Christ as his Saviour and Lord.

4. At a Eucharist in Ontario, as I prayed privately with an elderly lady, the Lord revealed to me that she had been abused as an adolescent by her father. The lady confirmed that this was so and the burden and shame of fifty years was dealt with in forgiveness and healing.

5. After a praiseful time of singing in tongues, a message was given in a tongue and interpreted. An astonished visitor later confirmed the word to be accu-rate as it had been delivered in a Hebrew dialect that was known to her.

Dramatic examples like this do not happen when *we* decide. Miracles may not happen on Tuesday at 7:30 p.m.! There are no easy answers to some ques-tions, but certainly charisms are given how and when God decides (providing we are not the instruments to get in the way!) (1 Cor. 12:11). When charisms are given, people leave the worship knowing they have met with God. Of course, when such gifts are not evident, the people of God also know they have met God in the mystery of Word and Sacrament.

Many spiritual gifts are natural rather than supernatural in form. St. Paul deems these to be important, as are people who think themselves to be insig-nificant (Rom. 12:6–8; 1 Cor. 12:22). Churches like the famous Willow Creek community are careful to enable a process of discernment.[38] The maxim in such cases should be: Handle carefully, but be open to the Spirit.

For spiritual gifts to be introduced into worship it is necessary that there be good preparation, sensitivity, courage, and wisdom in the discernment of time and place. However, after many years of professing to be in renewal, a goodly number of clergy are still reticent to let the Spirit move spontaneously among his people.

WORSHIP AND SERVICE

The work of the church is to bring the world to the worship of Almighty God, and to be a sign of the kingdom until creation is restored in Jesus Christ. Great mystics of prayer, like St. Paul and St. Teresa, never saw worship as a way to retreat from the world. Rather, it provided motivation to propel them into serv-ice.[39] These persons perfectly exemplify that worship is both *proskunaesis* and *latreia*.

It is interesting to note that, of the charismatics surveyed by David Reed,[40] 29 percent of the laity and 50 percent of the clergy claimed their spiritual gift to be in evangelism. Worship and service clearly go together![41] In relation to David Watson's comment, it has been my personal privilege to see many people offer their lives to Christ in charismatic services of worship, even before the sermon takes place!

CONCLUSION

Mark's Gospel concludes with the words, "The Lord worked with them and confirmed the message by the signs that attended it. Amen" (Mark 16:20). Confirmation of God acting in Word and Spirit is happening in marketplaces all over the world; it is also happening wherever, in decency and order, the Spirit is given freedom in the lives of worshippers.

Archbishop Carey reminds us that "attempts to revitalize forms of worship without first renewing the inner life and experiences out of which worship comes are doomed."[42]

In terms of worship, evangelism, and mission, the charismatic movement has much to offer the church. However, evangelism without renewal is hypocrisy if we preach good news and fail to support people in renewed lives and communities.

Come Holy Spirit, shine upon your Church in *Shekinah* glory and in Pentecostal power, that we also may shield our faces, move on trembling foundations, repent of our sin, cry out for salvation, and be empowered to serve.

SUGGESTED READING

A. M. Allchin, *The Kingdom of Love and Knowledge* (New York: Seabury Press, 1979).

Ronald Kydd, *Charismatic Gifts in the Early Church* (Peabody, Mass.: Hendrickson Publishers, 1984).

Michael Marshall, *Renewal in Worship* (London: Marshall's Paperbacks, 1982).

Ralph Martin, *Worship in the Early Church* (Grand Rapids: Eerdmans, 1964).

ENDNOTES

1. We may need to be reminded that God's self-revelation is the basis of Christian faith. Forces that shaped the "modernism" of the fifties through the seventies owe much to a form of Darwinism that sees culture as an evolving force to change the focus and shape of faith. God is ontologically constant; therefore his transcendence is the basis upon which revelation begins.

2. T. Smaille, *The Forgotten Father* (London: Hodder & Stoughton, 1980), p. 164.

3. J. Meyendorff, *St. Gregory Palamas and Orthodox Spirituality* (New York: St. Vladimir's Press, 1974), p. 127.

4. Gregory of Nyssa, *Life of Moses* (New York: Paulist Press, 1978), p. 15.

5. J. Meyendorff, *Living Tradition* (New York: St. Vladimir's Press, 1978), p. 171.

6. J. Finegan, *Myth and Mystery* (Michigan: Baker Book House, 1989), p. 15.

7. Austin Farrer, *The Essential Sermons* (Cambridge, Mass.: Cowley Publications, 1991), p. 8.

8. Sam Shoemaker, *With the Holy Spirit and with Fire* (Texas: Word Books, 1960), p. 44.

9. M. Marshall, *Renewal in Worship* (London: Marshall's Paperbacks, 1982), p. 32.

10. William J. Wolfe notes that Anglicans, holding this premise, are comfortable in dialogue with Eastern Orthodoxy. After the Cromwellian suppression, Anglicanism was re-established, not on the basis of a confession, but of the Book of Common

Prayer. William Wolfe, *The Spirit of Anglicanism* (Conn.: Morehouse-Barlow, 1979), pp. 161–162.

11. Donna Steichen, *Ungodly Rage* (San Francisco: Ignatius Press, 1991), pp. 27, 78.

12. A short paper by the Rev. Richard J. Salt, responding to the papers circulated at Essentials 94, advocates the need of such transformation as the church wrestles with pressing ethical and social issues of the day. He despairs that the church too easily adopts a secular mind in accepting that conditions such as homosexuality cannot be changed. "We find it difficult to believe in the promised miracle and so concur with the secular thinking that denies the possibility of transformation by the power of God." Declaring his witness to the transformation of such seemingly hopeless conditions, he presents two keys that make wholeness possible: "from the biblical perspective we are prepared for transformation by turning to Christ with total commitment and by starting to live a lifestyle which is pleasing to God." One may add a thought to this statement that we need not despair of the weakness of human effort. It is the work of the Holy Spirit (the Paraclete, the Helper) to form Christ in us (Gal. 4:19; John 14:16,18). To continue in the process of conversion/transformation, Richard Salt urges us to realize that we are constantly engaged in spiritual warfare. Those who are aware of Satan's tactics need to embrace four spiritual weapons: (1) Confession (James 5:16); (2) The Word of God (Heb. 4:12–13); (3) Deliverance/rescue from sin that controls us (1 Cor. 6:19–20); (4) Healing (Isa. 61:2). "Specific prayers for healing of the wounds and hurts of the past are an important part of the ministry that leads to wholeness." The paper concludes with the words, "Those seeking to be transformed should be able to receive that ministry at any and all Anglican churches across this land. Are we ready and prepared?" ("A Biblical Perspective on Wholeness and Healing," by Richard. J. Salt, Rector of Trinity Anglican Church, Sarnia, Ontario.)

13. J. R. Fison, *The Blessing of the Holy Spirit* (London: Longmans, Green and Co. Ltd., 1956).

14. Thomas F. Torrance, *Theology In Reconstruction* (London: SCM Press Ltd., 1965), pp. 240–258.

15. Eastern Orthodox theologians never thought in terms of total absorption into God (reminiscent of Pantheism). For an Orthodox view of *theosis* see John Meyendorff, *St. Gregory Palamas and Orthodox Spirituality* (New York: St. Vladimir's Press, 1974), pp. 35–47.

16. Ibid.

17. Ibid.

18. Karl Barth, *Church Dogmatics* (Edinburgh: T. & T. Clark, 1936-62), Vol. 1, Part 2.

19. Vladimir Lossky, *Orthodox Theology* (New York: St. Vladimir's Press, 1978), p. 33.

20. R. Lovelace, *Dynamics Of Spiritual Life* (Toronto: InterVarsity Press, 1979), p. 42.

21. Kallistos Ware, *The Orthodox Way* (New York: St. Vladimir's Press, 1986), p. 134.

22. This was the surprising finding of a clinical psychologist who attempted to determine a common personality profile for glossolalists. John Kildahl, *The Psychology of Speaking in Tongues* (New York: Harper and Row, 1972), p. 65.

23. Morton Kelsey, *Tongue Speaking* (New York: Doubleday, 1964), p. 168.

24. Smaille, *Forgotten Father*, pp. 14–17.

25. Ralph P. Martin, *Worship in the Early Church* (Grand Rapids: Eerdmans, 1964), p. 137.

26. Ronald Kydd, *Charismatic Gifts in the Early Church* (Peabody, Mass.: Hendrickson Publishers, 1984), p. 87.

27. Ibid., pp. 9, 17, 44.

28. Ibid., p. 9.

29. Ibid., p. 20.

30. Ibid., p. 26.

31. His book, based on his doctoral thesis, is very informative in appraising us that the Church was "normally charismatic" until the mid–third century. Ronald Kydd, *Charismatic Gifts in the Early Church* (Peabody, Mass.: Hendrickson Publishers, 1984).

32. Ibid., p. 57.

33. David A. Reed, "From Movement to Institution: A Case Study of Charismatic Renewal in Canada," *Summary Of Proceedings* (Forty-fifth Annual Conference, American Theological Library Assoc., Toronto, June 1991).

34. George Egerton, from a report on Prof. D. Reed's "Case Study," *Incourage Magazine*, 6:3 (Winter 1992/3).

35. A. M. Allchin, *The Kingdom of Love and Knowledge* (New York: Seabury Press, 1979), p. 47.

36. David Reed, "Evangelism Easier When Enjoyed," *Anglican Journal* (Dec. 1991), p. 9.

37. Reed, "From Movement to Institution," p. 181.

38. Charles Colson, *The Body* (Dallas: Word Publishing, 1992), p. 294.

39. Evelyn Underhill, *Mystics Of The Church* (Greenwood, S.C.: Attic Press, 1975), pp. 42–44.

40. Prof. David Reed, of Wycliffe College, Toronto, spent a sabbatical year surveying charismatic parishes across Canada. Interviewing laity, clergy, and bishops, he produced a summary paper, "From Movement to Institution: A Case Study of Charismatic Renewal in the Anglican Church of Canada." This paper was delivered to the Forty-fifth Annual Conference of the American Theological Library Association in June 1991.

41. David Reed, *The Logic of Evangelism in Charismatic Experience* (An address to the Anglican Congress on Evangelism, Geneva Park, Ontario, July 1993), p. 12.

42. George Carey, *Church in the Market Place* (Eastbourne: Kingsway Publications, 1989), p. 32.

CHAPTER 12

WORSHIP IN SPIRIT AND IN TRUTH
DESIGNING WORSHIP FOR TODAY'S CHURCH

ANTHONY BURTON

In his encounter with the Samaritan woman at the well, Jesus had occasion to speak about worship. He was prompted by the Samaritan woman who, having become aware of his authority, questioned him regarding one of the chief issues dividing the religious life of Jews and Samaritans: where is the right place to worship God—in the Jerusalem Temple or on Mount Gerizim? Jesus answered:

> Woman, believe me, the hour is coming when neither on this mountain nor in Jerusalem will you worship the Father. You worship what you do not know; we worship what we know, for salvation is from the Jews. But the hour is coming, and now is, when the true worshippers will worship the Father in spirit and truth, for such the Father seeks to worship him. God is spirit, and those who worship him must worship in spirit and in truth (John 4:21–24).

Liturgical dispute has a long history. So too do theological disputes fought on the battlefield of liturgy. While all liturgy embodies a theology of one sort or another, liturgy and theology are not the same thing: the confusion between the two has contributed immeasurably to the crisis in Canadian Anglicanism. To compound the problem, liturgy is not, as is commonly assumed, the same thing as worship. My intention in this chapter is to make some observations about the relationship between worship, liturgy, and theology and then to make some re-marks about the immediate future of liturgical revision in Canada.[1]

WHAT IS WORSHIP ABOUT?

Worship is the acknowledgement and response of the creature to a gracious Crea-tor. Christian worship is necessarily trinitarian in form and content. For it is both a response to God revealed in his trinitarian identity as Father, Son, and Holy Spirit, and a delightful sharing in the divine life to which he has redeemed us in Jesus Christ. Christ who is in our midst places us in the presence of the Father by the power of the Holy Spirit of their mutual love.

In worship we are called out of ourselves and into the presence of God and recognize our place in the drama of salvation. We play our part in the pageant of redemption, taking our place in God's story written out for us to read in Jesus Christ. Word-shaped and Spirit-governed, our worship signals our place in God's purposes: we respond "yes" to God's great "yes" to us in Jesus. In our worship we give voice to creation in praise of God. George Herbert put it best:

Of all the creatures both in sea and land
Onely to man thou hast made known thy wayes
And put the penne alone into his hands,
And made him Secretarie of thy praise.[2]

Jesus' response to the Samaritan woman was to tell her that the worship of both the Samaritans and the Jews would be transformed into what we now understand as worship in the Trinity. Jesus tells the Samaritan woman that "you worship what you do not know; we worship what we know, for salvation is from the Jews. But the hour is coming, and now is, when the true worshippers will worship the Father in spirit and truth"(John 4:22–23). In the hour of the Messiah, neither Gerizim nor Jerusalem counts any more. The body of Jesus is the new temple, destroyed and raised up within three days (John 2:19), the dwelling of God among humans. It is the Spirit given by the Father and the Son which is to stir up and give life to this new temple.

WORSHIP AND EDIFICATION

There are important distinctions to be made between *liturgy* and *worship*. Not all prayers are created equal. Consider this one, for example, from a collection of private prayers found among the papers of John Ward, an English member of Parliament:

O Lord, thou knowest that I have mine estates in the City of London; and likewise that I have lately purchased an estate in fee simple in the County of Essex. I beseech Thee to preserve the two counties of Middlesex and Essex from fire and earthquake and, as I have a mortgage in Hertfordshire, I beg Thee likewise to have an eye of compassion on that county. For the rest, of the counties Thou mayest deal with them as Thou art pleased.[3]

The problem with this little prayer is that it is, in a way, liturgy and not worship. It does not worship the God of the Bible but rather demeans him.

So it is not hair-splitting to want to have standards by which we can distinguish whether liturgy is worship or something else.

We are to worship not only "in spirit" but "in truth." "We worship what we know." Jesus specifies that worship should be in spirit *and* truth, which we must be careful not to oppose. For human beings the Spirit is mediated by Word and Sacrament. The Spirit's leading is not to be judged by what feels good or right, but what Christ has revealed to be true.

It is crucial then that our liturgies be "true." The fundamental test of forms of liturgy is not, "Do I like it?"; "Will newcomers like it?"; "Is it what I am used to?"; "Does it have an Hippolytan shape?"; "Is it beautiful?" The fundamental test is, "Is it true?" "Correlative to the freedom [in the Spirit] which Christ has given His Church in ordering its worship is its responsibility to see that these principles, taught by Christ, are constantly observed, and to judge all ... forms of worship by the light of them."[4]

To be true to God and his kingdom, worship must be scriptural. It must be deeply informed and shaped by the authoritative witness which Holy Scripture bears to God and his kingdom and its realization in Jesus Christ. And therefore the "scriptural" quality of liturgy is a multi-layered thing: it is not simply a question of the quantity of Scripture read, or whether something is a quotation from Scripture or not.

More deeply, it has to do with the way in which Scripture is read and heard. For Scripture is not simply text, or imagery, or ritualized exercise: Scripture is doctrinal—all its images, the force of its poetry, the history it records—are a means of teaching.[5] Scripture is addressed to the mind first, and then the heart. So liturgical texts must be informed by true scriptural doctrine, and must be tested by it.

A scriptural liturgy is one that speaks the message of salvation as clearly, fully, and powerfully as possible. In scriptural liturgy the great teachings of the Bible give shape, content, and direction to our prayers. The Trinity, for example, is not just an article of the creed to be invoked as a touchstone of orthodoxy, but a reality we meet in liturgy and in which we pray. In good liturgy we enter in heart and mind into the incarnation, the atonement, the resurrection, the work of the Spirit, and the hope of eternal glory.

Of late there has been much valid criticism of "prayed catechesis." Worship cannot simply be a device for enforcing assent to orthodox doctrine. Professor Webster points out that liturgy cannot be

> a kind of encoded confessional statement rather than ... prayer. But, for all that, prayer and rite are not immune from issues of truth and falsity: it is possible to do or say something which does not correspond to the gospel. Whatever else *lex orandi, lex credendi* may mean, it cannot mean that the liturgical life of the people of God is beyond the reach of critical, reflective activity which is one of the primary tasks of theology.[6]

Liturgy, then, is to order our lives into the pattern of saving doctrine as it is revealed in Scripture, and must be understood to extend beyond public worship on Sunday to an ordered routine of daily (and ideally common) prayer. Eugene Peterson finds this principle of ordering and edifying prayer in the liturgy of the Book of Revelation:

> Life as we encounter it is chaotic. The raw material served up by the day is disordered and turbulent. Nature is clamorous and many-headed. We ourselves are many-hearted and conflicted. How can we master such a mob? Is there any hope for harmony in such a chaos? The act of worship gathers in to its centring rituals and harmonizing rhythms every aspect of creation. Worship does not divide the spiritual from the natural, it coordinates them. Nature and supernature, creation and covenant, elders and animals are all gathered. Worship that scorns creation is impoverished. The rabble of creation "red in tooth and claw" comes to order before the throne and finds itself

more itself: each creature is alert (full of eyes) and soaring (six wings). In George Herbert's words, "All creatures of my God and king, lift up your voice and sing!"[7]

THE ROLE OF LITURGY IN IMAGINING THE KINGDOM

Bishop Rowan Williams has argued persuasively that one of the functions of liturgy is to help Christians perceive the spiritual kingdom in their particular circumstances. He writes that we need to tackle "the question of how Christians are to articulate in praise, repentance and intercession their accountability to the norms of God's Kingdom against the background of the communities in which their human identity is being shaped and tested. After all, no-one else seems interested or equipped to articulate the accountability of political society to something beyond itself."[8] He argues that one of the great and distinctive achievements of historic Anglican liturgy was to spell out the church's relation to the world (to which it has a mission) and to the kingdom of God (of which it is an anticipation). "The genius of the Prayer Book is to perform this liturgical task in a way which does not become human-centred, but continues to evoke the primacy of God's holiness and generosity."[9] This balance is an extremely difficult one to achieve, and recent liturgies have not been notably successful in evoking either the primacy of God's holiness or our accountability as a modern society.

PRAYER BOOK REVISION ?

The designing of liturgies is an act of great importance and not to be lightly undertaken. All liturgies are profoundly informed by the intention and theology of those who compose them. A good theologian may not be a good liturgist but a bad theologian cannot be. In a church with an authorized liturgy, liturgical revision of any but alternative liturgies should only be undertaken at a time of relative consensus in theology. Admittedly, most great liturgical changes were effected by autocrats, papal and political, but it is something which would be highly imprudent today. To attempt to impose the theology of a party on the whole church is simply unacceptable in an age of loose denominational loyalty.

Neither the Book of Common Prayer (BCP) nor the Book of Alternative Services (BAS) is perfect. The only perfect liturgy is the liturgy of heaven imaged, for example, in the books of Hebrews and Revelation. Our work in our worship is to come as close to this standard as we can. I earnestly wish I could say that the two worship books in our church taught the same thing or that their teachings complemented each other. Professor Alan Hayes of Wycliffe College, to name only one, has shown how the two liturgies express deeply divergent understandings of the church's identity and the Christian faith, and his conclusions have been echoed by the National BAS Evaluation Commission. Between the BAS and the BCP there is no easy reconciliation.

There is much that is excellent in the BAS. Its provision for an Old Testament Lesson in the Eucharist for example, its articulation of the work of God throughout the history of Israel, its Holy Week options, the accessibility of some of its language, are all welcome arrows in the Anglican quiver. To express reservations about some of the principles on which it is based is not to condemn the book nor to attack new and creative approaches to liturgy.

The BCP is undergirded by the orthodox view that the Christian faith is divinely revealed in Scripture, and that Scripture itself is a "doctrinal instrument of salvation." This is to say that the images of Scripture have a content embodied, for example, in the creeds. Scripture is not merely one authority in a convergence of criteria from which one might pick and choose at random. For the Prayer Book, Scripture and doctrine—as the distillation of what the Scriptures essentially teach—are the fundamental criteria for the order and life of the church and for the liturgical worship of God.[10] This is the clear teaching of Thomas Cranmer and Richard Hooker. It is altogether crucial for the understanding of worship as both the acknowledgement of God's truth and as participation in the divine life revealed in Jesus Christ, the Word and Son of God. As Cranmer puts it: "He that keepeth the word of Christ, is promised the love and favour of God, and that he shall be the dwelling-place or temple of the blessed Trinity."[11] The teachings of Scripture illuminate the path of our spiritual journey. They are used by the Spirit as food for our souls and as the measure and rule for our life and worship of God.

Not surprisingly, the BAS teaching on some Christian basics—such as the atonement, and the role of repentance and faith—are weak. The BAS effectively forbids the use of the Confession and Absolution at all services in which the Eucharist is combined with something else (e.g., baptisms, weddings, funerals, ordinations) and requires the use of the Confession only on Ash Wednesday. The scriptural insistence upon the central place of repentance in the life of faith is not integrated into the essential structure and pattern of public worship. The primacy of Scripture is further undermined in the BAS lectionary, which goes as far as to omit certain parts of the New Testament.

As with so many differences of opinion in the church, there appears to be an underlying difference between how the two books view the Bible. Is it the authoritative Word of God, as the BCP maintains, or is the Bible an incoherent collection of faith documents, inspiring tokens of the past belief systems of the people of God?

The understanding that the two books have of the Bible also has implications for the constitution of our church, the *Solemn Declaration of 1893*. The *Solemn Declaration* establishes the doctrine of the Book of Common Prayer as the doctrine of our church (BCP, p. viii). At the moment, the Prayer Book maintains that the church stands under the judgement of Scripture. In contrast, the BAS understands the Scripture as standing under the judgement of the church. If a combined book, containing a BAS view of Scripture as something subordinate to the church, were adopted as the new Book of Common Prayer, then the church's official position on Scripture would seem to change as well.

Many theological conservatives who prefer modern-language liturgies have accommodated themselves to the BAS, adjusting its shape and content to compensate for what they perceive to be its theological inadequacies. Such expedients may serve them as long as they have a bishop who is prepared to overlook these practices. In a church with authorized liturgies, however, such expedients can only be viewed as temporary. The bishop has a responsibility to see that the authorized liturgies of the church are used as printed in accordance with their rubrics—and he or she has the legal authority to enforce it. Moreover, by tying their parishes in to the exclusive use of alternatives, they lay them open to the enforced use of subsequent revisions of those alternatives. If the latest New Zealand liturgies are an example of the next stage of the liturgical movement, our future revised liturgies will be increasingly at variance with the norms of historic Christianity.

The bad news is this: though we may long for an end to liturgical debate, at this point there is no alternative to the status quo—two books, one the official standard, which is the inalienable right of all Anglicans to use; the other a permitted, but not required, alternative. Some long for a unified book—but such a book at this point would essentially be the BAS dressed up in a few superficial BCP features, but without a BCP theology. This would not end liturgical quarrelling; if anything, it would raise the temperature to new heights.

The good news is this: we can live with two books in status quo; that is, where the Prayer Book is the standard which Anglicans are free to use with integrity, without pressure to abandon it, but where the BAS is also available for use for those who find it helpful. With a certain amount of mutual forbearance and charity, liturgical differences can be constructive. Eventually, when the church returns renewed to a true understanding of the faith, there will exist the theological consensus to allow revision.

CONCLUSION

Worship has no purpose beyond itself. Good liturgy should help us to worship by articulating our place and the place of our community in God's story. We come to liturgies not so much to offer worship as to join in an offering continually going on. We "come not to initiate worship but to contribute to, and be carried up by, a worship which never ceases, the source and fountain of which lies in the external activity of Christ."[12] In worship we reflect the great "Amen" that God spoke when he created the world to delight in, and that he spoke again in the person of his Son. By the agency of the Spirit in us, one deep calls to another: we are drawn through Christ into the heart of the Father, and there find ourselves taken up in the chorus of all creation:

> Worthy is the Lamb that was slain to receive power, and riches, and wisdom, and strength, and honour, and glory, and blessing (Rev. 5:12).

SUGGESTED READING

Colin Dunlop, *Anglican Public Worship* (London: SCM Press Ltd., 1953).

Eugene H. Peterson, *Reversed Thunder: The Revelation of John and the Praying Imagination* (San Francisco: Harper, 1988).

Submission to the Book of Alternative Services Evaluation Commissioners (Prayer Book Society of Canada, 506 Orkney Lane, Ottawa, Ontario K2C 3M7, Tel. (613) 226-3722; Fax (613) 233-4399, 1993).

Thinking About the Book of Alternative Services: A Discussion Primer (Toronto: Anglican Book Centre, 1994).

ENDNOTES

1. The Rev. David Curry, the Rev. Gavin Dunbar, and the Rev. Anthony Bassett have given me invaluable assistance in the preparation of this chapter. In so far as it says anything true, it is to their credit. Its manifest errors and prejudices are entirely my own.

2. "Providence" in *The Temple* (Menston, Yorkshire: Scolar Press, 1968).

3. Quoted by the Rt. Rev. Michael Marshall in the video, "The Cultural Captivity of the Church."

4. J. I. Packer, "Gain and Loss," in *Towards a Modern Prayer Book: The New Services Examined*, ed. R. T. Beckwith (Appleford, Abingdon: Marcham Manor Press, 1966).

5. The distinction between prayed catechesis and prayed narrative can be overdrawn—and often is. Simple Judaic faith and simple Judaic scriptural imagery is falsely opposed to Greek philosophical theology and dogma. In fact, the two are complementary. Dogma informed by philosophical theology and validated by the universal church is necessary to guard the content and substance of Judaic imagery—particularly today when it is commonly deconstructed into metaphors and images to bolster feminist or Marxist ideology.

6. *Thinking About the Book of Alternative Services: A Discussion Primer* (Toronto: Anglican Book Centre, 1994), p. 30.

7. Eugene H. Peterson, *Reversed Thunder: The Revelation of John and the Praying Imagination* (San Francisco: Harper, 1988), p. 62.

8. Rowan Williams, "Imagining the Kingdom: Some Questions for Anglican Worship Today" in *The Identity of Anglican Worship*, eds. K. Stevenson and Bryan Spinks (Harris, Pa.: Morehouse, 1991), p. 12.

9. Ibid., p. 6.

10. Prayer Book Society of Canada, *Submission to the Book of Alternative Services Evaluation Commissioners* (1993), p. 4.

11. *The First Book of Homilies*, Homily 1, in *The Works of Thomas Cranmer*, ed. J. E. Cox (New York: Johnson Reprint Society, 1968).

12. Colin Dunlop, *Anglican Public Worship* (London: SCM Press Ltd., 1953), p. 17.

13

CHRISTIAN SEXUALITY AND SEXUAL ETHICS IN A PERMISSIVE SOCIETY

ELAINE POUNTNEY

Sex. Everywhere we look, everywhere we go, we are confronted with sex! At breakfast we start the day with Kellogg's Special K, marketed as a "sexualized" product promising to produce slim, sleek, sexy bodies. We end the day listening to the television news reporting more sex-related scandals, more sexual abuse, more sexual violence.

Sexual ethics in a permissive society is a gigantic topic and I must confess that I have felt overwhelmed in trying to address it. Like most other Christians, I struggle with the issues and the realities of sex and sexuality. We might acknowledge from the outset that while the Bible sets forth certain proscriptions and guidelines in the realm of sexual behaviour and sexuality, for those seeking to live as Christians in face of the seductions and complexities of modern permissive cultures, much is left to our discernment of God's will in interpreting and applying biblical wisdom to our sexual conduct. This chapter will consider biblical guidelines that help us understand more fully what sexuality from a Christian perspective means, and, extrapolating from the guidelines, will suggest how to approach decisions on sexual behaviour.

The first half of the discussion will present a three-part model for looking at issues of sexuality: it starts with *creation sexuality* (our ideology), then considers *fallen sexuality* (our reality), and concludes with *redemption sexuality* (our response). This three-part model is based on Mary Stewart Van Leeuwen's gender analysis[1] and Jennifer Harold's[2] gender paradigm (see fig. 1, p. 160). In creation sexuality, both female and male were created for equality and for interdependence. Both genders were created for accountable sociability to cooperate and be responsible for social relationships and for accountable dominion to make responsible decisions and to take responsible authority. This model will serve as the foundation for the second half of the analysis, which will attempt to apply the model to behaviour in the contexts of singleness, marriage, and divorce. Finally, the chapter will address abuses and misuses of sexuality.[3]

CREATION SEXUALITY: IDEOLOGY

Genesis, chapter one, describes God creating our world, and we get the sense that God is enjoying himself. Chapters one and two describe God creating sexuality, and he still seems to be enjoying himself. Each time God created a part of our world in Genesis 1, he stopped, stood back, looked, assessed what he had created and said that "it was good" (Gen. 1:4,10,12,18,21,25).[4] After God made humankind, he stopped, stood back, looked at "everything that he had made" and said that "it was *very* good" (Gen. 1:31, emphasis mine).

But sometime later God stopped, stood back and assessed what he had created and said, "It is not good that the man should be alone" (Gen. 2:18). This was the "one aspect of all creation that God observed to be not good"—note that it is God himself who declares this.[5] Adam had perfect fellowship with God but that relationship did not meet all of Adam's relational needs. Inherent in creation was "a need to relate to God as a creature relating to its creator" and also "a need to relate to others of his own kind as an aspect of imaging a trinitarian God of relationship ... the two relational needs of Adam were complementary but distinct, intertwining but with neither replacing the other."[6] And so, God made woman (Gen. 2:21–22).

God, not Adam, determined who the man's partner would be; Adam, in calling her "woman," rejoices in their mutuality and "delights in what God has already done in creating sexuality,"[7] saying, "bone of my bones and flesh of my flesh." Can't you just see Adam dancing around in all his naked glory as his joy and delight overflows to God and to woman! And Eve's surprised joy in response! What a delightful picture. So now there is both sexuality and community.

Sexuality Is about "Who I Am"; It's about My Identity

There is mystery in the sacredness of sexuality. The sacred meaning of sexuality is to be brought into the whole sacred meaning of what it means to be a human being. This is the mystery of our indivisible union of identity with sexuality throughout our whole existence. God created male and female in the image of the Godhead, then "blessed" them, saying it was "very good."

Human sexuality has to do with our creatureliness before God. "So God created humankind..." (Gen. 1:27,31). God is the creator, we are the created; human beings are different from God. There is an ultimate, absolute, ontological difference between the creator and the created.[8]

Human sexuality has to do with being created in the image of God. "So God created humankind in his image" (Gen. 1:27). We somehow reflect God, but we do not represent God. The fundamental and unique relationship that is between God and humankind—both male and female—determines and defines us as human beings in our sexuality. Our sexuality is thoroughly integrated in our humanness, and our humanness lives and moves and has its being in the divine; this is our "image-ness."

Human beings image the trinitarian Godhead, not Jesus the man. Genesis 1:26 states: "Let us make humankind in our image, according to our likeness," not "let us make humankind in your image," as if the Father and the Spirit are speaking to the Son.

Human beings image God in their completeness as human beings. So we "image" not just in our femaleness and maleness, not just in rationality, or sexuality, but in all ways in which we reflect the Godhead in our normal life activities—for example, in justice, in compassion, and especially in our capacity for sacrificial love.[9]

Sexuality, then, is much more than merely genital sex—it is about our very identity! Sexuality is about who I am, about my feelings, about my values; it is about energy and aesthetics, about social life; it is about economics and legislation; it is about faith and religion. There is no aspect of life that does not in some way affect our sexuality. Conversely there is no aspect of our sexuality that does not connect with some aspect of our life.

Sexuality Is about Gender: Femaleness and Maleness

Sexuality is about gender; that is, being female or male: "male and female he created them" (Gen. 1:27) with distinct separateness and complementarity. We know one another as "she"/"he" or "her"/"him," not "it." Gender is a biblical construct in creation theology; gender has its source in the will of God, not in societal construction. Using gender in this way is different from the commonly used definition of gender as a social construct that refers to learned behaviour or social differences within a particularized cultural context.[10] *Gender* is to be distinguished from *gender roles*, which do refer to culturally learned or assigned behaviour specific to women or men.

Gendered femaleness and maleness is sacred and worthy of celebration. As soon as Adam and Eve *were*, they "were" as male and female, and they related in a social construct—and it was still "very good" and blessed by God.

Femaleness and maleness is in children before they are born. Sexuality is not something that "becomes" at puberty or is activated the first time one has sexual intercourse. Children in their maleness or femaleness image God; they are full human beings, already "imaged," already reflecting God. Therefore, children's sexuality is to be honoured and protected.[11]

Human beings complete the image of God in their union as male and female. This completion is not only in an event of genital, erotic, "one-fleshness," but as we come together in communities of female and male. It is in community with God and with other gendered beings that we are defined as human beings.

Gendered female and male relationships are created to be equal and interdependent, to share symmetrical tasks requiring mutual honour.[12] Female and male are equally made in the image of God, equally created for accountable sociability in relationship and accountable dominion in managing the earth's resources (Gen. 1:27–28), equally and "inescapably social,"[13] and equally dependent upon each other.

Female and male are complementary. Each completes the other, each has an essential difference from the other.[14] This is not just the paradigm for sexual interaction but a pattern for ways in which female and male in community give us a more complete image of God.

Sexuality Is about Sexual Expression

Both erotic and non-erotic sexuality are intrinsically good and are to be celebrated. Genesis, chapter 1, links the goodness of human sexuality with procreation and pronounces a divine blessing: femaleness, maleness, and fertility are all good and blessed. Genesis 2 is a more intimate, relational account of sexuality that overcomes isolation, loneliness, and aloneness and establishes and blesses community and companionship of man and woman. Adam and Eve experienced no shame in their nakedness or sexuality. "Celebration is in the Old and New Testament, but the teaching of the Stoics, the Puritans, and a whole dismal string of Christian tradition has tended to inculcate both fear and contempt for sexual desire and sexual pleasure. Pleasure is something God has put into creation for us to enjoy"[15]—without guilt or shame!

Sexual and erotic pleasure is to be enjoyed and celebrated in the holy context of gendered male-female covenanted relationship. "Therefore a man leaves his father and his mother and clings to his wife, and they become one flesh" (Gen. 2:24). This "holy context" is what we understand as marriage. One leaves one's family of origin to form a new, blessed relationship where physical, emotional, and spiritual "one flesh-ness" is formed.

Being created in the image of God separates humankind from the animal kingdom. Human sex is different from animal sex. Human beings have control in shaping their sexuality in a way that animals do not. Human sexuality is more than a hormonal, biological drive.[16]

Sexuality Is about Whether God Is Female or Male; It's about Divine Gender

We move from considering human gender to addressing divine gender—a theme of great contemporary interest and controversy.

Our creator tells us who he is; the created do not determine or define God. The God of the Bible is not just any god but is "one Lord" who is "one particular God who has done particular things in particular times and places."[17] "Let us..." reveals the Godhead as plural, as a community working cooperatively in creation.

The Godhead ontologically transcends gender; God is spirit.[18] God of the Old Testament revealed himself as "I am;" this is a non-gendered response.[19] Although both male and female are created in God's image, neither gender is the complete ontological image of God.

Although God ontologically transcends gender, he relates to Adam and Eve and the world he created in personal ways. God was personally concerned for Adam[20] in his aloneness and created Eve (Gen. 2:18); God was personally concerned for the earth he had created and made "man" and "woman" stewards of it (Gen. 1:26–31). God's personal involvement with creation demanded a personal response.[21]

FALLEN SEXUALITY: REALITY

And the Lord God commanded the man, "You may freely eat of every tree of the garden; but of the tree of the knowledge of good and evil you shall not eat, for in the day that you eat of it you shall die." And the "crafty" serpent taunted Eve and challenged God. So when the woman saw that the tree was good for food, and that it was a delight to the eyes, and that the tree was to be desired to make one wise, she took of its fruit and ate; and she also gave some to her husband, who was with her, and he ate.... Then the eyes of both were opened, and they knew that they were naked ... and the man and his wife hid themselves from the presence of the Lord God.... (Gen. 2,3).

Paradise Lost

So paradise was lost. Now men and women bore a broken, scarred image of God; so, too, sexuality was broken and scarred. Adam and Eve disobeyed an ethical boundary set up by God for their good. Upon eating the fruit, they had "knowledge of good and evil" and they began to die. "The eyes of both were opened." Shame exploded into their identity, distorting and breaking their "image-ness," and fear ripped them into separateness and aloneness, forcing them to hide from their Image Maker and from each other, and to dissemble their own identity by clothing their bodies. As a result of the disobedience, there would be pain for the woman in childbearing and struggle for the man to be a good steward of his environment.

Identity Crisis

A great, hulking, six-foot-four man fidgeted in his chair, pushing back almost to merge with it. After forty minutes of struggling to say it, he finally whispered, "I'm a big man, aren't I?" I said, "Yes." "I'm really a big man, aren't I?" "Yes," I said. Long pause. As he shrank even more, "I'm really a big man, but I've got this little dick." It was painful to watch his agony and despair. (*From author's counselling files.*)

What a tragic example of distorted self-worth. Identity, created to have its source in the image of the creator, and to be integrated with sexuality, is here disassociated from its source and disintegrated from sexuality. Sexual identity for many men is understood in terms of genital size, sexual performance, and power over women, or domination.

Similarly, female worth is also defined mainly in sexual terms—the glamour of face, the shape of breasts, waist, hips, and thighs. Sexual identity for many women is understood in terms of relationship—whatever the cost. Accountable sociability is changed into a propensity to abdicate accountable authority and responsibility.

The fall changed sexuality, identity, and gender relationships. Human beings were not to use their position of stewardship and dominion to determine what was good and what was evil—this belonged to God. Nor were human beings to misuse their "one flesh" sociability to persuade each other to step beyond the boundaries set by God.[22] Nevertheless, Eve wanted "to know" good and evil and to be like God; Adam wanted to maintain sociability and did what Eve suggested, ignoring God's command. The result was that they betrayed each other and betrayed God's trust. Accountable sociability changed to enmeshment and accountable dominion changed to domination; shame entered their experience and gender communion deteriorated into gender enmity.

Gender Enmity

While visiting her Aunt's home in a small Alberta town, this thirteen-year-old girl went "walking the town" with her same-aged cousin and met some of his buddies. Within minutes they had burst into song—a tune you would know—singing: "Do your 'tits' hang low, do they wobble in the snow; can you tie them in a knot, can you tie them in a bow?", laughing jeeringly, highly amused at their wit and power. She stood there paralyzed and stunned, burning with shame as they assessed her worth as a female, mentally stripping her. (*From author's counselling files.*)

The reports of rape, abuse, and vengeance between men and women that fill our popular media constitute clearly recognized forms of gender enmity. Jokes and humour are another, sometimes more subtle, form. Language is a powerful tool to establish and maintain power. The jokes that begin in the school yard, and continue into the work-place, give expression to our desire to control each other. Moreover, our society is comfortable with a double standard in which the accepted norm is to demean women's bodies, deliberately controlling and shaming women.

Gender Enmity and Unfulfilled Desire

In addition to those two consequences of the fall—pain in childbirth and a curse on the ground that brings forth food—there is another important consequence that directly affects our discussion of sexuality. To the woman God said, "Yet[23] your desire shall be for your husband and he shall rule over you." Gilbert Bilezikian suggests this means that the "woman is being warned that she will experience an unreciprocated longing for intimacy with the man."[24] " The woman wants a mate and she gets a master; she wants a lover and she gets a lord; she wants a husband and she gets a hierarch."[25] As a counsellor, I have worked with countless women who are irrevocably drawn to men and to relationships that are abusive and destructive and are unable responsibly to step out of such painful circumstances.

So we now have both gender enmity and unfulfilled desire. We can readily look back and see how these have affected our personal experience as sexual beings. The combination of men's propensity to power and women's desire for a man is potent and deadly. It has led to hierarchical gender relationships with differential power bases. Not only have men been given power but, over the long term, prevailing attitudes have served to legitimate their "right" to power over women.[26] This gender pattern, when men lord it over women, is the embodiment of fallen sexuality and has been institutionalized in social and ecclesiastical structures. The commonly used term for this is patriarchy.

Patriarchy

Patriarchy—the male domination of the female—is a reality. It is sad that the church has so often participated in and upheld patriarchal values that keep women voiceless and powerless. The interminable discussions on "headship" reflect this. The question of "headship" is particularly poignant and complex; we need to take seriously the passion that this issue triggers[27] because the interpretation of "headship" determines not only who has power but who has the freedom and right to keep one gender under another. It is here we see fallen sexuality functioning hurtfully—with the pattern of male domination distorting the gender relationships intended in God's creation.[28]

The entrenchment of patriarchy is, in part, derivative from the influence of dualistic thinking in our cultural heritage and in church tradition.

Dualism

Dualistic thinking, generally regarded as a Greek concept, takes the value-neutral philosophic construct of dualism and applies it to gender identity. Dualism, which views the universe as split into two distinct, irreducible natures, sees a human being consisting, therefore, of two parts: spirit (or soul) and body. *Spirit* is associated with the rational, incorruptible, eternal, and pure; *body* is associated with the earthly, fleshly, corruptible, and lustful. The former is seen as superior and is exalted, and the latter, as inferior. When dualistic thinking identifies soul or spirit with maleness and body with femaleness, and when "through the projection of male fears and drives, women have been made the receptacles of the impulses and images that men have been conditioned by patriarchy to find unacceptable in themselves,"[29] then we have oppressive patriarchal attitudes which elevate men as superior and denigrate women as inferior. In turn, such attitudes exacerbate the problems of misogyny by both men and women, generating men's hatred of women, women's hatred of other women, women's hatred of themselves,[30] and also men's hatred of themselves.

In summary, we learn the following from the story of creation and the fall. Fallen sexual human beings challenge their image-ness and want to *be* God. That mysterious gift of sexuality and gender is changed into "sex," in turn to be bought and sold as entertainment or plied as a "profession."[31] Rather than being respected and upheld, gender differences are the object of scorn in jokes and sarcastic humour. Erotic sexual pleasure becomes an end in itself, reducing passion and desire to a biological, animal-like drive that must have instant gratification. "In the Fall, the human race experienced severe damage to everything relationally important for cohesive personhood.... Human attempts at goodness became pervasively tainted by sin."[32]

Figure 1: Gender Paradigm*

Creation   BOTH FEMALE AND MALE
Sexuality   CREATED FOR EQUALITY AND INTERDEPENDENCE

BOTH FEMALE AND MALE CREATED FOR

Accountable Sociability	*Accountable Dominion*
–cooperative interdependence	–responsible decision making
–responsible in relationships	–responsible authority

BOTH MALE AND FEMALE DISOBEY GOD'S CREATION BOUNDARIES

Fallen
Sexuality

Adam abused accountable sociability	*Eve abused accountable dominion*
–chose to do what Eve asked	–determined good and evil by herself
–crossed boundaries set by God	–crossed boundaries set by God

DIFFERING SEXUALITY CAUSES SEPARATENESS
SHAME AND GENDER ENMITY

Woman blamed the serpent	*Man first blamed God then blamed woman*
–did not acknowledge her own responsibility	–did not acknowledge his own responsibility

Woman rejected accountable dominion	*Man rejected accountable sociability*
–chose relationship at any cost; her temptation is to abdicate ac–countable authority and responsibility	–chose power and control; his temptation is to reject accountable responsibility in relationship

GENDER ENMITY
ALONENESS

Enmeshment	*Domination*
–Woman needs to be acknowledged and to be significant	–Man needs to control and to master

Redemption   REDEMPTION BY SERVANT KING
Sexuality   CONNECTEDNESS WITH GOD
                IDENTITY AND SEXUALITY ARE INTEGRATED
                MUTUALITY, EQUALITY, AND DIGNITY
                GENDER PEACE AND RESPECT

Woman chooses accountable dominion	*Man chooses accountable sociability*
and rejects abdication of responsibility	and rejects domination

BOTH WOMEN AND MEN, INDIVIDUALLY AND CORPORATELY, CHOOSE
ACCOUNTABLE DOMINION AND ACCOUNTABLE SOCIABILITY

*Based on Van Leeuwen's gender analysis.

REDEMPTION SEXUALITY: RESPONSE

Inasmuch as humanity needed and needs redemption, so too our human sexuality needed and needs redemption, individually and corporately. "It is clear that a major purpose in God's redemptive plan is the restoration of his image in the redeemed person individually and in the redeemed community corporately."[33] The third section of our trilogy shows how God, acting primarily through Jesus the Servant King, offers us a spirit-empowered way in which our sexuality can be redeemed.

Redemption Is God's Initiative, God's Revelation and God's Design

Redemption is God's plan of rescue; it is his ungendered love for us. God's plan of redemption started when Adam and Eve "sinned," and will end in the second coming of Jesus. God covenanted with a people through whom he could reveal himself to the world; he gave them the ten commandments. The voice of the prophets called God's people to justice, and faithfulness to "I Am." God's plan was accomplished through the work and death of Jesus and continues to be fleshed out in the "body of Christ" until Jesus returns. This plan is about God's personal interaction with, and commitment to, the creatures he created in his own image; this plan is about redeeming our whole being, which includes our identity and our sexuality.[34]

Redemption Sexuality Is through Jesus the Servant King

So far I have argued that redemption, which "rescues" our image-ness, identity, and sexuality, is God's initiative and God's plan. God revealed himself in personal terms and most fully in the person of Jesus the Servant King. In coming as a human being, Jesus stands against dualistic thinking; in coming as servant, Jesus stands against oppressive patriarchal thinking. Being male or female is secondary; what is primary is that Jesus came as a representative of human beings, both male and female, to bring redemption to all humanity and, therefore, to our identity and sexuality, through his death and resurrection.[35] "The Word was made flesh and lived among us, and we have seen his glory." Not since Eden was the presence of God so present to humankind.

In coming as body, flesh and blood, Jesus stands against dualist thinking that devalues women. Jesus did not "abhor the Virgin's womb" or abhor coming as flesh and blood. Jesus was born flesh and blood, he lived as body, he died as body, he rose as "resurrection body." In the Eucharist we celebrate the historic event of Jesus' bodily death and bodily resurrection.

Jesus also stands against dualistic thinking by affirming and valuing women. In the home of Simon the Pharisee, Jesus was anointed by a woman "who was a sinner." This is profound; here we see a socially unacceptable woman, a prostitute, weeping, drying Christ's feet with her hair. She was a woman whose hands had sexually caressed men's bodies, and whose hair had helped ply her trade. And Jesus received what the woman offered him. Jesus offered redemption through forgiveness and through dignity and mutuality in his personal interaction with the woman, and she accepted; Jesus offered Simon redemption through forgiveness for his selfishness and hardness, and he rejected it.

Jesus stands against oppressive patriarchy. Jesus established a new hierarchical order: "Whoever wants to be first must be last of all and servant of all" (Mark 9:35). In washing his disciples' feet (John 13:10–20), Jesus laid down the patriarchal privileges of a man and took up the servanthood of women as a model for discipleship. The ultimate stand against the power and status of patriarchal identity was Jesus becoming our sacrificial lamb, the slaughtered victim.

Jesus stands against abdicating responsibility. The Servant King model has two elements: servant and king. The model of *servant* is a call away from power and domination (responding to the propensity in men for power and control) to accountable sociability; the model of *king* is a call away from abdication of responsibility (responding to the propensity in women for enmeshment). Jesus' encounter with the Canaanite woman is an intriguing commendation for the woman's persistence and for her taking responsibility in that situation (Matt. 15:21–28).

Redemption Sexuality Is through the Holy Spirit

But how on earth are we actually to achieve redemption sexuality in our thinking and in our behaviour? All attempts to "be good," to reform ourselves, to fulfil "the Law," or to be socialized into righteousness, demonstrate that it's impossible—without the empowering by the Holy Spirit. When Jesus lived on earth, he was incarnate in a particular human body, in a particular culture, in a particular geographic place. When he left the earth, he gave both the individuals who believed in him, and the church, the gift of the Spirit, who would dwell within believers and be with them, individually and corporately, forever (John 14:16). So now the presence of God is within each believer; the God of the cosmos has chosen again to dwell with frail flesh of men and women, to reconnect relationally.

Direct communion with God is re-established with both male and female in their identity and sexuality. "In the last days it will be, God declares, that I will pour out my Spirit upon all flesh, and your sons and your daughters shall prophesy..." (Acts 2:17). Women and men are *equally* gifted and *equally* indwelt by the Holy Spirit. Neither the gift of the Holy Spirit nor the gifts of the Holy Spirit are gender specific. All believers are *equally* called to display the fruit of the Spirit: "love, joy, peace, patience, kindness, generosity, faithfulness, gentleness, and self-control" (Gal. 5:22–23).

Redemption Sexuality Is through the Establishment of New Community

Not only is redemption sexuality dependent on the Holy Spirit working within each individual, redemption sexuality is also dependent on the Holy Spirit working in the community of believers to uproot and overcome systemic injustices caused by patriarchal and dualistic thinking. This new community is to be a place of healing and nurture, of challenge and responsibility. It is likened to a body with many parts working together. "Just as the body is one and has many members, and all the members of the body, though many, are one body, so it is with Christ. For in the one Spirit we were all baptized into one body" (1 Cor. 12:12–13). But to function as one body in the midst of fallen sexuality and brokenness is also impossible—without the empowering of the Holy Spirit. This new community is to "bodily" express radical redemption sexuality. This redemption community is to overcome gender enmity where "there is no longer male or female" (Gal. 3:27–28) and where domination and abdication are dismantled. It is a place where light overcomes darkness, where we are no longer under the curse but are under the blessing of God. A place of celebration and joy in our identity and sexuality, where there is mutuality, equality and dignity; a place where there is justice and mercy, love and gentleness, truth and courage, grace and respect; a place where women choose accountable dominion and men choose accountable sociability; a place where we have peace with God and peace within gender difference.

CHRISTIAN SEXUAL ETHICS IN A PERMISSIVE SOCIETY

This new redemptive community is particularized in a society obsessed with sex. Lewis Smedes suggests that, as North Americans, we are fixated on sex as though it were a real thing:

> We talk about sex, write about sex, and teach our children about sex. But sex is nothing at all; only sexual persons are real. The ironic thing is that our obsession with an unreality called "sex" makes us prisoners of a myth. Perhaps this is why sex dominates so much of modern life: it is an abstraction promoted to the status of reality, and unreality turned into a myth tends to become a dominating force in life.[36]

Our obsessions reflect who we are, what we value and what we are committed to. In terms of sexual ethics, our behaviour is motivated by the source of our personal identity, and those things we believe affirm our worth and value. If our source of personal identity is from God, then we are motivated to do what God says regarding sexual ethical conduct; if our source of personal identity is from "fallen" needs to dominate or abdicate responsibility,[37] then we are motivated to fulfil and satisfy those needs. Our behaviour will reflect what motivates us or what we are "obsessed" with.

This part of the discussion will consider behaviour and motivation, or sexual ethics; we move from ideas to application. Ethics requires decision making, choosing from options, and then translating those decisions into behaviour. We will look at redemption sexuality as it applies to singleness and marriage, and to abuses of sexuality.

Basis of Sexual Ethics

What are the biblical guidelines for sexual ethics? The whole of the Bible provides the guidelines as it speaks to these profound and mysterious issues of value, worth, identity, and sexuality. However, the Bible does set boundaries on our sexual behaviour. So, for example, we take the ten commandments and the teaching in Leviticus concerning sexual behaviour seriously.[38] Similarly, our sexual behaviour is governed by such teachings as the Sermon on the Mount and the Pauline Epistles. The New Testament recognizes only two forms of sexual behaviour as appropriate for Christians: monogamous heterosexual marriage—the norm from creation—and celibacy.

But how many of us have been taught, explicitly or implicitly, that, because there are limitations on sexual expression, all sexual expression is "bad"? Limitations are placed on our sexuality because our sexuality is mysteriously linked with our very being and identity. To sin sexually is to sin against our own bodies and our own identity. Again, to cite Smedes:

> "Every other sin which a man commits is outside the body; but the immoral man sins against his own body" (1 Cor. 6:18). Now why does [St. Paul] say this? Over simplifying other sins to make his point, he seems to say that sins like stealing, coveting, even lying, do not infringe deeply on a person's own selfhood. But sexuality involves our very self. Sleeping with a prostitute commits a man's very person, even though he does not intend it to. The point is not that sexual acts are more serious than other acts because they are sensual. They are more serious because they are much more than merely sensual; they involve the deepest and most significant facets of our personhood. No Christian can make believe that sex with a whore is only a release of his bodily tension. Casual sex is a contradiction in terms.[39]

Helmut Thielicke puts it this way: "This is the reason why sexuality—contrary to what is commonly thought—does not merely split man into flesh and spirit, but rather divides the spirit within itself."[40] This is the mystery and sacredness of sexuality. Sexuality and identity are indivisible. If they are indivisible, then what we do sexually has the potential of maturing, integrating and harmonizing every part of our being, intrapersonally and interpersonally, or of disintegrating and destroying us.

1. Freedom in Christ

We experience freedom when our sexuality is integrated with our identity and when we express that integration of our sexual behaviour within the limits of biblical teaching. Christ lived and died that we might be free: "For freedom Christ has set us free" (Gal. 5:1); "Where the spirit of the Lord is, there is freedom" (2 Cor. 3:17). What does this mean in terms of our sexuality? It does not mean "freedom from sexuality"[41] where there would be no sexual drive, only some spiritualized numbness; nor does it mean "escape from responsibility," license to satisfy any sexual desire in whatever way possible.[42] It is freedom from the compulsion to use our physical sex drives to exploit others; freedom from guilt—real and false; freedom from the moral tyranny of oppressive rules within a community; freedom from the illusion that sexual technique is the route to personal joy; and freedom from the illusion of the imprisoning myth that sex is a real thing. It is freedom for loving service, freedom for "whole self" integration (with or without sexual intercourse), freedom for ultimate sexual relationship within biblical norms, freedom for covenanted relationship.[43]

2. Self-control

We have freedom, yes, but Christian freedom in union with self-control. Now, we do not like this word self-control! Especially when applied to our sexual behaviour. And yet repeatedly we are admonished to be self-controlled: Galatians 5:22 lists self-control as one of the fruits of the Spirit; 2 Peter 1:6 argues that in order to "escape from the corruption that is in the world," among other things, we are to "make every effort to support" our faith with self-control and endurance; and 1 Thessalonians 4:3–4 calls us to "abstain from fornication" and to "know how to control our own body in holiness and honour, not with lustful passion." We are admonished in Colossians to "put to death ... fornication, impurity, passion, evil desire, and greed" and we are to "get rid of all such things—anger, wrath, malice, slander, and abusive language from [our] mouth," not lying to one another, because we have "stripped off the old self with its practices" and we have clothed ourselves "with the new self, which is being renewed in knowledge according to the image of its creator" (Col. 3:5–10). We are to overcome and destroy those sexual activities that destroy the mystery and sacredness of our sexual identity. Then we are to get rid of emotional and verbal abuse that have the stench of gender enmity and the fall. The reason for this? Our "life is hidden with Christ in God" (Col. 3:3); we are redemption people, released from the curse of the fall; we are being made new. This is a call to put sexual activity in the context of a right relationship with our Creator and with fellow human beings; it is a call to accountable dominion over our sexual passion, lust, and desire and to accountable and responsible sociability in all our relationships as sexual beings.

To be a unified, integrated, free human being, all elements within a person must "be in harmony—even the sexual," which means that some elements have to be subordinate to others; "the raw energy of feeling or physical vitality must be harnessed and guided by the rational, ethical and spiritual self."[44] The physical act of coitus is not simply an animal-like, biological, hormonal response;[45] "it is a sensual act with spiritual implications, a physical act with an inner meaning."[46]

3. Journey

Let me now suggest that we all are journeying towards redemption sexuality. On this journey, most of us have strayed from the biblical norm that is "best" for us according to the instructions of our Maker. We have sinned. Jesus said, "Everyone who looks at a woman with lust has already committed adultery with her in his heart" (Matt. 5:27–30). If we have not sinned in deed, then we have most likely sinned in thought, whether our sin is from domination or abdication, malice or slander, adultery or abuse. If we deny we have sinned, there can be no redemption transaction with God. So let us call a sin a sin and open the door for healing through confession and forgiveness, which leads to right relationship with God and with other human beings.

Jesus' response to the woman caught in adultery (John 8:1–11) illustrates clearly the meaning of calling a sin a sin. The religious authorities, all male, brought a woman caught in adultery to Jesus (interesting that they did not bring the man caught in adultery as well); the woman was guilty; the purpose was to catch Jesus, not to uphold the sacredness of sex. While Jesus wrote something in the sand, his response to the trick question was, "Let anyone among you who is without sin be the first to throw a stone at her." Whatever Jesus wrote in the sand caused every accuser to leave, indicating they too were "sinners." Jesus' response to the woman is wonderful: "Has no one condemned you?" "No one, sir," she replies. "Neither do I condemn you. Go your way, and from now on do not sin again."

Jesus challenged the sinfulness of both the woman and the religious authorities. To the woman he said, "Do not sin again." Jesus' response is extraordinarily matter-of-fact, but he does not attack her identity. Consequently she went away forgiven. This passage does not record the accusers' response, but if they did not acknowledge their own sin before God, then God would be unable to extend forgiveness. Reconciliation through forgiveness necessitates open relationship between the accused and the forgiver. All of us are in need of forgiveness from God, and calling a sin a sin ought to produce mercy, gentleness, and grace, not critical condemnation.

Singleness

Keeping in mind that we are all sexual human beings on a journey looking for mentors and signposts that will help us on our journey, we now look to Jesus and what he modelled. Jesus very clearly demonstrated that genital sexual relations are not necessary for fulfilment as a human being sexually. Jesus was a gendered male and responded as a male to men and women around him but did not experience genital sex.[47] Jesus, in his gendered maleness, enjoyed intimate relationships in the community of disciples, male and female, who interacted with him and cared for him, who lived and travelled with him (Luke 8:3). Smedes says "There is no reason to suppose that he had no erotic feelings toward women ... nor is there any reason to suppose that women felt no erotic attraction toward him."[48]

The Christian church has many wonderful models of single people who are fulfilled and complete in their identity and in their sexuality as men and women. The reader can easily provide examples. Just think of their creative ministry through their vocations and what a gift that has been to the church. I believe we have seriously undermined the value and perhaps giftedness of both singleness and celibacy. Paul upheld celibacy as a gift that frees both men and women to be concerned about the Lord's affairs (1 Cor. 7:32–34). How often do we hear singles affirmed for their ministry rather than pitied in what is often perceived as their loneliness—"Poor dear, she has no one to care for her."

But the harsh reality for many is that singleness is not by choice. It is often by default, because of someone else's choice, because of divorce, because of disabilities, through death of a spouse, or through an emotional death within a relationship where one spouse is unable or unwilling to emotionally commit to the other.

> Her body shook as she sobbed uncontrollably. All she had ever really wanted was to have a family, build a home with a man she loved and who loved her. Now she was forty-seven, past the safe child-bearing age, single, professional, competent ... and alone. Why did God give her these desires if he wasn't going to satisfy them? (*From author's counselling files.*)

In these circumstances singleness is painful, lonely, and full of grief over lost possibilities of loving and being loved, of expressing oneself in a genitally sexual way. The fallenness of our society often stigmatizes women who have never married and those who are divorced, saying, "It's their fault ... they're not good enough ... who'd want her." Men feel just as much pain and loneliness as women but a woman's intrinsic worth is assessed on her ability to have and keep a man.

Whether celibate or single by default, singles need a community of redemption and resurrection where they are free to come in the joy of their singleness or with their pain and brokenness. It is because of this that the church must take very seriously the challenge to form a dynamic, vibrant community that responds to the needs of singles—not by forming a "singles' group" as a dating service, but rather by providing a place of interaction and intimacy, of respect and service; a place to celebrate sexuality in non-erotic ways.

Marriage

The norm and ideal for expressed erotic, genital sex in the New Testament is monogamous, heterosexual relationship that is rooted in covenanted, committed love. For Christians then, marriage is the only place where sexual intercourse is sanctioned. Christian marriage is built on covenant love which is characterized by commitment, caring, fidelity, justice, compassion and fairness. It is permanent and binding. Covenant love guards and protects the giving of oneself to another sexually.

Sexual relations are contained within marriage because there is mutual authority and mutual submission between husband and wife (Eph. 5:21; 1 Cor. 7:3–4). The husband has "authority" over his wife's body and the wife has "authority" over the husband's body. This indicates symmetrical rights and responsibilities in the full giving of bodies to one another in sexual intercourse, in love, in openness, in trust, in faithfulness, and in honesty; there is mutual honouring and mutual right to each other sexually.[49]

1 Corinthians 7 admonishes husband and wife not to deprive one another sexually, except by mutual agreement. If a wife or a husband does not want to engage in sexual intercourse with the other, there is to be mutual agreement for a set time. The reason needs to be stated: if it's for a time of sexual fasting and prayer, clarify that; if it's for some reason other than prayer, then that needs to be stated and the situation resolved, with outside help if necessary; if it's because one partner wants to engage in sexual behaviour that the other does not want to engage in, respecting the other's boundaries is imperative.

In marriage, living within redemptive sexuality norms that are governed by the gift of the presence of God within us and by the gifts of the Holy Spirit, we continue our journey towards equal and accountable sociability and dominion. Within individual marriages we are mutually to determine the roles and cultural uniqueness that will characterize a particular marriage relationship. Roles and distribution of responsibilities will be decided according to circumstances and personality. Some men are gentle and prefer jobs with relational emphasis; some women are strong leaders and very able to play roles traditionally reserved for men. Marriage enables us to break free of stereotypic roles that are rooted in fallen sexuality and to respect and enjoy the exploration of individuality within intimacy.[50]

If a couple bring children into their relationship, then these principles of sexuality are modelled and incorporated into the family experience. Our families are places where we delight as the Holy Spirit invigorates and energizes the sexuality of each member within the family. Behaviour that demonstrates accountable dominion and accountable sociability allows for non-gendered expression of the fruits of the Spirit: "joy, peace, patience, kindness, generosity, faithfulness, gentleness, and self-control" (Gal. 5:22).

Fallen Sexuality

When biblical ideals for sexual behaviour in singleness or in marriage are abandoned, then identity, sexuality, worth, and image are distorted and destroyed. Fallen sexuality is the result of abandonment of the ideals for which God created sexuality and sexual relationships, abandonment to ego-centric, power-dominated behaviour. The following examples, drawn from counselling experience, illustrate briefly the realities of fallen sexuality.

1. Abandonment of public commitment

There seemed no room for discussion. "We don't need an artificial ritual with a piece of paper to give us permission to live together. We love each other; we've committed ourselves to each other. We don't need a passé religious institution telling us what to do—it's our business what we do. Besides, if we do split up, it's much cleaner and easier than divorce..." (*From author's counselling files.*)

I wondered how the couple I was counselling would build deep trust without commitment. And their idea of commitment seemed to be contradictory. Marriage includes the following essentials: a single man and a single woman setting themselves apart, exclusively, in genuine, permanent commitment to each other; a relationship that accords with God's pleasure such that God can "set them apart" for blessing; and a public declaration before God, the community of believers, and the larger social and cultural community. Marriage is not simply a private affair of two individuals. It is a public event that joins not only two individuals but also two families together, embracing values, gender role expectations, family patterns, and histories. Paul Avis says, "The sacred is always social, always public, always cosmic, always greater than the individual and his or her private concerns. The sacred has to do with the way the world is—'the divine order.'"[51] This public proclamation of intent is important to Christians. It allows family and community to celebrate, support, and bless a ceremony that involves the mystery of what is sacred.[52]

2. Abandonment to betrayal

There was no question mistaking that emotion: anger; pure, unadulterated anger. After thirty-two years of marriage, four children, and three known adulterous "relationships" (her husband didn't like the word "affairs"), her husband said he was seeking a divorce because he wanted to marry his twenty-one-year-old colleague. Her husband was a church official with a position of authority, and both he and his "colleague" were Christian believers. They felt that their relationship was acceptable before God, and they would live together until the divorce was finalized and they could get married. My client felt totally abandoned by God. Totally abandoned by her husband that she had "tolerated through three affairs." Totally abandoned in a culture where she had no obvious marketable skills. (*From author's counselling files.*)

The husband in this scenario abandoned his wife of thirty-two years. What a deep betrayal. Divorce is not the original intent or will of God but divorce is allowed because of "hardheartedness" (Matt. 19:1–9). Divorce expresses fallen sexuality, breaking apart a relationship that was set apart to be holy. Thielicke makes an interesting point: the New Testament teaching is addressed to men because women did not have the right or authority to divorce—only men did. So the teaching on divorce is directed at men. A man could very easily dismiss a woman in divorce in Jewish New Testament times. When this authority was misused it was men once again rejecting responsibility in relationship and choosing ego-centric, power-based behaviour.

Am I saying that the woman in this scenario had no responsibility in what happened? No. I am saying that men more often make ego-centric decisions because they have more power in the relationship. And I am saying that adultery and divorce is a deep betrayal of covenant relationship that leaves scars on both spouses. It is easy to see how divorce can be the result of men and women rejecting both accountable dominion and accountable sociability within the relationship. Divorce is uniquely complex and requires much more discussion than allowed here.

3. Abandonment to sexual pleasure

She sat in my office obviously weighted down with guilt and confusion. How could she keep the relationship if she didn't respond to the sexual demands of her boyfriend? His sexual demands made her uneasy and guilty. He argued that biblical teaching indicated that only vaginal intercourse was prohibited before marriage—nudity, oral intercourse, anal intercourse, living together were all okay—and he expected her to engage in oral sex. (*From author's counselling files.*)

In this situation, the young man abandoned himself to pleasure on his terms and for his own gratification at the expense of the young woman's need for a guilt-free relationship, for affection, and for affirmation of her intrinsic worth. And how did he manipulate this situation? Through a legalistic argument. If the Bible doesn't say oral intercourse is wrong, then is it okay? No. The prime question here is not whether oral sex is right or wrong. It's a question of personal values and the needs of this woman, which were less important than her boyfriend's need for sexual gratification. Mutuality and equality were not being expressed in this relationship. He was dominating and she was enmeshed. This is fallen sexuality. He was self-centred and she was pressured to abandon her own sexual boundaries.

Teenage girls and women often consent to sexual intercourse when what they really want and need is affection and relationship—not sex. Teenage boys often insist that their girlfriends do it to prove they really love them, to prove their male prowess to their buddies. Both are trapped by their need for identity affirmation. So often erotic love is used as a substitute for a deeper need. Experience and statistics reflect that the majority of singles, including teens, are saying yes to intercourse outside of marriage. Just because this is what is happening does not mean that it is good, right, or acceptable before God. It simply means that this is what is happening. And it does not mean that God's intended design is faulty; it simply means that the road to holiness in sexuality is the narrow road (though I recognize that walking this road is far from simple). Choosing God's standards is not necessarily being "narrow-minded," but it may be a choice to uphold the mysterious sacredness of sex and sexuality.

4. Abandonment to sexual experience

His body distorted in pain and shame as he forced himself to talk about his sexual fantasies and his compulsive masturbation. Every time this young Christian man tried to pray, his mind would fill with pornographic images and pictures of penises. He despaired of ever finding healing or freedom in this area—and whenever he made attempts to "just pray," study, or serve others, he only ended up with more guilt and despair because it didn't work. (*From author's counselling files.*)

This young man abandoned himself to the experience of orgasm. Again, there is no biblical text that refers to masturbation. So we are left to look at the principles of sexuality to make a decision about masturbation.

Contrary to oft-quoted myths, masturbation does not cause mental illness; you are not condemned if you masturbate. Masturbation is autostimulation and it does nothing to bring sexual expression into community of loving relationship; it is "love turned inward."[53] Because of this, the experience of orgasm, although momentarily pleasurable, is incomplete. Sexual expression was created to overcome loneliness and aloneness. Masturbation abandons a person to loneliness—although it is temporarily, physically satisfying. Even if it doesn't feel like it, individuals do have control over their own bodies sexually, unlike animals who are driven by automatic responses.[54]

This young man also abandoned himself to the use of pornography to stimulate orgasm. Pornography is highly addictive, enslaving the person feeding on it and demeaning the individuals used to produce the material. Masturbation, when addictive and compulsive, and when coupled with pornography or fetishes, is complex and powerful. Compulsive masturbation and obsession with pornography are means to satisfying needs that were not properly met at some point in our lives. We need the power of the Holy Spirit, counselling, prayer, and a loving community to bring healing and freedom in these areas.

5. Abandonment to violence and betrayal

Abandonment to violence and betrayal results in rape, incest, and sexual abuse. The Lambeth Conference Report of 1988 had this response to sexual abuse:

> There is universal agreement that respect, reverence and mutuality are necessary in all human relationships. This agreement about the fundamentals of human relations, including sexual relations, leads to a firm judgment and condemnation of sexual abuse and exploitation.... Sexual abuse is self-gratification by exploitation. It makes an impersonal object of the other person, abusing both the person and sexuality itself. Abuse occurs in a wide range of sexual activities: always in rape and child molestation, usually in adultery and prostitution, and sometimes even in marriage.... The Church must be clear about these violations of sexual intimacy. It must be explicit in its teaching about these particular aberrations of sexual relations, aggressively proactive about its social policy and action touching on these areas, and forthright in dealing with violations in its own community.[55]

One form of abandonment to violence is rape. Rape is not about sex and genitals; it is about power and gender. Rape is one person disregarding another person's sexuality, violently exerting power over them. The more powerful persons snatch sexually whatever they choose. Rape is wrong and unacceptable, in marriage or out of marriage, on a casual date or in a "friendship." Rape is accountable authority turned into violent domination and responsible relationship turned into ego-centric self-gratification. This is not just a secular problem—Christians are also guilty of this crime.

> He's an abuser; he's a Christian; he sexually molested his daughter for years creating scars that will last a lifetime, robbing her of her childhood, sexualizing her before she ever should have been burdened with the awesome responsibility for sexual behaviour, impregnating her with mistrust and denial and self-rejection.(*From author's counselling files.*)

Incest is abandonment to violence and to betrayal. It is one of the worst betrayals a child can experience. Parents are to protect and nurture their children, but incest abuses and misuses a child for selfish power needs. When this happens—in Christian homes, by Christian parents in particular—it is incredibly destructive and hypocritical. Incest violates the trust of the child who is powerless to protect himself or herself against such abuse, and it damages normal childhood development of trust, identity, self-esteem, and sexuality.

The "body of Christ" is to be a place of healing for both the survivor of incest and for the perpetrator. The healing process for both is long and painful. The survivor needs patient, loving care and a place to talk openly, directly, and honestly about the abuse experience in an atmosphere of trust, safety, and confidentiality. The perpetrator needs patient, loving care and a place to be confronted with the responsibility of his or her actions of abuse that will lead to confession, remorse, restitution, and restoration in an atmosphere of justice, truth, mercy, and grace. The healing and freedom of both survivor and perpetrator requires the profound healing power by the Holy Spirit. Reconciliation will come as God heals the deep brokenness within both the survivor and the perpetrator—and will take time, sometimes a long time.[56]

> There they sat, stiff, defensive, around the table. There I sat with the parents of my client, a young woman. The church leadership, all male, was defending a colleague who had admitted to having sexually abused my client for seven years of her childhood, wanting the parents of my client to immediately put aside their pain and anger—"Just forgive, it's the Christian thing to do." (*From author's counselling files.*)

Sexual abuse by a church leader has incredible impact on the individuals involved, the church, and the whole community. Church leaders have been entrusted with the spiritual care and development of children, and when that trust is abused, a child not only mistrusts people in authority but also learns to mistrust God. The "National Policy and Protocol Regarding Sexual Assault and Sexual Harassment"[57] has set guidelines for responding to allegations of sexual abuse within the church. It is critical when abuse is exposed that the church leadership respond very quickly to the accusations, affirming the potential seriousness if abuse occurred, and promising to investigate the allegations. Sexual violation by a church leader is a gross misuse of power and authority; inaction, indifference, or aggression by church leadership after hearing of allegations of abuse is also a misuse of power and authority within the church—it has the effect of re-victimizing the victim.

REDEMPTION COMMUNITY: THE BODY OF CHRIST

I believe that what we need most to live as sexually redeemed human beings in our world today is a redemption community where we can journey together in love and mercy.

We need the "body of Christ" to be a place where, as gendered human beings, we are loved and ministered to in a non-erotic sexual way; a place where we experience the wholeness of the "image-ness" of God as we celebrate and delight in our sexuality and the wholeness of community; a place that upholds the sacred mystery that binds sexuality and identity together.

We need the body of Christ to be a place of healing for our broken sexuality; a place that has the smell of ointment and healing salve about it; a place where we will define and clarify what it means to be a gendered, sexual being.

We need the body of Christ to be a place of education and teaching about biblical sexuality; a place where we will teach "redemption sexuality" for both genders of all ages, infants to grandparents; a place where young children will celebrate their "girlness" and "boyness" in a community that respects and loves both genders in their similarities and in their complementarity; a place where fifteen-year-olds will learn that sexual relationships have to do with mystery, commitment, and trust; a place where we will teach loving responsibility and accountability in our sexual behaviour; a place where we will talk respectfully and directly about sexuality.

We need the body of Christ to be a place where we do not judge or criticize one another on the grounds of gender, sexuality, or stereotypes.

We need the body of Christ to be a place where the resurrection power and the healing presence of Jesus are seen bringing good news to the captive, recovery of sight to the blind, and freedom to the oppressed (Luke 4:18–19)—in all areas of sexuality; a place where prayer is central in discerning and understanding sexual brokenness; a place where individuals are delivered from the powers of darkness.

We need the body of Christ to be a place where together we walk in mercy and grace on our journey to sexual wholeness; a place where we call a sexual sin a sexual sin; a place where we find forgiveness and freedom at the cross of Jesus Christ; a place where we invite the Holy Spirit to dwell within to comfort.

We need the body of Christ to affirm that we are children of God, living in the light of Jesus Christ, empowered by the Holy Spirit to be a royal priesthood and a holy nation (1 Pet. 2:9).

SUGGESTED READING

Dan B. Allender and Tremper Longman III, *Bold Love* (Colorado Springs, Col.: NavPress, 1992).

Louis Smedes, *Sex for Christians* (Grand Rapids, Mich.: W. B. Eerdmans, 1976).

John Stott, *Decisive Issues Facing Christians Today* (Grand Rapids, Mich.: Fleming H. Revell, 1990).

Mary Stewart Van Leeuwen, *Gender and Grace* (Downers Grove, Ill.: InterVarsity Press, 1990).

John White, *Eros Redeemed* (Downers Grove, Ill.: InterVarsity Press, 1993).

ENDNOTES

1. Mary Stewart Van Leeuwen, *Gender and Grace* (Downers Grove, Ill.: InterVarsity Press, 1990).

2. Jennifer Harold, "Men, Women, History, Vision," seminar presented at 17th Student Mission Convention, Urbana Student Mission Conference '93 (Urbana, Illinois, Dec. 26–31, 1993).

3. Robert W. Prichard (*A Wholesome Example: Sexual Morality and the Episcopal Church* [Lexington, Ky.: Bristol Books, 1992]) suggests that the Anglican Church has been built on four pillars of authority: the Bible, tradition, reason, and recently, experience. These four authorities "do not stand on equal footing ... but in a dynamic hierarchy," with the Bible being first and primary, followed by tradition, then human reason, and, lastly, experience. Consequently, we will start our explanation of human sexuality by considering the biblical view of sexuality.

4. The New Revised Standard Version will be used throughout this chapter.

5. Jeanne L. Jensma, "Kohut's Tragic Man and the *Imago Dei:* Human Relational Needs in Creation, the Fall, and Redemption," *Journal of Psychology and Theology, 21:4 (Winter), pp. 288–296.*

6. Ibid., p. 289.

7. Van Leeuwen, *Gender and Grace*, p. 41.

8. See Elaine Storkey, *London Lectures in Contemporary Christianity: God and Sexuality,* lectures presented at the Institute for Contemporary Christianity (St. Peter's Church, Vere St. London, W1M 9HP), May 1993. It is not a difference of degree but a difference ontologically, of substance and of "being-ness."

9. Storkey, *London Lectures,* no. 3.

10. This definition of gender is significantly different from the position taken by social feminists and proponents of "Queer Theory" who see gender as an empty, meaningless category.

11. Storkey, *London Lectures,* no. 3.

12. Ibid.

13. Van Leeuwen, *Gender and Grace*, p. 39.

14. Queer Theory argues that male and female are empty categories and that any identity out of the social construct of gender is only nurture, not nature. (See Michael Warner, ed., *Fear of a Queer Planet: Queer Politics and Social Theory* [Minneapolis, Minn.: University of Minnesota Press, 1993].) But I believe God created two distinct genders, male and female.

15. Storkey, *London Lectures,* no. 3.

16. Helmut Thielicke points out some differences between the sex drives of animals and humans. Animal copulation is an automatic response to a biologically determined behaviour, that is, animals being "in heat." When animals are "in heat," their sexual drive cannot be interrupted except by some forcible external intervention. When the automatic sexual process is interrupted, this leads to manifestations of aggression. By contrast, human beings have control of shaping their sexuality and can separate themselves from sexual expression. Human beings are capable of transforming the absence of sexual expression with another human being into something creative and loving without copulation. In *Theological Ethics: Sex* (Grand Rapids, Mich.: W. B. Eerdmans, 1979), pp. 56–58.

17. Elizabeth Achtemeier, "Why God Is Not Mother," *Christianity Today* (August 16, 1993), p. 20.

18. lvin F. Kimel, ed., *Speaking the Christian God: The Holy Trinity and the Challenge of Feminism* (Grand Rapids, Mich.: W. B. Eerdmans, 1992), p. 30. The Old Testament God is quite different from the gods of the surrounding cultures and nations; he is unlike the gendered gods of the Baals, not needing a consort to be made complete.

19. Achtemeier, "Why God Is Not Mother," p. 20.

20. Whether "Adam" is the particular, first male God created or representative "man," God has established personal relationship with the creation of humanity with accountability in that relationship.

21. Achtemeier, "Why God Is Not Mother," p. 20.

22. Van Leeuwen, *Gender and Grace*, pp. 43–45.

23. The "yet" is intriguing in God's dialogue with Eve, suggesting that in spite of the pain in childbearing, a direct result of sexual intimacy and intercourse, she will still desire her husband in sexual intimacy, running the risk of further pain in bearing children.

24. Gilbert Bilezikian in Mary Stewart Van Leeuwen, *Gender and Grace*, p. 44.

25. Bilezikian's more complete quote is: "[The woman's] desire will be for her husband, so as to perpetuate the intimacy that had characterized their relationship in paradise lost. But her nostalgia for the relation of love and mutuality that existed between them before the fall, when they both desired each other, will not be reciprocated by her husband. Instead of meeting her desire, he will rule over her." In *Gender and Grace*, p. 44.

26. We are indebted to current feminist writers and to academics who continue to illumine our understanding of femaleness and maleness. Carol Gilligan, *In a Different Voice: Psychological Theory and Women's Development* (Cambridge: Harvard University Press, 1993), and M. F. Belenky et al., *Women's Ways of Knowing* (New York: Basic Books, 1986), indicate significant differences in the way women and men "know" and make moral decisions. Women use the metaphor of voice that emphasizes speaking, listening, and closeness between subject and object, while men use a visual metaphor that emphasizes distance in interaction. (And how surprising to have Gilligan point out that Piaget and Kohlberg built their development studies on virtually all male subjects.) Deborah Tannen (*You Just Don't Understand: Women and Men in Conversation* [New York: Ballantine Books, 1990]) suggests that women's focus on intimacy, connectedness, and community, and men's focus on independence and success, can leave men subject to vulnerabilities around power issues and women subject to vulnerabilities around the need to be significant.

27. See Maxine Hancock, "Silenced Servants, Shouting Stones," *Faith Today* (November/December 1993), p. 37.

28. Gilbert Bilezikian (*Beyond Sex Roles: What the Bible Says about a Woman's Place in Church and Family* [Grand Rapids, Mich.: Baker Book House, 1985], pp. 134–144) presents a persuasive, well-reasoned, and biblical response to the "headship" issue. He states that three clues aid the comprehension of 1 Cor. 11:2–16: (1) the different symbolic meaning of man's physical head and woman's physical head; (2) the relevance of head covering for worship; and (3) the significance of worship on earth to the world above. John Stott presents three interpretive positions on "headship": (1) the traditionalist, hardline view that headship equals lordship, which clearly restricts and forbids women from speaking in church or teaching men; (2) the view that sees "any and every concept of masculine headship as being irreconcilable with the unity of the sexes in Christ," bringing up the debate of whether the male "headship" concept is creational or cultural; and (3) the view interpreting headship not as "chief" or "ruler" but rather as "source" or "beginning" and holding that when Paul described man as woman's "origin," it was a reference to priority in creation (*Decisive Issues Facing Christians Today* [Grand Rapids, Mich.: Fleming H. Revell, 1990], pp. 264-281). In a series of articles in *Faith Today* (1993), these positions are debated by Kassian and Badley in one article and by Kassian, Horban, Badley, and Quast in another.

29. Paul Avis, *Eros and the Sacred* (London: SPCK, 1989), pp. vi–ix.

30. Mario Bergner and Mary Pomrening, Misogyny Seminar presented at Restoring Personal Wholeness through Healing Prayer with Leanne Payne (Pittsburgh, April 13–17, 1993), Tapes #10 & #11.

31. See Lewis B. Smedes, *Sex for Christians* (Grand Rapids, Mich.: W. B. Eerdmans, 1976), p. 87.

32. Jensma, "Kohut's Tragic Man," p. 291.

33. Jensma, "Kohut's Tragic Man," p. 290. Biblical references: Eph. 4:24, Col. 3:10 and Rom. 8:28–30.

34. This is not the place to engage at length with the question of the revelation of Jesus and God in masculine terms and the problems this presents, particularly to women who have suffered abuse at the hands of males, other than to state that efforts to sexualize God as female, androgenous, or gynandrous are more reflections of our fallen sexuality than rightful efforts to capture the multidimensional images of God's ungendered qualities of nurturing mother and loving father symbolized in Scripture. Jesus had no name for God but Father, and taught us to address God as Father (Matt. 6:9). See Wolfhart Pannenberg, *An Introduction to Systematic Theology* (Grand Rapids: W. B. Eerdmans, 1991), pp. 31–32, and Elizabeth Achtemeier, "Why God Is Not Mother," cited above.

35. One of the difficulties with Jesus being a human male and Jesus teaching us to call God "Father" is the sense of alienation that some women have felt because men have used this to reinforce patriarchal attitudes to demean women. One feminist option is to leave the patriarchal, androcentric, ecclesiastical systems. This is expressed by Mary Daly's now famous sermon (quoted by Storkey, *London Lectures*, no. 2): "Sisterhood of man cannot happen without a real exodus. We have to go out from the land of our fathers into an unknown place. We can this morning demonstrate our exodus from sexist religion, a break which for many of us has already taken place spiritually. We can give physical expression to our exodus

community that we must go away. We cannot really belong to institutional religion as it exists. It's not good enough to be token preacher; it isn't good enough to have our energies drained and co-opted singing sexist hymns, praying to a male god. Breaking our spirits makes us less than human. The crushing weight of this tradition and this power structure tells us we do not even exist. Let us affirm our faith in ourselves and our transcendence by rising and walking out together." Daphne Hanson affirms this view: "Christianity is irredeemably sexist and by the time you strip away from Christianity what it has done to women's sexuality in particular but to women's spirit in general, then you have nothing left of Christianity to redeem." It is important to listen to what these feminists are saying and attack the systemic gender injustices and inequalities.

36. Lewis Smedes, *Sex for Christians*, p. 87.

37. I am assuming that the reader is familiar with the first half of this chapter and will be familiar with the three point model (creation sexuality, fallen sexuality, and redemption sexuality).

38. Robert Pritchard states that the ten commandments set forth the "basic elements of personal morality—a rejection of the dishonouring of parents, murder, marital infidelity, theft, perjury, and covetousness—at the heart of what it means to be a covenant people, faithful to God.... Anglicanism has consistently held ... that the moral commandments of the Old Testament (but not the ceremonial, civil, or other commandments) continue to be valid for the Christian." *A Wholesome Example: Sexual Morality and the Episcopal Church* (Lexington, Ky.: Bristol Books, 1992), p. 23. Leviticus 18 and 20 indicate unacceptable sexual behaviours: incest, adultery, homosexual relations, and bestiality. References: incest (Lev. 18:6–18; 20:11–12); adultery (Lev. 18:20; 20:10,17,19–20); homosexual relations (Lev. 18:22; 20:13); bestiality (Lev. 18:23; 20:15–16).

39. Smedes, *Sex for Christians*, pp. 81–2.

40. Thielicke, *Theological Ethics*, p. 74.

41. Smedes, *Sex for Christians*, p. 82.

42. Ibid.

43. Ibid., pp. 82–89.

44. *Issues in Human Sexuality: General Synod of the Church of England*, A Statement by the House of Bishops (Harrisburg: Morehouse Publishing, 1991), p. 29. The House of Bishops in England emphasized that unity within a human being necessitates growing "to love every God-given aspect of our human nature ... including the sexual" and that "all elements within an individual need to be in harmony—even the sexual."

45. See Thielicke, *Theological Ethics*, pp. 52–58.

46. Smedes, *Sex for Christians*, p. 134.

47. You may ask how I know that. By deduction: If Jesus had sexual relations when not married, the religious authorities would certainly have accused Jesus of being immoral and breaking the law. But they didn't. Hebrews 4:14-16 says he was without sin.

48. Smedes, *Sex for Christians*, p. 78.

49. Storkey, *London Lectures*, no. 4.

50. Ibid.

51. Avis, *Eros and the Sacred*, p. 143.

52. I encourage the reader to look closely at the words of the Marriage Celebration in both the Book of Common Prayer and the Book of Alternative Services. The BAS directly asks the members of the families of the bride and groom to give their blessing to the marriage, as well as asking all witnesses present to do all in their power "to support and uphold this marriage." I must admit I find that an awesome response every time I witness a marriage.

53. Leanne Payne, *Restoring the Christian Soul through Healing Prayer* (Wheaton, Ill.: Crossway Books, 1991), p. 38.

54. John White, *Eros Defiled: The Christian and Sexual Sin* (Downers Grove, Ill.: InterVarsity Press, 1977) is an excellent response by a psychiatrist to the issue of masturbation.

55. Lambeth Conference Report (1988) as quoted in Anglican Church of Canada, *Guidelines for the Implementation of the National Policy on Sexual Harassment and Sexual Assault Applicable to National Staff and National Volunteers*, accepted by National Executive Council on November 6, 1993.

56. Dan B. Allender's two books, *Bold Love* (Colorado Springs, Col.: NavPress, 1992), co-authored by T. Longman III, and *The Wounded Heart: Hope for Adult Victims of Childhood Sexual Abuse* (Colorado Springs, Col.: NavPress, 1990), are excellent resources for working through the experience of sexual abuse and subsequent forgiveness.

57. *Guidelines for the Implementation of the National Policy.*

CHAPTER

14

"AND SUCH WERE SOME OF YOU"
THE CHURCH AND HOMOSEXUALITY TODAY

PETER C. MOORE

Seated across the table in a Toronto café was a young man in his late twenties who had recently begun attending Little Trinity, the church I serve. Glen was a graduate student who had come east from Vancouver to complete his studies. As dessert was served, he asked if he could share something personal with me. Sensing what was coming, I encouraged him to talk and to try to be as honest as possible.

What unfolded as Glen encapsulated the story of his life was not that atypical in this sexually revolutionized culture in which we live: a distant father, a heightened desire to please, efforts to date followed by growing suspicion of latent homosexuality, encouragement to "come out" by openly gay friends, and finally surrender to the deep impulses within. Glen had spent several years in Toronto's active gay community, had no doubt about his sexual orientation despite having been voted "best potential husband" by the girls in his high school graduating class, and was about to reveal his lifestyle to all his friends and colleagues, fully cognizant of the limitations that disclosure would lead to in later life.

A man to whom he was sexually attracted had befriended him. This man turned out to be a committed Christian. They began discussing religion and the importance of Christ. Glen was urged to read *Mere Christianity* by C. S. Lewis and throughout was challenged to end his current long-term relationship with an older man. He began attending Little Trinity at the suggestion of his new friend who was a member of another church. Meanwhile the gospel began to work its own unique power.

As Glen came out to me he relayed his dissatisfaction with his life and his growing desire to make a break. I listened and empathized as best I could. Later Glen wrote that while he feared condemnation from our meeting, he found grace. I told him that as a follower of Christ he should recognize sin as sin, and put the gay lifestyle behind him. I sought to encourage him to look for possible long-term healing in his sexual orientation, although I offered no illusions as to how easy that might be. I pointed him in the direction of a Christian support ministry for homosexuals,[1] and promised that if he wished to be accountable to me in the coming weeks, I was there for him.

Today, several years later, Glen and his wife—a deeply sensitive woman who married him fully aware of his background—live outside of Toronto, attend an Anglican Church, where they lead a small house church group, and have started a family. "I still have occasional struggles with homosexual feelings," Glen writes, "but it is increasingly further and further behind me every day."

It is incidents like these that make pastoral ministry both difficult and exciting. But should I have said what I did to Glen? Should I rather have encouraged him to accept his homosexuality, learn to live with it as best he could, and hope that in God's time he might find a permanent partner with whom to share his life? Would it have been better had I merely listened, been non-judgmental, and left Glen to garner his own conclusions? Or was I right to call him out of his present lifestyle, and offer him some hope of healing through Jesus Christ? These are the choices confronting those in pastoral ministry today on this thorny issue.

TWO SOLITUDES

I realize that to begin a chapter on homosexuality and the church with Glen's story immediately raises difficulties. It might lead traditional church folk to think that the issue of homosexuality can be settled easily. It cannot. Glen's story is an uncommon one. The great majority of homosexuals outside the church appear to desire no change in either their behaviour or orientation, and increasingly within the church the story is the same. Moreover, others are able to produce quite different stories about homosexuals who, after considerable struggle, have failed to find any release from their homophile orientation and have yearned for the church to give some guidance on how to live as Christians fully accepting who they are. Moreover, there are now within the church articulate advocates who insist that homosexuals who desire to live within committed monogamous relationships should be fully accepted both as "paid up" members and as candidates for all levels of leadership—including the ordained ministry.[2]

The battle of opposing views has heated up in Canada, fuelled by the United Church's decision to make sexual orientation (and practice) no obstacle to full participation and leadership within the church, by the much publicized trial of The Rev. James Ferry, and by the tragic death of the Rev. Warren Eling in Montreal. These and other incidents have made us painfully aware that the struggle for homosexual rights, while not yet a fully global issue, is certainly a Western civilization issue which must be faced in this generation.

The complexity of the issue is heightened by the apparent inability of the two sides to talk rationally with one another. It is presumed that the reason for this is the high stakes involved. Many people have defined the church (as distinct from the world around it) specifically in terms of what behaviour it will tolerate and what it will not. Therefore, while greed, dishonesty, gossip, gluttony, indifference towards the poor, and divorce will be tolerated (though not approved), stealing, drunkenness, adultery, and homosexuality will not. The issue becomes one of identity. Hence, when it is argued that inclusivity should include people whose behaviour many will not tolerate, it goes to the heart of our sense of who we are.

I would argue, however, that the reasons for this lack of communication go far deeper and that neither biblical proof-texting on one side nor compassion for victims of oppression on the other will bring about the necessary engagement essential to see the church through this seriously divisive issue.

THE MEANING OF PERSONS

We are all aware of the enormous changes in sexual consciousness and freedom that have taken place in our culture in comparatively recent years. The Pill (before and after), the legality and frequency of abortion, the availability of pornography, the impact of the film, television, and rock music industries in shaping attitudes towards sexual behaviour, to name just a few, have led to both a new openness to sexual expression and a new tolerance of it (greatly encouraged by the media) among the general populace. Pollsters Bibby and Posterski tell us that 55 percent of Canadian teenagers are sexually active, and comment that "young people of today give every indication of engaging in sex on a level probably never before matched in Canadian history."[3]

What we are not so aware of, however, is the changing understanding of self or personhood that underlies this new openness. Throughout the Western world, since the seventeenth century, the concept of individual rights has been fundamental to our concept of society. This autonomy, widely perceived to have been won from oppressive political and religious authorities, has in our own day been given new resonance and power through its marriage to a new idea of the *self* coming out of the therapeutic revolution.

The *self* is defined subjectively, not by any external qualities, such as role, social status, race, or clan. Inwardness is the only path towards the knowledge of one's identity. Each self is endowed with abilities that in the course of everyday life must be discovered, nourished, and encouraged to grow. Thus the self makes contact with its own depths and finds its satisfaction in expressing this discovery in daily life.[4]

THE MORAL DIFFERENCE

It should become obvious that this new cultural understanding of the self has important moral implications, especially in the area of sexual behaviour. Previously the self was seen in relationship—first to God, and then to those others to whom in the providence of God it was joined: parents, spouse, children, fellow believers, neighbours. Love was "owed" to each of these in special ways, and was a task that, while not always pleasant to fulfil, brought its own deep rewards. Persons were understood to flourish in patterns of relationship that are understood to be normative. Within this order, sex existed to fulfil two main functions: unitive and procreative. It was therefore to be used within the committed relationship of marriage to serve both the individual and the common good.

The new understanding of the self, however, has shifted the ground beneath us. Love, once conceived of as an offering to the other, is now conceived of as a feeling arising from the depths within. Actions, specifically sexual actions, must be limited only by their intention to be benevolent, and by their reception as acts of generosity. Justice must, of course, be served in the respect accorded the rights of others; and the aim of life is the promotion of happiness and the elimination of suffering. Morality has thus shifted from being something inherent in an act itself to being something determined solely by the intentions of the individuals involved.[5]

One could argue that as a corrective to rigorism or legalism, or as a reaction to Victorian prudery, this is not all bad. Most of us now believe that self-love is a prerequisite for other-love. We would also insist (with Jesus) that motive is an essential part of any ethical undertaking. Our acceptance of the idea of rape within marriage is witness to this fact.

But, of course, this new understanding of the self makes the traditional teachings of the churches seem to many of our contemporaries—if not most—to be neither benevolent, just, nor loving and furthermore to be calculated to cause suffering. Those consigned to singleness feel deprived of a perceived right to sexual expression, while those encased in less than ideal marriages feel trapped. If sex is natural, indeed, if sex is inescapably linked to the depths of our being, then why should it not be expressed in contexts where it is perceived to be generous, non-compulsive, and pleasurable?

PANSEXUALITY

We must go one step further in our exploration of the new understanding of the self, which is allied to the deepest streams of modernity, and consider the new science of sexology. Building on the work of Freud, who saw sex as *the* fundamental human drive, of Kinsey, whose two studies in the sexual behaviour of the human male (1948) and female (1953) were enormously influential, and of Masters and Johnson, whose clinical observations of the human sexual response (1979) put the stamp of scientific objectivity on this emerging field, the current leadership of sexologists claim to approach sex in a value-free, neutral way. The most visible sexologists are, of course, pop media personalities Dr. Sue Johanson (Canada) and Dr. Ruth Westheimer (United States). They bring the findings of this field into the living rooms of every North American. But behind them are many psychologists, clinicians, and educators whose work has extended into universities, where sex educators for the public school system are trained, and institutes to which government agencies look for guidelines on policy matters.

Despite the impression of objectivity, it appears that those who set the pace in this field are rooted in what Aldous Huxley called the "perennial philosophy," a monist understanding of the cosmos that C. S. Lewis argued was the natural religion of humankind. Unfortunately, an exploration of this is beyond the scope of this chapter.[6] But what we can be certain of—thanks to the critical work of Dr. Judith Reisman and Mr. Edward Eichel, whose book *Kinsey, Sex and Fraud* received high praise from, among others, the British Medical Association—is that the leaders in this field are operating from a pansexual understanding of human nature in which gender is a subset under sexual attainment. That is to say, everyone is essentially bisexual, and orgasm is identical whether the sexual partner is of the same or opposite gender.

The means whereby these conclusions were drawn involved highly questionable methods that would undoubtedly be classified as criminal in any court of law. Hundreds of children, for instance, from two months of age to fifteen years, were subjected to adult sexual stimulation to the point, in some cases, of violent convulsions, gasping, groaning, screaming, and an abundance of tears, obviously under restraint, and often for hours at a time until orgasm brought temporary relief— only to have the procedure begin again! Such data is elaborately detailed in chapter five of Kinsey's study, *Sexual Behavior in the Human Male*.[7] This would be almost too painful to recount in a chapter like this were it not for the fact that Kinsey is so often cited as the authority behind the biological determinism which sees that there is no inherent sexual behaviour appropriate to a male or a female. He taught that what is forever seeking fulfilment, thrusting upwards into the conscious from deep wells in the unconscious, is an undifferentiated sexual drive.

This new knowledge, or so it is presented, when paired with modernity's focus on the autonomous individual self, leads to the conclusion that social constraints that hinder the flow of sexual energy through us, or seek to channel them in one direction to the exclusion of another, are evil. Feelings, having become the final arbiters of right and wrong, effectively sever sex from relationships where it was presumed there would be a mutual sharing of lives. Sex is thereby freed from its calling to be, in biblical terminology, sacramental, both of our creation in the divine image as male and female and of our redemption as rooted in Christ's love for the church.[8] Earle Fox opines, "It might well be that the Freud-Kinsey-Masters-Johnson development of sexology, more than any other single factor, [has] contributed to the virtual demolition of the Judeo-Christian sense of sexual morality in America, and perhaps in western culture."[9]

THE HOMOSEXUAL DEBATE

All this may seem very far from the current debate on homosexuality in the church. But it governs the terms of the debate, at least from one side, more than might appear, and it certainly hinders ordinary church people from grasping what the church has been saying about sexuality over the centuries or from understanding why norms that prevailed in a culture far removed from our own should be binding today.

Some would like us to confine our discussion to the clear-cut cases of monogamous homosexuals (both gay and lesbian) who seek the church's blessing on their love and in some cases believe they have heard a call to ministry. Unfortunately, the issue is not so simple, for there is by no means unanimity among advocates of the homosexual cause that the issue should be so confined. Some, like Carter Heyward of the Episcopal Divinity School, and the Rev. Robert Williams, a gay priest ordained by Bishop John S. Spong, believe that monogamy is neither healthy nor necessarily moral. Williams, until his death from AIDS, advocated multiple partners, and Heyward suggests marriage be replaced by "sexual friendships."[10]

Clearly they, and others, are arguing from a fundamentally different ground than the church has done throughout its history. The linkage between their assumptions and those of the contemporary culture as outlined above are unmistakable. They presume a new paradigm in which reality is no longer seen as divided into distinct categories in hierarchical relationships, but interwoven into an undifferentiated whole. The old polarities of masculine and feminine, subject and object, God and the cosmos, even good and evil, are indissolubly joined together, and life is viewed as a process rather than an order.[11]

The appeal of this personalist ethic is three-fold. It speaks to the hope so many in our alienating culture have that the private sphere can be intensely meaningful. Here is where people really touch each other. Secondly, it turns the spotlight on those areas where the church's traditional teaching on sex appears not to be working. Christian divorces—even clergy divorces—witness to the unequal, oppressive, and even exploitative relationships the church has countenanced. And thirdly, it appears to champion the biblical language of love and justice.[12]

But it is not without its own inherent contradictions. Once traditional categories for defining the self have been abandoned in favour of what McGill philosopher Charles Taylor calls the "expressivist self," with its roots in Descartes, Locke, Rousseau, and Montaigne. There is no guarantee that the "self" has any concrete reality. Detached from theism, Taylor argues, the self no longer corresponds to any order (outward or inward) and is purely a product of self-creation. This is why the "personalist ethic" may be an oxymoron, since the idea that there are any moral qualities to which the self must conform presupposes a reference point outside the self—that is, an order of some sort. Those who live on the far side of this destructuring project are left with the utopian hope that, freed from past oppressions, the self will choose ethical (that is, healthy and life-affirming) forms of expression. But this is based on a view of human nature that neither the Bible nor history support.[13]

A good telling of this personalist ethic may be found in *To Live According to Our Nature*, a 137-page monograph self-published by Bruce Pellegrin of the Atlantic School of Theology in Halifax.[14] Pellegrin, in a spasm of reactive apologetic, uncritically follows the simple formula that homosexual relations are to be judged on the same basis as heterosexual ones: are they loving, mutual, respectful, healthy, and so on? This leads him to draw a one-to-one parallel between "committed long-term homosexual" relations and "exclusive life-long heterosexual" ones without seeing the fundamental difference. Pellegrin presents his personalist ethic as the only legitimate Christian one, sweeping aside the classical Anglican point of view, which, in contrast to the Roman Catholic one, has hesitated to define ethics in very specific terms, rather preferring broad principles that leave details to individual consciences. Hence, when Pellegrin calls the Anglican Church to come up with a code of acceptable gay behaviour, he is parting from the Anglican tradition and inviting the church to enter where it has historically stayed away—the bedrooms of the faithful. While there clearly are forms of sexual abuse within marriage, the church has rightly, I think, resisted the invitation to spell out in detail just what forms of erotic expression are acceptable and unacceptable. Rather, the church trusts the individual consciences of those involved to sort this out within the context of a loving covenant. Thankfully, it is the context of marriage that the church is primarily concerned with, not whether or not a given sexual act is loving, healthy, mutual, and so on. How could it begin to judge such things?[15]

THE BIBLICAL ETHOS

It should be clear, given the popularity and widespread acceptance of this new personalist ethic within the church, why a straightforward rebuttal of it by use of biblical texts will not carry the day. This is not to say that biblical texts should not be normative. Indeed, they are considered normative by every branch of the church and especially our own, which officially recognizes Scripture as the supreme authority in matters of faith and morals. What this simply recognizes is the fact that even if it were proven beyond a shadow of a doubt that the Bible condemns homosexuality—a viewpoint surprisingly still questioned by some—not all will be persuaded.

For us this raises the deeply troubling question of how the church is to find and submit to the mind of Christ if a major portion of it refuses to find that "mind" where the church has historically found it—in the Scriptures, interpreted by tradition and sanctified reason. Many view "experience," which they understand as the collective reflection of Christians seeking to live out their faith in relation to contemporary culture, as taking precedence over Scripture in those areas where Scripture is said to be an inadequate or flawed witness.[16] Much effort is expended and a great deal of ink is spilled attempting to separate the biblical prohibitions from our modern context—by saying either that the biblical prohibitions are not really prohibitions or that our context differs so drastically from the biblical one that a bridge cannot be built between them.[17]

We are told that there is very little actually said about homosexuality in the Bible—and nothing said by Jesus himself. Of course, the argument from silence is notoriously weak, especially where those passages that do speak of homosexuality do so with a consistent voice and emphasis.

The stories of Sodom (Gen. 19) and Gibeah (Judg. 19) clearly mention homosexuality disapprovingly. The Holiness Code in Leviticus (chapters 18 and 20) considers homosexuality an "abomination"—using a strong Hebrew word that, in context, indicated that the practice was not just cultically unclean (as some have maintained) but a high offence against God and humanity. Incest was also an abomination, as was the use of uneven weights. Neither bore any special relation to pagan cults.

St. Paul's mention of homosexuality (including lesbianism) in Romans 1 is, of course, the classic New Testament text and has therefore been subject to great efforts at reinterpretation. Some have said that Paul is not condemning true homosexuals, only those heterosexuals who engage in homosexual activity. But they are assuming that homosexual orientation, as opposed to homosexual practice, was a known phenomenon in the ancient world. By this they read a modern understanding of homosexuality back into the New Testament and engage in a classic form of eisegesis. Others focus on the phrase "against nature" (verse 27) and seek to limit Paul's understanding of "nature" either to the human natures of the people involved or to the views of what was considered natural in the society of his day.[18] Two arguments tell against these. First, the context clearly takes us back to the creation and fall where what is natural and unnatural is governed by Paul's intuitive conception of what ought to be in the world as designed by God. And second, Paul is not dealing in Romans 1–3 with the personal biographies of individual sinners, but with the human condition as a whole in its rebellion against God. The passage, then, refers to a breach of universal norms.[19]

Beyond these passages are references in I Corinthians 6 to *porneia*, which seems to be a catch-all phrase for irregular genital contact. Vancouver philologist P. D. M. Turner believes this most likely included male commercial and ritual prostitution.[20] *Porneia* is a word Jesus uses, according to Matthew (5:32; 19:9). Also *malakoi* and *arsenokoites* (literally, "soft" and "one who lies with men") most likely refer to those who play the female and male parts, respectively, in homosexual intercourse. Paul apparently composed the latter word himself to tie his list of vices in with the Septuagint (the Greek translation of the Old Testament), particularly by the Holiness Code in Leviticus 18 and 20.[21]

It is hard to resist the conclusion, even on the basis of this brief survey, that the biblical witness taken as a whole strongly disapproves of homosexual behaviour.[22]

THE DESEXUALIZATION OF GOD

But it is important to place this essentially negative assessment within the overall positive view that the Bible has of heterosexual relationships, including marriage and sexual love. Nor in this respect was the Bible merely a reflection of its times. The ancient world, according to Greenberg, was heavily influenced by the images of deities who were highly sexual. Seduction, polygamy, adultery, abduction, masturbation, rape, and homosexuality were all attributed to various deities in Egyptian, Babylonian, Hindu, Greek, and Roman religion. Sexuality therefore infused virtually all of society. Homosexuality was tolerated as a concession to the polymorphous sexual nature of men in particular and was widespread. Hardly an ancient society—from the ancient Near East, Greece and Rome, to pre-Columbian Americas, to China and the Arab world—was without its significant expression.

Within Hebrew society, however, it was not tolerated.[23] Why? Because the Hebrew ideal was monogamous marriage.[24] To preserve this ideal, all forms of nonmarital sex were considered deviant. Women and men were made for each other, according to Genesis 2, and in their complementarity they would discover something of what it meant to be created in the image of God, according to Genesis 1. The creation of woman from man's rib, while often misused to indicate submission, can quite naturally mean its opposite, according to University of Toronto Old Testament scholar Stanley D. Walters. Since the rib cage protects the essential organs of heart and lungs, and the muscles of the diaphram, the rib can be seen as the bone that draws breath, and therefore the creation of Eve "establishes an intimate, life-giving, and lively reciprocity between man and woman" that could be shared by no other created being.[25]

The value placed on this basic unit of marriage, reinforced by its linkage with the divine covenant as the prophets constantly reiterated,[26] was responsible not only for the conviction that the family (rather than the nation or the individual) was the most basic unit of society but also for the dignity accorded to women. It is well known that when homosexuality flourishes, as it did in ancient Greece, the role of women declines, and an idealized concept of man becomes the focus of intellectual and physical activities.

Jewish apologist Dennis Prager strongly argues that Western civilization owes its strength to the sexual revolution initiated by Judaism and later carried forward by Christianity. Only by the constant delaying of gratification and a rechanneling of natural instincts was Western civilization in its Judaeo-Christian aspect made possible.

> To a world which divided human sexuality between penetrator and penetrated, Judaism said, "You are wrong—sexuality is to be divided between male and female." To a world which saw women as baby producers unworthy of romantic and sexual attention, Judaism said, "You are wrong—women must be the sole focus of men's erotic love." To a world which said that sensual feelings and physical beauty were life's supreme values, Judaism said, "You are wrong—ethics and holiness are the supreme values."[27]

Prager seems to be echoing J. D. Unwin's thesis, as set out in his monumental study, *Sex and Culture*. Unwin claimed that "any human society is free to choose either to display great energy or to enjoy sexual freedom; the evidence is that it cannot do both for more than one generation."[28]

COMPULSION OR CHOICE

The attempt to undo this revolution, which has received significant support from within the church in our day, has involved a paradigm shift from the idea of the self as existing for God first, others next, and self last, to one which places the needs of the self at the top of the agenda. It has been buttressed by the growing evidence that sexual orientation may not be a choice but rather a given. Many homophiles confess to never having had sexual feelings other than towards their own gender. Studies attempting to show a biological predisposition to homosexuality have received wide publicity in the media while studies showing that these same people may have had a prevalence of disordered familial backgrounds have not. The verdict is still out on whether, or to what degree, there might be a determining factor, although it seems certain that without environmental encouragement there is no evidence that even those with genetic, hormonal, or neurological predispositions would turn out exclusively homosexual. Otherwise, how would we account for the disparity in numbers of active homosexuals and the great variety in types of homosexual expression that exist in different eras and in different parts of the globe? Moreover, many feminist scientists, in reaction to how Darwinian theory has been used to reinforce prejudices against women, are now declaring that "biological predisposition does not mean biological destiny," and that "inherited characteristics [can] be deeply modified through learning, environment or conscious decisions."[29]

There must be a continued willingness on the part of all, especially within the church where we believe that all truth is God's truth, to confront the objective data of science. However, there should be a reticence to whitewash the moral question simply because it may someday be proven that there is a biologic predisposition to homosexuality. We have known for years that some people are biologically disposed to alcoholism and mental illness, and while we now see these as tragedies rather than sin, we still believe people can and should seek change. Besides, can a genetic or psychological explanation for a person's condition ever say whether that condition is good or bad? Someday we may even find a scientific cause of criminal behaviour. Behind much of the research for a biologic cause of homosexuality, and certainly behind the media coverage it receives, is the assumption that anyone doomed either to live life in denial of their basic sexual orientation or to seek a change that may be impossible or extremely difficult and invariably partial is being deprived of their essential humanness.

ESSENTIAL HUMANNESS

For the church to find its way through the emotionally charged mine-field of the contemporary debate, it must begin at the beginning with a fresh look at biblical anthropology. This is important for two reasons. First, the personalist ethic described above is fuelled by the determinist assumptions of the modern field of sexology. If an undifferentiated sexual drive lies at the root of our natures, and if discovering and expressing the depth of our being is essential to our personhood, then it is a foregone conclusion where the argument over homosexuality will end. Second, it is the experience of so many homosexuals that a confused identity has led to a disordered lifestyle. How persons see themselves, including how others see them (parents, friends, the culture as a whole), influences greatly how they will behave.

A biblical anthropology will inevitably have its roots in Genesis, especially in the two accounts of creation: the cosmic story in chapter one, and the human story in chapter two. The two were joined by Jesus, who in Mark 10:6–7 takes phrases from both to argue for the sacredness of the marriage bond. A reading of these passages raises the vital question: What does it mean to be made in the image of God? Does it have something to do with gender?

MALE AND FEMALE

Helmut Thielicke, building on the work of Barth and others, believes that in Genesis, sex differentiation, while not exhaustive of the image of God, is certainly contained in it. "Sex differentiation ... is one of the media in which, through which, and despite which ... [our relationship with God] is realized."[30] This seems an obvious deduction from Genesis 1:27, whatever the literary relationship is between the three phrases that comprise this verse in our Bibles. Gender existed in the mind of God—that is, as maleness and femaleness—even though, if Scripture is our guide, God neither has a gender nor is androgynous (the latter sometimes taken as justification for the ascription of both *Mother* and *Father* to God).

It seems, then, that both complementarity and differentness are essential to our natures, according to the Bible. Since both of these exist prior to the experience of sex (chapter 2), they therefore cannot be linked solely to its expression. The expression of genital sex within heterosexual monogamy, as the Bible reiterates, is highly valued both for its physical and spiritual import. But it is not essential to our natures. What is essential is the expression of our distinctness and our unity as male and female in relation to God and to one another.

We must not hesitate to point to the differences between the genders out of fear of transgressing the boundaries of political correctness. These gender differences do not necessarily determine specific roles either in the family or society. However, they are well documented in scientific research.[31] While we must take care not to misuse gender differences to stereotype and stigmatize others, we can celebrate them as part of the diversity of our creator.

Through the fall, the relationship between the male and the female was distorted, but it will one day be totally healed. Marriage serves as a partial symbol of this healing. As John Stott writes, it is a kind of reunion of two persons who were originally one but become alien to each other, and then, through the sexual encounter of marriage, come together again.[32] But marriage points beyond itself to something greater—the ultimate healing of our painful divisions through the love of God in Christ. It is in the Christian community where we see that unity in the Spirit that witnesses to this ultimate togetherness. Marriage is thus not to be romanticized, for the reconciliation that husbands and wives enjoy is always partial and must be received as both gift and task.

A REDEMPTIVE PARADIGM

The reason, then, why the church should not bless homosexual unions or ordain those who, by word and deed, advocate homosexual behaviour is that it is called to bless only those relationships capable of pointing to the ultimate reconciliation that God's redemption will accomplish.[33] Even when the church honours celibacy, it assumes, particularly in Roman Catholic teaching, a marital metaphor, for those pledged to celibacy are married either to Christ or to the church.

Those in spiritual leadership must be wholesome examples to the flock, and signs of the healing possible between men and women.[34] Those who, like Jesus, remain single are capable of witnessing to this reconciliation between the sexes through the quality and purity of their relationships with the opposite sex. Nevertheless, familial life will remain the principal place where this reconciliation is demonstrated. For this reason, probably the best place to counter the pansexual drift of modern society (whose pop-expression is "unisex") is in the homes of God's people. Healthy, loving homes where parents manifest to their children the reconciling power of Christ, and where they are emotionally available to those children, may be the best insurance we can provide against the development of disordered sexual patterns. Conversely, it appears that the increase in single-parent families, which because of their tragedy deserve all the support the local church can provide, makes our society more prone to increasing numbers of people expressing homosexual orientation and behaviour.

Those who feel the pull of homo-erotic feelings should be called not only to chastity (or fidelity if they are married) but to involvement in supportive fellowships where men and women discover, through common discipleship to Christ, their true identities. Pat Allan, Director of New Directions for Life, Toronto, and Vice-President of Exodus, North America, has helped hundreds of people come out of the gay lifestyle. She says that homosexuals need to gain a new sense of their God-given identity, freed from the lies they have bought into from other people, and even from their own inner voice—for both ultimately come from the "Father of lies" himself. "Names do hurt us, despite the often heard children's maxim," she says. "To be the man or woman God wants us to be, we must draw close to God and remember that in his love he will bring to completion the work he has started." Allan offers hope to many homosexuals, being a former lesbian herself, but counsels that gaining a new identity requires patient hard work as well as the healing power of Jesus Christ.

A redemptive model will hold out hope of healing for the homosexual, but not always in the sense of complete sexual reorientation. For as long as we are still "in the flesh," most healings will be partial, and all will be temporal. But since gender precedes genital sexual activity in our understanding of true humanness, we will look for healing in those relationships that have affected and been affected by sexual disorder. Many homosexuals have discovered significant healing in attitudes towards parents and vice versa, and many have derived new strength from the discovery that tender relationships with the opposite sex are made newly possible by grace.

Beyond that, we will encourage one another with the knowledge that denial, however painful it may seem at the time, serves a higher purpose in the economy of God. To say "no" to one form of behaviour is coupled with saying "yes" to another, writes Philip Turner:

> To say "yes" to life in the Spirit is in fact the only way to end self-deceptive denial and harmful repression. The Spirit of God is the Spirit of truth and life rather than repression and denial. It calls for us to present ourselves at

each moment to God as we are, with as much knowledge of ourselves as we can muster, with all our desires and intentions exposed, and in so doing ask for guidance, help, and the transfiguration of our lives. God will not answer yes to many of the desires presented, but in saying no he will say yes to deeper desires and deeper loves—both for God and for the men and women with whom God has surrounded us.[35]

As for our attitude towards those who, despite all our urging, still feel compelled to pursue overt homosexual activity, and who wish to be considered brothers and sisters in the Christian fellowship, we must take great care not to fall into the pharisaic trap of thinking of ourselves without sin. Sin is a bondage that holds us all in its grip and which only the grace of God in Jesus Christ can and does break. Obviously we must confess any lingering homophobia, in the sense of an irrational fear or loathing of homosexuals. But such a confession must be accompanied by a willingness to meet, talk to, befriend, and, as far as possible, walk with homosexuals. One of the great needs homosexuals have is for real friends in the straight world.

Within the Christian fellowship, unity is discovered at the foot of the cross, and if that is to have more than a sentimental meaning, it must include—at least—the collective admission that we are all sinners and that one of the most common forms of sin is self-deception. Therefore the homosexual who declines the offer of healing (assuming it is given with love and understanding) is obligated to persuade the fellowship that he or she can do no other, and that he or she lives by the same grace and answers to the same holy calling. He or she must understand why the church cannot bless same-sex unions or ordain those who practice them, and must receive that verdict with the same accepting spirit by which he or she desires to be accepted.

Acceptance of the Christian homosexual who is not pledged to chastity will be similar to the acceptance of the Christian alcoholic who is not pledged to sobriety. They will always be treated with loving understanding but will not be invited to share in the church's leadership nor be put in positions where their particular weaknesses will be unduly tested. Ideally they should be linked with someone of their own sex who is more mature in the faith and who can provide wise counsel and support while consistently maintaining biblical standards.

The homosexual must be helped to see that, within the Christian fellowship, no one's value is determined by his or her level of sanctification any more than it is by the good works that he or she does. Homosexuals are as valuable as heterosexuals, because all together belong to the world for which Christ died. However, the church is commissioned to call one and all to the wholeness that is our birthright as males and females made in the image of God. And the church serves to proclaim the grace by which we are all enabled to begin that journey.

SUGGESTED READING

Richard B. Hays, "Relations Natural and Unnatural: A Response to John Boswell's Exegesis of Romans 1," *Journal of Religious Ethics*, Vol. 14/1 (Spring 1986).

Donald L. Faris, *The Homosexual Challenge: A Christian Response to an Age of Sexual Politics* (Markham: Faith Today Publications, 1993).

House of Bishops of the General Synod of the Church of England, *Issues in Human Sexuality* (London: Church House, 1991).

Laity of Little Trinity Church, *A Discussion Paper on Homosexuality*, submitted to the Task Force on Lesbian and Gay People in the Anglican Church, Diocese of Toronto, 1993. Obtainable c/o Little Trinity Church, 425 King St., E., Toronto, ON, M5A 1L3.

Robert W. Prichard, ed., *A Wholesome Example: Sexual Morality and the Episcopal Church* (Lexington: Bristol House, 1993).

ENDNOTES

1. New Directions for Life, P.O. Box 1078, Station F, Toronto, ON, M4Y 2T7. A partial listing of healing and support groups for homosexuals is found in an appendix of Denyse O'Leary, *A Crisis of Understanding: Homosexuality and the Canadian Church* (Burlington, Ont.: Welch, 1988).

2. See John S. Spong, *Living in Sin?* (San Francisco: Harper and Row, 1988). See also an analysis and critique of the United Church of Canada's *Toward a Christian Understanding of Sexual Orientation, Lifestyles and Ministry* in *A Crisis of Understanding*, op cit, pp. 35–50. The Human Affairs Commission Report to the 1991 General Convention of the Episcopal Church recommended developing liturgies to bless same-sex unions and to ordain sexually active homosexual persons to Holy Orders.

3. Reginald Bibby and Donald Posterski, *Teen Trends: A Nation in Motion* (Toronto: Stoddart, 1992), pp. 38–9.

4. For a fuller discussion of this new concept of the self see David A. Scott "Traditional Sexual Ethics: Making a Case" in *A Wholesome Example: Sexual Morality in the Episcopal Church*, Robert W. Prichard, ed. (Lexington: Bristol, 1993), pp. 107–118.

5. See Philip Turner, "Sex and the Single Life," *First Things*, No. 33 (May 1993), pp. 15–21.

6. See F. Earle Fox, *Biblical Sexuality and the Battle for Science* (Emmaus Ministries, P.O. Box 21, Ambridge, PA 15003), for a full discussion and evaluation of the work of Kinsey and other sexologists.

7. (Philadelphia: W. B. Saunders Co., 1948).

8. See Genesis 1:27 and Ephesians 5:32.

9. Fox, *Biblical Sexuality*, p. 140.

10. Prichard, *A Wholesome Example*, p. 125–6.

11. An effort to justify panentheism as an inherently Christian idea may be found in Urban T. Holmes III, *What is Anglicanism?* (Toronto: Anglican Book Centre, 1982), pp. 27–32.

12. Prichard, *A Wholesome Example*, p. 112.

13. See a review of Taylor's *Sources of the Self: The Making of the Modern Identity* (Harvard) by Gilbert Meilaender of Oberlin University in *First Things* (August/September 1990). See also Anthony Giddens, *The Transformation of Intimacy: Sexuality, Love and Eroticism in Modern Societies* (Cambridge: Polity Press, 1992). Arguing for a "plastic sexuality" whereby through life choices people construct an answer to the question

"Who am I?", Giddens admits: "Nobody knows if sexual relations will become a wasteland of impermanent liasons, marked by emotional antipathy as much as by love, and scarred by violence. There are good grounds for optimism in each case, but in a culture that has given up providentialism, futures have to be worked for against a background of acknowledged risk" (p. 196). This is precisely why the church must resist the personalist argument which Taylor calls "insidious" and Meilaender, "satanic."

14. V. B. H. Pellegrin, *To Live According to Our Nature* (R.R. #2, Newport, NS, B0N 2A0), pp. 96–7.

15. Robert W. Prichard writes: "There is no specific canon condemning sexual relations outside of heterosexual marriage for clergy, because [Anglican] canons have never been an exhaustive code of behavior. [Anglicans] ... generally do not follow such examples as Roman Law or the Napoleonic Code. They do not construct intricate systems of morality and ethics that cover every eventuality. Rather, in the English common law tradition, [Anglicans] have been content with a few basic principles, a body of laws drafted to deal with a few difficult circumstances, and an accumulated history of judicial decisions." *A Wholesome Example*, pp. 49–50.

16. Arguing for a reinterpretation of biblical passages traditionally held to be against homosexual practice, "Homosexuality—is it wrong? Does the Bible tell me so?", a discussion resource produced by the Unit on Human Rights for the Anglican Church of Canada (June 1992), says: "New traditions" (about slavery, divorce, etc.) contravene certain biblical imperatives, [therefore] many would say our understanding of the Bible's truth has evolved out of our experience, sound reasoning, and the consideration of new awareness. The evolution, they would argue, is towards a fuller understanding of the Gospel. They would even say that belief in a compassionate God of love *demands* that we continue to reinterpret some traditional teachings—to allow love to be more fully expressed—and that this is the work of the Holy Spirit in our time."

17. Examples of both attempts are found in Pim Pronk's *Against Nature: Types of Moral Argumentation Regarding Homosexuality* (Grand Rapids: Eerdmans, 1993) [Dutch Reformed]; Pamela Dickey Young, *Theological Reflections on Ministry and Sexual Orientation* (Burlington: Trinity, 1990) [United Church of Canada]; L. W. Countryman *Dirt, Greed and Sex* (Philadelphia: Fortress, 1988) [Episcopal Church, U.S.A.]; and J. J. McNeill, *The Church and the Homosexual* (Kansas City: Sheed Andrews and McMeel, 1978) [Roman Catholic].

18. John Boswell in *Christianity, Social Tolerance, and Homosexuality* (Chicago: University of Chicago Press, 1980) asserts that there is no clear condemnation of homosexual acts in Romans 1, only a recognition that these acts are "extraordinary or peculiar." He denies that Paul had a concept of "natural law" because such an idea was not developed for a thousand years. But Richard B. Hays gives examples that show that the common Hellenistic polemic against homosexual acts found in many Greek writers (Dio Chrysostom, Plutarch, and Plato), and later reflected in the Hellenistic Jewish condemnation of homosexuality in the first century (Josephus and Philo), clearly identified "nature" with the created order. Moreover, says Hays, Boswell completely ignores the plain sense of the meaning of Romans 1 which places "explicit reference to homosexuality in direct parallelism with the 'base and improper conduct' which the vice list of 1:29–31 elaborates." *Journal Of Religious Ethics*, Vol. 14/1 (Spring 1986), pp. 192–199.

19. P. D. M. Turner in her unpublished paper entitled "Biblical Texts Relevant to

Homosexual Orientation and Practice: Some Notes on Philology and Interpretation."

20. David F. Greenberg cites several scholars who challenge John Boswell's claim that *arsenokoitai* referred only to male prostitutes and who say that this was a neologism created because the Greeks did not have a word for homosexuality—only specific homosexual relations. *The Construction of Homosexuality* (Chicago: University of Chicago Press, 1988), pp. 213–4.

21. It is regrettable that Bruce Pellegrin (*To Live According to Our Nature*) treats this classical passage so briefly, echoing only the views of John Boswell without taking into consideration the extensive rebuttals of his work by contemporary scholars like Hays and Greenberg.

22. A summary of the conclusions of others may be found in the position paper on homosexuality prepared by the laity of Little Trinity Church as a submission to the Task Force on Lesbian and Gay People in the Diocese of Toronto (c/o Little Trinity Church, 425 King St. E., Toronto, ON, M5A 1L3).

23. Greenberg (*Construction of Homosexuality*) believes that the Hebrews had no prohibition against homosexuality prior to the Babylonian exile in 586 BC, save as it was associated with pagan religious cults. But he overlooks the possibility that one of the reasons for official opposition to these cults may have been their tolerance of (male and female) prostitution (p. 441). Following Martin Noth, he also argues that Leviticus is a post-exilic document containing later additions to earlier lists of prohibitions. He includes those against homosexuality, although his evidence for this is thin (pp. 190–5). Generalizing on his findings, he says that early civilizations began to legislate against homosexuality when religion shifted from the veneration of deities who are immanent in the world to the worship of transcendent gods (pp. 182–3).

24. See Dennis Prager, "Judaism, Homosexuality and Civilization," *Ultimate Issues*, Vol. 6, No. 2 (April/June 1990; 6020 Washington Blvd., Culver City, CA 90232).

25. Many scholars have noted that the Sumerian *TI* means both "life" and "rib." Walters believes that the original polyvalence of "rib" was known to the writer. In any event, if in the Old Testament woman was made from man, in St. Paul's letters, it is man that is made from woman (1 Cor. 11:12). Personal correspondence with Dr. Walters. Used with permission.

26. Isa. 54:5; 62:1–5; Jer. 2:2; 31:32; Ezek. 16:23; Hos. 1–3.

27. Prager, "Judaism, Homosexuality and Civiliation."

28. Oxford University Press, 1934.

29. See "A Little Elbow Room, Please, Dr. Darwin," a *New York Times* feature article about a conference at the University of Georgia on Evolutionary Biology and Feminism. (Reprinted in the *Globe and Mail*, July 2, 1994).

30. In *Theological Ethics*, Vol. 3 (Grand Rapids, Mich.: Eerdmans, 1964), p. 6.

31. See Stephen B. Clark, *Man and Woman in Christ* (Ann Arbor: Servant, 1980), pp. 371–465. See also Corinne Hutt, *Males and Females* (Baltimore: Penguin, 1972).

32. John Stott, *Issues Facing Christians Today* (Basingstoke: Marshalls, 1984), p. 311.

33. This is why the "blessing of the hounds" in parishes that serve the country gentry is a charade.

34. 1 Tim. 3:12; Titus 1:6; Eph. 5:21–33.

35. "Sex and the Single Life," *First Things*, No. 33 (May 1993), p. 20.

Chapter 15

CHRISTIAN HOLINESS
A HOMILY

REGINALD HOLLIS

HOLY GOD, HOLY PEOPLE

We regularly proclaim our belief in the "one holy, catholic and apostolic church," but do we seek the holiness we proclaim?

Seeking holiness is clearly an expectation of the early church as portrayed in the New Testament. St. Peter writes, "As he who called you is holy, be holy yourselves in all your conduct; for it is written, 'You shall be holy, for I am holy'" (1 Pet. 1:15,16). He is affirming the old covenant as set out in Leviticus 29:2: "You shall be holy for I the Lord your God am holy." Peter goes on to affirm the Christian community as a holy priesthood (1 Pet. 2:5), and a holy nation (1 Pet. 2:9). The church, as the new Israel, is to fulfil the calling given to the people of the covenant God made with Abraham. Israel was chosen for responsibility: "The whole earth is mine, but you shall be for me a priestly kingdom and a holy nation" (Ex. 19:6). That holiness came from their relationship with God, but in the early days much of the holiness was expressed in cultic observances, including adherence to food rules. Such observances kept the people from pagan religions. However, loyalty to God clearly involved an ethical element: "You will remember all the commandments of the Lord and do them, and not follow the lust of your own heart and your own eyes" (Num. 15:39). The prophets associated the holy God with righteousness: "The Lord of Hosts is exalted by justice, and the Holy God shows himself holy by righteousness" (Isa. 5:16). Jeremiah sees this devotion to the Lord's way as a sign of holiness: "I remember the devotion of your youth, your love as a bride, how you followed me in the wilderness.... Israel was holy to the Lord, the first fruits of his harvest" (Jer. 2:3). Habakkuk writes concerning the Holy One, "Your eyes are too pure to behold evil, and you cannot look on wrongdoing" (Hab. 1:13).

HOLINESS AS A GIFT

To define the holiness of God is beyond the limitations of our minds, just as it is beyond our human comprehension to define fully the love of God. God is holy. God is love. We are finite and God is infinite. It is as people have encountered the holiness of God that they have known their humanity. The prophet Isaiah had a vision in which he saw the seraphs calling to one another, "Holy, holy, holy is the Lord of hosts; the whole earth is full of his glory." His reaction was, "Woe is me! I am lost, for I am a man of unclean lips, and I live among a people of unclean lips; yet my eyes have seen the King, the Lord of hosts!" (Isa. 6:3–5).

Visions like Isaiah's have not been a common experience for men and women. What is a common experience is that when men and women become deeply aware of God in his holiness, they also know their unworthiness and their need for forgiveness. John Henry Newman expressed this: "As God's grace elicits our faith, so His holiness stirs our fear, and His glory kindles our love."[1]

It is no wonder that, for St. Paul, there is a strong association of righteousness with holiness. Yet, the cry for forgiveness and the seeking of righteousness are not just a response to an awareness of God's holiness. For Paul, it is a righteousness with its foundation in the work of Christ: "Christ loved the church and gave himself up for her in order to make her holy by cleansing her with the washing of water by the word, so as to present the church to himself in splendour, without a spot or wrinkle or anything of the kind—yes, so that she may be holy and without blemish" (Eph. 5:26). It is Christ's death that deals with our humanity, and enables us to relate to God in his holiness: "By a single offering he has perfected for all time those who are sanctified" (Heb. 10:10).[2] St. Peter writes his first Epistle to the exiles "who have been chosen and destined by God the Father and sanctified by the Spirit to be obedient to Jesus Christ and to be sprinkled with his blood" (1 Pet. 1:2). It follows from the emphasis on Christ's death that holiness is not primarily achieved but is received.

It is of the utmost importance to hold on to this truth that holiness is received. Sanctity is not primarily achieved by working to be holy. This is a basic principle laid down by many spiritual guides. The English writer Martin Thornton explained, "In Christianity fact precedes feeling; what we do depends on what we are."[3] The Bible teacher Oswald Chambers emphasized time and again in his devotional writings that sanctification is God's action in Christ, and that only from that action can people hope to grow in holiness of life. He wrote:

> Sanctification is not drawing from Jesus the power to be holy; it is drawing from Jesus the holiness that was manifested in Him, and He manifests it in me. Sanctification is an impartation, not an imitation. In Jesus Christ is the perfection of everything, and the mystery of sanctification is that all the perfections of Jesus are at my disposal, and slowly and surely I begin to live a life of ineffable order and sanity and holiness "kept by the power of God."[4]

THE LORD'S INDWELLING PRESENCE

It is because God is holy, and because this holy God dwells with his people, that his people become holy. The high and lofty one "who inhabits eternity, whose name is Holy, says: 'I dwell in the high and holy place, and also with those who are contrite and humble in spirit'" (Isa. 57:15). His dwelling with his people is declared in Emmanuel, God with us. So Paul can write, "In him the whole structure is joined together and grows into a holy temple in the Lord; in whom you also are built together in the Spirit into a dwelling place for God" (Eph. 2:21). The presence of the Holy Spirit sanctifies. Paul knows that his ministry is dependent on that, "so that the offering of the Gentiles may be acceptable, sanctified by the Holy Spirit" (Rom. 15:16).

The indwelling presence of Christ in the believer is what brings a new status, a new being. Baptism sacramentally expresses the death of the old being so that "just as Christ was raised from the dead by the glory of the Father, so we too might walk in newness of life" (Rom. 6:4). Chambers writes elsewhere, "Sanctification makes me one with Jesus Christ, and in Him one with God, and it is done only through the superb Atonement of Christ. Never put the effect as the cause. The effect in me is obedience and service and prayer, and is the outcome of speechless thanks and adoration for the marvellous sanctification wrought out in me because of the Atonement."[5]

At the heart of this understanding of sanctification is the awareness that the Lord is with us. It was very significant for St. Paul to move in his writing from his traditional thinking of God as dwelling in the holy place, the holy of holies, to God as being present in the new community. The community forms the new temple: "Do you not know that you are God's temple and that God's Spirit dwells in you?... God's temple is holy, and you are that temple" (1 Cor. 3:16,17). Paul goes on to individualize this truth: "Do you not know that your body is a temple of the Holy Spirit within you, which you have from God, and that you are not your own?" (1 Cor. 6:19). For Paul, at the heart of Christian hope is the mystery of Christ dwelling in the believer: "the glory of this mystery, which is Christ in you, the hope of glory" (Col. 1:27). Paul prays for the Ephesians that they might "know the love of Christ that surpasses knowledge, so that you may be filled with all the fullness of God" (Eph. 3:19). The Christian at prayer experiences this awareness that God is with us. Seventeenth-century spiritual writer Bishop Jeremy Taylor is prepared to say in his still basic manual, *The Rule and Exercise of Holy Living*, that "God dwells in our heart by faith, and Christ by his Spirit, so that we are also cabinets of the mysterious trinity."[6]

HOLINESS AND THE DIVINE IMAGE

This awareness of the presence of God is the beginning of the process of sanctification. Dr. Eric Mascall put it this way: "The truth is not merely that in Christ the new creation was effected on our behalf, but that through our union with him it is to be brought about in each one of us."[7] Oswald Chambers expresses it simply: "Sanctification is not something Jesus Christ puts into me; it is Himself in me."[8] To become holy does not begin with following rules of conduct. It begins with the action of God within us, and then that action calls forth a response in us. Our response is a holiness of life that reflects the divine image.

God's people are to be like God, for they were made in the divine image. That image was badly distorted, but in Christ there is a new person who fully reflects the divine. Christ's life, death, and resurrection, and the gift of the Spirit are the means whereby the image reflected in Christ might be reflected in all believers. Paul writes, "All of us, seeing the glory of the Lord as though reflected in a mirror, are being transformed into the same image from one degree of glory to another; for this comes from the Lord, the Spirit" (2 Cor. 3:18). In the same vein, G. C. Morgan defines holiness as "approximation to the character of God, indeed it is the character of God reproduced at the centre of personality."[9]

To be in the divine image is primarily *to love*. It was love that marked the life of Jesus, and Paul writes that God "chose us in Christ before the foundation of the world to be holy and blameless before him in love" (Eph. 1:4). Paul writes of the incarnation that Jesus humbled himself and became obedient (see Phil. 2:6–8). Humility—a humility that removes self-satisfaction and self-assertion from the attitude with which life is faced—is an essential mark of the holy life. Obedience to God is clearly seen in Jesus' life. He declared, "I have come down from heaven, not to do my own will, but the will of him who sent me" (John 6:38). He lived that obedience in facing the cross. Obedience to the will of God, to the full extent that God's will is perceived, is an essential mark of holiness. The holy person seeks that will through prayer, Bible study, and consulting with fellow Christians. This desire to be in the image of God would seem hopeless without the sense of the Lord's indwelling and empowerment. That empowerment is real, as can be seen in St. Paul's recognition that love is a basic ingredient of the fruit of the Spirit. The love that is the embodiment of holiness is not primarily an effort to love but, rather, the gift of the Spirit.

In seeking how to live out love, humility, and obedience in daily life, every member of the church ought to be asking the question posed by St. Peter: "What sort of persons ought you to be in leading lives of holiness and godliness?" (2 Pet. 3:11). A basic answer is given by St. Paul when, after writing of the wonder of our redemption in Christ, he encourages Roman believers: "I appeal to you therefore, brothers and sisters, by the mercies of God, to present your bodies as a living sacrifice, which is your spiritual worship. Do not be conformed to this world, but be transformed by the renewing of your minds, so that you may discern what is the will of God—what is good and acceptable and perfect" (Rom. 12:1,2). Clearly, holiness entails a questioning of all commonly accepted ethical standards and all that merely satisfies personal desires. Jesus said, "If any want to become my followers, let them deny themselves" (Mark 8:34). Peter writes, "Like obedient children, do not be conformed to the desires that you formerly had in ignorance. Instead, as he who has called you is holy, be holy yourselves in all your conduct" (1 Pet. 1:14,15). For the early Christians, there was obviously a challenging change in lifestyle. Paul, after listing some of the lifestyles that do not belong in the kingdom of God, writes, "This is what some of you used to be. But you were washed, you were sanctified, you were justified in the name of the Lord Jesus Christ and in the Spirit of our God" (1 Cor. 6:10). Similarly, he writes to the Colossians, "You who were once estranged and hostile in mind, doing evil deeds, he has now reconciled in his fleshly body through death, so as to present you holy and blameless and irreproachable before him" (Col. 1:21,22). Today's Christians can equally recognize "desires formerly had in ignorance" and times when, overcome by desires for self-satisfaction, they were "estranged and hostile in mind, doing evil deeds." But today's Christian can also affirm that he or she has been "sanctified, justified in the name of the Lord Jesus Christ," and reconciled to God.

HOLY LIVING

The prophets clearly teach that obedience to God means living honestly and treating others with justice. Isaiah proclaims, "The Lord is a God of justice"

(Isa. 30:18). To be a Christian, to reflect the image of God, to grow in the holiness that God gives, a person must regularly ensure that his or her relationship with others is marked by fairness and justice.

It was almost inevitable that St. Paul, living in a society where sexual morality was very loose, should write to a number of his congregations about how living in holiness must affect sexual morals. He writes to the Thessalonians, "This is the will of God, your sanctification: that you abstain from fornication; that each of you know how to control your own body in holiness and honour, not with lustful passion, like the Gentiles who do not know God" (1 Thess. 4:3). Basing his exhortation on the promise of a new relationship with God through Jesus, Paul writes, "Since we have these promises, beloved, let us cleanse ourselves from every defilement of body and of spirit, making holiness perfect in the fear of God" (2 Cor. 7:1). Sexuality is a gift of God in the original creation. Therefore it is not surprising that it is an area of our lives where we need to be responsible to God. However, it is an area where passions are strong and self-fulfilment can overrule any obedience to what we know is right. Twentieth-century moral standards and ethical openness are no help to a Christian seeking to grow in holiness. This is an area where Christians need "not to be conformed to this world, but transformed by the renewing of their minds." Among other things, that means not feeding the mind on the loose lifestyles portrayed in many movies and current novels.

Clearly the call to holiness and love is not focused on sexuality alone but on the whole personality. Baron Friedrich von Hugel, having written of the work of the Spirit in the soul, writes, "The Soul is primarily a Force and an Energy, and Holiness is a growth of that Energy in Love, in Full Being and in Creative Spiritual Personality."[10] Paul writes, "As God's chosen ones, holy and beloved, clothe yourselves with compassion, kindness, humility, meekness and patience" (Col. 3:12). He goes on from there to speak of the need for forgiving one another and then summarizes, "Above all, clothe yourselves with love, which binds everything together in perfect harmony" (Col. 3:14). Maybe the best description of what characterizes the person living in holiness is Paul's description of the fruit of the Spirit: "love, joy, peace, patience, kindness, generosity, faithfulness, gentleness, and self-control" (Gal. 5:22). Holiness, for the Christian, means holy living. Oswald Chambers writes, "Holiness is not only what God gives me, but what I manifest that God has given me."[11]

Another of the marks of holiness is the recognition that one is a servant of God, and therefore his witness. Under the old covenant, Israel experienced God's holiness not only for Israel's own spiritual life but also that it might fulfil its mission. It was said to Israel, "The whole earth is mine, but you shall be for me a priestly kingdom and a holy nation" (Ex. 19:6). Living as God's servant, as a holy nation, was meant to bring to pass the word of the One who is Lord of the whole earth: "To me every knee shall bow, every tongue shall swear" (Isa. 45:23). This same mission is given to the people of the new covenant, the church: "You are a chosen race, a royal priesthood, a holy nation, God's own people, in order that you may proclaim the mighty acts of him who called you out of darkness into his marvelous light" (1 Pet. 2:9). Holiness is marked by a witness, in word and life, to the love and holiness of God so that others may come to believe in him.

Surely it is obvious that Christians seeking to live out holiness must be daily in prayer, being aware of God's presence within, and of the holy God before whom they stand. Eric Mascall writes, "Being a Christian is an ontological fact, resulting from an act of God."[12] To pray is to be deeply aware of that act of God. It is to know that our life in Christ depends on him. This awareness is strengthened by reading and meditating on the written account of his actions in Holy Scripture. Daily prayer and Bible reading are a must for growth in holiness.

A HISTORICAL PERSPECTIVE

Throughout the church's history, awakenings to new life have begun with a new awareness of God, of his holiness and love. Professor Albert C. Outler writes of John Wesley that he had "a conscious awareness of the vital presence of God."[13] No wonder he and his associates at Oxford were known as "the Holy Club." Through the years there were significant steps of growth in his awareness of the holy God and of his relationship to God through the grace of Jesus Christ. This led to the commitment of his life "to beget, preserve, and increase the life of God in the souls of men."[14] It has been said of his ministry and the ministry of his brother Charles that "the Wesleys transformed the spiritual atmosphere of Britain in the eighteenth century."[15]

Another example of new life in the church was the Tractarian Movement in the Church of England in the nineteenth century. Archbishop Michael Ramsey said of the Tractarians that they had "an intense call for holiness." This was because they had a new vision of the holy God. Ramsey writes, "They were looking back to the Caroline divines and the ancient Fathers of the church—but also looking up, because the church was to them a supernatural society, the body on earth of the risen Jesus, who through the Holy Spirit sanctifies men and women and makes saints."[16] The Tractarian Movement was the means God used to bring many to faith; to develop a new awareness in the church that when the Christian community gathers to celebrate the Eucharist, the Lord is with them; and to deepen a sense of the mission of the church. The truth is that "the core idea of Tractarian spirituality is that we may become by grace what Christ is by nature; we are transfigured by the divine indwelling."[17] Wherever this spirituality has been clearly focused, it has meant new life in the Anglican Communion.

ESSENTIAL HOLINESS

Human nature being what it is, externals can sometimes hide the inner spirituality. It is demanding to emphasize and live the righteousness that belongs with holiness, and often it is easy to be more concerned with externals than with the renewal of spirit. Thus, in many churches in the earlier part of this century, the emphasis was put on holy rules about worship, the sanctuary, and the sacrament (for instance, unveiled members of the altar guild were not to enter the sanctuary; there were clear rules about the ablutions; and so on), although many of these rules have now quietly slipped away. All too often there was an awareness of holiness in a "cultic" sense: respect for holy ground and holy things but not worship of the holy God. It has been easy for the church to miss out in other ways on the sense of the holy God. In the nineteenth century, in England, F. D. Maurice wrote, "We have been dosing our people with religion when what they want is not that but the living God."

While an emphasis on cultic holiness can obscure our awareness of the holiness of God, over-emphasising service or skills can have the same effect. In words that ring true today, English devotional writer Evelyn Underhill wrote in the 1920s, "We are drifting towards a religion which consciously or unconsciously keeps its eye on humanity rather than on Deity—which lays all the stress on service, and hardly any of the stress on awe; and that is a type of religion, which in practice does not wear well.... It does not lead to sanctity; and sanctity after all is the religious goal."[18] Recently, Chinese pastor Chua Wee-Hian complained that "biblical holiness means godliness; true godliness is always rooted in God-centredness. In many of our churches we rate skills over sanctity, programs over prayer. Holiness has a low priority."[19] Neither of these writers would want to deny the importance of service to others, the use of our skills, or the development of programmes in serving the holy God. Their concern has to do with relating to God himself.

HOLINESS AND THE CHURCH'S MISSION

Any failing to be aware of the holy God and to seek to live out his holiness weakens our church in its mission. Having ministered for sixteen years as a diocesan bishop in Canada, and having served for eleven of those years on the National Executive Council of the church, I now believe that two important tasks lie before the Anglican Church of Canada today:

1. The first responsibility is to help members come to a deeper awareness of the presence of God-with-us. We are in Christ. The Holy Spirit dwells in us. This awareness that "the Lord is in his holy temple" will bring a sense of holiness and will develop the relationship expressed in prayer. The baptismal covenant, which is frequently renewed these days, is one in which we know we are God's people. We need to emphasize that God says to his people, "You shall be holy, for I the Lord your God am holy."

2. The second task before the church is to help its members to understand what holy living is in today's context. As the sense of holiness develops in the context of a relationship with the Lord, so will the awareness of the need to respond in righteousness. This will involve deeper Bible study, a seeking together to "discern what is the will of God—what is good and acceptable and perfect." The Christian must be able to hear, not only the voice of current society, but a teaching voice in the church based on the Scriptures and on the tradition that has given guidance through the centuries. At the official level of its teachings, the church needs to develop statements on ethical

matters that grow in response to holiness. The church needs to be responsive to human distress and cognizant of new scientific research, but any position developed solely from these understandings without also starting from the Christian's call to holiness would show an inadequate understanding of the essentials of our faith. General Synod holds a pivotal position in the life of the Canadian Church in this regard. If General Synod, or any other governing body in the church, is to speak with the authority needed to guide the church, its members must be daily seeking to renew their lives in holiness in the presence of the holy God. Only a God-centred church can proclaim the truth of the Holy One—the true one—and so fulfil his mission.

ENDNOTES

1. John Henry Newman, *Lectures on Justification* (Oxford: J. H. Parker, 1838), p. 337.

2. The richness of the English language sometimes obscures in translation the single-minded intensity of the original Greek of the New Testament. *Sanctification* is simply another way for us to speak of being made holy. We must remember that a saint in the New Testament is, literally, "a holy one." The use of a Latin root makes this less clear, but it is very important to be aware of the meaning in reading English translations of the New Testament. These separate expressions, *sanctify* and *holiness*, aren't in the original Greek text. *Hagios* and its derivatives cover both *sanctify* and *holiness*.

3. Martin Thornton, *Christian Proficiency* (Cambridge, Mass.: Cowley Press, 1988), p. 3.

4. Oswald Chambers, *My Utmost for His Highest* (London: Marshall, Morgan Scott, 1955), p. 205.

5. Ibid., p. 294.

6. Jeremy Taylor, *The Rule and Exercises of Holy Living* (The Langford Press, 1970), p. 22.

7. Eric Mascall, *Christ, the Christian, and the Church* (London: Longman, Green, 1955), p. 78.

8. Chambers, *My Utmost for His Highest*, p. 204.

9. G. C. Morgan, *The Westminster Pulpit* (Old Tappan, N.J.: F. H. Revell Co., 1954), vol. 3.

10. Baron Friedrich von Hugel, *Eternal Life* (Edinburgh: T. & T. Clark, 1912).

11. Chambers, *My Utmost for His Highest*, p. 245.

12. Mascall, *Christ, the Christian, and the Church*, p. 77.

13. A. C. Outler, *John and Charles Wesley* (New York: Paulist Press, 1981), p. xiii.

14. F. L. Cross, *Oxford Dictionary of the Christian Church* (London: Oxford University Press, 1957) p. 1446.

15. F. Whaling, *John and Charles Wesley* (New York: Paulist Press, 1981), p. xix.

16. Michael Ramsey, *The Anglican Spirit* (Cambridge, Mass.: Cowley Publications, 1991), p. 50.

17. R. D. Townsend, in *The Study of Spirituality*, ed. C. Jones, G. Wainwright, E. Yarnold (London: SPCK, 1992), p. 467.

18. Evelyn Underhill, *Concerning the Inner Life* (London: Methuen, 1947; first pub. 1926), p. 4.

19. Chua Wee-Hian, in *The Cross and the Crown*, ed. D. Porter (Carlisle: OM Publishing, 1992).

SECTION IV

OUTREACH

16

EVANGELISM
THE UNCHANGING ESSENTIALS

MICHAEL GREEN

A bishop and a theologian sit in a hotel lounge in the jungles of Sabah and lead the hotel manager and the finance manager in a prayer of commitment to Christ.

A man is brought, unwillingly, to an evangelistic breakfast for men. He is overwhelmed by what he hears, and within an hour after the meeting he pulls off the freeway, cries his way into the kingdom, and begins a life which will change dramatically from what it has been.

Or come, in imagination, to an English cathedral where the gospel has just been proclaimed to a large congregation, and see the verger, with his gown and silver-tipped wand, conducting the preacher to lead the instruction talk on personal faith.

Come to a bonfire on November 5, a day when the British let off fireworks. Four hundred people are gathered around a hay wagon, eating burgers, watching jugglers, and eventually listening to a preacher. Many totally unchurched young people come to faith. One youth worker later writes: "Three of our group got saved and two began to seek. On Sunday they went to a Youth Fellowship for the first time. On Monday morning, I found them avidly reading the Bible. On Tuesday, they came and told me they needed to get baptized. Wednesday they told me that through their witnessing two more had become Christians and one of the seekers had become a Christian. We are now a group of ten."

These are examples of evangelism, and it is what Jesus Christ commanded his church on earth to make a top priority.

What exactly do we mean by *evangelism*? There is vast confusion on this subject in our church. I have heard a bishop describe the new Prayer Book as evangelism. I was preaching in an American cathedral recently and found the evangelism group hard at work—selling name tags for dogs. That too is evangelism, apparently.

But the word is quite precise in meaning: it is telling good news. To be sure, there must be a credible lifestyle, and warm relationships, but there is an inescapably vocal element in evangelism. It involves opening our lips to tell others of what God has done for them. You will recall Charles Spurgeon's famous definition of evangelism as "one beggar telling another beggar where to get bread." Archbishop William Temple put it well when he defined it as follows: "To evangelize is so to present Jesus Christ in the power of the Holy Spirit that men and women may come to put their faith in God through him, to accept him as their

Saviour and to serve him as their King in the fellowship of his church." That is evangelism. That is what we are talking about. And it is not in very plentiful supply these days in the Anglicanism of the Western world. It is one of the many areas where we need to learn from our colleagues in Third World countries.

I want in this chapter to be very direct and basic; other chapters will address more specifically than I can the current Canadian context. I offer you ten essentials, as I see them, for giving evangelism the priority it deserves in our church life.

1. AN ANALYSIS OF OUR FAILURE

We Canadian Anglicans are not celebrated for our evangelism. We used to be, and much of the pioneer evangelization of this country was done by intrepid Anglican missionaries. But such is not now the case. Indeed, in the years when I was working here and speaking in many parts of the country and to a variety of denominations, it often amazed them that I was an Anglican. They somehow did not associate evangelism with our Anglican Church. Great numbers of people who used to be keen Anglicans have left us and gone to join other churches where evangelism is more to the fore.

Why have we become so weak at it? There are a number of obvious reasons. We have surrendered very much to the spirit of the age in our theology, and have moved a long way from the biblical foundations which once made the Anglican Church strong. We frankly do not believe that there is much good news to tell; it is more a matter of church-going and being kind and generous to others. We do not believe that people will be lost without Christ: it is not important that they come to trust him. We are often very weak on the deity of Jesus Christ. We do not lay much stress on the power and reality of the Holy Spirit. Our members are often unsure about their own standing with God and are therefore quite unable to help anyone else to get clear about it. Our clergy have never been trained in evangelism at their seminaries, and have for the most part been taught that it is inappropriate in the pluralist culture in which we live. Naturally, therefore, they are not equipped to train lay members of the congregation. We tend, moreover, so to concentrate on the Holy Communion that we have no conception of providing seeker-friendly services for unchurched friends, and this in an age when people know less and less about the tenets of Christianity. In a word, we are introverted; many Anglicans live out their religion in a churchly ghetto. No wonder we find evangelism impossible.

2. A VISION OF THE NEED

We are told that when Jesus saw the crowds, he had compassion on them because they were harassed and helpless, like sheep without a shepherd. When Jesus saw this, his heart was stirred within him. Alas, we are so conditioned by the climate of pluralism and relativism around us that we often do not see that people are "without God and without hope in the world," as St. Paul put it. But consider the emptiness of belief and purpose, the terrible divisions in this lovely land, the moral desert, the spiritual blindness and decay. Canada has become one of the most godless countries in the world, and our church seems to do little to confront it. Indeed, we all seem tarred with the same brush. The church is almost indistinguishable from the rest of society in its lifestyle, as study after study has made plain. We seem to be blind to the situation in which people all round us live; blind and careless. And all the while, the New Testament is reminding us of the truth that we are not all going the same way, are not all equally secure and danger-free. It speaks of building on the sand or building on the rock. It speaks of sheep and goats, of a broad way that leads to destruction, and a narrow way that leads to life. It speaks of being in Christ or without Christ, saved or lost, for Jesus or against him. It speaks of a final destination, heaven or hell. Much as we would love to find justification in the Bible for our genial wish that we are all travelling the same way, and that it will be well for one and all at the end, the New Testament forbids us to hold such a view—not through one or two proof texts, but by the combined force of the whole of New Testament theology. It matters eternally whether we belong to Christ or not. And in our church we have lost the passion and conviction for that truth. Yet without passion, we are not likely to cause much of stir through evangelism.

3. AN EXCITEMENT WITH JESUS

You have only to visit somewhere like Sabah or Tanzania to find Christians deeply excited with Jesus. He is the one who has rescued them from a variety of enemies with which they struggled ineffectually before: drugs, sexual bondage, fear of death, guilt, loneliness, lack of meaning; and fear of demons, which runs deep in the animistic cultures prevalent in much of Asia, Africa, and Latin America. These Christian men, women, and children have a sense of joy, of discovery, about them. It is their prevailing attitude. As a result, they are anxious to make Jesus known to their friends and acquaintances. For once you have found treasure, you are keen to give it away if you have an ounce of generosity in you. You do not say, "These people have their own ways to God; it would be wrong for me to mention Jesus to them." No, you have the excitement of the newly engaged who rush around their friends extolling the virtues of their beloved. It is not church or Anglicanism or liturgy or ethics that these Christians are so excited about. It is Jesus. The magnetism, the spell of the Great Lover has gripped them. And they can't keep quiet about him.

I find that very moving, very attractive, very hard to resist. But I have to say that I find it very rare among Canadian Anglicans. Until we regain that thrill of knowing God personally through Jesus, I do not think we will penetrate this tough, secular culture very much.

Actually I am wrong: it is far from secular. A great many of our compatriots have realized the sterility of mere materialism and are looking for something deeper to satisfy them. That is why they are turning to the New Age, to Buddhism, or to one of the many self-help popular psychologies that flourish throughout North America. But Jesus brings to the soul of humankind a joy, a peace, and a sense of fulfilment that nothing in the world can match. Until people see that we have fallen in love with Jesus, and are excited about him, they are unlikely to be impressed—or changed.

4. A VIBRANT CHURCH LIFE

The main instrument for effective evangelism is, without question, the local church. That church is there all the time, in contrast to the ephemeral evangelistic campaign. It is made up of many people, not one high-powered evangelist. Its lifestyle is apparent for all to see. And therein lies both the glory and the shame of the church. When church people leave their service looking gloomy; when there are disputes between them; when there is a chilly atmosphere in the congregation; when there is incompetence, authoritarianism, or a bad reputation in the minister; then it will be useless to talk of evangelism. People will not come to such a church. They have troubles of their own and do not want to compound them by difficult associations. When the church does not have programmes that are appropriate for the neighbourhood, when its services are dull or repetitive, when there is little concern for the non-member, who can blame people if they keep well clear? And if, in modern Canada, the type of worship is predominantly English in style and not truly indigenous, that is another obstacle to those considering the possibility of joining. The gap between the church and society at large is now so great that it is imperative to have clear, well-presented teaching in non-ecclesiastical language, with opportunities for discussion and debate.

Renewal in the church is an indispensable prerequisite to evangelism from the church. The following ingredients are central in this new life. First, there must be love; for love is the language of heaven, the language of the Holy Trinity. Unless there is love, nobody will be drawn in. Second, there must be prayer, because prayer tells God that we can do nothing of ourselves, but are totally dependent on him for fruitfulness and growth. Third, there must be an openness to the Holy Spirit and his gifts. The power of the Spirit is given to equip us for mission, and we marginalize him at our peril. For far too long the church has done just this, so much so that if the Holy Spirit were totally withdrawn, most churches would continue precisely as they are.

Another element that I have found indispensable in church life all over the world is the small cell group, the living embodiment in street and home of the church it helps to constitute. It is here that love can flow, relationships can flower, and ministry, both within the church and beyond it, can be orchestrated. It is here that a lot of shared learning can take place, and prayer can become a way of life.

It is obvious from all this that we need in our Anglican churches to recover the central New Testament teaching about the body of Christ. Often our church has been run as a benevolent monarchy by the vicar, with a little help from the vestry. Before we can evangelize effectively, we need to insist that all Christians are called to minister, that God has given them appropriate gifts for the work he wants them to do, and that the church will be impoverished unless they contribute that gifting. The idea that attendance on Sunday and money in the plate are all that is required of most members of the congregation must be firmly rejected. I would find it hard to regard anyone as a real member unless they recognize and exercise some gifting for the good of the body as a whole.

Before leaving this aspect of a vibrant church life, I must mention one other area that needs a great deal of attention. We need to have people ready at the drop of a hat to lead a nurture group for the new Christians we are praying to God to give us. He has no intention of bringing new births into being unless there are warm cribs, so to speak, in which they can be received, where they can learn the rudiments of the good news and the lifestyle that goes with it, and can experience the beginnings of Bible reading, prayer, and fellowship. It is in these groups, too, that early problems can be discussed and issues like baptism and confirmation pursued. God does not put live chicks under dead hens, and if we want to see numerical growth in our churches, we must give priority to the quality of spiritual life in our congregations.

5. A SENSE OF CHALLENGE AND PRIVILEGE

The early Christians relished the fight with unbelief. They were thrilled to see themselves as the carriers of the Lord's message. He had not entrusted it to angels, nor to people, however gifted, who were not his disciples. Instead, he had given the privilege of being his ambassadors to them—humble and inadequate though so many of them felt themselves to be. It amazed them that they had this high privilege of being his representatives. It thrilled them that they should be his go-betweens.

I do not see a great deal of this enthusiasm in our churches today. For too long we have assumed it is not our job to tell good news to all and sundry. We have surrendered to the clericalization of the church. And that is disastrous for growth.

I think of Christians in Argentina who get on a tram on Sunday and shout out *Gloria Dios* until the whole tram is shouting it. Many of the occupants follow these unlettered but excited Christians into their places of worship. We could do with a little more of the Canadian equivalent of that sense of enthusiasm and privilege. The same is true of the challenge of being Christ's messengers. After all, he depends on us—just as we depend on him. The head and the body are inextricably united: both need the other. Jesus challenges us to go in his name and make him known. It is our responsibility, and the challenge is a stimulus and a joy. When we face up to any challenge it makes us grow. And as we take seriously this challenge, we find ourselves growing spiritually. Being unashamed about our allegiance becomes a habit. It is attractive to find Christians who live like that. The churches they belong to grow. There are plenty of such churches in Canada, but few of them, alas, are Anglican—as yet.

6. AN EQUIPPING MINISTRY

A very important and much neglected prerequisite for effective, long-term evangelism is the equipping of members of the congregation. Ours has been a pastoral church for many years, going back in its ethos to England where the conversion of the country and division into parishes took place within a hundred years of St. Augustine's arrival in the sixth century. Naturally, therefore, clergy were trained to conserve what had been gained, to teach, and to care pastorally for the people within their parish. Evangelism was not the name of the game, for the whole country was, notionally at least, Christian. But, particularly since the last Lambeth Conference, there has been an enormous emphasis in Anglicanism on the need to evangelize, because the conditions have radically changed; pluralism in matters of religion is the norm, while ignorance and unbelief are widespread.

Our clergy, therefore, need to be trained both to believe New Testament Christianity and to learn how to win new disciples to their Lord. Both areas have been very weak for a long time. A theological skepticism, rooted in the now-questioned assumptions of the Enlightenment, has ruled the roost in the university departments of religion—and worse, in the theological seminaries of the West. This has been rather extreme in Canada. I am aware of only one Anglican theological seminary that is thoroughly committed to grounding its students in biblical Christianity. I have been in one in the United States that has a self-confessed witch on the faculty, and many faculty members are cynical about evangelism and dominated by issues rather than the theology and practice of the New Testament.

This has led to confused clergy emerging from the seminaries, unsure of what to believe—and vast numbers of good lay people leaving the Anglican Church for other denominations because they do not get the scriptural nourishment they seek. God does not owe any denomination a living, and I fear that unless there is a return in our seminaries to a serious grappling with the New Testament and its teaching, Anglicanism will die within two generations, probably sooner. And that would be tragic; Anglicanism has so much of balanced Christianity to offer to the world once it becomes true to its foundation documents again, something it is already doing in many parts of the world. Biblical training has to start with the clergy, most of whom have not been trained in this way.

And if the biblical training of the clergy has been weak, their training in evangelism has been non-existent. Hardly any seminaries take seriously the apologetics and evangelism which are essential for clergy who hope to make an impact in today's secular society. Consequently they have no idea how to go about bringing someone to Christian faith, even the easiest of seekers. They can at best only encourage their flock to evangelize; but they have no idea how to train them. The laity are rightly frustrated by all this. The hungry sheep look up and are not fed. There are, mercifully, plenty of training courses in the fundamentals of personal evangelism and effective preaching for a decision, if we will only humble ourselves and seize the opportunity to learn. But a clergyman who does not know how to win someone else for Christ and train others to do so is rather like a lifeguard who does not know how to swim.

I trust that one of the results of the Essentials 94 conference will be a great cry from clergy for help in training their congregations in evangelism. We need to avail ourselves of the expertise of people like Dr. Don Moore, coordinator of Vision 2000, who gives all his time to helping churches to go forward in evangelism and church planning. And we need to work and pray and strategize for more theological seminaries that will train men and women effectively for mission in the latter years of this century and into the next.

7. AN OUTWARD ORIENTATION IN CHURCH LIFE

One has only to speak of priorities like these to find clergy stopping their ears. There are so many pressures on their lives all the time that it seems unrealistic to be asked to do evangelism as well. However, I am not pleading for one more thing, but a different attitude. Evangelism is not so much an action as it is a way of life. It can and should affect how we do everything in our church and personal life. It affects our attitudes towards our neighbours: at the back of our minds is the longing to share with them the most important thing in our lives. It affects our attitude at work, in leisure pursuits, and in civic relationships. Wherever we go, and whomever we meet, there is that underlying hope that the way may open up for us to be a link in the chain (by no means always the last one) drawing them to Christ. If you watch Christians in Singapore or Sabah, you will find that this is their orientation. They are so fulfilled in their relationship with Christ that they are only too willing for it to overflow.

With that attitude, the Moms and Toddlers Club takes on an outward look, and so does every other aspect of the church's life. Gradually the optimistic dictum of Archbishop William Temple becomes more true: "The church is the only organization in the world which exists for the benefit of the non-member." Naturally, this attitude will be embodied in the leadership. The clergy will see wedding and baptism preparation, funeral and crisis visitation as marvellous opportunities to get close to people with some aspect of the good news of Jesus. They will not talk about the church or the weather, but about Jesus and the help that he can bring in these varied situations — thus paving the way for men and women to be drawn into the Saviour's embrace. It is impossible to exaggerate the importance of this outward-looking attitude at all levels of the church's life. It is evangelism at grass-roots level.

8. AN ENGAGEMENT IN SPIRITUAL WARFARE

I know the phrase "spiritual warfare" has become something of a cliché these days, but it is important to understand its reality and relation to evangelism. The consistent teaching of the Bible is that we are engaged in a battle where we cannot see the enemy; but we neglect him at our peril. Satan and his forces were an ever-present reality to Jesus and his apostles. Paul reminds us that we do not battle merely with flesh and blood when we are trying to advance the kingdom of God, but with principalities and powers of darkness. A great deal has been written on this subject in recent years, and even more has been experienced.

Many stories are emerging from Argentina, for example, of the way a major advance for the gospel takes place in a city, once the place has been soaked in prayer for a considerable time and its prevailing characteristic has been discerned and prayed against. Prayer and fasting are the supreme tools God has given us to enable the Holy Spirit to move freely in a situation that otherwise seems hopeless. But the Western church is very weak on prayer: we believe in methodologies instead. As for fasting, it happens nowadays not as a spiritual discipline but as an aid to slimming. So long as we retain this mindset, we will not even discern the features of our enemy, let alone dethrone him.

I believe this is one of the most important lessons that our brothers and sisters in the Two-Thirds World can teach us. They know how to pray, to pray sacrificially, and at length. They know how to fast for a spiritual purpose. They need no persuading of the power of dark forces hemming in their lives and impeding the advance of the gospel. And if we want to emulate their fruitfulness, we shall need to abjure that Enlightenment rationalism that affects to despise the reality of the devil. We shall need to take him as an awesome but defeated foe, just as our Master taught us. We shall need to confront him with believing, specific prayer, and rely on the blood of Christ and the power of the Holy Spirit to break his stranglehold of skepticism and materialism in the West, like the stranglehold of animism in the East.

It so happens that in this "postmodern" age we shall not find the climate as strongly against us as it was a decade ago. The foundations of Enlightenment skepticism have been eroded, and its two-and-one-half-century spell over modern thought effectively demolished, though there will be a hangover for many years to come. The challenge to us and our own prayer life, as well as the prayer life of our families and churches, is plain. Without prevailing, believing prayer, there will be no effective evangelism; for evangelism is God at work, and God works when his people pray. That is the thing his satanic enemy is most keen to prevent.

9. A HUMBLE WILLINGNESS TO LEARN

Anglicans have a reputation, not wholly undeserved I fear, for arrogance. We have little enough to be arrogant about, in all conscience, but the suspicion remains. We regard ourselves as just a touch better than other denominations, and we treat ourselves as the establishment even in countries where such pretensions are eminently absurd. This introversion has rendered us very unwilling to learn from other denominations, particularly in the matter of evangelism. The Pentecostals, for example, are far better at evangelism than we are; they have an enthusiasm, a courage, and a willingness to involve everyone. The Baptists are far better at it than we are. They are intentional about their evangelism and increasingly imaginative in their approach to it. Both the Salvation Army and the Pentecostals are to be found witnessing among the poorest and neediest of our society. We prefer to give money rather than get our hands dirty. The Mennonite Brethren are only a small denomination in Canada, as we ourselves are. But they have a clear and effective policy of church planting on an annual basis. Their Antioch Plan is something we could profitably examine and learn from.

Perhaps we are blinded by our assumption that if people have been baptized they must be all right, even if there has been no profession, let alone reality, of repentance and faith. Perhaps we have hoodwinked ourselves into thinking that if people are in church, they must be Christians. Nothing could be further from the truth. People are to be found in church for all manner of reasons. In any event, we are decidedly ineffective at evangelism; and yet, instead of learning from other denominations, we affect to ignore them. The Roman Catholics gain many members through their marriage counselling. They gain many more by advertising instruction courses in the faith. We seem to have no serious policy for reaching the unevangelised masses all around us. If it is to be done at all, it needs to be done in partnership with other denominations. A joint trans-denominational outreach in a city makes so much impact. People see that we stand together: they are amazed, and many of them are prepared to listen. I do not merely hope this is true; from my experience over the years here in Canada I know it is.

10. AN ATTEMPT TO PENETRATE THE STRUCTURES

From the earliest days we find the first Christians seeking to penetrate the power structures of their world. They certainly did not neglect the poor and the powerless but they also sought out the proconsul, the governor, the Roman cities, and even proclaimed Christ before the emperor himself. In the limited time and with the limited resources at our disposal, we need to take a lesson from them. One of the results of the Essentials 94 conference could be a determined attempt to befriend leaders in our towns, in industry, in government, and in the media. I know that this is what a large group of ministers did, with remarkable results, in Calgary recently. We are bidden to pray for those in authority over us; if we both pray and befriend, there is no knowing where it will lead.

It has been a privilege to do something of the sort with parliamentarians in the United Kingdom in recent months, and my colleague Michael Marshall has been able to do the same, also with heads of industry. One of my friends in parliament has been able to make representations to the Saudi ambassador about the persecution of Christians in his country. My friend and his colleagues have been working on a powerful indictment of the state of the nation. People like this are no more valuable to God than anyone else, but they can touch far more lives than most of us, and therefore we should pay heed to them, and encourage them.

But in particular, I want to urge that we attempt to penetrate the national structures on Jarvis Street. Our Anglican Church in this country has been very tightly controlled by the central bureaucracy and by the bishops, since here we do not have the checks and balances to ecclesiastical power that exist in some other countries. It stands to reason, therefore, that we should seek, on merit, to gain a hearing in the places where major decisions are made. The Anglican newspaper is one obvious example, and another is the staff of theological seminaries. We constantly stand in need of courageous bishops, committed to Christ and the Scriptures, and we need good representation on General Synod.

Many evangelical and charismatic church leaders eschew ecclesiastical responsibilities, preferring to get on with the job. But this is short-sighted. If we want to wield influence for the gospel in our church, we need to speak where many listen, and write what many read. If, for example, we are to be heard when the next revision of the Prayer Book takes place, we need to produce liturgiologists who can command a place on the appropriate committee by proven competence. And for that we need to start now. We have a lot of ground to make up. Compared with the situation in most countries, our representation of evangelical and charismatic church leaders in the main structures that influence the church's life is very small. That must change if we hope to advance. My colleague Bishop Colin Buchanan has given us an example. He was a real pain in the neck to the English establishment as a young man, constantly pointing out uncomfortable truths in the church papers. But all the while, he was educating himself in liturgy. He was invited onto the Liturgical Commission, and in due course, by sheer competence, toughness, and clear-sightedness, he began to exercise an enormous amount of influence on that commission. Indeed, it is due to him that the Alternative Service Book of 1980 in Britain is as useful and theologically reputable as it is. We need Colin Buchanans in many spheres in the Canadian Anglican Church. And to get there, they will have to be not just as good as the liberal establishment but manifestly superior. That takes hard work and planning, but it has to happen.

POSTSCRIPT: A PASSION FOR SOULS

The New Testament prefers to speak of *people* rather than disembodied *souls*, but we know well enough what our ancestors meant by "a passion for souls." If we are going to affect this great nation for God, we need to have a passionate fire blazing inside us. If we do not, we shall be overwhelmed by the many everyday tasks that crowd in upon us. Evangelism is difficult. It is demanding. There is every reason to persuade ourselves that it cannot be as pressing as all that, and that we have more urgent concerns that take priority. That attitude has prevailed too long among us. It is in direct contrast to the attitude of our Lord, who had a deep concern to seek and save the lost, and was always doing it.

I shall never forget the visit to our ministers' fraternal in Oxford of a priest called Fr. Diamond from the East End of London. He had spent all his life in that tough area, and he had a tremendous rapport with the largely unchurched locals. He left us all to ponder this question: "Do we burn with a passion that is almost a pain in order to bring other people to Christ?" If we have to confess that we do not, let us beg the Lord to ignite this passion within each of us. Not until that happens will we see a wide-spread revival of evangelism in the Anglican Church of Canada.

CHAPTER 17

EVANGELISM AND THE
ANGLICAN CHURCH OF CANADA

HAROLD PERCY

SHARING GOOD NEWS

Given the rather low profile of evangelism in the Anglican Church of Canada until fairly recently, it is important to clarify exactly what it is we are talking about at the beginning of any discussion of evangelism. Most of us have heard by now that evangelism has to do with sharing good news. But we must be more precise than this. Unfortunately, many discussions on evangelism get to this point only to draw the conclusion that everything we do in and through our churches that represents good news to someone constitutes evangelism. Indeed, it is not unusual to hear the comment that "everything we do is evangelism."

Of course every congregation and every Christian should be involved in as many "good news" activities as possible, but we should not make the mistake of concluding that all of these activities are forms of evangelism. For Christians, the good news that we share in evangelism has a specific content. It is the good news of what God has done for us through the life, death, and resurrection of Jesus Christ. In perhaps its most concise form, this good news is the announcement that through the death and resurrection of Jesus, God has defeated the powers of evil that seek to destroy God's creation, and we can be set free to live a new life in the light and truth of God's reign.

The deeper truth that lies behind this formulation of the good news is the biblical insistence that through the pernicious and permeating influence of evil, humanity and all of creation have been estranged from their creator. Human history has been played out in a state of alienation from God. In 2 Corinthians 5, St. Paul uses the language of reconciliation to describe the good news that Christians have to share. He writes:

> If anyone is in Christ, there is a new creation: everything old has passed away; see, everything has become new! All this is from God, who reconciled us to himself through Christ, and has given us the ministry of reconciliation; that is, in Christ God was reconciling the world to himself, not counting their trespasses against them, and entrusting the message of reconciliation to us. So we are ambassadors for Christ, since God is making his appeal through us; we entreat you on behalf of Christ, be reconciled to God. For our sake he made him to be sin who knew no sin, so that in him we might become the righteousness of God (2 Cor. 5:17–21, NRSV).

We live in a culture in which the language of reconciliation has particular relevance. Most people in Canada are aware of some dimension of alienation and estrangement at the personal or societal level, and understand the importance of reconciliation. People who are gifted at the work of effecting reconciliation are highly valued in our society. The good news that we share in evangelism is an offer of reconciliation. To those who are estranged and alienated from God, we bring God's offer of reconciliation and friendship. The language of reconciliation provides a ready-made, culturally "hot" category for the proclamation of the gospel.

But there is more to evangelism than the simple sharing or proclamation of this good news. This good news should always be shared in the form of an invitation. The task of the church is not simply to announce the good news, but to invite people to accept it. Indeed, the work of evangelism involves persuading people to accept God's offer. It is easy for us to forget how important this is to God, and the terrible price that was paid to make this offer possible. Evangelism is not an indifferent, take-it-or-leave-it announcement of God's invitation, but a passionate and determined attempt to persuade people to respond affirmatively and to turn to Christ. Obviously, this must be done sensitively, giving people all the time and space they need to make a thoughtful, well-considered response, but we should never forget that the goal is to encourage and help them to make that response.

WHEN SHARING GOOD NEWS SEEMS LIKE BAD NEWS

In order to make any progress in our ability to engage effectively in the ministry of evangelism, it is important to be completely honest and admit that, for many (most?) of us, the prospect of being involved in evangelism is rather daunting. There are many areas of the church's life and ministry to which we respond more enthusiastically than the call to evangelism. It is legitimate and important to ask the question, "If evangelism is sharing good news, why does the call to evangelism sound like bad news?" There are many reasons why this is so.

Cultural Values

One of the biggest reasons for our reluctance is cultural. I have frequently discussed this reluctance about evangelism with groups of Christians. To several groups I have said something like this: "If we read a good book, we are eager to share it with a friend; if we find a good restaurant, we are eager to tell our friends about it; if we see a good movie, we like to recommend it to others. Shouldn't it be natural, then, when we accept the good news about Jesus to want to share it with our friends? If we enjoy our church, isn't it natural to want to invite our friends to join us there?" Invariably, the response to this question is a resounding, "No!"

"You are missing the point," these groups tell me. "When we share the news of a good book or a good movie or a good restaurant with our friends, they hear this news as an overture and expression of friendship. They understand that we are offering them an opportunity for enjoyment and enrichment. When we talk to them about Christian faith, or invite them to church, there is a good chance that they will not hear it as an offer of enjoyment and enrichment. They are more likely to feel that we are passing judgement on them; that we are saying that they are not good enough; that we are trying to change their lifestyle or their values."

There is a strong cultural force at work in this. We are increasingly being shaped by a society that places a high value on tolerance. We are part of a nation that cherishes pluralism. In such a climate there is a very strong pressure not to tamper with the belief (or non-belief) structures of others. This has very serious implications for how evangelism is done. For the moment I will limit myself to two brief observations.

The first is that we should remember Don Posterski's repeated reminders to the church in Canada that "pluralism is a friend of the faith." Pluralism offers the climate for a free and vigorous exchange of ideas and values. The Christian monopoly on religious discourse in this country is long gone, but that is not a fact that should be particularly lamented. We live in a marketplace of ideas and convictions. The task is to be able to articulate our convictions clearly and persuasively, and to listen carefully, in order to understand the values and convictions of those with whom we are sharing. Pluralism has the ability to change the face of evangelism for the better because it demands that the evangelist be both sensitive and caring.

The second observation is that the gospel will not be heard as "good news" by everyone. To those who are settled and content, the news that God wants to be involved in their lives will only sound like an unwelcome intrusion. I strongly believe that the gospel is really only heard as good news by those who know they are needy. Because people have differing needs, different aspects of the gospel will resonate more strongly for one than for another, but I believe it to be a spiritual truth that the gospel is heard as good news only by those who realize that they are "poor in spirit." This means that effective evangelism must always begin with listening, in order that the good news might be shared in a way that reaches the "felt need."

Personal Reasons

There are also a number of personal reasons for our reluctance to embrace the call to evangelism with enthusiasm. Perhaps the most obvious has to do with temperament. It is simply a fact that some people are more outgoing than others, and that they find it easier to initiate and guide conversations about topics they wish to discuss. If the church is going to be faithful in its ministry of evangelism, it must be prepared to help people to be involved in ways that do not demand an extroverted, highly energized personality.

For many Anglicans, our reluctance about the task of evangelism has to do with some stereotypes that are hard to put to rest. First among these is that of the flamboyant American television evangelist. The audacious materialism, the confrontational style, the simplistic answers to the deepest mysteries of life, the unabashed hucksterism in appealing for money, all characteristic of so many of these people, simply puts us off. Many of these personalities have given evangelism a bad reputation, and sensitive people find themselves wanting to pass by on the other side of the street.

There are other stereotypes as well. The memories of various sects who have sent their members knocking on our doors scare us half to death. I have heard many variations on the theme: "If evangelism is about knocking on doors, you can count me out." Others raise the objection that evangelism seems to be about the church trying to find more people to help it survive. Such people rightly discern that if the church's interest in evangelism is for the sake of its own well-being rather than for the benefit of those it is seeking to reach, then evangelism is really little more than recruitment for self-preservation. Such manipulation lacks integrity.

A Lack of Confidence

I fear, however, that the resistance many Anglicans have towards evangelism goes much deeper than the reasons outlined so far. I believe that much of our reluctance stems from a crisis of faith. It is a basic rule of evangelism that you cannot share what you do not have. Long experience has taught me the simple truth: that many people who are faithful attenders and supporters of their church are not at all confident that they understand the basic content of the Christian faith well enough to explain it to themselves, let alone attempt to share it with somebody else. In addition, many of our members are personally quite confused and unclear about their own identity as Christians.

Over the past few years I have taught a course entitled "Christian Basics" a number of times. One of the questions that is asked again and again in these groups is, "How can I be certain that I am a Christian?" This question does not always come from "outsiders." It is asked by people who have been faithful church members for many years. It is interesting to observe that the answer, "If you have been baptized then you are a Christian," annoys them more frequently than it satisfies them. People who ask this question are hungering for an experience of God's presence in their lives. It is hard to motivate people to share good news if they are not sure what the good news is, or if they know that they have never experienced it themselves.

For some church members the issue goes much deeper than their own sense of identity as Christians. Many of our people have questions and reservations about the truth of the gospel. I suspect that many Anglicans are saying the creeds with their fingers crossed behind their backs. This frequently has to do with the quality of preaching and teaching to which they have had access over the years. When the clergy and leadership of the church are given to expressing their doubts about the historic truth of the faith, it is hard for the general membership to be convinced and excited. I suspect that many of our most faithful members are essentially relativists, whose core belief is that "this works for me, but it might not be true for you." Such people will never make enthusiastic evangelists.

It is also a fact to be recognized that the present leadership of our church has not been trained for the ministry of evangelism. During my three years in seminary preparing for ministry, I doubt that I ever heard the word *evangelism* spoken, let alone discussed in class or considered as to its place in parish ministry. I know that I am not alone in this. I would be willing to wager that 95 percent of the present leadership of the Canadian Anglican Church has not had ten minutes of formal training in how to equip their people for the ministry of evangelism. (This is the void that the Wycliffe College Institute of Evangelism is attempting to fill, both within the college and the Anglican Church of Canada.)

Most clergy that I know don't go out of their way looking for opportunities to make themselves look bad in front of their people. Their lack of enthusiasm to take on yet another area of ministry, especially an area for which they themselves are not equipped, should hardly come as a surprise.

So What Should We Do?

Given the undeniable fact that the church has been called by Jesus Christ to make the ministry of evangelism an absolute priority, and given the many reasons for our fear and reluctance to do so, what is the way ahead? There are two imperatives that must be attended to if we are to make progress in this area. The first has to do with disabusing ourselves of the stereotypes of evangelism outlined above and beginning to develop a form of evangelism that is more congenial to the mainstream Anglican temperament and ethos. The second has to do with the acceptance of a new operative paradigm for parish ministry.

THE EVANGELIZING COMMUNITY— AN "ANGLICAN-FRIENDLY" APPROACH TO EVANGELISM

To begin with, I believe there is a ready consensus among Anglicans that any form of evangelism that we would find acceptable has to be parish based. For us, evangelism must emerge from the life of a parish community and lead to the incorporation of new believers into the life of that community. We need to take seriously the concept of the parish as an "evangelizing community" if we are going to lay to rest many of the reservations our people have about this sudden focus of our church on evangelism.

With this model of evangelism, the task is to help the local congregation develop into a loving, caring, healing community that is alive to the presence of God and eager to share in the mission of God. The members of this community understand that they are "disciples-in-the-making" as they encourage and help one another to grow towards Christian maturity. As they do so, they are more and more concerned to reach out to those who are outside of the faith. Their method is to invite those within their natural spheres of influence to come and sample the life of this Christian community. They can do this happily because they know those they bring will find a genuinely warm acceptance and be offered a place to belong. Within the loving, nurturing, healing environment of this community, these newcomers will hear and experience the love and grace of God, shared sensitively over time, and will be invited to accept God's offer of reconciliation and friendship.

The strength of this form of evangelism is that it takes seriously the biblical concept of the church as the "people of God." In evangelism it is important always to remember that God's purposes in redemption do not begin or end with the individual. In the Bible, God is always in the process of forming a distinctive community of people who will live in the world as a light in the darkness. In the New Testament, this community is the church. The mission of the church is to bear witness to the truth of the gospel, to live as a sign and model of the reign of God, and to work for the reconciliation of the entire world to God through Jesus Christ. Individuals who respond to the invitation of the gospel become a part of this community and begin to take their place in its ongoing mission.

The weakness of this form of evangelism is simply the present condition of the church. It is only fair to say that perhaps the majority of our local congregations are a long way from being the type of community through which the good news is clearly proclaimed to those outside the community and into which new believers can be readily assimilated and equipped for their place in the church's mission. This points out clearly the present task for the church if we are to be faithful in the ministry of evangelism to which God is calling us. We must develop a new model of parish ministry.

A NEW MODEL OF PARISH MINISTRY

The three core values in this new model will be the development of genuine community, the making of mature disciples, and the building of bridges into the local community. This will require a new understanding of what parish ministry is all about and, in most cases, the acquisition of new skill sets by our clergy as they find themselves ministering in situations far different from those for which they were prepared in seminary.

The new job description for clergy will be "building community, building people, and building bridges." We should not underestimate what a radical change this is from a traditional understanding of parish ministry. The traditional form of parish ministry has been shaped by the church as it enjoyed the belief and worldview consensus of Christendom. For such a church, the appropriate form of parish ministry was the pastoral mode, in which the priest, trained in pastoral ministry, took care of the "faithful flock." People naturally looked to the church to provide meaning to their lives and expected the church to provide its pastoral services and rites at the appropriate times and seasons.

The challenge the church is facing today is that Christendom is dead. The church is just one voice among many in the marketplace of ideas, and people no longer automatically turn to it as the possessor of truth and the shaper of values. However, many of our parishes are still attempting to operate on the Christendom model. It won't work. We can't turn back the clock, nor should we try to deny reality. The times have changed, and our models of church and ministry must change if we are to be effective. Of course, many congregations will simply refuse to change, and eventually they will die.

The terminology presently being used to describe the required paradigm shift in parish ministry is that of *maintenance* and *mission*. *Maintenance* describes the "business as usual" approach to ministry. The emphasis is on maintaining the present forms and structures of ministry, emphasizing traditional forms of worship and pastoral care dispensed by the parish priest. As the numbers of those attending worship and requesting the pastoral services of the priest decline, a major concern of such a parish increasingly becomes that of its own survival. For many such parishes today, mere survival is viewed as success.

The weakness of the maintenance model of ministry, with its focus on individual pastoral care, is that it tends to keep people in perpetual dependence upon the clergy. It is not at all uncommon to find people who have spent their entire adult lives actively participating in the life of a parish but are still unable to say a simple prayer aloud in a group of their fellow parishioners, who would have no confidence in their ability to read the Bible on their own and understand it, and who could not write a simple paragraph on the basic essentials of the Christian faith.

This model of ministry has simply not placed a high value on helping our people grow towards spiritual maturity. This is nothing short of a tragedy. It is undeniable that the New Testament Epistles place a high value on believers growing towards maturity and being equipped for their place in the ministry of the church. No wonder many people have left the church in frustration, pronouncing it irrelevant to their lives.

A further weakness of this model of ministry is that it has not always helped church members to understand the organic nature of church life. The New Testament is quite clear that as "the people of God" we belong to one another. Each of us is a part of the "body of Christ"; we form an interconnected whole. This concept is little more than irrelevant church talk to many of our people. It is certainly accurate to say that *congregation* does not automatically mean *community*. Many congregations remain collections of individuals who gather at the same time in the same place to say their prayers and receive their communion, but who otherwise have very little to do with one another. They would be aghast at the suggestion that they have any responsibility, to or for one another, beyond paying their fair share of the costs to keep the building maintained and pay the salary of the priest. From such congregations arises the oft-cited caricature of "God's frozen people."

Parishes operating on this model don't have a hope as far as evangelism is concerned. But they are probably not too worried about it either. If your predominant understanding of the church is as a place where you go to be cared for, it is difficult to get very excited about reaching out to others. Or if you are not growing deeper and deeper in your understanding of the Christian faith and your awareness of what God is doing in the world, you are not likely to develop much of a sense of the importance of evangelism to God as he seeks to reach a lost and hurting world through the community of his people. As one church warden put it when questioned about the work of his parish in evangelism, "The door is unlocked on Sunday morning, and the sign says 'Everyone Welcome'— what's the problem?"

Mission describes an outward-focused ministry that recognizes the death of Christendom and realizes that the church is living in a missionary situation. The culture is no longer Christian, and the church can no longer automatically assume that the institutions and structures of the surrounding culture are its allies. Whereas in Christendom, society supported the work of the church, in post-Christendom, society challenges the church. The post-Christendom societal momentum pulls people out of the churches rather than pushing them in. The mission-focused church realizes that its calling is to proclaim the gospel in a post-Christian cultural environment. Rather than simply caring for the faithful, its task is to share the gospel with the unconverted with the intention of encouraging them to accept God's offer of reconciliation and to share in the life of the people of God.

The mission-focused parish is constantly seeking to find and create new opportunities for reaching people with the good news about Jesus. It understands that evangelism is done most effectively through a partnership between the leadership, the congregation as a whole, and the individual members. The members of such a parish regard the church as a centre for mission and realize that they are an integral part of that mission. The leadership provides the teaching and equipping necessary to build people up in the faith and prepare them for ministry; the congregation provides a caring, magnetic community environment into which the individual members can invite their friends who are still outside the faith.

The individual members are constantly looking for opportunities to invite their family and friends. As they grow towards maturity in the faith and become more and more aware of what constitutes ministry in a post-Christian world, they come to place a high value on inviting those within their natural spheres of influence to come and sample the life and teaching of this Christian community. They are learning to share in a short and simple format what their faith and the life of this Christian community mean to them. They are learning to listen for signs of openness and searching that will provide opportunities for them to share their personal word of witness and an invitation to "come and see" what this community is all about. So important is the Christian community to evangelism that, if its members cannot say with confidence "come and see," they should never be encouraged to "go and tell." Without a caring community into which to invite new or prospective Christians, evangelism simply has no integrity.

The leadership of such a parish recognizes that their primary focus must be on building their people up in the faith and developing a loving, caring community into which people can be invited to experience the grace of God mediated through his people. To be sure, such a parish offers good pastoral care, but never as an end in itself. Pastoral care is offered as a part of the ministry of the parish in order to help its members grow to maturity and wholeness as they deal with those issues in their lives that keep them from their rightful place in the mission of the church. One of the most pronounced characteristics of such a parish is the fact that the members are taking primary responsibility for caring for one another. The age-old pattern of every member's dependence on the priest has been broken. (We should not underestimate how traumatic this change may be for many—both clergy and laity—in maintenance-minded parishes.)

GETTING STARTED

The first task of parishes wishing to grow into genuinely evangelizing communities is to provide opportunities for the spiritual growth of their current members. In many cases, the first group of people to be targeted for evangelism should be those who are already in the pews. Many faithful churchgoers are still waiting to be converted to Christ and helped to get started on the exciting adventure of Christian discipleship. In his book *Biblical Perspectives on Evangelism* (Abingdon, 1993), Walter Brueggemann says that one of the goals of evangelism is to help "forgetters become rememberers."

Many of our people have spiritual amnesia. They have forgotten what it means to be the "people of God." For many parishes, the first order of business should be an in-depth focus on the nature and purpose of the church. It would help mightily if many parishes were to suspend all other activities until they have reached a clear understanding of what God intends the church to do and to be. Parishes that cannot answer the question, "What are we here for?", should suspend all other activities until they are able to give a clear and concise answer to this question.

The preliminary teaching required to begin changing the focus of a typical "maintenance-minded" congregation to that of a "mission-focused, evangelizing community" has to do with what it means to be the church of Jesus Christ. The most basic form of this question is, "Why does God want there to be a church?" In order for our congregations and individual members to be motivated and energized for evangelism, we must help them answer that question. Many churches could do a lot worse than to focus almost exclusively on that one question for the better part of a year. We need to understand and say clearly that we are a community of people who have been reconciled to God through Jesus Christ and that our mission is to bear witness to God's saving grace revealed in the life, death, and resurrection of Jesus. We are called to proclaim the wonderful acts of God in Jesus and to invite people to turn to Christ for forgiveness, healing, and new life.

MAKING DISCIPLES

Beyond this basic understanding of who we are as the church and what our calling is, we need to help people to make discernible progress in their journey towards spiritual maturity. At its most elementary level, this teaching will include instruction about the God who has made himself known to us in Scripture and in Jesus Christ. It will explain the human dilemma of estrangement from God and God's offer of reconciliation through Christ. It will explain the importance of making an intentional decision to turn to Christ and beginning to learn to live as a dedicated follower of Jesus. Through this instruction, not surprisingly, many people will discover that until now they have really been spectators rather than disciples. That discovery will come as a tremendous relief to them as they realize why they have always felt slightly confused about what Christian faith is all about. Their joy in their new identity as intentional followers of Jesus will be infectious!

For new and renewed disciples-in-the-making, instruction will include practical help in reading and understanding the Bible and some basic help in learning to pray (alone and in groups) with confidence. They will need help in understanding the nature of the local church as an organic community and the importance of their active participation in the life of that community. They will need to learn more about the mission of God in the world and how they have been gifted to share in that mission. They will also need to be trained in the use of their gifts in order to share in the adventure of authentic ministry. Through all of this, they will need to be made aware of God's continuing presence and provision of power to them through the work of the Holy Spirit in their lives and in the church community.

None of this will happen overnight. In some congregations, it won't happen at all. But in others, by the grace of God, the challenge will be seized and a new direction for ministry undertaken. And God will bless such communities. They will discover more and more the adventure of faith to which we are called in our post-Christendom situation, and through their joyful and difficult efforts, many will make the marvellous passage from darkness to light.

Suggested Reading

Michael Green, *Evangelism through the Local Church* (London: Hodder & Stoughton, 1990).

Howard Hanckey, *Church Growth and the Power of Evangelism* (Cambridge, Mass.: Cowley, 1990).

Donald C. Posterski and Irwin Barker, *Where's a Good Church?* (Winfield, B.C.: Wood Lake Books, 1993).

CHAPTER

18

REDISCOVERING THE CLOSENESS OF GOD

POSTMODERNISM, "NATURE SPIRITUALITY,"
AND THE CHRISTIAN GOSPEL

LOREN WILKINSON

The God who made the world and everything in it is the Lord of heaven
and earth.... He himself gives life and breath and everything else.... God
did this so that men would seek him and perhaps reach out for him and
find him, though he is not far from each one of us.
— From Paul's sermon in Athens, Acts 17

"Religion" may be on decline in the modern Western world. But "spirituality"
(or at least interest in spirituality) is increasing. A wide assortment of spiritualities
are available in the current marketplace: "native," "pagan," "feminist," and
"nature" (or "creation"), to name a few. Indeed there are few areas of activity—
ranging from sex to business—where someone has not discovered and promoted
an appropriate "spirituality." The titles of workshops at a thriving west coast
island "retreat centre" make the point: "Native Culture and Spirituality"; "Spiritual Retreat for Couples"; "Science and Spirituality"; "Spirit of the Drum."

There is also, within the church, a growing interest in Christian spirituality.
Most of us have benefited from this resurgence. Much of the charismatic renewal movement (for example) is a product of it. But the fact that this up-well-
ing of interest in spirituality is occurring both inside and outside the church (and
within the church is usually not accompanied by an accompanying interest in
theology) certainly raises questions for us about the relationship between "Christian spirituality" and our society's interest in "spirituality" in general. What is
"spirituality"? What (or whose) is the spirit (or are the spirits) of which it speaks?
Why, in this most materialist of ages, do we find this sudden interest in the
spiritual? Should the general interest in spirituality encourage—or discourage—
an interest in Christian spirituality? How is Christian spirituality related to Christian theology?

I cannot hope to answer all these questions adequately, but I would at least
like to provide a framework in which they can be answered. First, I'd like to try
to describe the cultural soil in which this contemporary preoccupation with "spirituality" has grown. To do this I will consider the emerging mood of
"postmodernism." Second, I want to focus on one particular cluster of
"spiritualities" that has great—and increasing—appeal: "creation" or

"ecofeminist" spiritualities, dealing with our relationship to the created world. Third, I want to speak of some of the resources in orthodox Christianity that enable us both to discriminate among "spiritualities" and to share more fully in the life of the triune God.

Saying No to Modernity's Exclusion of the Spiritual

The interest in spirituality in general is a major ingredient in what is now increasingly called "postmodernism." The very name of this mix makes it plain that we must understand the "postmodern" against the backdrop of "the modern."

For our purposes, "the modern" (or "modernity") can be defined as a determined attempt to exclude "the spiritual" from our experience and understanding. The origins of modernity are hard to pinpoint, but something like it first emerges as a potent intellectual force in the seventeenth century. In that period a wide range of thinkers were trying to devise new methods for knowing and manipulating the world. These new methods countered old ways of knowing, which took some sort of spiritual reality seriously. In nature (and "Nature" itself was a spiritual force), even objects moved according to an inner impulse. For example: water "seeks" its level; nature "abhors" a vacuum. In human affairs, no one questioned that the most important thing about men and women was their spiritual nature, and that political affairs were anchored by a spiritual status residing in the king. The ultimate authority for this was the church: a spiritual power founded on an inspired revelation.

The new methods developed in the seventeenth century sought a new authority, based on empirical observation and the disciplined use of reason. (The suspiciously "spiritual" nature of reason itself was generally overlooked.) We call the cluster of new methods "science." By no means was the new science seen as an un-Christian activity, nor should we see it so today. It did, however, place emphasis on methods for knowing the material world that implicitly minimized the spiritual.

We see the marginalization of the spiritual in the fragmentation of the inductive method of Francis Bacon, who argued that we should learn through the accumulation of facts rather than through the imposition on the facts of ideas arrived at through non-empirical or "spiritual" reasons. In this new emphasis on what can be measured, weighed and counted, there is an implicit assumption that what can't be empirically described is unimportant.

We see the same dwindling of the spirit in the methodological detachment of Rene Descartes, who maintained that the mind is "thinking substance," aloof from the world it thinks about, which is merely "extended substance." There is indeed in the mind something like "spirit" (it has been characterized as "the ghost in the machine"); but the rest of the world, including the body, is a different sort of thing altogether: dead matter, operating according to physical laws that the mind can know, describe, and control.

This modern attraction towards mechanism is evident in Isaac Newton's thought—which he made spectacularly convincing in the theory of gravitation— that the universe is matter in motion in a kind of cosmic machine whose laws we can figure out. By the end of the seventeenth century, the image of the universe as a kind of cosmic clockwork had become popular, and we are still trying to get free of it. Much of Christianity had accommodated itself to this picture of a sheerly material universe by seeing God as the great machinist who set up the clockwork, then withdrew—intervening only occasionally, if at all, in the well-designed machine of creation.

Taken together, these attitudes have had the effect, to use a phrase first popularized by Max Weber, of "desacralizing" the cosmos, including ourselves. C. S. Lewis describes that process of "despiritualizing":

> At the outset ... the universe appears packed with will, intelligence, life and positive qualities; every tree is a nymph and every planet a god. Man himself is akin to the gods. The advance of knowledge gradually empties this rich and genial universe: first of its gods, then of its colors, smells, sounds and tastes, finally of solidity itself as solidity was originally imagined. As these items are taken from the world, they are transferred to the subjective side of the account: classified as our sensations, thoughts, images or emotions. The Subject becomes gorged, inflated, at the expense of the Object. But the matter does not end there. The same method which has emptied the world now proceeds to empty ourselves. The masters of the method soon announce that we were just as mistaken, and mistaken in much the same way, when we attributed "souls," or "selves" or "minds" to human organisms, as when we attributed Dryads to the trees.... We, who have personified all other things, turn out to be ourselves mere personifications.[1]

We don't feel at home in such a universe, for one of the things it dissolves is our very personal selves. And it has become increasingly obvious that the picture of science that modernity assumes—and that postmodernism questions—is deeply flawed. Science is not now—and never was—a mechanical accumulation of facts issuing in knowledge. The very nature of the reality we are investigating is not so clearly "mechanical" or even physical, and it has become abundantly clear that personality cannot be excluded from our understanding of science.

But for now we need to understand how profoundly modernity has excluded "the spiritual" from our thought and experience. The attitudes of fragmentation (learning more and more about less and less), detachment (assuming that knowledge is necessarily impersonal), and mechanization (reducing knowledge to laws of matter in motion) have had the effect of alienating us from the universe, from our bodies, even from our own minds and emotions. We have found it harder and harder to live in the kind of structures we have concluded that we ourselves are, because that explanation of our world has excluded "the spiritual" as a meaningful category.

This attitude was summed up by Joy Davidman, describing the casual materialism of her Marxist youth: "Life is only an electrochemical reaction. Love, art and altruism are only sex. The universe is only matter. Matter is only energy. I forget what I said energy is only."[2] She meant it ironically. But an eloquent spokesman for the modern mind, Bertrand Russell, meant it seriously when he wrote in "A Free Man's Worship" this starkly modern statement of belief:

> That man is the product of causes which had no prevision of the end they were achieving; that his origin, his growth, his hopes and fears, his loves and his beliefs, are but the outcome of accidental collocations of atoms; that no fire, no heroism, no intensity of thought and feeling, can preserve an individual life beyond the grave; that all the labors of the ages, all the devotion, all the inspiration, all the noonday brightness of the human genius, are destined to extinction in the vast death of the solar system, and that the whole temple of man's achievement must inevitably be buried beneath the debris of a universe in ruins—all these things, if not quite beyond dispute, are yet so nearly certain that no philosophy which rejects them can hope to stand. Only within the scaffolding of these truths, only on the firm foundation of unyielding despair, can the soul's habitation henceforth be safely built.[3]

Russell wrote that statement early in the twentieth century when it did indeed seem to many that the mechanistic explanation of the universe was "nearly certain." His words describe the foundation of liberal modernity. However, the science of the intervening decades has made his confident despair a good deal less certain and the universe, and our place in it, a good deal more mysterious. (He wrote, for example, before the discovery that the universe had an origin in time; before the "anthropic principle," which acknowledges that the universe we live in is anything but "an accidental collocation of atoms"; before theories of chaos that point to ordering principles deeply embedded in so-called random processes of change.) His modern despair is courageous. But it has proven to be not only wrong in its science but unacceptable in its blueprint for human habitation.

Russell's use of the metaphor of habitation is particularly suggestive. He speaks of building a "soul's habitation" on the foundation of "unyielding despair" that a random cosmos requires. (One of the ironies, of course, is that such a cosmos excludes as well the possibility of a soul.) And one of the most spectacular triumphs of modernity is a particular kind of "habitation": "modern architecture." These impressively rational boxes of glass, concrete, and steel that mark the horizon of the modern city have been described as "machines for living." That phrase excludes the human spirit, as do the buildings themselves. Yet in the fifties and sixties there was a great flurry in many of our world's cities to build whole communities of such "machines for living" as a rational, modern way of doing away with squalor. The attempt is universally acknowledged to have failed, even though all over the world long blocks of such spirit-less dwellings stand like tombstones. Indeed, some have dated the beginning of "postmodernism" and its irrepressible cry for some sort of "spirituality" with a particular moment in architectural history (July 15, 1972, 3:32 p.m.), when a whole series of such buildings in St. Louis, the Pruitt-Igoe complex, was dynamited because it had proven to be an "uninhabitable environment."[4] So much for the "firm foundation of unyielding despair."

"Modernism," then, is a movement that for the last several centuries has tried to define human nature in terms of mechanistic, cause-and-effect laws that excluded "spirit," whether spirit was understood as spirit of God or spirit of the earth or human spirit. But we have grown tired of being modern. Of course, our postmodern weariness is highly selective (we are more than happy to take advantage of the modern technologies of medicine, transportation, information, and so on). Nevertheless, in Western culture, where modernity was invented, growing numbers of people are aware that the modern hope of a golden age of human fulfilment brought about through the application of science and technology to human problems—a hope we have lived with for at least a hundred years—has faded. And nowhere is the fading of this modern hope so clear as in the vigour with which we seek "the spiritual."

Modernity, for all its accomplishments, has thus created a kind of spiritual desert: people are thirsty for the spiritual, but do not know what they are thirsty for. Here are some of the things that define that thirst.

1. We long to be at home in our bodies. Thus we are beginning to question modern techniques and attitudes that detach us from the physical, leaving the body with less and less to do. The great appeal of "body work"—such as Yoga, massage, or simply "working out"—is that such techniques promise, and up to a point deliver, a reconciliation between body and spirit. The great appeal of meditation, with emphasis on posture, relaxation, and breathing, draws on this desire for integration of body and spirit.

2. We long for community. As small communities have dwindled and cities have grown, people feel a nostalgia for connectedness with other people. Though the optimistic era of "intentional communities" is at least a couple of decades behind us, most of our contemporaries long for some kind of human connectedness. The Personal Classified sections of city newspapers reveal more than a desire for sexual companionship: they speak of a deep, sad longing for meaningful human community.

3. We long for a healing of the alienation from creation: "nature," the earth. The world of modernity is increasingly a human construction. The more we acquiesce, for our own comfort, in these late stages of a process that began with simple needs for warmth and shelter, the more we want to be challenged by the non-human. Not surprisingly, the continuing growth of interest in "wilderness"—with its complex promise of spiritual renewal—is centred in the cities.

4. We long for a reconciliation with God. This is the deepest longing of all, and hence it is usually not recognized for what it is. The other longings are all substitutes for this hunger for relationship with God, and the reason why

none of them will be ultimately satisfying. No community or companionship or wilderness experience can meet the deep desire for a relationship with the living God.

Most contemporary "spiritualities" are an attempt to heal some of these alienations. And the word "spirit" is often used in connection with the elusive goal in each. To be in touch with one's body is a "spiritual" experience. Relationships, sexual or otherwise, are "spiritual"; the experience of the earth is often described in terms of "spirituality." And all are short-lived substitutes for the relationship, through the Holy Spirit, with the triune God, the relationship that brings the others to lasting life.

CREATION SPIRITUALITY AND ECOFEMINISM

Much of the current concern for spirituality is focused on "nature spirituality," whether it is pagan, understood as a revival of Wicca or European nature magic, or shamanism, understood as some form of native religion; or "creation spirituality," using some of the language and imagery of Christianity. "Creation Spirituality," popularized by the former Dominican priest Matthew Fox (he has recently been evicted from the order), is perhaps the most aggressively proposed of these spiritualities and the one most likely to appeal to contemporary Anglicans. The movement publishes a journal, *Creation Spirituality*, which includes this definition in its masthead:

> Creation Spirituality strives to awaken authentic mysticism, revitalize Western religion and culture, and promote social and ecological justice by mining the wisdom of ancient spiritual traditions and the insights of contemporary science. Creation Spirituality teaches panentheism, the belief that divinity permeates all things. It is the earliest tradition of the Hebrew Bible and was celebrated by the Rhineland mystics of medieval Europe. It is a tradition that honors women's experience and the cosmologies of Native cultures around the planet.

Creation spirituality has in many cases merged with "ecofeminism," a widespread coalition of "deep ecology" and feminism around the idea that the earth is Goddess, mother, of whom we are a part. "Creation spirituality" is thus almost inseparable from "women's spirituality." The reasons for this in a movement that is self-consciously anti-modern are not hard to find. In the three characteristics of the modern that I have highlighted—fragmentation, detachment, mechanism—the argument is that masculine ways of seeing and thinking have predominated. Men are more inclined to distance themselves from their bodies, hence from the earth, and to promote a "spirituality" of dominion. Men are thus more likely to describe the world and themselves in terms of pieces, fragments; not "wholisticly." Men are more likely to image the world as a machine, whereas women are more likely to image the world as an organism, a growing thing, a womb.

In every case, "modern" traits, understood as contributing to the despiritualizing, desacralizing movement of modernity, are linked to the masculine. The spiritual is seen as a feminine force, countering sterile modernity with life and nurturing. The appeal of ecofeminism is that it embodies attitudes that are equally attractive to men and women, for they hold out the promise of healing all four of the alienations we have just described.

1. For a variety of obvious reasons, mostly related to childbirth and nursing, women are less likely to pretend that they are, in their essence, merely a mind thinking about dead matter. Thus the women's movement has nourished a *greater comfort with a person's being a body*. It is, perhaps, easier for women to be at home with their bodies than for men, which may be one of the reasons why sexuality means different things to men and women. So it is not surprising that a part of the women's movement has been its opposition to anything that reflects an attitude towards the body as a mere thing: pornography, rape, and loveless intercourse—all of which are primarily male ways of trying to come to terms with alienated masculine existence.[5] By challenging those sadly inadequate ways of being masculine, feminism has thus been indirectly responsible for the "men's movement," in which men explore how to be men in a way that acknowledges their weaknesses, their feelings, and much that has traditionally been dismissed as "womanly."

2. Likewise, ecofeminism holds out the prospect of *a genuine community* that is not marred by the patriarchy—or by hierarchy of any kind—that, it is said, has done such damage to modern civilization. Indeed, a spiritless modernity is sometimes seen as patriarchy's chief monument. The symbol of such a genuine community is the circle: decision by consensus rather than decision from above or without. Ecofeminism speaks of a mythic, non-hierarchical, goddess-worshipping past of genuine community in which there was no war and men and women lived at peace with each other, their bodies, and nature. This reconstructed history is largely wishful thinking (goddesses and matriarchies seem to have been no less bloodthirsty than their masculine equivalents), but it represents an age-old longing for a lost golden age—a glimpse, perhaps, of Eden.

3. Most fundamentally, ecofeminism argues that much of our *alienation from the earth is the result of the dominance of masculine ideas of exploitation*. Common phrases such as "rape of the land" and "virgin forest" support the claim. At the "Global Forum" of the Earth Summit in Rio in 1992, by far the most lively and vital of the various centres was a large tent called "Planeta Femea" in which women from all over the world shared their concerns for their children, their communities, and their planet. Time after time the close link between women and agriculture, women and the soil, was underlined, and a convincing case was made that if women had more say in human affairs, the lot of the earth would be better. Much of this argument turns on a woman's biological—and psychological—preparation for giving birth and nurturing. The introduction to *Reweaving the World*, an important collection of ecofeminist

writings, makes the point in its dedication to one of the pioneers of the environmental movement, Rachel Carson:

Men of science have believed for hundreds of years that naming preceded owning, that owning preceded using, and that using naturally preceded using up. Some even believed that scientific understanding of the world would, if shrewdly managed, become something human beings could with considerable profit do to one another.... We have so many hard jobs ahead of us, so much education, so much organizing, so much action. But we do have that other way of understanding, a revolutionary understanding that we call feminist and ecological, in which we share the world with all creatures and living things and know that their stories are our own.[6]

4. Finally, ecofeminism suggests that most of the problems of modernity can be understood as the consequences of worshipping a God who is imaged in masculine terms—thus placing as the source and meaning of all things a detached, distant being. It is no surprise, goes this line of argument, that the worship of such a deity produced the self-alienating, spirit-destroying aberrations of thought that we have been characterizing as modernity. The *worship of the Goddess replaces the worship of God* in ecofeminism.

Central to this whole way of thinking is Gaia, the goddess of the earth, whose name was half-whimsically re-introduced into modern culture in the serious science of James Lovelock, who used Gaia as a name for the self-regulating capacities of the planet's living environment. The analogy with a planetary goddess has proven irresistible; thus much contemporary spirituality is "ecofeminist" or "gaia" or "goddess" spirituality.

A highly influential vehicle for the blend of "women's spirituality" and "earth spirituality" that I have been describing is a series of films produced by the National Film Board of Canada under the overall title "Women and Spirituality." The first, *Goddess Remembered*, makes a case for the now-familiar idea that all over Europe an earlier benign goddess religion reigned until about five thousand years ago. Then gradually it was supplanted by a patriarchal warrior religion that spoke of male deities and opened the door to most of the oppression and evil of our times. The second film, *The Burning Times*, considers some of that oppression in the European attitude towards witches.

The most recent of the films, *Full Circle*, pictures an emerging pagan spirituality that is essentially a religion of the earth. The film is beautifully done, with music by Loreena McKennit and eloquent footage of scenes as diverse as Stonehenge, Mexican temples, the American Southwest, and Canadian forests and waterfalls. Throughout the film, women's voices and women's faces, in a blend of sincerity and self-consciousness, try to describe an emerging spirituality. Author Anne Cameron, with obvious bitterness towards Christianity, declares, "When you get beyond the religion of Churchianity and get into the religions of the people, I don't care where on the face of the earth you go, that religion was the same. It was creation-honoring, it was woman-honoring, it was earth-nurturing."

The follower of Wicca, Starhawk, who in the film declares that she still feels close to her Jewish roots, says, "For me the goddess is immanent; she is the world, she is us, she is nature, she is the changing of the seasons, she is the earth herself. It is as if the whole universe were one living being that we are a part of." Here the implicit monism of this new spirituality is clear. (Monism is any philosophy or religion which declares that people, nature and God are all one.) And it is set over against a theism that distances God from creation, where God (that is, the deity spoken of as masculine) is found outside the world.

The same sentiment appears in the essays of *Reweaving the World*. Susan Griffin writes of the immanence of the divine as "a concept foreign to those raised in Judeao-Christianity.... [T]he view that we've grown up with is that the divine and matter are separate and that matter is really dangerous."[7] Ever since, so the argument goes, there has been a deep suspicion of the body, the feminine, and "nature," or the earth. The manifestation of this suspicion is in the growth of "patriarchy," which argues for the superiority of mind over body, male over female, and "man" (humanity) over "nature."

The growing movement of ecofeminist spirituality has nurtured both the trivial and the profound. On the trivial side is the aggressive marketing in some circles of something called "Amulets of the Goddess." In the words of an advertisement:

> The first time you consult the *Amulets of the Goddess* you could be facing an important decision.... [Y]ou reach into the black velvet pouch. Your fingertips brush softly against the amulets, the slight roughness of their surface reminiscent of an old adobe building or perhaps an ancient temple wall. You choose an amulet from the pouch and draw it into the light. Gazing at the amulet, tracing the engraved lines, the ancient symbols, you are drawn back to an earlier, more balanced time—a time when the law of nature was the law of the people and the Goddess was the oracle that taught the law....

Elsewhere the advertisement suggests, "Just think of it as your portable Sacred Space."

Trivial it may be; but the advertisement appeals very well to the spiritual longings of postmodern people, both women and men. It speaks of the longing for some kind of spiritual guide; it appeals vividly to our longing for something old, timeless, significant, something that transcends the fads of the age (faddish as the amulets themselves might be); it appeals to our longing for reintegration of fragments ("a more balanced time" when the law of people, nature, and Goddess was the same); above all, it appeals to a longing for closeness to the source of the spiritual (in this case the amulets themselves). Less obviously, perhaps, the "amulets" reflect our penchant for making "the spiritual" a handy, portable guide completely within our control.

More thoughtful, perhaps, is the re-visioning of Christian theology being done by some feminist theologians. Here are some observations from an interview with Brazilian feminist theologian Ivone Gebara.

> I am saying that our understanding of God must change. We can no longer posit a God who is Being-unto-himself, omnipotent, above all. This image of God is no longer adequate; we can no longer give obedience to someone "up there." This is the God built by patriarchy! Instead our intuition tells us that we dwell in Mystery larger than ourselves. We are part of this Mystery, which, like us, is evolving. This Mystery is what we call the Divine. But this Mystery is not a being, not a person. There is no God sitting on a throne who will judge us when we die. Our brothers and sisters on this earth are our only judges.

In response to the question, "Is there a personal God"?, Gebara answers:

> If God were a person, God would be an autonomous being, which is the same thing as the patriarchal concept of God who is "above" and "over" life itself. God is not a person, but we humans are persons so this is how we tend to relate to Divine Mystery. Because we are persons, we are able to initiate a dialogue, and we personalize all our relationships.... But what is the fear here? There is no "one God" to manipulate, as the "mono" theists have done.... This God is an entirely political God, a God whose main job is to dominate and control. Holistic ecofeminism holds that God is in all—and therefore all is sacred. We speak of panentheism. This is much closer to what primitive peoples have believed....
>
> What we are trying to do is relativize Christianity. It is one experience of how human beings explain Divine Mystery. The Jesus movement offers one response to humanity's search for meaning. But the Christian experience is only one response, not the response....
>
> We are speaking here of a change in paradigms. The patriarchal paradigm has lasted for more than 5,000 years. But everywhere that paradigm is falling apart. The old clothes no longer fit. We must look for new clothes, new constructs which we probably won't live to see firmly in place. But we are called to do so by the future, by our grandchildren.[8]

I quote Gebara at some length because she expresses fairly clearly both the ideological pressures and the spiritual longings that shape the environment in which contemporary Christians now live. Gebara assumes a great deal about Christian belief that is simply wrong, though unquestionably the church has been guilty of perpetuating some of the ideas she criticizes. And many of her suggestions for a more "user-friendly" theology are deeply wrong themselves, because she profoundly misunderstands the shape of Christian thought. Despite that, her complaint against what she calls patriarchal Christianity invites us to reaffirm the bases of an authentic Christian spirituality.

A CHRISTIAN RESPONSE

The sources of Christian spirituality lie where they have always lain, in the tri-une God, Creator and Redeemer, whom we meet decisively in history in Jesus, on the cross and in the witness of the Spirit to the reality of the resurrected Christ. We mouth these great truths regularly, but it is another thing to live them. Indeed, one of the problems of Anglican Christianity, which was born at the same time as what we have been calling "modernity," is that the truths embod-ied in our liturgies and confessions have been steadily diminished through re-interpretation as the hold of modernity has increased. Now, in a postmodernity that is deeply pluralistic, the gospel's scandal of particularity—that the way God made to himself is in a particular place, person, and time—has never been more scandalous. Nevertheless, the postmodern thirst for spirituality—which is uni-versal—should lead us back to a recovery of neglected truths of the scandal of the Christian gospel as a source for healing the wounds of modern alienation. The central answer for the confused syncretism of modern spirituality is a fuller understanding of God's closeness. Paul's words to the pagans of another period sets the tone well. At Lystra and again at Athens, he identifies the gifts and goodness of creation as the gifts and goodness of the creator God. "God did this," says Paul (referring to those gifts), "so that men would seek him and per-haps reach out for him and find him, though he is not far from each of us." The major task of Christian spirituality is to discover the closeness of the God glimpsed in creation and made flesh in Jesus, the only one who can heal the wounds of modern alienation.

THE TRANSCENDENT AND IMMANENT CREATOR

The alienation that underlies the contemporary quest for "spirituality" is our alienation from the God who made us, and who seeks to be our friend. Longing for connection with something, modern people seek a variety of connections—with the earth, with their body, with other people—in an attempt to find a con-nection with their creator. The alienation from God is rooted in human sin, a concept for which there is little room in contemporary spirituality (though it is given a variety of other labels, ranging from "patriarchalism" to "codependency").

But our feeling of distance from God does not mean that God is indeed dis-tant. We cannot affirm too much the transcendence of God, but we often do so to the exclusion of God's immanence, his closeness to creation. We have de-fended so ardently the Genesis account of creation "in the beginning" that we overlook the abundant biblical testimony of God's continuing, upholding care both for the cosmos and for each person. Indeed, one of the tragedies of our time is that when our whole society is crying out for a concept of the earth as "crea-tion" and a relationship with its creator-source, a cry expressed in the environ-mental movement and in ecofeminism in particular, Christians have diminished that concept by squabbling over the "how" and "when" of Creation. We have neglected to wonder at the "that" of creation now, and have thus been closed to the abundant evidence of God's spirit in the created world.

On the whole, the poets have done better at glorying in God's closeness to the creation than have the theologians. Thus the poet Gerard Manley Hopkins proclaimed in the first line of one sonnet: "The world is charged with the grandeur of God"[9] ; and in the last lines of another,

> All things counter, original, spare, strange;
> Whatever is fickle, freckled (who knows how?)
> With swift, slow; sweet, sour; adazzle, dim;
> He fathers-forth whose beauty is past change:
> Praise him.[10]

The result of this neglect of God's immanence has been a kind of Christian deism, which pictures God as distant and implacable: far off, generally angry, and breaking through only in occasional miraculous events. This is the machinist-God, the distant God of modernity, and it is no surprise that our culture, sensing the activity of God's spirit in creation, has sought a more intimate relation with that spirit.

But, on the whole, the more "evangelical" our theology, the more we have seen the incarnation not as "the word without [whom] nothing was made" but only as a kind of divine rescue mission, necessary to save God's image-bearer, man, from a cursed and doomed creation, like a child from a burning house.

The biblical picture is of a much closer relationship between creator and creation. God is presented as everywhere present to his creation, but nowhere confused with it: the closeness would be impossible were it not for his infinite greatness. Hopkins (not only a great poet but also a good theologian) puts very well this paradox:

> God is so deeply present to everything that it would be impossible for him, but for his infinity, not to be identified with them or, from the other side, impossible but for his infinity so to be present to them. This is oddly expressed I see; I mean, a being so intimately present as God is to other things would be identified with them were it not for God's infinity, or were it not for God's infinity he could not be so intimately present to things.[11]

Several biblical passages make the point clearly. One is Psalm 104, which is loosely patterned after the order of Genesis 1. Unlike Genesis 1, however, many of God's creative acts are here presented, not as taking place in some archetypal beginning, but continually, now:

> He makes springs pour water into the ravines... (verse 10).
> He waters the mountains from his upper chambers... (verse 13).
> He makes grass grow for the cattle, and plants for man to cultivate—bringing forth food from the earth (verse 14).
> These all look to you to give them their food at the proper time (verse 27).
> When you send your Spirit they are created, and you renew the face of the earth (verse 30).

This is certainly not pantheism (a heresy to which Christians sometimes fear an emphasis on God's immanence will lead). For the Psalmist never confuses creator and creation, though he sees God's goodness and self-giving love as present here and now. In the New Testament, the little we see of Paul's sermons to the pagan world suggests that he takes seriously the pagan recognition of the over-flowing goodness of creation, but turns it back to its proper source: the God who (in Paul's words on Mars Hill) "is not far from each one of us.... In him we live and move and have our being" (Acts 17:27–28). In another pagan setting, at Lystra, Paul urges the people to turn to "the living God who made heaven and earth and sea and everything in them" (Acts 14:15). But Paul goes on to make clear that this creator is not distant in space or time: "He has not left himself without testimony: He has shown kindness by giving you rain from heaven and crops in their seasons; he provides you with plenty of food and fills your hearts with joy" (Acts 14:17).

Another text which speaks powerfully of the intimacy of God is Psalm 139. A few lines make the point: "You know when I sit and when I rise.... / Where can I go from your Spirit? / ... you created my inmost being; / You knit me together in my mother's womb." The recovery of this deep and immediate relationship of God to creation, and to each person in his or her uniqueness, is essential for the nurturing of a genuine Christian spirituality.

Another Christian truth that needs recovering as postmodern men and women begin to respond to the God who (in Paul's words) "is not far from each one of us" is the truth of the Trinity. The "Creator Spirit" that waters the hills and knits us in the womb is God; Jesus, who in the hours before his death tells his friends, "Unless I go away, the Counsellor will not come to you," is God; and the God to whom we pray "our Father," in whom we "live and move and have our being," who loves us with the love of father and mother together, is God.

The God of the Bible is neither the aloof and lonely deity whose watch-maker relationship to creation shaped modernity; nor is the God of the Bible the impersonal, all-pervasive world spirit, the Gaia-goddess of ecofeminism whom we discover when we meditate on our own inwardness. Rather, the God of the Bible is the loving and self-giving communion whose very nature is to be in relationship. It is this relationship which we long to enter.

It is described very well in the great fourteenth-century Rublev icon that depicts the Trinity as the three messengers sent to Abraham. They sit on three sides of a table; the fourth place, empty, faces us. Food is on the table. The gestures of the messengers invite us to sit. And, in a sublime disregard of the laws of perspective, the vanishing point in the picture is where we stand; in the icon, the lines widen into infinity. We are invited to move, through the food offered by the triune God, from the vanishing point of our shrunken modernity out into the infinite life of the Trinity, who is (in the words of the title of a recent book on the subject) "Being as Communion." It is above all this relationship that our alienated, fragmented postmodern sensibility longs for.

Redemption

Another truth that we need to recover is a full biblical picture of redemption. Though the legal language of substitution is indeed a part of the biblical picture, we have tended to understand and proclaim it solely in terms of a satisfaction to an angry God, a punishment meted out by the aloof law-giver to a willing, sinless victim. The alternative, in liberal Anglican circles, has been to see the death of Jesus as an invitation to imitate the love of God.

The one picture portrays the justice of God but does not clearly show the love of the God who, through Isaiah, says, "In all your afflictions I am afflicted." The other portrays God's love but does not adequately picture the consequences of sin, the world-breaking devastation of our own itch to be gods on our own terms. By distancing God the creator from Christ the innocent victim, we drive apart the relationships in the Trinity, obscuring the fact that in Christ it is our creator who suffers. By making Jesus simply a good example of that full humanity that, with God's help, we all can all become, we likewise overlook the trinitarian truth that it is God who suffers. The result in both cases has been a shrinking of the effects of the atonement to the merely private and interior world—a characteristically modern (and postmodern) problem. Frederick Dillstone, in his study of various understandings of the atonement, describes this irony:

> The smaller the dimensions of man's world, the more wide-ranging is likely to be his systematic account of reconciliation. As his world expands, so his system seems to contract. When the limits of his universe have vanished into far-off distances, his concentration of concern tends to be focussed upon the small-scale world of the isolated inner self. Such a sequence can certainly be seen in the history of theories of the Atonement.[12]

A much richer picture of the atonement is based on the overarching biblical story of the movement from God's good creation, through sin, to a restoration, in Christ, of creation: new creation. The first articulation of such an understanding is in the writings of the early church father Irenaeus:

> For the Lord, taking dust from the earth, moulded man; and it was upon his behalf that all the dispensation of the Lord's advent took place. He had Himself, therefore, flesh and blood, *recapitulating in Himself not a certain other, but that original handiwork of the Father*, seeking out that thing which had perished.[13]

Irenaeus stresses here what is obscured in the more recent Western understanding of the atonement; that is, the fact that we are redeemed not simply by a sinless man, the perfect victim, but by God himself, our creator. If we take seriously the New Testament passages that link Christ to creation, we must take seriously as well the implications of the atonement for the whole creation. Irenaeus puts eloquently this summing up and restoring of all things in Christ:

For the Creator of the world is truly the Word of God: and this is our Lord, who in the last times was made man, existing in this world, and who, in an invisible manner contains all things created, and is inherent in the entire creation, since the Word of God governs and arranges all things; and therefore He came to His own in a visible manner, and was made flesh, and hung upon the tree, that He might sum up all things in Himself.[14]

Nor is this understanding of the atonement as "recapitulation" peculiar to Irenaeus. As Gustav Aulen points out in *Christus Victor*, it was central to the theology of all the fathers "to mention only the most important names, Origen, Athanasius, Basil the Great, Gregory of Nyssa, Gregory of Nazianus, Cyril of Alexandria, Cyril of Jerusalem, and Chrysostom...."

Athanasius' words put very eloquently the same link between Christ and Creation that Irenaeus saw:

We will begin, then, with the creation of the world and with God its Maker, for the first fact that you must grasp is this: the renewal of creation has been wrought by the Self-same Word Who made it in the beginning. There is thus no inconsistency between creation and salvation; for the One Father has employed the same Agent for both works, effecting the salvation of the world through the same Word Who made it at the first.[15]

The postmodern longing for the spiritual described early in this article is a longing for re-connection that can only be achieved by God. But it is reconnection and reintegration, not only with God, but with our very nature and with the rest of God's creation. We cannot accomplish this reintegration ourselves, though a wide range of spiritual techniques are proposed to help us do so. It is God's work: but the God whom we meet in Christ is the same one who, in the Psalmist's words, "created my inmost being." The deep, divinely enabled humanism of this picture of the atonement is expressed beautifully by Athanasius:

You know what happens when a portrait that has been painted on a panel becomes obliterated through external stains. The artist does not throw away the panel, but the subject of the portrait has to come and sit for it again, and then the likeness is re-drawn on the same material. Even so it was with the All-Holy Son of God. He, the Image of the Father, came and dwelt in our midst, in order that he might renew mankind made after Himself.[16]

This restoration and reintegration of ourselves, by the suffering maker who shaped us in the womb, is the basis for a genuine Christian spirituality, and it is the kind of reintegration that the spiritually lonely postmodernism of our culture is seeking.

CHRISTIAN SPIRITUALITY IN A POSTMODERN AGE

A final truth that needs to be recovered if we are to nourish a Christian spirituality in our age is the living of a genuine Christian community. There are many movements in this direction in the church today—particularly in the experience of small groups. Yet we need to go much further, recovering the full picture spoken of by Joel, and reiterated, in its Christian fulfilment, by Peter at Pentecost: "In the last days, God says, I will pour out my Spirit on all people. Your sons and daughters will prophesy, your young men will see visions, your old men will dream dreams... (Acts. 2:17). Our churches, our families, our lives need to be evidence of this life of the Spirit, a spirit which does not leave creation behind. Thus it should draw on the biblical images of sabbath, celebration, and restored wholeness that we have often neglected.

Our postmodern society is no closer than the modernity it rejects to a full life of wholeness. Only in God will that life be found, but it will not be found so long as we live lives that, in their busyness, their desperation, their consumerism, their subjection to the promptings of television and advertising, are no different from those of our spiritually wandering contemporaries. The spirituality we need will be seen in a healing of relationships: fundamentally with God through Christ, but also with other people, with our own bodies, and with creation itself, the creation in which so many people dimly glimpse something of the triune Creator God revealed in Christ the Word "without whom nothing was made."

Isaiah describes such a spirituality: "You will be like a well-watered garden, / Like a spring whose waters never fail. / Your people will rebuild the ancient ruins / and will raise up the age-old foundations (Isa. 58:11).

His words are, I think, a promise not only to the exiles of Israel but also to the church in Canada, this beloved but increasingly alien land where we are asked to make a home.

SUGGESTED READING

James Houston, *The Transforming Friendship* (Oxford: Lion, 1989).
Roger Lundin, *The Culture of Interpretation: Christian Faith and the Postmodern World* (Grand Rapids, Mich.: Eerdmans, 1993).
Lesslie Newbigin, *Foolishness to the Greeks* (Grand Rapids, Mich.: Eerdmans, 1986).

ENDNOTES

1. C. S. Lewis, in preface to D. E. Harding, *Hierarchy of Heaven and Earth* (London: Faber and Faber, 1952), p. 9.
2. Cited by C. S. Lewis in preface to Joy Davidman, *Smoke on the Mountain* (Philadelphia: Westminster Press, 1954).
3. Bertrand Russell, *Why I Am Not a Christian* (New York: Simon & Schuster, 1957), p. 107.
4. David Harvey, *The Condition of Postmodernity* (Oxford: Blackwell, 1990), p. 39.
5. In his superb study of modern spiritual homelessness called *Lost in the Cosmos*, Walker Percy suggests that the average modern man is "a ghost with an erection." Caricaturing the male attitude, Percy writes, "not cogito ergo sum [I think, therefore I am] ... but rather: if I enter you, I am alive, even human" (New York: Farrar, Strauss and Giroux, 1983), p. 44.

6. Irene Diamond and Gloria Feman Orenstein, eds., *Reweaving the World: The Emergence of Ecofeminism* (San Francisco: Sierra Club Books, 1990), p. iii.

7. Susan Griffin, "Curves Along the Road," in Diamond and Orenstein, *Reweaving the World*.

8. "Cosmic Theology, Ecofeminism and Panentheism," an interview by Mary Judith Ress with Ivone Gebara, *Creation Spirituality* (November/December, 1993), p. 11.

9. Gerard Manley Hopkins, "God's Grandeur," *Poems of Gerard Manley Hopkins*, ed. W. H. Gardner and N. H. MacKenzie (London: Oxford University Press, 1967), p. 31.

10. Hopkins, "Pied Beauty," in *Poems*, p. 70.

11. In *Sermons and Writings of G. M. Hopkins*, ed. Christopher Devlin, S.J. (London: Oxford University Press, 1959), p. 128.

12. F. W. Dillstone, *The Christian Understanding of Atonement* (Welwyn: James Nisbet, 1968), p. 406.

13. Irenaeus, in *Against Heresies: Early Christian Fathers*, ed. and trans. Edward Rocie Hardy (Philadelphia: Westminster Press, 1955), p. 541, emphasis added.

14. Hardy, *Against Heresies*, p. 385.

15. St. Athanasius, *On the Incarnation*. Translated and edited by Penelope Lawson (Crestwood, New York: St. Vladimir's Orthodox Theological Seminary, 1953), p. 26.

16. Ibid., p. 44.

CHRIST AND THE CULTURES
AN ESSAY IN CANADIAN MULTICULTURALISM

CRAIG M. GAY

THE POLITICS OF PLURALISM, RECOGNITION, AND RELATIVISM

The challenge of relating Christianity to culture is obviously not a new problem, but has become particularly complicated lately by cultural plurality. The challenge today is not simply that of deciding how to speak Christianly within a single culture, but of deciding how to relate the gospel to the multiplicity of cultures that together make up the societies of many modern nations.

The problem is perhaps especially acute in Canada, given our current express national commitment to a policy of "multiculturalism." This internationally unique commitment—obviously rooted in Canada's troubled bilateral history—first surfaced in 1971 in "The Report of the Royal Commission on Bilingualism and Biculturalism," and culminated in the Multiculturalism Act of 1988. Situated within the broad framework of civil, political, and language rights, the act states that the Government of Canada is committed to recognizing the diversity of Canadians as a fundamental characteristic of Canadian society, and it commits the government to preserving and enhancing the multicultural heritage of Canadians while preserving the economic and social equality of all cultural groups.

On the one hand, Canada's official commitment to multiculturalism appears profoundly humane in its regard for cultural distinctives and particularity. And yet, as Canadian sociologist Reginald Bibby has recently pointed out, the results of this commitment thus far are somewhat ambiguous. Canada's commitment to preserving and enhancing the multicultural heritage of all Canadians may actually—albeit unintentionally—foster relativism and individualism, both of which are profoundly destructive of communal life. "In its zeal to promote coexistence," Bibby fears, "Canada may find itself a world leader in promoting the breakdown of group life, and the abandonment of the pursuit of the best. Individually, we are emancipated; socially, we are in disarray.... Such is the madness characterizing the country today...."[1]

At the heart of Canada's commitment to multiculturalism is what McGill political philosopher Charles Taylor recently labelled "the politics of recognition."[2] Advocates of "recognition" contend that a person's individual identity is shaped—at least in part—by the larger society's recognition of that person's cultural ancestry. Hence, the absence of such recognition or the mis-recognition of the value of a person's cultural identity—as in racism or prejudice—translates into real personal injury. As Taylor points out, there is an important anthropological insight embedded in such a position; namely, that human beings are "dialogical creatures" whose identities are decisively shaped, not simply by internal cultural conversations with others, but also by the "conversation" of their particular culture with other cultures in the larger society. The politics of recognition is thus a plea for wider public and especially political recognition of the value of distinctive cultural groups towards the end of affirming the value of those who have been shaped within these cultures. Wider public recognition is thus held to be essential to the survival of cultures and ultimately to the survival of individual persons.

But, of course, the politics of recognition begs a number of thorny questions that have received an increasing amount of media attention of late, not the least of which is whether certain cultures—or at least certain features of them—really deserve to be recognized as valuable and, if so (or if not), how this should be decided. Are all cultures equally valuable? Equally good? Can such a thing be determined in principle? What if there is a conflict between cultures? What if one culture's virtue is another culture's vice? What if the recognition of other cultures is proscribed within a particular culture? And what about conflict between cultures and individuals? Should the recognition of a culture supersede the rights of those who inhabit it? Or should the rights and liberties of individuals be upheld even at the expense of cultural solidarity? Such questions are difficult enough when considered individually. Taken together, they constitute a genuine conundrum. One very basic problem that surfaces is that the facile affirmation of the "equality" of all cultures simply cannot be made the basis for national unity. Canadian historian John Stackhouse recently noted in an article entitled "What's a Country For?" that "if all [cultures] are equally good, none better in any way than another, then I and my group have nothing important to learn from you or yours. And if Canada *does* restrict the free exercise of any individual's or culture's preferences, then so much for Canada."[3]

And the matter is made even more difficult when we realize that we cannot decide, in principle, for the equality of all cultures without emptying the notion of "recognition" of content. After all, what would such recognition be for? Simply for a culture's existence? This would hardly satisfy the aforementioned anthropological requirement for recognition. And yet, because any genuine recognition of a culture's value will entail discrimination and evaluation, subjecting a culture to such critical scrutiny will necessarily run the risk that certain features of it may not be valued, or that they will only be recognized in a negative sense. The recognition of a culture's value, it seems, cannot be guaranteed in advance without rendering the concept of recognition somewhat less than meaningful.

Yet if we refuse to affirm the equality, in principle, of all cultures, don't we thereby threaten the recognition of cultural particularity? Isn't this simply to leave minority cultures at the mercy of the dominant culture? Doesn't such a refusal lie at the root of cultural imperialism? Clearly, we face something of a paradox with respect to Canada's national commitment to multiculturalism. The genuine recognition of the truth, goodness, and beauty of distinctive cultures inevitably calls for judgement; and yet judgement—if it is to be taken seriously— cannot guarantee the equality of recognition *a priori*.

In Christian circles, the paradoxical challenge of multiculturalism is reflected in the paradoxical relation of "conservative" and "liberal" attempts to respond to it. "Conservatives" have, just as their postmodern accusers have suggested, tended to confuse their theological commitment to the unity of truth with the basic contours of WASP culture. The concern for biblical truth has all too fre- quently become a vehicle for the defence of the market economy, the bourgeois family, and other features of North American conservative Protestant culture. "Liberals," on the other hand, have become so concerned to recognize cultural diversity that they have either embraced a kind of relativism that is incapable of recognizing anything in particular, or become culturally "radicalized" in such a way as to make it is impossible for them to recognize anything beyond the par- ticularity of their own chosen cause or group.

ADDRESSING THE PARADOX OF MULTICULTURALISM

Resolving the paradoxical problem of multiculturalism to everyone's satisfac- tion will not be easy—perhaps it is impossible—but I want to suggest two theses that will hopefully contribute to Christian thinking on it. The first thesis, fol- lowing Taylor, is that pluralism and relativism undermine the value of recogni- tion. Thus, although the commitment to multiculturalism represents a legiti- mate entreaty for the recognition of the value of cultures in the face of serious threats to such recognition, such a commitment makes genuine recognition im- possible to the extent that this multiculturalism requires us to embrace plural- ism and/or relativism—both of which emphasize particularity at the expense of truth. While this may seem an obvious point to make, it is apparently not so obvious. Indeed, one of the problems we face today is that recognition is most often advocated in such a way that cultural particularity is either collapsed into liberal individualism or else stressed so dogmatically that it makes genuine rec- ognition impossible. Put differently, the attempt to mandate recognition seems to betray the fact that either culture is not really being taken very seriously after all or a single culture is being taken so seriously that all others are, in effect, excluded *a priori*.

There are so many ambiguities and ironies that attach to this issue of multiculturalism that we may be tempted to write the matter off as, in the words of one recent observer, "the masochistic celebration of Canadian nothingness";[4] but this would be a mistake, especially for Christians. There is far too much at stake in this matter. The anthropological assumptions underlying the politics of recognition and its protest against non- or mis-recognition suggest a high valua- tion of individuality, relationality, and personhood, all of which the gospel af- firms wholeheartedly. At the same time, the relativism that seems so often to go hand in hand with the contemporary commitment to multiculturalism obviously poses a very serious threat to Christian truth. And so the question is not whether we ought, as Christians, to speak out on this issue of multiculturalism, but rather *what* we are going to say. It is here that we need to recognize that Christian theology is remarkably and uniquely capable of resisting pluralism and/or relativism, while genuinely recognizing and affirming cultural diversity.

My second thesis, then, is that Christianity is uniquely capable of squaring the circle of multiculturalism. It would be relatively easy to demonstrate this second thesis historically, to demonstrate that the church has, for the most part, accommodated and affirmed cultural plurality within the broad limits of orthodoxy over the course of its long history and will probably continue to do so into the future. And yet, while this kind of historical reasoning is illuminating, it is not really adequate to the task at hand, for two reasons. The first is that most people, probably including many Christians, assume that Christianity's recognition of cultural diversity is really only a kind of historical accident: the failure of Christians to conquer the culture completely. The second reason, which is obviously closely related to the first, is that many people (again, many Christians included) don't understand how it is theologically possible for Christianity to recognize cultural plurality without also embracing relativism.

Thus for the church's remarkable historical record to be truly appreciated, it must be shown to be theologically explicable. The church's recognition of cultural diversity must be shown to arise out of basic doctrinal commitments. Along this line, I want to suggest that the affirmation of cultural particularity is essential to the kind of "good news" the Christian gospel claims to be; and indeed that the affirmation of cultural particularity, and hence of individual human persons, is a necessary implication of the central doctrines of the Christian faith.

Before developing this thesis further, however, it will help to take a closer look at "the politics of recognition" and at the nature of modern society; for we need to recognize that the most profound threat to the recognition of cultures today does not really stem from racism or prejudice but, instead, from the tendency towards homogeneity inherent in the process of modernization. Culture, according to *Webster's Dictionary*, is "the integrated pattern of human behavior that includes thought, speech, action, and artifacts and depends upon man's capacity for learning and transmitting knowledge to succeeding generations." Put somewhat less technically, culture is made up of the answers we give to the questions our children ask about the world. Such questions range from the trivial (Why can't I eat with my fingers?) to the profound (What does it mean to die? What is God like?). The answers we give to these questions are already partly built into the languages we use to answer them. Hence the vital connection between language and culture. But a culture is more than simply a language; it is an attempt to use language to fashion truthful answers to real human questions. And while few cultures are ever monolithic, a culture's integrity will depend upon how well or poorly its answers correlate with one another and with real human experience of the world. As Philip Rieff noted a number of years ago, "superior to and encompassing the different modes in which it appears, a culture must communicate ideals, setting as internalities those distinctions between right actions and wrong that unite men and permit them the fundamental pleasure of agreement. Culture is another name for a design of motives directing the self outward, toward those communal purposes in which alone the self can be realized and satisfied."[5]

"Multiculturalism," then, implies the coexistence of a number of different ideas about what ought to constitute communal purposes within a single society. The use of the term normally implies two kinds of assumptions. The first are cognitive assumptions about what is in fact the case in the contemporary situation; for example, the assumption that Canadian society is ethnically, religiously, and culturally plural. The second kind of assumption is typically normative and has to do with what implications the purported fact of cultural plurality ought to have for ongoing thought and practice. Almost all of the controversy over multiculturalism has to do with this second kind of assumption; that is, with conflicting opinions about what difference the fact of cultural plurality ought to make for us.

To get to the heart of this controversy, it will help to delineate four different ways the term "multiculturalism" is currently being used. Each holds a different social ideal in view. The first common use of the term multiculturalism today is largely pragmatic and rests upon two basic assumptions. The first is that there is apt to be something of value in all cultures and that, therefore, the pooling of our cultural resources is probably, on balance, a good thing to do. The second assumption is that, given the fact of cultural plurality, we're going to need to learn to get along with each other, and this will require, at the very least, trying to understand one another. Multiculturalism, from this perspective, then, is respectful of cultures but is principally pragmatic in orientation. This use of the term occasionally functions ideologically to the extent that Canada's commitment to multiculturalism is supposedly what distinguishes Canadian society from the American "melting pot." But for the most part this understanding of multiculturalism simply implies a broad strategy for education and socialization. It is our commitment to multiculturalism, so the argument runs, that will hopefully enable us somehow to take advantage of the "good" aspects of cultures while neutralizing the threat that certain "bad" aspects of cultures pose to social order.

Multiculturalism is also used today as a kind of "up-to-date" synonym for pluralism; that is, it is used to denote a classically liberal commitment to rational social order, to combating irrational (read: "traditional") sources of discrimination, and to guaranteeing an equality of opportunity for all individuals to participate in the larger society. Although such a commitment is very much in evidence in Canada's Charter of Rights and Freedoms, this kind of pluralist multiculturalism is most commonly associated with the American Bill of Rights, which basically calls for the sacrifice of cultural distinctness when the issue of equality is at stake. Cultural commitments, so the argument runs, cannot be allowed to impede the autonomy of the individual and his or her ability to participate in the society. Such an understanding forms the basis of the American social experiment captured in the famous motto *e pluribus unum*, "from many, one."

Not surprisingly, the classically liberal commitment to multiculturalism (pluralism) requires a culturally neutral state. While different people may well have different ideas about what constitutes "the good life," so the argument runs, we ought to agree to treat each other fairly and equally in spite of these differences. The way forward, therefore, is not necessarily to adopt or enforce some particular view of the good life, but simply to unite around a strong procedural commitment to treat all people, all cultures, with due respect.[6] The state's job, then, is to police this commitment from a position of neutrality.

Charles Taylor recently attempted to delineate a third use of the term multiculturalism within the context of what he considers to be a more hospitable version of liberalism. A hospitable liberalism, Taylor suggests, would, unlike the American model, be better able to appreciate communal and cultural convictions. Of course, it would discipline such convictions with a commitment to guarantee certain fundamental individual liberties, but hospitable liberalism would allow the state to sponsor certain communal cultural projects. This, Taylor argues, is basically what Quebeckers sought in having Quebec designated a "distinct society" in the failed Meech Lake Accord. Quebeckers thought it both possible and desirable to preserve a particular cultural vision, the preservation of Francophone culture in North America, while at the same time maintaining a reasonable commitment to the rights of individuals. Such a view is very much in keeping with the actual development of Canada's policy of multiculturalism, which emerged out of the discussion about biculturalism and is still set forth within a bilingual framework. Of course, Taylor recognizes that drawing the balance between cultural commitments and individual rights will not be as easy as it appears to be in the classical-liberal American model; but he points out that even the classical-liberal model is required to strike such a balance. Hence, the only real difference between the two models is that Taylor's hospitable liberalism is not as suspicious of culture as the American alternative.

A fourth use of the term multiculturalism—the use that has attracted the most media attention of late—is what might be called the "radical" or "ideological" use. It is multiculturalism in this sense that has generated such an acrimonious debate on university campuses and among cultural elites; and for good reason, for multiculturalism from this perspective is divisive by definition. As the equalization of power among competing socio-cultural groups is the only real moral absolute, so the argument runs, multiculturalism requires advocating the interests of minority cultures over and against the purportedly repressive hegemony of bourgeois culture. The politics of recognition, accordingly, become the politics of advocacy and solidarity on behalf of purportedly repressed minorities. "Recognition" from this perspective grows out of the barrel of a gun, to paraphrase the celebrated proverb of Mao Zedong.

CULTURAL HOMOGENIZATION

So what are we to make of these different and to some extent conflicting uses of the term multiculturalism? Perhaps the first thing to note is that the commitment to multiculturalism betrays certain vested interests. It has been observed, for example, that cultural leaders are far more likely to be concerned about multiculturalism than are the rank and file.[7] This is hardly surprising. The politics of recognition are, after all, about the formation and maintenance of cultural identities, and those whose business it is to shape and police such identities obviously stand to benefit from this project more tangibly than others. This would appear to hold true not simply for ethnic elites but for the leaders of all cultural groups whose identities depend in part upon finding fault with what they perceive to be the dominant culture. While the policies of multiculturalism are always defended in terms of the so-called man on the street, elites benefit from such policies most directly.

On the other hand, it has also been plausibly argued that the policy of multiculturalism in Canada finally amounts to a kind of "divide and rule" strategy on the part of the English-speaking majority culture.[8] From the perspective of certain French-Canadian critics, for example, the policy represents a *de facto* denial of Canada's fundamental biculturalism. Indeed, multiculturalism reduces the French language and culture to just another cultural minority, perhaps slightly ahead of Ukrainian culture numerically speaking, but far behind English language and culture in national importance.[9]

And there is evidence that certain immigrant groups are not entirely convinced of the merits of Canada's commitment to multiculturalism either. This is particularly true of groups that take religion seriously, for members of these groups recognize that whatever else the advocates of multiculturalism may say about the cultural importance of religion, they are wholly unwilling to allow certain religious commitments to function as cultural universals. Religious commitments are considered too potentially divisive. "In the final analysis," one author suggests concerning the Muslim experience in Canada, "Canadian multiculturalism is political ideology, even perhaps a subtle device to melt the variant immigrants down into homogeneous stew."[10]

This last observation is particularly significant, and it is important to see that all of the four variants of multiculturalism discussed above do, in fact, tend in the direction of cultural homogeneity. They also tend, albeit unwittingly and unintentionally, to foster relativism and individualism. This is perhaps most obvious with the classical-liberal or pluralist version of multiculturalism, which essentially requires the public square to be emptied of cultural and, particularly, religious commitments. Curiously, the tendency towards homogeneity floats quite close to the surface in the various radical versions of multiculturalism as well. For although radicals purport to defend the interests and integrity of minority cultures, they also typically demand an unwavering commitment to secular ideological dogma, usually some variant of neo-Marxism or neo-Nietzschianism. Just as with all "radical" programmes, this kind of commitment to multiculturalism is ultimately critical, reductionist, and dogmatically unified around a certain set of non-negotiable principles.

It is important to stress, however, that even the purely pragmatic version of multiculturalism and Taylor's more hospitable liberalism also tend in the direction of cultural homogeneity. The pragmatic approach points towards a social and cultural order in which peace and prosperity ("bread and circuses") become the only working universals; and it is not entirely clear that Taylor's modified liberalism really represents anything beyond a slight variation on the classical-liberal theme. In both versions of liberalism, when push comes to shove, the rights of individuals will always eventually prevail over the rights of cultural groups.

In effect, the policy of multiculturalism seems to need to neutralize cultural particularity in order to preserve it. The policy acts as a kind of cultural Trojan Horse, promising to preserve and enhance "cultural heritages," and yet insidiously neutralizing cultural particularity; and in neutralizing cultural particularity, leaving the door open to individualism, relativism, and the loss of cultural integrity and meaning. Interestingly, the problem may be even more acute in Canada than in the United States. Canada's commitment to communal life has historically been expressed in terms of submission to governmental authority, and not in terms of commitment to religious, cultural, and/or voluntary associations. To the extent that the Government of Canada becomes a kind of neutral arbiter of individual, or cultural, rights, so the society is left, in effect, with no cultural counterbalance to individualism. This is why Bibby characterizes the contemporary Canadian situation as one of "mosaic madness." "Our obsession with the individual and choice, our mosaic madness," he argues, "is carrying considerable costs. It is affecting our everyday interactions, our most personal relationships, our institutional involvements. The madness is highly destructive, keeping us from experiencing the best possible quality of life, individually and collectively."[11]

Considerable light is shed on the problem if we consider multiculturalism as a characteristically modern phenomenon and, more specifically, as a reflection of a process John Murray Cuddihy called "the ordeal of civility."[12] Developing one of the principal insights of American sociologist Talcott Parsons, Cuddihy contends that the process of modernization is one of progressive "differentiation," that is, of the separation of any number of things that have traditionally been unified in human cultures. A typically modern society, for example, is one that requires the separation of nuclear from extended families, of home from job, of economics from politics, of politics from religion, of religion from culture, of public from private, of fact from value, of theory from praxis, of means from ends, and, finally, of culture from personality, or of people themselves from the ideas they hold.[13] While space does not permit a detailed discussion of the reasons for this "differentiation" here, the process appears to have largely to do with the rationalized logic of the modern technological economy, which requires ever-increasing specialization and the progressive compartmentalization of social order. Cuddihy suggests that while this process of relentless differentiation does enable us "to live with unknown others without transforming them into either brothers or enemies,"[14] it also dissolves, and eventually destroys, traditional cultures—hence the phrase "ordeal of civility." Culture, particularly religion, is civilized, privatized, trivialized, and reduced either to such things as folk dance, costume, and cuisine or to mass-marketed products. Put differently, culture in a modern society is all but prevented from providing serious answers to serious human questions about the world. The end result of "the ordeal of civility" is really a kind of cultural homogeneity. As one observer recently suggested, "modernity promised us a culture of unintimidated, curious, rational, self-reliant individuals, and it produced ... a herd society, a race of anxious, timid, conformist 'sheep,' and a culture of utter banality."[15]

The modern "ordeal of civility," Cuddihy continues, is profoundly traumatizing, particularly for cultural groups that have immigrated into modern societies and so have been forced to cope with this process suddenly and abruptly. Indeed, Cuddihy interprets a great deal of modern intellectual culture in terms of its resistance to the process of modernization. "Beneath the politics of the oppositional intelligentsia," he writes, "the antimodernist thrust is all too audible. Demodernization, from Marx to Mao, is dedifferentiation."[16] That the "oppositional intelligentsia" have taken up the cause of multiculturalism so visibly and vociferously in recent years is perhaps an indication that multiculturalism is now functioning, at least in part, as a protest, not simply against such things as racism and prejudice, but more broadly as a protest against modernity's absorption and trivialization of all cultures.

But if this is true—if multiculturalism really is, at root, a kind of romantic protest against cultural homogenization—then this calls its basic cognitive assumption, the purported fact of cultural plurality, into question. The actual state of affairs may be quite different. Instead of a plurality of cultures, Canadian society may more accurately be described as a typically modern society in which cultural plurality is rather routinely absorbed into a kind of technological and commercial homogeneity. This was the central contention of Canadian political philosopher George Grant's celebrated *Lament for a Nation* (1965).[17] "Modern civilization," Grant observed, "makes all local cultures anachronistic.... [W]hen men are committed to technology, they are also committed to continual change in institutions and customs. Freedom must be a first political principle, the freedom to change any order that stands in the way of technological advance. Such a society cannot take seriously the conception of an eternal order by which human actions are measured and defined."[18] The society committed to technology and economic growth, in other words, cannot also be seriously committed to culture. Indeed, the workings of the technological economy may actually be impeded by serious reflections about ultimate human purposes. Instead, the only thing that really matters in such a society is to keep the process going. As American scholar Philip Rieff noted in a study entitled *The Triumph of the Therapeutic* (1966), "Western culture is changing already into a symbol system unprecedented in its plasticity and absorptive capacity. Nothing much can oppose it really, and it welcomes all criticism, for, in a sense, it stands for nothing."[19] Another observer recently coined the term "McDonaldization" to describe the ways in which culture is reduced in modern societies to the lowest possible common denominator.[20]

It is in this light that we can begin to appreciate how deeply ironic it is that the Government of Canada has sought to generate support for multiculturalism with the slogan "multiculturalism means business." For however else one may feel about business, it is not difficult to see that the logic of modern commercial activity poses a fairly serious threat to survival of cultural particularity. As British Anglican theologian Colin Gunton has recently noted, "the spectre at the banquet of the modern world [is] homogeneity.... The pressures for homogeneity are various: philosophical, political, social but above all perhaps commercial...."[21]

THE THEOLOGICAL TASK

In sum, we might say that although the case for multiculturalism is most often made in terms of more or less obvious threats to cultural recognition—racism, prejudice, discrimination, inequality—the concern for multiculturalism probably also betrays a kind of inarticulate hunger for serious culture *as such* in the face of modernity's erosion of cultural integrity. And yet, ironically, this commitment to multiculturalism, at least as it is commonly expressed today, is itself profoundly modern, secular, individualistic, and hence finally homogenizing. Put somewhat differently, while the commitment to multiculturalism may plausibly be interpreted as a cry for more adequate answers to basic human questions than the culture of modernity has to offer, this cry still rests upon typically modern assumptions. It is, for example, still circumscribed by the characteristically modern suspicion of religious culture. Indeed, the contemporary tension between longing for serious culture, and yet not wanting this culture to be religious in any serious way, is one of the more peculiar, and indeed tragic, features of late modernity.

And so the theological task we face is perhaps more complicated than we thought. The problem is not simply one of providing a theological basis for the recognition of cultural diversity, it is also one of trying to speak real meaning, real culture, into a society that, by virtue of the way it is structured, is increasingly bereft of meaning. Exposing the ironies and hypocrisies in our commitment to pluralism and multiculturalism is perhaps an important first step along this path. But the situation obviously calls for affirmation as well as criticism.

It is here that we need to see the gospel of Jesus Christ as "good news" precisely because it speaks to both of the problems just cited. On the one hand, the gospel obviously provides real answers to very real human questions and so comes as very good news in the context of a society increasingly bereft of serious meaning. We know this, of course. Christians have been saying this for a long time and will hopefully continue to say it. What we have not been saying, however, (and perhaps because we do not yet believe it) is that the gospel does not amount to a denial of human culture as much as it presents a radical affirmation of cultural particularity. Indeed, the gospel is so affirming of human culture that this has historically been an offence to those outside of the church and something of an embarrassment to those on the inside. After all, the radical affirmation of cultural particularity can be seen as a correlate of Christianity's so-called scandal of particularity. The fact that the eternal God would choose to speak to particular people in particular cultural situations, and indeed that this God would become flesh and dwell among us as a first-century Palestinian Jew, has always been hard to swallow. While this may not make much sense from the perspective of the "universal truths of reason," it is profoundly good news for real people who are themselves embedded in real historical cultures. The incarnation is nothing if it is not an affirmation of cultural particularity and, finally, of real human existence. That the Christian God takes human culture seriously is evidenced by the fact that he does not reveal himself in such a way as to annihilate culture and history, but instead he came, and continues to come, into our cultures, our traditions, our languages. This God has gone to very great lengths, indeed even to the extent of suffering an asphyxiating death on a first-century Roman cross, to communicate with real people who are embedded in real culture and history. And so, as Colin Gunton has recently noted, "it is often said that one of the intellectual drawbacks of Christianity is its elements of particularity ... [but] contrary to the received view that particularity is a disadvantage, a theology giving central place to particularity is precisely what the modern age needs...."[22] The gospel is not homogenizing but profoundly and essentially particularizing.

And yet, while Christianity's affirmation of cultural particularity is most profoundly evident in the incarnation, it begins with the doctrine of creation. This is the thrust of Colin Gunton's 1992 Bampton Lectures on "God, Creation and the Culture of Modernity." Gunton observes that both ancient and modern cultures show a persistent disposition towards cultural homogeneity, towards the absorption of all particularity into some kind of unity. In both cases, Gunton argues, this tendency is a reflection finally of philosophical and/or theological monism, that is, a reflection of a commitment to a single principle of unity in the world. This is not to say that there has not been protracted disagreement over just what this unifying principle is, or ought to be; but the general tendency has been to subsume cultural particularity, and indeed particularity as such, under some principle of unity. This has not tended to be very good news for minority cultures.

In contrast to ancient and modern monisms, Christianity affirms, or at least it ought to affirm, the significance and ultimate realness of created particularity as such, for it is Christianity that teaches that the creation is not simply a kind of emanation of God's essence, but an act of love and generosity. That this was possible points to the reality of particularity and unity in the one God who is also three persons. Because this God is eternally "being in communion," he did not have to create the world in order to have something to love, and the world does not eventually have to be re-absorbed back into his being. The creation is real, and its reality is the gift of grace. The world, including the nations and cultures of the world, is created so that it might share in the love that eternally unifies the Father, Son, and Holy Spirit.

Hence, it is no accident that the affirmation of the Trinity is the first of our Thirty-Nine Articles of Religion. This article affirms that God's essential being is not monochromatic but communal and personal, that he has created a world that reflects the richness of his communal and personal essence, and that our destiny is to share eternally in this personal communion. While the implications of God's essential tri-unity are far too numerous to be developed here, suffice it to say that the doctrine of the Trinity is very good news for cultural particularity. Such an understanding, as Gunton suggests, "can surely enable us better to conceive something of the unity in variety of human culture ... [for] if the triune God is the source of all being, meaning and truth, we should be able to develop a theology of the unity of culture without depriving each of its dimensions of its distinctive approach and validity."[23] Of course, it should be noted here that Gunton's chief concern is that Western Christianity has not tended to appreciate just how radical the implications of a truly trinitarian understanding are for a theology of culture. But given modernity's relentless homogenization of all cultural differences, Gunton suggests that the time is ripe for a rediscovery of trinitarian understanding.

It must also be stressed, however, that the gospel's profound recognition and affirmation of cultural plurality is neither pluralistic nor relativistic; for both effectively deny meaning in history and so undermine the biblical narrative of creation, fall, and redemption. As Bishop Lesslie Newbigin recently noted in *The Gospel in a Pluralist Society*,

> the gospel endorses an immensely wide diversity among human cultures, but it does not endorse a total relativism. There is good and bad in every culture and there are developments continually going on in every culture which may be either creative or destructive, either in line with the purpose of God as revealed in Christ for all human beings, or else out of that line. The criteria for making judgments between the one and the other cannot arise from one culture. That is the familiar error of cultural imperialism. There can only be criteria if God has in fact shown us what his will is. He has done so in Christ. If that is denied in the name of religious pluralism, then there is no valid criterion by which the positive and negative developments in human culture can be assessed. On the other hand, the content of the revelation in Christ, defined crucially by the twin events of cross and resurrection, provides the basis on which the great diversity of cultures can be welcomed and cherished and that claim of one culture to dominance can be resisted.[24]

Thus we must stress that the nations of the world are not affirmed in their fallenness and in their rebellion against God. Such an affirmation would hardly achieve the ends of love and communion. Indeed, were we to affirm cultures "in revolt," to use Brunner's suggestive term, we would only impede the reconciliation of the creation to its creator. Rather, the nations, and, finally, each one of us, must be baptized into the death and resurrection of Jesus Christ. Every culture must be washed in his blood if it is to rise up with him in resurrected life. We get a glimpse of resurrected multiculturalism in the apostle's description of the New Jerusalem in Revelation 21:23–24: "The city does not need the sun or the moon to shine on it, for the glory of God gives it light, and the Lamb is its lamp. The nations will walk by its light, and the kings of the earth will bring their splendor into it."

CONCLUSION

In conclusion, let us briefly review the argument. We have seen that the challenge of relating the gospel to culture today is not simply one of deciding how to speak Christianly within a single culture (perhaps it never really has been), but rather of deciding how to be "salt" and "light" in the midst of the multiplicity of cultures that together make up contemporary Canadian society. And yet, the challenge is not simply one of providing a theological basis for the recognition of cultural diversity, but also one of trying to inject real culture, real meaning, into a context in which there are profound pressures to reduce all cultures to homogeneity, cultures which are therefore increasingly bereft of meaning. In this context, we need to stress that the church's historical ability to recognize cultural diversity, however imperfect, is not accidental. It has stemmed from the central articles of Christian faith, and particularly from the Christian affirmation that the world and all of its rich diversity are the work of a God who is himself diversity in the unity of love.

To be sure, this gospel will continue to be a "stumbling block to Jews and foolishness to the Greeks" for a variety of reasons. But at least we can defend the Christian social vision against the accusations that it must be culturally monolithic or repressive, as though the gospel somehow requires the obliteration of cultural particularity. While many ancient and almost all modern visions of social order do require this, the Christian vision, because it is grounded in an understanding of God essentially "being in communion," is quite unique in its affirmation of cultural diversity and its celebration of individual personality.

SUGGESTED READING

Reginald Bibby, *Mosaic Madness: The Poverty and Potential of Life in Canada* (Toronto: Stoddart, 1990).

George Grant, *Lament for a Nation: The Defeat of Canadian Nationalism* (Ottawa: Carleton University Press, 1989 [1965]).

———, *Technology and Empire* (Toronto: Anansi, 1969).

Colin E. Gunton, *The One, The Three and the Many: God, Creation and the Culture of Modernity* (Cambridge: Cambridge University Press, 1993).

Charles Taylor, "The Politics of Recognition," in *Multiculturalism and "The Politics of Recognition,"* ed. Amy Gutman (Princeton: Princeton University Press, 1992).

ENDNOTES

1. Reginald W. Bibby, *Mosaic Madness: The Poverty and Potential of Life in Canada* (Toronto: Stoddart, 1990), p. 15.

2. Charles Taylor, "The Politics of Recognition," in *Multiculturalism and "The Politics of Recognition,"* ed. Amy Gutman (Princeton: Princeton University Press, 1992), pp. 25–73.

3. John G. Stackhouse Jr., "What's a Country For?" in *Crux: A Quarterly Journal of Christian Thought and Opinion*, Vol. 27 (Regent College, 1991), pp. 7–9.

4. Gad Horowitz (University of Toronto), cited in Bibby, *Mosaic Madness*, p. 92.

5. Philip Rieff, *The Triumph of the Therapeutic: Uses of Faith After Freud* (London: Chatto & Windus, 1966), p. 4.

6. Taylor, "The Politics of Recognition," p. 56. Taylor suggests that American scholar Ronald Dworkin is perhaps the most able representative of this position.

7. Ronald Wardhaugh, *Language and Nationhood: The Canadian Experience* (Vancouver, B.C.: New Star Books, 1983), p. 210.

8. Ibid., p. 214.

9. Ibid., p. 213.

10. Harold Barclay, "The Muslim Experience in Canada," in *Religion and Ethnicity*, eds. Harold Coward and Leslie Kawamura (Waterloo, Ont.: The Calgary Institute for the Humanities, 1978), p. 111.

11. Bibby, *Mosaic Madness*, p. 155.

12. John Murray Cuddihy, *The Ordeal of Civility: Freud, Marx, Levi-Strauss, and the Jewish Struggle with Modernity* (New York: Basic Books, 1974).

13. Ibid., p. 98.

14. Ibid., p. 12.

15. Robert Pippin, *Modernism and a Philosophical Problem* (Oxford: Blackwell, 1990), p. 22.

16. Cuddihy, *Ordeal of Civility*, p. 10.

17. George Grant, *Lament for a Nation: The Defeat of Canadian Nationalism* (Ottawa: Carleton University Press, 1989 [1965]).

18. Ibid., pp. 54, 72–73.

19. Rieff, *The Triumph of the Therapeutic*, p. 65.

20. George Ritzer, *The McDonaldization of Society* (Newbury Park, Calif.: Pine Forge, 1993).

21. Colin E. Gunton, *The One, The Three and the Many: God, Creation and the Culture of Modernity* (Cambridge: Cambridge University Press, 1993), p. 180.

22. Ibid., p. 181.

23. Ibid., p. 177.

24. Lesslie Newbigin, *The Gospel in a Pluralist Society* (Grand Rapids, Mich.: Eerdmans, 1989), p. 197.

CHAPTER
20

PROPHETIC OR CIVIL RELIGION
THE ANGLICAN DILEMMA

RON DART

The task of the church is not to preserve the status quo but to transform society in accordance with God's will.... [T]he move to include development in the mandate of the Primate's Fund was an important theological development—a recognition that it was called to a more prophetic role: at the heart of the Third World's movement out of suffering was a profound plea for justice.

> —Ian Stuchberry, *We Are the Branches:*
> *The Primate's World Relief and Development Fund,*
> *The First Twenty-five Years*

The theological roots of the Anglican social tradition in Canada are different from the roots of the Canadian Social Gospel tradition and the Roman Catholic social tradition in Canada. The Anglican tradition, therefore, can make a distinctive contribution towards the development of a Canadian public policy.

> —William Crockett, "The Anglican Social Tradition:
> Resource for Canadian Public Theology"

The view of traditional philosophy and religion is that justice is the overriding order which we do not measure or define, but in terms of which we are measured and defined. The view of modern thought is that justice is a way which we choose in freedom, both individually and publicly, once we have taken our fate into our hands, and know that we are responsible for what happens.

> —George Grant, *English Speaking Justice*

We need no longer belabour *whether* the Bible calls us to political practise—only *what kind* of practise.

> —Ched Myers, *Binding the Strong Man:*
> *A Political Reading of Mark's Story of Jesus*

INTRODUCTION

Religious renewal, if it is to be substantial, must unpack the social and political dimensions of our faith.[1] The era of the naked public square is over; religion that continues to focus only on the inner terrain of spirituality, cult, worship, belief, textual study, or a selective personal morality, reflects, in a clear and distinct way, the modern split between church and state, private and public, sacred and profane. This fragmented way of thinking is foreign to the Bible, the Christian tradition, sanctified reason, and a generous and full understanding of human experience. It is essential when catholics, evangelicals and charismatics link affectionate and ecumenical arms, as they do in this volume, that they do not ignore the positive insights of the liberals[2] and the rigorous demands of social and political responsibility.

Theology can not, in good conscience, turn its back on such crucial issues as the meaning of justice, environmental devastation, global poverty, and state-sanctioned violence in our feudal world order; if it does, it becomes a cloistered activity that legitimates a questionable social order.[3] We, as Christians, must be seriously concerned about reclaiming and sounding the depths and richness of our creeds and councils; we must also, though, be equally concerned about knowing how such institutions as the World Bank (WB), International Monetary Fund (IMF) and Multinational Corporations (MNCs) operate in our global village.[4] If theology is about God's word, and the God of the Jewish-Christian tradition is a God of justice and mercy, then good theology will deal with God's good news of both "justification" and justice for our troubled time.

The search, though, for justice and peace in the public square is fraught with ambiguity and tension. The task of being attentive, as Simone Weil understood, is not easy.[5] James Skillen, in his fine book *The Scattered Voice: Christians at Odds in the Public Square*,[6] clearly articulates the dilemma: there are so many voices, loud and quiet, near and distant, right, sensible centre, and left, each claiming to speak the authoritative word about the common good, yet each defining the means and end in a different way. The language of peace, justice, and the integrity of creation has a tendency, chameleon-like, to change colour in different settings. Who really speaks the prophetic message for the Christian community in our time? There is so much static in the air, it seems almost impossible at times to be fully attentive to the redemptive power of the still quiet voice. Is it possible, within the Anglican Church of Canada (ACC), faithfully to reflect the essentials of our faith, in word and deed, for our unique moment?

The ACC has obviously played a significant and ongoing role within Canadian politics.[7] The Anglican Church is much older than its Canadian jurisdiction, and it legitimately claims to be part of the "one, holy, catholic, and apostolic church." This ancient tradition has thought deeply, thoroughly, and historically about the relationship between the "Divine City" and the "Human City." The many truths that have been gleaned in the past can inform and assist us, if we are open and attentive, to understand the important differences between a prophetic church and an institution that merely props up and reinforces the trendy intellectual, social, and political fashions of a season. It is impossible to address adequately our modern times without acknowledging our indebtedness to the great cloud of witnesses that have gone before us. Hence, in this chapter, past and present will join hands as we seek to know and transmit the essentials of our common and catholic faith.[8] We must, in doing so, heed Richard Baxter's sagacious advice: unity in things necessary; liberty in things doubtful; charity in all things.

THE METHODOLOGICAL DILEMMA

We live in a time when, on the one hand, hermeneutical suspicion reigns supreme, and, on the other, anti-rational authoritarianism is making a bid to sit on the throne. Postmodernists like Foucault, Derrida, Lyotard, and Lacan have tried to convince us, in their different ways, that we are all trapped in the maze of our subjectivity, and we necessarily and inevitably bend and twist all things to gratify our perceived needs, desires, and impulses. Postmodernists, for the most part, reduce ethics and virtues to values we manufacture to confirm our ideology; this means that, for postmodernists, justice, truth, and beauty are merely arbitrary fictions.[9] The reaction to postmodernism is fundamentalism. Fundamentalists falsely assume sacred texts can be easily mined for absolute certainty on any troubling question. Both positions, of course, fail to understand that we indeed can and do see, but we see through a glass darkly. The quest for an authentic understanding of authority constantly seems to elude us, and it is too easy to be beguiled by counterfeits.[10]

The Anglican tradition has consciously and consistently emphasized the *via media* or middle way. The middle way has never been an end in itself; it has taken root in the sacred soil of the Bible, blossomed within the nurturing aspects of tradition, been tended by sanctified and educated reason, and tested by a broad understanding of human experience. Hence, whenever the Bible, tradition, reason, and experience agree, the consensus of the faithful (*consensus fidelium*) proclaims something essential about our faith. Anglican tradition views creation in a sacramental way; justice and peace are basic to our faith, and the church, in Christ through the Holy Spirit, is expected to be light, salt, and yeast in the world. Hence the church is the matrix within which we form our prophetic perspective.

THE CHURCH AS CHRIST'S BODY

The sacramental principle affirms the startling fact that God's grace is mediated to all creation in history. This means that all existence is constantly nurtured and sustained by God's generous presence. The world is, to quote G. M. Hopkins, "charged with the grandeur of God." The visible church, though, is the primary means of God's redeeming and sanctifying goodness. The church is, despite its finitude and fallenness, Christ's body and representative on earth. We cannot, in good faith, separate Christ from his body, the church. The church is the legs, hands, eyes, ears, and breath of God in the world. Salvation flows from the Father, through Christ, in the Spirit, to believers who constitute the church. Hence, in a very real sense, there is no salvation outside the church. The church, at its best and truest, is the means by which the glory of God is embodied and permeates and pervades all things; and it is the church that lifts all things up to God.

When we see the church as a sacramental community celebrating the sacredness of all things in Christ, we realize the church has a necessary role to play in the social and political realm.

This truth was clearly recognized by Stewart Headlam, who founded the Guild of St. Matthew in 1877. Headlam threaded together, in a fully integrated manner, the redemptive power of F. D. Maurice's view of the kingdom of Christ and the Oxford movement's high church liturgy. Headlam, unknown to many Anglicans today, stood for a truly catholic view of the church as a sacramental community that existed to renew all things in Christ; this meant the task was laid upon the church to challenge and transform culture and politics when and wherever injustice, indifference, or apathy dominated. As the church realized its oneness in Christ, it further recognized that it was called to represent Christ on earth. And Jesus the Christ, while on earth, spent the bulk of his time with the poor, outcast, marginalized, and needy. When he encountered either the religious elite or political establishment, he usually collided with them.

RELIGION AND POLITICS: TWO TEMPTATIONS

There are two temptations that, from different directions, tease those who struggle to make sense of religion and politics: the first claims that the Divine City and the Human City must exist in two separate spheres; the second argues that the Divine City equals the Human City. The task of being in the world and not of it, or giving to Caesar and God their respective due, is not easy to resolve.

The first temptation is to sever the chord that joins religion and politics; this is the way of religious separatists. Christianity, however, has a persistent political dimension to it, although there is more to Christianity than the "social principle" and the "political principle." The fact that there has been, in the last two hundred years, a split between church and state, and the fact that this principle still persists in some religious communities, reflects how deeply substantial segments of the church have been taken captive by the spirit of the age. The historical reason for the separation of church and state has a great deal to do with intolerance and violence between denominations in the sixteenth and seventeenth centuries in Europe and England. Liberalism, in its earliest years, attempted to check the brutal and scandalous infighting of Christians. Important political theorists, such as Hobbes and Locke, watched in horror as religious communities tore one another to pieces in the English Civil War (1642–1660) and the Thirty Years War in Europe (1618–1648). They decided, for different reasons, that the contractual state should replace religion at the core of society. This meant that religion could continue to exist, but it was increasingly stripped of its social and political role. The church fought against this, but the writing was on the wall. The new liberal contractual state agreed to allow religion to exist, but only in a domesticated and marginalized way. The church could now busy itself with cultic activities, theological squabbles, textual analysis and spirituality, but for the most part it was denied a substantial voice on important state-controlled social and political issues.

There are those who resisted this segregation, and we need to remember them, but they were a waning minority. The evangelical Anglican tradition refused to roll over passively just because the increasingly secular state told it to do so. The evangelicals had much to say in the political realm. Wilberforce, Shaftesbury, and many evangelical philanthropic, mercy, or charity organizations played a central role in ending the slave trade and challenging the injustices in Industrial England. Although the evangelical Anglicans have been criticized because they tended to be paternalistic and did not push the issue of structural justice to a deeper level, it is important that we faithfully remember that at least they did not turn their backs on the social and political spheres.

The broader Anglican tradition also addressed social questions in an integrated way. Hooker's *Of the Laws of Ecclesiastical Polity* (1593), S. T. Coleridge's *The Constitution of Church and State* (1829) and *The Statesman Manual* (1832), Maurice's *The Kingdom of Christ* (1842), and Temple's *Christianity and the Social Order* (1942) have set important standards to guide Anglicans in thinking about the relationship between theology and politics. Hooker, Coleridge, Maurice, and Temple, like the evangelical Anglicans, had their strengths and weaknesses; but they did strive to understand what the kingdom of God meant in their moment in history. In 1922, R. H. Tawney delivered the lectures that became the book *Religion and the Rise of Capitalism*. Tawney clearly diagnosed why and how (historically) Christianity had become linked to a capitalist system in the post-Reformation era; he also directed the work on the "Fifth Report," which was endorsed by the Lambeth Conference of 1920. It was Tawney's thorough work that laid the historical, economic, social, and political foundations for William Temple's *Christianity and the Social Order* (1942).

The fullest expression of Anglican social theory was articulated in a series of essays edited by Charles Gore and published as *Lux Mundi* (1889), and by the Conference on Christian Politics, Economics, and Citizenship (COPEC), held in Burmingham, which affirmed *Lux Mundi*'s vision of the church's social mission. This conference pulled together the best insights of the Christian Social Movement (Ludlow, Maurice, Kingsley) and the wisdom of Westcott, Gore, and Holland.[11] COPEC sent forth a strong signal that Anglicanism should not turn inwards and be relegated to the private sphere. We are, without doubt, desperately in need of a *Lux Mundi* II to provide a visionary perspective for our own era. The Anglican tradition, in the main, has upheld the idea that Christ, and thus the church, is the transformer of culture; any form of Anglicanism that ignores this tradition denies its heritage. The Malvern Conference in 1941 consolidated a sound theology of Anglican social action that demonstrated a commitment to critique the standards of the secular state. The best features of the liberal catholic tradition today can be found in Kenneth Leech's *The Sacred God* (1985), *Subversive Orthodoxy* (1992), and *The Eye of the Storm* (1993), and in Charles Elliot's *Praying the Kingdom* (1985) and *Comfortable Compassion* (1987).

The second temptation, though—equating the Divine City with the Human City—is more of a serious problem for Anglicans. The Anglican tradition, given its sacramental view of the world and history, has often yielded to this temptation, and the mistakes of the past have sent many scurrying for safety and cover. But, a cloistered and reactive virtue serves no one in a meaningful way. When Henry VIII declared himself "supreme head of the church," most clerics bowed dutifully before their new Caesar. We can be grateful for Thomas More who sounded the alarm on such an unholy union, although, like most prophets, he paid the predictable price for doing so. It was a short step from Henry's pretentious claim to Laud's divine right of kings and divine right of episcopacy. Hooker would have been aghast at such folly. When the interests of monarch and archbishop are one and the same, civil religion reigns, and the prophetic flame is usually smothered by one means or another. The Puritan reaction to Laud, although understandable, tended to mirror many of Laud's authoritarian tendencies. Many Puritans felt that Cromwell, "God's Englishman," was about to usher in the kingdom of God in England's fair and pleasant land. When religion enters the public square, the temptation always exists for the religious vision to hitch itself uncritically to the ruling elite or to some variant of the opposition or counter-culture. David Walsh's *After Ideology* (1987) and Glen Tinder's *The Political Meaning of Christianity* (1989) have exposed this tendency.

The political vision of the kingdom of God cannot be reduced to any of the political manifestos of the Human City. When John Keble, for example, preached his Assize sermon of July 14, 1833, on "national apostasy," he was clearly insisting that the state had no business in deciding how the church fulfilled its apostolic ministry; but the sermon only made sense because the state was attempting to steer the ship of the church. Keble, of course, was no separatist in the Anabaptist sense; but he did believe the interests of the church should not be swallowed up by or subordinated to the interests of the state.

Modern Anglicanism lives in a world that differs greatly from classical Anglicanism. When Anglicanism began, England was, in principle, a Christian culture; hence, church and state had a great deal in common. But as the state has become more secular, Anglicans have realized that their interests and the state's often collide rather than converge. It is only when we recognize how thoroughly the interests of the modern secular state have changed that we see the need to move from an Erastian to a prophetic paradigm of church-state relations. This move, for many Anglicans, entails a painful transformation where the cost of discipleship is high. When the church is truly a prophetic community, it walks a razor's edge. It must be careful of extremes on all sides: separatism and assimilationism will constantly present various and tempting guises. The church as the body of Christ is to be in the world as a kingdom that stands for justice and peace. We need now to discuss the principles that inform our understanding of how we are to be the kingdom of God in this world.

WILLIAM TEMPLE: PRINCIPLES AND PRECEPTS

William Temple (1881–1944) was a man for all seasons. He drew deeply from the insights of Hooker, Maurice, and Gore; yet in many important aspects, he deepened their social analysis. *Christianity and the Social Order* (1942) sums up many of Temple's major concerns. Temple cogently argues against those who insist that the church has no role to play outside its sacred setting; he insists that the church is part of the kingdom of God, which, like all kingdoms, is vitally concerned with all aspects of life. The history of the church, he continually points out, verifies this rather obvious conclusion. But, although it is a significant truth for the modern world, stating this fact only gets us to the starting gate; the race is yet to begin. If the church is to be involved and interfere in matters of the state, what are the theological principles that justify such actions? What should be the attitude towards precepts that flow from principles, and what sort of actions are considered legitimate?

Briefly put, Temple argues that there are "primary" and "derivative" principles that should motivate and animate Christian social and political thought. These principles must be priorized, then fleshed out into precepts that have an impact on state policy. The primary principles for Temple are "God and His Purpose" and "Man: His Dignity, Tragedy and Destiny." God has, through Christ, called all creation to be one, restored and complete. However, while bearing the image of God, humanity continues to wear the smudge of sin. Christ has, in principle, restored all things, but the tragedy of human existence testifies to the sustained impact of sin. In short, we are still very much on the human journey, and on this journey, dignity and tragedy underwrite all human activity. These primary principles ward off utopianism on the one hand, and *real politik*, with its too eager embrace of the tragic and power-hungry tendency of human nature, on the other.

Temple then moves on to discuss three derivative principles: freedom, social fellowship, and service. These principles obviously have some overlap with the liberal principles of freedom, equality, and fraternity, but the differences are important. Temple further argues that justice and love are the glue that holds all things together; without this adhesive the principles move off in all directions. But these principles must also be translated into prescriptions for policies.

Temple was insistent that principles create the conditions within which prescriptions can be discussed; if people disagree on the issue of principles, it is difficult to move on to a serious discussion of prescriptions. Hence, for Temple, there are Christian principles, primary and derivative, that are not negotiable, but prescriptions can err and must not be pushed with the same intensity as principles. This distinction between principles, prescriptions, and application tends to frustrate many political activists who meld and melt everything together, then equate union of their principle-prescription and lobby method with a prophetic stance. It is important to note, though, that many political theorists have a tendency to hide behind the garment of principles and remain silent on particular policy and lobby issues. Most people consider poverty, unemployment, environmental devastation, human rights violations, and militarism to be issues that must be dealt with in principle, but the prescriptions and policies that are articulated to deal with these pressing problems tend to move off in different directions. All groups marshal facts and statistics to prove their positions, and the facts usually end up confirming the prejudices of the lobby group. In *Christianity and the Social Order*, Temple clearly articulates principles and prescriptions for the state in his day, and he further argues that these prescriptions must be pressed by negotiation, due process of law, education, and various forms of political action. But Temple's mild and restrained prophetic attitude needs to be nudged yet further, and this will lead us deeper into the meaning of social and political *praxis*.

WILLIAM STRINGFELLOW AND KINGDOM PRAXIS

Once, when leaving the United States, Karl Barth said, "Stringfellow is the man America should be listening to." William Stringfellow (1929–1985) was a lawyer, a lay theologian, and a faithful and committed member of the Episcopal church. *Time* magazine referred to Stringfellow as "one of the most persuasive of Christianity's critics-from-within," and the 68th Convention of the Episcopal Church, at Stringfellow's death, "gave thanks to God for the life, witness and ministry of William Stringfellow." *Sojourners* magazine claimed poignantly that "while liberals ignored the Bible and evangelicals argued over its inspiration, Stringfellow applied the Biblical word like no other contemporary Christian."[12] When Pierre Berton's *The Comfortable Pew*, commissioned by the ACC, was published in 1965, Stringfellow wrote one of the most powerful responses: "The Case against Christendom and the Case against Pierre Berton" (in *The Restless Church*, 1966).

If the Anglican Church of Canada is going to be renewed in a prophetic way, sitting at the feet of Stringfellow is a good place to start. Stringfellow was seriously concerned about the rather tame and safe way First World Christians applied their social ethics. First World theology, Stringfellow argued, had a predictable tendency towards ignoring the plight of the poor and going limp and silent on important political issues.[13] Stringfellow was one of the first critics of the Vietnam War. As a lawyer, he also realized how the courts served the interests of the rich and self-righteously punished the poor for lesser crimes. He further argued that the Cold War and the nuclear threat meant that the god of "techne," personified by the Greek god Mars, ruled America, rather than the God of the Jewish-Christian prophetic tradition. Stringfellow headed with his legal training into East Harlem and committed himself to a poverty law practice and inner-city ministry. He remained throughout his life a gadfly to the Episcopal church, but the religious establishment could not deny the integrity of his life and the firmness of his conscience. Stringfellow, unlike many liberals, did not spend a great deal of time talking about structural change or reform; neither did he waste his time sitting on countless committees that wrestled with ideas (*doxa*) but rarely translated the ideas into action (*praxis*).[14] Stringfellow firmly believed in action as education rather than education for action, and he was convinced that when action included personal, social, and political components, serious *praxis* was afoot. Stringfellow, like most classical political philosophers, argued that our life of willing and acting must have a social and political element because we are social and political animals. But Stringfellow went a step beyond this. He argued that *praxis* must both stand by the side of the poor, marginalized, and victims, and, just as importantly, challenge those who create and profit from an unjust world order. It is this important move along the *praxis* spectrum that makes Stringfellow a compelling thinker for our moment, and in some ways unites him with some strands of political and liberation theology. Stringfellow, of course, would have had a certain suspicion of Moltmann and Metz's state-supported political theology, and he would have questioned some elements of Marxist liberation theology, but he was firm on the point that essential prophetic theology must push ever deeper into the realm of *praxis*,[15] and that this would often mean siding with the poor (without idealizing or romanticizing them) and being quick to critique power elites (without demonizing them). Stringfellow takes us much deeper than Temple, and it is the relationship between civil disobedience and *praxis* to which I will now turn.

PRAXIS AND CIVIL DISOBEDIENCE

Christianity began as an illegal religion (*religio illicitia*) in the Roman Empire. Hence, to be a Christian meant breaking the law. This important point must always be kept on front stage. Until the Constantinian settlement, the church began and sustained itself with one continuous boycott of Roman values. The name for the book of Acts, in Greek, is *Praxis*. Most of the early Christians, by being Christians, broke the law, and many of course were killed for differing with the *Pax Romana*. The Christian belief that an unjust law is no law (*lex iniusta non est lex*) also raises the important connection between law and justice today. What should a Christian of good conscience do when the laws of the state are unjust? Temple raised the important issue of principles, the need to priorize them, the important task of articulating prescriptions, and the need to lobby them about town. What happens, though, when the various means used are perpetually frustrated? Is it legitimate to resort to the *praxis* of civil disobedience when the state consciously and deliberately violates the principles and prescriptions of the kingdom of God?

The history of biblical *praxis* and church tradition is abundant with those who have obeyed God rather human law. When the state supports abortion on demand, the state must be critiqued and challenged; the rights of the most vulnerable are being violated in such actions. When the state steals the lucrative land of indigenous peoples, or uses the land for military purposes, the state must be admonished. When nuclear testing and the various forms of pollutants are dumped in the air, soil, and water, the state must be stared down. When national security is used to justify the worship of Mars, the church must protest that it worships another God.

Political *praxis* takes on a tougher demand when the move is made from negotiation, to political action, to direct action. This is not to suggest that one method is superior to another, but the modern Western church tends to be rather slow and hesitant about stretching *praxis* to include civil disobedience; in doing so, it negates its own tradition. Whether we reflect on the courageous lives of Philip Berrigan and Liz McAlister (who protest against American militarism), Lane and Kathy Walker (who regularly protest at the abortion clinic in Vancouver) or Loren, Mary Ruth, and Heidi Wilkinson (who used civil disobedience to protest the destruction of old-growth forests at Clayoquot Sound), we are rightly dealing with people who are using their freedom to challenge injustice in high places and are calling the church to a deeper understanding of political *praxis*.

THE PRIMATE'S WORLD RELIEF AND DEVELOPMENT FUND

We live in a world of about 5.5 billion people. Our feudal world order puts a few of us in a comfortable position at the top of the hierarchy and most of the population near the bottom of the pyramid. Here are a few consequences of the way the world is ordered:

- 40,000 children die each day of hunger-related causes (14 million a year);
- 2.5 billion people live in a constant state of absolute or relative poverty;
- 29 percent of the world's population (First World) has 80 percent of the world's wealth;
- $150 billion is spent each year on Research and Development (R&D); less than 5 percent of R&D is spent on improving conditions in the Third World where 75 percent of humanity lives;
- there are about 45 million refugees in the world (this includes internally displaced refugees);
- Canada and the United States are moving, in their aid and development funds, further away from the United Nations standard of 0.7 percent of gross national product. Aid from the United States is the lowest of the First World states (0.24 percent) and Canada's aid hovers at about 0.4 percent.

We in the First World are protected and sheltered from a great deal of human suffering by a sophisticated military, economic, and political coalition that protects our affluence. The Gulf War of 1991 is a classic case in point. The world purrs along when the flow of oil is uninterrupted and controlled by the First World. The "Seven Sisters" oil conglomerates individually have larger annual incomes than more than 150 states in the world. When Iraq invaded Kuwait, neither human rights nor state sovereignty was the sole or primary issue. If human rights were the real concern of the First World coalition, then the plight of the Tibetans in China, the Kurds in the Middle East, the Mayans in Guatemala, the Palestinians under Israeli rule, and the East Timorese, Aheh, and Papuans in Indonesia should receive more publicity. But Kuwait (with 10 percent of the world's known oil reserves), unlike the Tibetans, Timorese, Kurds, Mayans, Palestinians, Irish, or Marsh Arabs, plays an important economic role for the prosperity of the West. China, Indonesia, Turkey, Guatemala, and Israel are also close friends with the West. So, when our interests are threatened, Mars is quickly called in to protect them. These First World–enforced political inequities raise serious questions for the Primate's World Relief and Development Fund (PWRDF).

Since its beginning in 1960, PWRDF has attempted to address the question of stark world inequalities in three ways: through relief, development, and justice. Relief and support for victims of natural disasters will always be a necessary component in alleviating the immediate and surface causes of human suffering. But the deeper questions of why poverty persists takes us to another level of analysis. Non-governmental organizations (NGOs) attempt in a grassroots way to bypass the state definitions of development, whereby funds for various types of megaprojects are channelled through bilateral and multinational structures. Seventy-eight percent of Canadian development aid is bilateral and multilateral funding. By working in solidarity with the marginalized themselves, however, PWRDF is more concerned with empowering people in the Third World to shape their own future. The debates within the development field between NGOs, and, more strenuously, between NGOs like PWRDF, and mega-state projects that do little to serve the poorest, are always heated. But the internal debates about development often falter when they fail to factor in the interests of the First World. When there is a collision, as there often is (for instance, in the 1991 Gulf War), between First World interests in Third World states and the interests of the common people in Third World states, the First World (in conjunction with the elites in the Third World) tends to protect its interests with whatever force seems necessary.

PWRDF is often caught on the horns of a difficult dilemma. The question of how much a relief-development agency (significantly funded by CIDA) should get involved in rigorous political and national security questions raises the justice issue; a prophetic church will attempt to deal with the three-fold relief-development-justice challenge in a non-ideological but firm way. The fact that some of the states that receive the largest amounts of Canadian development funding (China, Indonesia, India, Bangladesh) have some of the worst human rights records should concern us. Canada is also one of the largest arms suppliers to Turkey, and Turkey, without doubt, is brutal in its treatment of the Kurdish people.

The issue of relief-development-justice raises some pressing issues for First World theology.[16] It is too easy to slip into a relief-development syndrome (with all its debates, differences, and distinctions) and shut down discussion on the justice imperative. Theology, if it is going to be prophetic and seriously serve the church, must look at the macrostructures in our feudal world order that condition and limit what can be done in the field of relief and development. When theology and the church properly dialogue on the relief-development-justice continuum, the mission of PWRDF and the ecumenical coalitions will be enhanced.

In the Anglican church now, however, 80 percent of parish income stays in the parish, 14 percent goes to the dioceses, 5 percent goes through the dioceses to the national church, and only 1 percent is contributed to PWRDF.[17] When we reflect on the immense disparities between the wealthy First World and impoverished Third World, or when we further reflect on the sobering fact that we only give 1 percent of our parish income to PWRDF, we need to stop and ask ourselves about our real concerns as a church for "the least of these." The church, if it ignores the essentials of responsible and sacrificial *praxis*, will merely be building bigger barns that feed the First World but force the Third World to beg for scraps from the rich man's table. This, of course, is the lament of liberation theology. Liberation theology argues that most forms of First World aid and development conceal Western imperialism and sustain an unjust world order. Liberation theologians equate liberation and justice, and they use these terms to critique the milder form of Western compassion that we call aid and development. Hence, liberation theology is not only a critique of doctrine cut loose from *praxis*, it is also a vigorous critique of First World *praxis*.

CONCLUSION

As we have seen, the Anglican tradition affirms the fact that our faith has social and political dimensions. The church, as Christ's agent and ambassador on earth, should incarnate the Christ-like life in this world, a life that has strong justice and mercy aspects to it. William Temple clearly articulated some principles that can aid us in making sense of what it means to be a just people, and how principles must inform prescriptions. William Stringfellow takes us deeper into the realm of political *praxis*, and there is a sense in which he is a conservative like Temple, but more radical than Temple. Temple and Stringfellow, when read together, can aid us as we attempt to sort out the tensions between aid, development, and justice. The global perspective of PWRDF must be nurtured by a theological tradition that gives it focus and direction; Temple and Stringfellow offer such a prophetic perspective, and when their insights feed into PWRDF, the relief-development-justice tensions will take on a sharper focus.

The Primate's World Relief and Development Fund offers Anglicans a compassionate agency through which funds can be directed, in a discerning way, to the Third World. But the giving of money is only a beginning. Each of us, at the parish level, should be consciously and keenly aware of needs in our local community, town, or city. In short, the church, at its best, is meant to provide a mediating structure between the state and individuals. The church should critique the state when the state legitimates injustice; but the church must also embody an alternative way. Each parish, along with its "normal" pastoral and ecclesiastical responsibilities, should incarnate our new life in Christ. As unemployment and underemployment (currently for 25 percent of the population) continue to grow and as poverty increases (now affecting three million people in Canada), we should be moved by God's merciful and compassionate spirit to identify and genuinely share with those who suffer. We need to be aware of stewardship programmes and participate in activities that alert us to injustice on the local, national, and international levels. Each parish, of course, must discover what particular service it is called to; but if our faith is to be genuine, our proclamation of the gospel must equally recognize the gospel imperatives of love and justice.

PWRDF opens up to us an international perspective. The Anglican Church in Canada is also involved with many different types of ecumenical coalitions, and each of these coalitions highlights how the universal church can work together in unity on issues of aid, development, and justice. Project Ploughshares, one of the ecumenical coalitions the ACC belongs to, monitors Canada's complicity in the arms trade. For example, Canada is among the top 10 percent of countries exporting military equipment. Local Ploughshares groups in many cities support the national work. Members of parishes could participate on a local level with groups like Project Ploughshares or other coalitions. Groups like Amnesty International and World Vision also provide an excellent forum for education and action. There are obviously many different ways and means by which our desires for mercy and justice can work themselves out, but the process of action and reflection, and reflection and action, forms a crucial part of our being involved in this world as Anglicans on parish, diocesan, national, and international levels.

SUGGESTED READING

Hannah Arendt, *The Human Condition* (Chicago: University of Chicago Press, 1959).
——, *The Life of the Mind* (New York: Harcourt, Brace, Jovanovich, 1971).
Paul Avis, *Anglicanism and the Christian Church* (Minneapolis: Fortress Press, 1989).
Noam Chomsky, *Deterring Democracy* (New York: Hill and Wang, 1992).
William Crockett, "Canadian Anglicans and Social Justice" (unpublished paper).
George Grant, *Technology and Empire* (Toronto: Anansi, 1969).
——, *English Speaking Justice* (Toronto: Anansi, 1974).
Bonnie Greene, ed., *Canadian Churches and Foreign Policy* (Toronto: James Lorimer and Co., 1990).
Stanley Hauerwas, *After Christendom* (Nashville: Abingdon Press, 1991).
Mary Jo Leddy, *Reweaving Religious Life: Beyond the Liberal Model* (Connecticut: Twenty-Third Publications, 1991).
R. Matthews and C. Pratt, *Human Rights in Canadian Foreign Policy* (Montreal: McGill-Queen's University Press, 1988).
J. Moltmann and H. Küng, eds., *Who Has the Say in the Church?* (New York: The Seabury Press, 1981).
Ched Myers, *Binding the Strong Man: A Political Reading of Mark's Story of Jesus* (New York: Maryknoll, 1988).
C. Pratt and R. Hutchinson, eds., *Christian Faith and Economic Justice: Toward a Canadian Perspective* (Burlington: Trinity Press, 1988).
William Stringfellow, *Dissenter in a Great Society* (New York: Abingdon Press, 1966).
William Temple, *Christianity and the Social Order* (Toronto: Penguin, 1942).
E. Voegelin, *The New Science of Politics* (Chicago: The University of Chicago Press, 1952).
Simone Weil, *The Need for Roots* (New York: G.P. Putnam's Sons, 1952).

ENDNOTES

1. Hannah Arendt, probably one of the finest political philosophers in the West in the twentieth century, has consistently argued that we must clearly distinguish between "the social principle" and "the political principle," and we must further know the difference between "intellectual events" and "historical events." It is when the social and political principles move from the realm of intellectual events to historical events that we move from the life of the mind to the life of the will. She suggests that political *praxis*, at its most significant, deals with the subtle and dialectical interplay of thinking, judging, and willing.

   P. Avis's *Anglicanism and the Christian Church* (Minneapolis: Fortress Press, 1989) is a fine complement to Arendt's astute political analysis. Avis is a liberal catholic, in the best sense, and his distinction between an "Erastian Paradigm" and an "Apostolic Paradigm," and the way he uses reason to distinguish between the essential and accidental in the past and present, is most apt and pertinent. A blend of Arendt's thinking, judging, and willing and Avis's Erastian-Apostolic paradigms can lead us a good way along the path in making sense of the modern dialogue between theory and practise.

2. D. Edwards and J. Stott, *A Liberal-Evangelical Dialogue* (Toronto: Hodder and Stoughton, 1988). See also John Habgood, *Confessions of a Conservative Liberal* (London: SPCK, 1988).

3. Philip Lee, *Against the Protestant Gnostics* (Oxford: Oxford University Press, 1987).

4. C. Pratt and R. Hutchinson, *Christian Faith and Economic Justice: Toward a Canadian Perspective* (Burlington: Trinity Press, 1988).

5. Simone Weil, *Waiting for God* (London: Harper and Row, 1951).

6. James Skillen, *Scattered Voice: Christians at Odds in the Public Square* (Grand Rapids, Mich.: Zondervan, 1990).

7. John W. Grant, *The Church in the Canadian Era* (Burlington: Welch Publishing Co., 1988).

8. Compare Alister McGrath's, *The Renewal of Anglicanism* (Harrisburg: Morehouse Publishing, 1993) with Geoffrey Rowell, ed., *Tradition Renewed: The Oxford Movement Conference Papers* (London: Darton, Longman and Todd Ltd., 1986). See also S. Sykes, *The Integrity of Anglicanism* (London: Mowbrays, 1978).

9. Pauline M. Rosenau, *Postmodernism and the Social Sciences: Insights, Inroads and Intrusions* (Princeton, New Jersey: Princeton University Press, 1992).

10. Hannah Arendt, *Between Past and Future: Six Exercises in Political Thought* (New York: Viking, 1965).

11. J. Carpenter, *Gore: A Study in Liberal Catholic Thought* (London: Faith Press, 1960); C. Gore, ed., *Lux Mundi* (New York: E. and J. B. Young, 1890); A. M. Ramsey, *New Era in Anglican Theology: From Gore to Temple* (New York: Scribners, 1960); R. Page, *New Directions in Anglican Theology: A Survey From Temple to Robinson* (New York: Seabury, 1965).

12. J. Wallis, *Sojourners* (December 1985), p. 5.

13. William Stringfellow, *Dissenter in a Great Society: A Christian View of America in Crisis* (New York: Abingdon Press, 1966).

14. Political activist Philip Berrigan wrote in his letter to me of 22 November 1993: "As for the Stringfellow revival—it is long overdue. It is impossible to lessen his significance as a prophetic voice of Biblical thought.... Unfortunately the same

trend marks Bill's revival, i.e., that of liberals intellectualizing his work as they did with Thomas Merton. In brief, no action."

15. I received another letter from Philip Berrigan, dated 17 January 1994. He said, "I am not familiar with the liberal/radical dialogue going on in Catholic circles. The radical Catholics spend most of their time trying to live it. As for a distinction between the two, liberals consistently choose what they see as the lesser evil; radicals are primarily interested in the truth—Gospel truth, non-violent truth." Stringfellow and Berrigan very much represent a radical view of action; such a position tests all thought by the fruit of sacrificial action. Liberals often agree with radicals on the level of ideas (*doxa*), but they do not wed thought and will in such an intimate way.

16. Bonnie Green, ed., *Canadian Churches and Foreign Policy* (Toronto: James Lorimer and Co., 1990).

17. "Answers," ACC paper on disbursement of funds (1994).

21

REFOCUSING CROSS-CULTURAL MISSION IN THE ANGLICAN CHURCH OF CANADA

DONALD M. LEWIS AND TONY TYNDALE

Though there are notable exceptions, the dominant model of the church within the Anglican Communion is a pastoral one. Emphasis in all aspects of the church's life tends to be placed upon care and nurture, rather than proclamation and service. The pressing needs of today's world demand that there be a massive shift to a "mission" orientation throughout the communion....

—*Report on Mission and Ministry for the Lambeth Conference of Bishops*, 1988

As the 1988 Lambeth Conference makes clear, evangelism is actually something to which the *underdeveloped* nations are calling the *developed* nations—a total inversion of the situation envisaged by the "evangelism-as-domination" school. The demand for increased priority to be given to evangelism [at the 1988 Lambeth Conference] came especially from the bishops of east Africa, with powerful support from the east Asian bishops; the greatest resistance to this suggestion appears to have come from the English and American bishops.

—Alister E. McGrath, *The Renewal of Anglicanism*

Anglicanism is growing and thriving in many parts of the world: dioceses in south-of-the-Sahara Africa, in parts of Asia, and in Latin America represent some of the liveliest forms of the Christian faith. Many of these dioceses are experiencing rapid expansion and are reaching out to other nations in cross-cultural mission. It is clear that the centre of world Anglicanism has shifted from the West and North to the East and South.

This global picture of Anglicanism may come as a surprise to many Canadian Anglicans. We seem to have become used to bad news: rumours from Britain of schism; reports of secession to Rome; and divisions within the American Episcopal Church that are causing some of its largest and liveliest congregations to withdraw from the denomination. At home, alarm is raised by the predictions of a leading Canadian sociologist of religion, Professor Reginald Bibby, who foresees the virtual collapse of Canadian Anglicanism in the next twenty years. Based on current trends, Bibby predicts that the number of Anglicans worshippers on a given Sunday will fall from the current 220,000 to about 100,000 and membership will decrease from 720,000 to 500,000.[1]

We are only too aware that growth and expansion are not problems that preoccupy us. Rather than our churches being filled with enthusiastic young people, the typical Canadian Anglican is much older than the general population: the denomination is greying around the temple and attracting fewer and fewer of the younger generation. The eventual extinction of the Anglican Church of Canada seems to be a real possibility. Many Canadian Anglicans are thus profoundly discouraged about the future of their church; possibly our clergy are the most disheartened.

This growing despair is not relieved by acknowledgements such as the following by Bishop John Spong of the American Episcopal Church:

> The churches that do attempt to interact with the emerging world are for the most part the liberal Protestant mainline churches that shrink every day in membership and the silent liberal [Roman] Catholic minority that attracts very few adherents. Both are, almost by definition, fuzzy, imprecise and relatively unappealing. They might claim to be honest, but for the most part they have no real message. They tinker with words, redefine concepts, and retreat slowly behind the rear guard protection of a few pseudo-radical thinkers. I have sought to live in this arena. It shrinks daily.[2]

The issue of mission needs thus to be considered against this backdrop of Anglican decline in the West and the resurgence of Anglicanism elsewhere. Clearly Canadian Anglicans need to learn what mission is and it is obvious that non-Western Anglicanism has much to teach us. The old Sunday school image of Western missionaries imparting the Christian gospel along with supposedly superior Western culture to the world's less fortunate has to be set aside; it is the Canadian church that needs humbly to learn how Anglican churches in other countries are able to function and grow in settings as multicultural and multifaith as any of our major cities. This has begun to happen in some places; bishops and other Anglican leaders from Africa and Latin America are able to speak and be heard in North American contexts where Canadian and American Anglicans are not being heard.

ANGLICAN CHURCH OF CANADA: THE PRODUCT OF OVERSEAS MISSION

As we begin to consider this question, we should perhaps remind ourselves that the Canadian Anglican Church is largely the product of missionary endeavour! For a long time the Canadian Church was a "missionary-receiving" church, benefiting from the work of several British Anglican missionary societies from the early eighteenth century onward: the Society for the Propagation of the Gospel (very active in eastern Canada); the Church Missionary Society (active especially in the west and north); the Colonial and Continental Missionary Society (especially active in Newfoundland, but also in parts of eastern Canada); and the Bible Churchmen's Missionary Society (active in northern Canada). And at the turn of the twentieth century, the Anglican Church of Canada had a large number of missionaries serving overseas.

At the end of the twentieth century there does not seem to be much interest in or commitment among Canadian Anglicans to cross-cultural mission and evangelism overseas—and this is the case in spite of the commendable efforts by the World Mission department to encourage mission awareness. We have far fewer missionaries working abroad now than we did at the beginning of the century.

Two agencies of the national church work in the area of mission. The Primate's World Relief and Development Fund (PWRDF) is concerned with relief and development; it is funded through voluntary gifts and matching government grants where applicable. Partners in World Mission (PWM), funded by the apportionment budget of the national church, is concerned with mission education and promotion. PWM, through its three regional desks (Africa and the Middle East; Asia and the Pacific; Latin American and the Caribbean), and its Canadian education and resource programmes, acts as a facilitator of reciprocal relationships in mission between twenty-five Anglican provinces and the Anglican Church of Canada. PWM does this through specific programmes designed to assist Canadian Anglicans to be in partnership with the worldwide Anglican and ecumenical community. These programmes provide opportunities for mutual learning, sharing of gifts, building of personal links, and supporting common mission and work. The programmes of PWM include the People Exchange Program, the Partnership Visit programme, the Mission Personnel Placement programme, Volunteers in Mission, and the Companion Dioceses programme.[3]

There are currently eighteen Canadian Anglican missionaries who are sponsored in the field by PWM (and another ten on their way). Most of these are lay people who will serve abroad for two-year (renewable) terms under the Volunteers in Mission programme of PWM. Such ministries are important and call for our strong support. It is distressing to the authors, however, that we seem to have lost sight of the need for long-term missionaries willing to work in cross-cultural evangelism. We are convinced that the era of cross-cultural evangelism is not over; there are many areas of the world not yet evangelized.

Both the Primate's World Relief and Development Fund and Partners in World Mission programmes continue to remind us of the truth proclaimed by the 1963 Anglican Congress in Toronto: "The Church that lives to itself, will die by itself." If we are to learn again what it means to live for others, we perhaps need to begin by asking the question: what is mission?

WHAT IS MISSION?

Emil Brunner has observed that "the church lives by mission as a fire lives by burning."[4] Alister McGrath, commenting on Brunner's remark, has written: "Mission is something intrinsic to the identity of the church—not an optional add-on, but something that is part and parcel of the very being of the church. The church exists for many reasons—and one such reason is being the bearer and proclaimer of the good news of Jesus Christ."[5]

Today the term "mission" means many things to many people. In Anglican circles it is often interpreted as meaning everything that the church is sent into the world to do. Often this task is divided into two broad categories: service and evangelism. The first, service, includes the church's social responsibility (including relief and development work as well as efforts to bring justice to the poor and oppressed). Evangelism, the other aspect of mission, involves the declaration in word and deed of the death and resurrection of Jesus in order that "men and women may respond in penitence and faith to him, thus establishing a life-changing new relationship which is both individual and collective, and which has eternal consequences."[6]

THE BIBLE AND MISSION

The need for evangelism has been underlined by the bishops of our communion who have designated the 1990s as the "Decade of Evangelism." Scripture is clear: our God is a missionary God. He has sent his Son to reconcile the world to himself at the cost of the cross—which is central to our gospel. He has sent his Spirit to draw all people to his Son, that by believing in him they might be rescued from their rebellion against him. The Thirty-Nine Articles of Religion powerfully affirm this central teaching.

The biblical basis for mission has been clearly outlined in the documents of the 1988 Lambeth Conference of Anglican bishops:

(a) *We are inspired* by God's deep love for the world as demonstrated in the sending of the Son to live and die for and among us. "For the love of Christ controls us, because we are convinced that one had died for all.... [T]herefore, we regard no one from a human point of view (2 Cor. 5:14,16).

(b) *We are compelled* by our understanding that God is a calling and a sending God. Abraham is called and sent. Moses and the prophets are called and sent. The Father sends the Son. The Holy Spirit is sent at Pentecost. Jesus sends the disciples.

(c) *We are challenged* by the example of Jesus' mission as inaugurating the Kingdom of God—"The Kingdom of God is at hand; repent and believe in the gospel" (Mark 1:15)..... This aim Jesus accomplished primarily through preaching, teaching and healing, and through his life, death and resurrection. These become the Church's model for mission.

(d) *We are empowered* by the Holy Spirit for mission. In the exuberance of the joy we have experienced in being healed, restored, forgiven and freed from bondage, we seek to proclaim and demonstrate the good news of the Kingdom....

(e) *We see signs* of the Kingdom's presence as Jesus promised....[7]

This is the biblical basis of mission. Cyril Okorocha, secretary for mission and evangelism and officer for the Decade of Evangelism with the Anglican Consultative Council, has written: "In short, the Word of God comes to humankind with or as an apostolic mandate. In other words, the proof of having heard the word on the part of any person or group is their apostolicity."[8] Okorocha outlines five inseparable aspects of this task:

> Because it is a holistic venture, that mission of the Church in the world involves hazards as well as joyful harvests. But it must include five inseparable aspects ... [namely] proclamation, demonstration, preservation, anticipation and participation in partnership. We declare the Good News, that is the perfect atonement in Christ and thus the possibility of adoption into God's family, we demonstrate it in our lives in qualitative conduct and by loving deeds; we preserve it in the natural order, i.e., by preserving God's hand in and respecting creation, and God's moral values in human behavior as revealed in the Word from God, and as we struggle to bring hope into a hopeless and needy world; we involve all of God's people irrespective of ethnicity, gender, race or social class in this great and exciting mission and thus assert God's impartiality and universal love. This is the meaning of mission and evangelism, according to Scripture, the bringing of God's Good News to everyone in context.[9]

THE EVANGELISTIC PRIORITY IN MISSION

In the twentieth century the Christian church has had great difficulty in holding together the two aspects of mission, evangelism and service. Instead it has often emphasized one at the expense of the other. Dr. Alan Cole, a leading figure in Anglican mission-thinking has noted that the Great Commission to "go into all the world and preach the Gospel..." (Mark 16:15) is closely linked to the Great Commandment to "love your neighbor" (Matt. 22:39). Increasingly it is being realized in both Catholic and Protestant circles that the priority in mission has to be given to proclamation, as it was in the ministry of Jesus. Pope John Paul II recently wrote: "Proclamation is the permanent priority of mission. The Church cannot elude Christ's explicit mandate, nor deprive men and women of the 'Good News'...."[10] Dr. Cole has argued that some would see such prioritization as reflecting

> a privatized or personalized view of the Gospel. This [however] is what Jesus himself did. So far as we know, Jesus in his lifetime never actually delivered anyone from prison, not even John the Baptist or himself. Nor did he embark on a program of social or political reform, whether peaceful or violent, so he cannot have regarded the remission of debts as part of the gospel, while it may be one of the fruits of the Gospel proclaimed in society.

Further reflecting on the scriptural accounts, Dr. Cole argues: "There is no hint in the whole of the New Testament that the preaching of the Gospel initially involved the preaching of better economics, social or political conditions to the poor, or indeed to any other stratum of society, while these may well be inevitable glad consequences of the gospel-yeast when it is mixed in the dough of a particular society."[11]

In recognition of the importance of mission as proclamation, the 1986 Anglican Consultative Council affirmed the following: "It is imperative that our Communion recover an emphasis on personal evangelism, recognizing that the call to repentance and faith is addressed to those within the church as well as to those beyond it. We need to acknowledge afresh our responsibility to share the gospel with people of other faiths and no faith, always remembering the need for sensitive listening and dialogue."[12]

Cross-cultural mission thus involves a national church's expression of its call to serve and to evangelize beyond its own national boundaries. In many cases this will involve the national church in cooperative relationships with other Anglican dioceses that indicate a need for such assistance, and in places where there is little or no Christian presence.

THE NEED FOR SENSITIVE LISTENING AND DIALOGUE

In this context, therefore, the Consultative Council's appeal for sensitive listening and dialogue is important. Cross-cultural mission today needs to be understood in terms of partnership—many countries that historically have been "missionary-receiving" countries now have well-established national churches. Mission now involves reciprocity between equal partners—decisions cannot be made in the West as to what is best for non-Western contexts. As the 1988 study on Mission and Ministry puts it: "In all these movements, like Peter and Cornelius, both evangelists and the evangelized are transformed by a fresh apprehension of the Good News (Acts 10). Structures are re-thought in the face of new situations and Christ is continually disclosed afresh in a world which is increasingly a melting-pot of faiths and cultures."[13]

Regarding the changes that have affected the Western churches, and are beginning to disturb the other churches, the study noted that

it is here that the Churches in the Western world can give help to forewarn and forearm, as they have learned hard lessons from their experience of the onslaught of the forces that have swept their countries.... But the Western Churches also need both the ancient and the newer non-Western Churches to help bring about a deep re-conversion of the soul of the West. Above all it is these Churches that can help to rekindle a passionate concern for sinners, sufferers, victims of injustice, the confused and the lost.[14]

Mutuality can go a long way toward dissolving the resentment that easily develops among those who are on the receiving end of help—resentment against those who are perennially perceived as the donors. Such resentment can in turn cause anger and hurt on the part of those who feel their generosity is being slighted.

Clearly for Canadian Anglicans, this means that we need to serve Anglican dioceses overseas by making every effort to be sensitively aware of the needs expressed by our partners. Second, we need to become conversant with the strengths of our sisters and brothers overseas. Their strengths—especially in church-planting and evangelism—may well be more needed here in Canada than our strengths there!

In discussing partnership in mission, one has to consider the issue of finance. Clearly it is of the utmost importance that gradual steps be taken to reduce dependency upon outside giving. If the local church is to be healthy, whether in the Chaco of Argentina or in the Cameroons, in Chicoutami or the Canadian North, the work must be becoming increasingly self-supporting. This, however, does not mean that the financial responsibility of the financially richer churches is lessened.

Western Anglicans involved in cross-cultural mission need especially to heed the Consultative Council's caution to listen: we must be careful not to repeat the errors of Anglicanism's colonial past when Western missionaries assumed that they had the cultural and political answers to other nations' problems. Today, the "cultural baggage" Western missionaries bring often reflects Western theological agendas that may have little relevance to non-Western Christians. Jurgen Moltmann has pointed out that Latin American liberation theology has little about it which is demonstrably Latin American,[15] and one might suggest that the agenda of radical feminist theology and its talk of "Sophia"-worship has more to say about Western theological confusion than it does about the non-Western churches' analyses of their own problems and need for solutions. The recent talk about "Western church guilt" may well have more to say about the anxiety of the Western churches wanting to emphasize their continuing central role in the worldwide church than about Western modesty. Modesty would tend to cause one to eschew offering Western answers to non-Western needs.[16]

STEPS ON THE WAY FORWARD

As we noted at the beginning of this chapter, the 1988 Lambeth Conference of Bishops called for "a massive shift" from a pastoral and maintenance model "to a 'mission' orientation throughout the communion...."[17] How, in practical terms, can we begin to see this change begin in our local churches, in our dioceses, and at the national level?

Here are some practical suggestions and ideas:

1. *Evangelism at home must be made a priority* if evangelism abroad is ever to become a priority. All Anglicans must be taught that they are the ministers of the church of God. As the bishops have observed, "at the heart of this [missionary movement] would be a revolution in the role of the laity. Such a revolution would enable us to see every Christian as an agent of mission."[18]

2. *We must be open to listening to and then doing what the Holy Spirit directs.* Again, our bishops have been so helpful when they acknowledge that the revolution called for above "will never be simply a matter of technique or programmes, important as they are, but the result of openness to the same Holy

Spirit who sent the New Testament church to turn the world upside down (Acts 17:6)."

3. *We need to get to know and to support Anglicans involved in cross-cultural missions.* It is hard to become enthusiastic and supportive of a cause in which you know none of the participants. As mentioned above, there are currently some eighteen missionaries in the field associated with the Anglican Church of Canada (and another ten preparing to go).[19] The World Mission department of the Anglican Church of Canada would, I am sure, be delighted to provide parishes with information on the work of these individuals.[20] A number of these missionaries serve in the Volunteers in Mission programme, which links individual Canadian Anglicans with specific needs in dioceses overseas.

There are also significant numbers of Anglicans who are working abroad with other organizations and in close cooperation with Anglican communions. Every Anglican parish should seek to establish personal, nurturing links with at least one Anglican missionary and get to know what he or she is doing. Surely national church headquarters would be only too happy to know of such enthusiasm! Furthermore, the recently-formed Mission Awareness Program, based in Vancouver, is seeking to identify Canadian Anglicans who are serving abroad with agencies other than the Anglican Church of Canada and could prove to be a helpful link in establishing such ties. It has also sought to work closely with the World Mission department.

4. *The* Anglican Journal *and local diocesan papers might consider a regular page or column focused on cross-cultural missions* that would keep people informed as to what both our communion as a body and individual Anglicans are doing in this area. Such pages could include information on mission projects, discussion of the theology of mission, reviews of books on mission, Volunteers in Mission's "Letters from Overseas," articles by missionaries, and so on.

5. *Missionaries to Canada from overseas have much to contribute,* as the Diocese of Rupert's Land discovered when the Rev. Godfry Majjewe of Uganda was appointed through the Partners in World Mission programme to do mission work among the First Nations people and those living in several small communities associated with reserves.

ENDNOTES

1. Reginald Bibby, *Unknown Gods: The Ongoing Story of Religion in Canada* (Toronto: Stoddart,1993), p. 104.

2. John Spong, *Rescuing the Bible from Fundamentalism* (San Francisco: HarperCollins, 1992), pp. 25–6.

3. See the Mission Statement of Partners in World Mission (Minutes, PWM Unit meeting, September 25–28, 1993). See also Primate's World Relief and Development Fund 1993 Annual Report, *Anglican Journal* (May 1994).

4. Alister E. McGrath, *The Renewal of Anglicanism* (Harrisburg, Pa.: Morehouse Publishing, 1993), p. 49.

5. Ibid.

6. Alan Cole as quoted in Alan Nichols, *Equal Partners: Issues of Mission and Partnership in the Anglican World* (Sydney Square, Australia: Anglican Consultative Committee, 1987).

7. *The Truth Shall Make You Free: The Lambeth Conference 1988* (London: Anglican Consultative Council, 1988), Mission and Ministry Section Report, pp. 30–1.

8. "Scripture, Mission and Evangelism," a paper delivered to the Evangelical Fellowship in the Anglican Communion (June 1993), p. 1.

9. Ibid., p. 3.

10. *Redemptoris Missio: Encyclical Letter of the Supreme Pontiff John Paul II on the Permanent Validity of the Church's Missionary Mandate* (London: Catholic Truth Society, 1991), par. 44; quoted by McGrath in *Renewal of Anglicanism*, p. 53.

11. In Nichols, *Equal Partners*, p. 20.

12. Ibid., p. 51.

13. *The Truth Shall Make You Free*, Section 16, p. 33.

14. Ibid., Sections 29 and 30, p. 36.

15. McGrath, *Renewal of Anglicanism*, p. 18.

16. Compare Jonathan Mills, *The Malarkion*, Vol. XXIV, No. 4 (December 1988), pp. 6–7.

17. *The Truth Shall Make You Free*, p. 32.

18. Ibid.

19. Letter from the Rev. Canon John H. B. Rye, World Mission Staff, to the author, 28 April 1994.

20. Parishes can write to: World Mission, 600 Jarvis Street, Toronto, ON M4Y 2J6.

CHAPTER

22

SHORT-TERM MISSIONS
VOCATIONS OLD AND NEW

FRED CARSON

Jesus has mandated his church to have a missionary thrust: "Go into all the world ... and make disciples of all nations" (Matt. 28:19). In this concise command, our Lord has underscored the purpose of his church; to be a witness and a testimony to the love of the great I AM and to share the good news of salvation in Jesus Christ both locally and globally. I would like to emphasize that as Christians we are not so much called to *do* mission as we are called to *be* mission. "You are witnesses of these things," said Jesus (Luke 24:48). And Paul proclaimed to the elders of the Ephesian church: "You yourselves know how I lived among you ... testifying to both Jews and to Greeks of repentance to God and of faith in our Lord Jesus Christ" (Acts 20:18b–21).

Mission is not a recent invention of the church to gain membership, for God himself is the author. Indeed, it could be argued that in the opening chapters of Genesis, as he reaches out to his creation with challenge and correction, the Almighty was really doing his own missionary work. Is this not the case when God warns Adam and Eve of the consequences of disobedience (Gen. 3:3)? God's missionary involvement is further demonstrated in the lives of Noah and his family, as God calls them to be saved through obedience. In faithfulness Noah responded to God's beckoning and "did all that God commanded him" (Gen. 6:22). As a result of God reaching out and Noah's faithful response, eight people were saved from the perils of the flood.

"In many and various ways God spoke of old to our fathers by the prophets, but in these last days he has spoken to us by a Son" (Heb. 1:1-2a). The hand and mission of God has never been seen with as much clarity as when he became incarnate and "dwelt among us." Jesus was The Great Missioner for he was both the messenger and the message: the good news of God's salvation is revealed uniquely in him who is the crucified and resurrected Messiah, the Christ.

Since the time of the early Christians, mission activity has been the hallmark of the church. Jesus' promise that "you will receive power when the Holy Spirit comes on you; and you will be my witnesses in Jerusalem, and in all Judea and Samaria, and to the ends of the earth" (Acts 1:8) is fulfilled. Remarkably, at Pentecost, the first time Peter preached, three thousand people were converted to Christ (Acts 2:41).

The church has always taken its mission seriously. Untold millions have come to know Christ, because some Christian somewhere shared the gospel. Many men and women have gone into foreign lands and unknown situations to share the love of God. Centuries of reaching out to a world that needs Christ has produced many disciples. Going into primitive and dangerous lands, without concern for one's own safety or well-being, has borne much fruit. Missionaries have sacrificed themselves so that others may know the Living Hope.

Until recently, missionaries were generally expected to commit themselves for long periods of time. It was, after all, a career choice that would span many years for some, and a lifetime for others, who would return home only for brief periods of furlough to rest and do deputation work. Part of the theory of missiology seemed to be, with some justification, that one needed to get to know the people, their culture, and their language before one's mission would have any real influence. Many months and even years would be spent in learning the language and way of life of the people among whom one would minister.

The career missionary is still very much in evidence as people of all walks of life give up the security and comfort of home and family to answer the call, whether as teachers or agriculturalists in Uganda, doctors or nurses in Somalia, construction workers in Central America, social workers in Calcutta, or pastors in Beijing. God has need of both professionals and non-professionals who wish only to serve him on the mission field. The career missionary has had, and will continue to have, a valid and valuable place in this world of lost souls.

While the long-term missionary will continue to have a place in the outreach of the church, God has been doing a remarkably new thing. With the advent of the technological age, the airplane, computer, and fax, long distance travel and communication have become relatively easy. This means that today we can consider ministry opportunities that even two decades ago would have been difficult. People with varying gifts and expertise are able to experience other cultures and ministries while giving themselves and their time in service to their Lord and others. The short-term missionary is now a major component of the global church, as men and women with varying backgrounds offer themselves in service for anywhere from two weeks to three years.

But we must ask ourselves if short-term mission is indeed new. Is it in fact unique to our generation? I think that even a cursory reading of the Bible will help us to realize that short-term mission really is very old. Look at Jonah, for example, and how God used him after his initial rebellion to warn Nineveh of the impending overthrow. After the great city repented, God had pity on them and blessed them. Jonah was only in the city a few days, perhaps only three, but he was in a sense God's catalyst, who turned Nineveh from disaster; he was the messenger who delivered the divinely inspired word.

Next to Jesus, whose special public ministry and mission were completed in only three years, Paul, the Apostle to the Gentiles, whose journeys included much of the known world, is the most famous of the short-term missioners. Indeed, although he didn't start all of the Gentile churches, he had tremendous influence over them. In his absence, his Epistles served to encourage, exhort, and challenge the new believers, and often reminded them about the "kind of men we proved to be among you for your sake" (1 Thess. 1:5).

As recent as a decade ago, there were only a handful of short-term mission agencies, but today there are more than 450 operating globally. The numbers of groups that are being raised up are phenomenal. These agencies are varied and diverse. There are those who respond to so-called practical needs, like feeding the hungry or drilling wells in a drought-stricken land. Others frequently spend their vacations sharing their knowledge and expertise in the classroom or out in the farmer's field. Still others answer God's call to go out into the "mission field" to evangelize or minister in the local church.

While there are significant differences among the agencies, the one factor they hold in common besides their love for and devotion to the Lord Jesus Christ is that the team members all have other occupations and professions. They receive little training as missionaries and generally spend only a few weeks to a few months in the field—at their own expense.

The South American Missionary Society (SAMS) is well known for the long-term missionary work it does in South and Central America. It has a proven track record of sending solid Christian leadership into areas where the church requires assistance with a long-term need, whether for spiritual direction for a congregation, youth ministry, service among university students, or teaching among students of theology.

Perhaps not so well known is the short-term component of SAMS, where teams of people of various ages may be organized for differing purposes. For example, it is not uncommon for teams of medical personnel, teachers, or contractors to go on a Short-term With A Purpose (SWAP) mission to minister in a physical, hands-on, practical way. Or a student may be given a theological placement under supervision as part of his or her missiological experience. At other times, parish and youth teams are despatched to carry out construction or cleanup jobs, or to partake of teaching opportunities. Even healthy retired persons have an opportunity to be involved in the Sharing Experience and Expertise Resources (SEER) ministry.

"Do everything to the glory of the Lord Jesus Christ in fulfilling the Great Commission"—so reads the mission statement of African Community Technical Services (ACTS). ACTS is committed to providing technical assistance in Africa, particularly in East Africa, in partnership with the national church of the area where the work is to be done. ACTS is an "interdenominational" agency begun by engineer Jim Wardroper, who recognized a need and believed that his professional background would not only enable him to help others with a real physical need but would also give him special opportunities to share the gospel of Jesus Christ.

In response to requests from bishops and other church authorities, ACTS recruits professionals to do such things as drill wells, enhance the existing water supply, or provide training in useful trades such as carpentry. ACTS recently had the opportunity to provide much-needed bicycles in one diocese, where cycling is the only mode of transportation. ACTS provides the necessities of life while helping others to help themselves, bringing to the people both physical and spiritual nourishment.

Sharing of Ministries Abroad (SOMA; the Greek word for body) attempts to take seriously Paul's analogy of the relationship between the church and the human body (1 Cor. 12) and its exemplary interdependent nature. The body of Christ is both local and universal and, thus, when teams are commissioned, it is as one part of the family responding to the needs of another part, even though it means going to an entirely different culture on the other side of the world. Similarly, as a network of friends and contacts bound together by the shared experience of the renewing power of the Holy Spirit, SOMA understands the church to be effective only when the saints are equipped for ministry. For this reason, SOMA concentrates its ministry on building up the body of believers. Its mandate is not to proselytize or do street evangelism but to work with the nationals, providing teaching and instruction compatible with their requirements and requests. Small teams of normally three to six people, in consultation with the local bishop or designated leader, go into dioceses and parishes to share and teach. "Let the word of Christ dwell in you richly," says Paul, "as you teach and admonish one another in all wisdom, and as you sing songs and hymns and spiritual songs with thankfulness in your hearts to God" (Col. 3:16).

But Sharing Of Ministries Abroad involves more than sending teams out to another country; for SOMA's mandate is to build up the body—the church. We are called to minister to one another, transculturally, ecumenically, and interracially. It is not uncommon, for example, to find SOMA teams composed of various races and different denominations. While SOMA's leadership remains Anglican, its ministry is to the whole church.

SOMA is often requested to teach the basics of evangelism, discipleship, and spiritual gifts. It is common for bishops to request teaching on divine healing or assistance for the clergy or lay leaders in developing their ministries. Increasingly, SOMA is asked to deal with spiritual warfare, "for though we live in the world we are not carrying on a worldly war" (2 Cor. 10:3). It is SOMA's purpose to assist in preparing the body of Christ for ministry through sharing the faith and teaching sound doctrine.

The developing world is indeed in need of sound teaching. The church is growing at a phenomenal rate in much of the Two-Thirds World, and with such rapid expansion, problems are often encountered. (In Canada we might wish we could have such growth-related problems!) The church is outgrowing its leadership—too few shepherds for too many people. As an African visitor to Canada recently stated, "What we really need are good Bible teachers to disciple our people." If there is neither sound teaching nor a good discipleship programme, new converts easily return to their old ways, or bring customs and lifestyles into the church without realizing there may be a conflict. Just as Judas (Barsabbas) and Silas went with Paul and Barnabas to Antioch to encourage and exhort the people of God, so one crucial element of short-term mission is God's anointed ministry to the new Christians of the young church, to build up and strengthen the body.

In 1986, the General Synod of the Anglican Church of Canada, in partnership with the Evangelical Lutheran Church in Canada, recognized a need in the wider church. They launched a new, short-term mission programme to enable people of all walks of life to volunteer their gifts and time for one to two years, largely at their own expense. The Volunteers in Mission (VIM) programme continues to provide an opportunity for qualified men and women to respond to specific needs identified by partner churches and institutions. The national church acts as a sort of clearing house, coordinating, facilitating, and processing applications, soliciting requests, and matching the volunteer with the requested ministry. The needs are as diverse as the church itself; Christian Canadians with appropriate expertise and a desire to serve Christ and his church answer the call. VIM provides an opportunity to learn first-hand about the life, work, worship, and witness of Christians in different cultures and/or countries, and in Canada. Desiring to be a true partner with the wider church, the Anglican Church of Canada, through Volunteers in Mission, strives to share in their life and mission, their struggles and victories, sorrows and joys, and attempts to then interpret the global picture for the local Canadian context.

For centuries missionary activity was largely a Western enterprise of *sending* missionaries; Africa, Asia, and Latin America have been the *recipients* of missionary work in the past. While Christian workers continue to go out to assist underdeveloped nations, it is now becoming more common to discover that an evangelist in Canada may in fact be from the Caribbean or East Africa. The short-term mission agencies mentioned above are not only concerned with sending teams out to meet the needs of the young church but are equally concerned with bringing Christians from other cultures to Canada to encourage and exhort the church here to be all that it can be in Christ.

Someone might ask, "Why short-term missions? What could possibly happen in two or three weeks that is worthwhile? How can one justify the expense?" Perhaps all things are relative, but one cannot help but wonder what the results would have been if the early apostles had used such questions to approach their ministry. Not only did they proselytize but they later returned to minister to the Christians, "strengthening the churches," generally for short periods of time. The scriptural precedence for short-term missions is well established. The Acts of the Apostles is an exciting testimony to the Holy Spirit's activity in the early church, and how the disciples were used to teach, exhort, and minister with the gifts of the Holy Spirit.

Like many short-term agencies today, the early church leaders spent time building up and encouraging the body through sound teaching and personal ministry. We only need to read the Epistles, especially the Corinthian Epistles, to know that the first-century church was not without its problems. It needed correction and challenge. It needed encouragement and instruction. "Now concerning spiritual gifts, brethren, I do not want you to be uninformed" (1 Cor. 12:1). Should we want any less for today's church?

Short-term mission provides opportunities for more people to experience the church in another area of God's world, usually in a very different culture. Sometimes people are asked to go into poor areas where water may be a luxury, while others are commissioned for ministry in a modern community. Lifestyles may contrast, but the spiritual needs are the same: to know Christ as Saviour and serve him as Lord, in the power of the Holy Spirit. As with any ministry, one cannot go on a short-term mission without being positively affected by the experience. There are few short-term missioners who would not say that it was the greatest experience of their Christian lives. And virtually everyone who has shared Christ in another culture will never be the same.

But what makes short-term missions so attractive is the way in which everyone who is remotely involved is touched and spiritually strengthened. When the team returns home, they share their experiences far and wide; their home church, of course, is touched dramatically. The local part of the body may have contributed financially to the mission; and certainly, brothers and sisters at home will have been praying for the ministry. Imagine, if you will, the church's excited anticipation of the team's return and the experiences and stories that would be recalled: how a little child who could not walk is now able to run; how the person involved in witchcraft is now free; how the clergy ministering in predominantly non-Christian and anti-Christian lands have been strengthened and encouraged. As the team returns home with remarkable stories of God's grace, the local community feels very much a part of the experience.

When a short-term team or individual is commissioned for ministry in another land, the sending churches, the receiving churches, and the participants all gain from sharing their ministries with the whole church; for this is the nature of the ministry to which we have all been called by virtue of our membership in the one body. To God be the glory!

Section V

Advance

HOPE WHICH DOES NOT DISAPPOINT
THE PATH TO GENUINE RENEWAL

ROBERT CROUSE

A TRINITY OF VIRTUES

Early in the fifth century, perhaps AD 420, a young man by the name of Laurentius asked the great North African bishop St. Augustine to provide him with a handbook that set out the essentials of Christian faith and practice. We still have the bishop's response: a very substantial little book called *Enchiridion: On Faith, Hope and Charity*, in which St. Augustine works through the Pauline trilogy of Christian virtues (1 Cor. 13) in the form of meditations on the articles of the Apostle's Creed and the petitions of the Lord's Prayer,[1] because, he says, "Faith believes and hope and charity pray"[2] and "these are the things which must be chiefly, nay solely, sought after in religion."[3]

Such a direct and simple statement of essentials strikes us, perhaps, as quite remarkable; and especially so if we recall to mind the very complex and troubled circumstances of the Christian church in St. Augustine's time. Christianity was by then the religion of the empire, but there was little comfort or security in that, for the empire was rapidly falling into ruin, vexed by corruptions within and invaders from without. Ten years before the *Enchiridion* was written, the city of Rome itself had been sacked by Alaric and his Gothic invaders; ten years after the *Enchiridion*, St. Augustine's own episcopal city of Hippo was besieged by invading Vandals while the aged bishop lay dying within the walls. "The mind shudders," said St. Jerome, a contemporary of St. Augustine, "when dwelling upon the ruin of our day,"[4] but that shudder finds no echo in St. Augustine's statement of essentials. Just as there is no worldly aspiration there, so there is no dismay at worldly ruin.

The world was, indeed, in ruins, and the Christian church, within itself, was also painfully divided. The Arian heresy, which denied the truth of the Holy Trinity in an effort to conform to the most sophisticated thought of the age, was still widely influential. New controversies about the humanity and divinity of Christ were in the making, and the Pelagian and Donatist controversies, which raised extremely difficult questions about the Christian moral life and the efficacy of divine grace, were in full spate in St. Augustine's own North African church. But although the saintly bishop was capable of trading hot polemical phrases with the best of them, in the *Enchiridion* he adopted and promoted what St. Paul, at the end of 1 Corinthians 12, calls the "still more excellent way"—the way of the essential Christian virtues of faith and hope and charity. And, inasmuch as these virtues are not just a matter of hearing but also a matter of living, St. Augustine reminded Laurentius that "it will not suffice to place a small manual in one's hands; rather, it will be necessary to enkindle a great zeal in one's heart."[5]

I have begun with this little historical digression, not because I wish to belabour the thought of parallels between the ruin of St. Augustine's time and the ruin of our own—although I do think that there is scope for interesting and instructive comparisons in matters both intellectual and moral, and every current newspaper, perhaps especially every church newspaper, seems designed to elicit mental shudders. But what I want to suggest, rather, is the importance, especially in such times of chaos and confusion, of concentrating our attention and focusing our energies positively upon the essential principles of Christian spiritual life, which that great doctor and apologist of the Elizabethan Settlement, Richard Hooker, sketches so admirably:

> ... concerning Faith, the principal object whereof is that eternal Verity which hath discovered the treasures of hidden wisdom in Christ; concerning Hope, the highest object whereof is that everlasting Goodness which in Christ doth quicken the dead; concerning Charity, the final object whereof is that incomprehensible Beauty which shineth in the countenance of Christ the Son of the Living God...[6]

In those great virtues, says St. Zeno of Verona, "the foundations of the Christian life subsist,"[7] and St. Augustine, with a bold image, remarks that the whole "machinery" of the Sacred Books exists precisely for the up-building in our souls of that faith by which we believe what we do not yet see, and that hope and love whereby we look for, and long for, and reach out to embrace the very substance of the gracious promises of God.[8] Taken together, these virtues represent the whole work of redeeming grace in our lives, God's presence and indwelling in our souls by his Word and Holy Spirit. Thus, the great Franciscan theologian St. Bonaventure, basing his thought on St. Augustine's doctrine of the created image of the Holy Trinity in the three-fold powers of memory, understanding, and will within the unity of human personality, puts the matter in this way:

> Just as in man's creation, the image of God was created in a trinity of powers with a unity of essence, so in man's recreation the image of God consists in a trinity of virtues with a unity of grace. Through these virtues, the soul is borne upward to the supreme Trinity in a way which corresponds to the attributes of the three Persons. Thus, faith, by believing and assenting, leads to the highest Truth; hope, by trust and expectation, leads to the loftiest Height; charity, by loving and desiring, leads to the highest Good.[9]

A trinity of virtues, and a unity of grace: by faith our understanding is redeemed by the eternal Word revealed; by hope, our feeble will is fortified by the Holy Ghost, the Comforter; and by God's precious gift of charity, our whole being is united to that eternal Good which faith discerns and hope expects. A unity of grace: in their trinitarian pattern these three virtues that constitute the very substance of our spiritual life are interrelated inseparably. Where there is no faith, hope is empty; but where there is no hope, faith itself is dead. And where there is no faith discerning what we do not yet see, and no hope willing what we do not yet possess, there can be no bond of charity uniting us to God and to one another in him. William of St. Thierry, a great twelfth-century spiritual teacher, commenting on St. Paul's Epistle to the Romans, makes the point succinctly: "Faith in its progress is hope, and in its perfection is charity."[10]

ATTENDING TO THE ESSENTIAL VIRTUES TODAY

The Christian church in our time is sorely vexed, distressed by intellectual and moral confusions, and increasingly divided. The spirit of the age, the *potentia saecularis*[11]—the power of the unbelieving, unhoping, unloving world—seems to press insistently upon us. It is quite possible, of course, to exaggerate our current troubles, and while we are in the midst of them, it is difficult to see them in true perspective. Perhaps ours are neither the best nor the worst of times; and indeed, in the wisdom of God's eternal providence, the times that seem to us the worst may be the best. After all, the road of salvation is a journey through the wilderness;[12] and, as Karl Barth remarked, "faith which presses onward and leads to sight does not wait for sight in order that it may believe. It believes in the midst of tribulation and persecution."[13] St. Paul makes that point emphatically in the fifth chapter of Romans, verses 3 to 5: "...we glory in tribulations also, knowing that tribulation worketh patience; And patience, experience; and experience, hope: And hope maketh not ashamed; because the love of God is shed abroad in our hearts by the Holy Ghost which is given unto us"(KJV).

We know ourselves to be set in the midst of dangers; that recognition is, of course, the whole reason for such a conference as Essentials 94. In the light of the Word of God, we seek to make sense of our situation, and we try to understand what is God's will for us as individuals and as a church. If we do that earnestly and prayerfully, surely our very tribulations will be a blessing: our faith, so often pervaded with secular assumptions, will be purified of worldly conformities; our hope, frustrated by failed ambitions and disciplined by worldly defeats, will learn to look solely to the promises of God; and our charity, with all worldly *eros* crucified, will find its rest in God.

Fundamental to any genuine renewal of Christian life in our church and in ourselves must be renewal in these essential virtues, in which the whole substance of our spiritual life consists. Our only real enemies are the infidelity that erodes our faith, and the temptation to despair, which would contradict our hope. Faith and hope are the basis (the *preambula*, says St. Thomas), and when they are destroyed, our charity also is uprooted and destroyed.[14] These virtues are gifts of grace in us, but it is our part to persevere in them and exercise them continually, for it is only thus that they will live and grow in us. A great seventeenth-century Puritan divine, John Owen, speaks with the voice of the whole tradition of Christian moral theology when he says, "Frequency of acts doth naturally increase and strengthen the habits whence they proceed. And in spiritual habits [e.g., faith, hope, love] it is so, moreover, by God's appointment.... They grow and thrive in and by their exercise ... the want thereof is the principal means of their decay."[15]

Our exercise of faith is principally our attentiveness to the Word of God revealed, audible in the words of Holy Scripture and visible and tangible in Holy Sacraments.[16] Our exercise of hope is primarily our activity of prayer, which is, as St. Thomas Aquinas aptly says, "interpretative of hope."[17] Our faith is nurtured and supported by centuries of devout and learned meditation on the Word of God, and our hope is supported by patterns of prayer certified by the holy lives of saints and martyrs and the faithful witness of humble men and women from one generation to another. All of this is the gift of God the Holy Spirit; all of it belongs to our heritage as Anglicans, and in our heritage lie great resources for renewal. Anglicans in particular possess in the liturgy of the Book of Common Prayer, and its traditional lectionary, a superb system of spiritual direction, faithful to the Word of God revealed, and attentive to the profoundest human need.[18]

I think that nothing has been more destructive of spiritual life among us than the pernicious persuasion that this heritage—ancient, ecumenical, and Anglican—is now somehow outmoded and inappropriate. That persuasion, and the widespread destruction of theological and liturgical tradition that it implies, has resulted in confusion, failure of confidence, and a weariness and lethargy that, in the souls of many, borders on despair, that most dangerous of all sins.[19] Our spiritual health depends crucially upon a recovery of hope.

In the Middle Ages, Christian artists sought to set the essentials of Christian faith and life before Christian people in a language of pictures, executed in glass and wood and stone, constituting a kind of *Biblia pauperum*—a Bible for the poor. Thus, on the facade of the vast and magnificent thirteenth-century cathedral of Amiens, for instance, just at the side of the central portal and beneath the great figures of Christ and his apostles and prophets, the artist has carved at eye level, in medallions in bas-relief, representations of the Christian virtues and their opposite vices. Leading the procession, of course, are faith, hope, and charity, with their opposites, idolatry, despair, and avarice. But hope deserves an especially close look. There she is, seated upon the rock of faith, because faith is hope's only solid ground. Her hand is outstretched towards heaven, from which we see the crown of righteousness descending. Beside her stands the golden banner, symbolic of Christ's resurrection, which is hope's unshakable assurance. In the series of the vices, hope's opposite is despair, represented by a woman all alone, piercing her breast with her own sword.[20]

Our Christian hope is surely established in the promises of God; our despair is all our own and of our own making. But hope is no Pollyanna: Christian hope is always, and must always expect to be, embattled in this world, tried and troubled, always reaching out towards a good not yet possessed. As Jesus told his bewildered disciples (John 15), it is only through pains of travail that new life in the Spirit comes to birth in us. For St. Paul, the great paragon of hope is Abraham, who "contrary to hope, believed in hope" (Rom. 4:18–21); Abraham, who saw in Isaac the fulfilment of God's promise that his seed would be blessed; Abraham, who was then called to bring that son to the altar of sacrifice; Abraham, who was torn between earth and heaven. Yet, "contrary to hope, he believed in hope." "That is to say," comments Henry Bullinger, "there he had a constant hope, where notwithstanding he had nothing to hope after, if all things had been weighed according to the manner of this world. But hope is a most firm and undoubted looking after those things which we believe: so that we see that the apostle did make faith manifest by hope, and by the certainty of hope did declare the assured constancy of faith."[21]

We know not the day nor the hour of hope's fulfilment; nor do we know the precise manner of it, nor the form it will take. We can only sow in hope; the harvest is God's business, and he will give the increase. "But you must know," says Meister Eckhart, in his wonderfully paradoxical way, "that God's friends are never without consolation, for whatever God wills is for them the greatest consolation of all, whether it be consolation or desolation."[22]

ENDNOTES

1. Augustine, *Faith, Hope and Charity*, tr. L. Arand, Ancient Christian Writers Series, no. 3 (Westminster, Md.: Newman Bookshop, 1947). Centuries later, St. Thomas Aquinas followed precisely St. Augustine's example in designing his own *Compendium of Theology*, tr. C. Vollert (St. Louis: B. Herder Book Co., 1949).

2. Augustine, *Enchiridion*, II, 7.

3. Ibid., I, 4.

4. Jerome, *Epistle 60*.

5. *Enchiridion*, I, 6.

6. Richard Hooker, *Of the Laws of Ecclesiastical Polity*, I, xi, 6.

7. Zeno of Verona, *Tractatus*, I, 36; *De spe, fide et caritate*, I, 1.

8. Augustine, *De trinitate*, VIII, 4, 6.

9. Bonaventure, *Breviloquium*, Pt. 5, c. 4, n. 4. Compare J. G. Bougerol, *La théologie de la espérance aux xiie et xiiie siècles* (Paris, 1985), Vol. I, p. 267. On the doctrine in Augustine, compare R. Crouse, *In multa defluximus: Confessions* X, 29–43, and "St. Augustine's Theory of Personality," in H. Blumenthal and R. Markus, *Neoplatonism and Early Christian Thought* (London: Valorium Publication, 1981), pp. 180–185.

10. William of St. Thierry, *Exposition on the Epistle to the Romans*, ed. J. Anderson (Kalamazoo, Mich.: Cistercian Publications, 1980), p. 85, on Romans 4:18–19.

11. The phrase comes from St. Thomas Aquinas, *Super epistolas S. Pauli lectura*, II, ad *Thess.*, c. 2, lect. 2, 49.

12. I have explored this theme, from Genesis to Dante, in *Images of Pilgrimage: Paradise and Wilderness in Christian Spirituality* (Charlottetown, 1986).

13. Karl Barth, *The Epistle to the Romans*, tr. E. Hoskyns (London: Oxford University Press, 1933), p. 154.

14. Thomas Aquinas, *Quaestiones de malo*, Q. 2, a. 10, ad. 2.

15. As quoted in J. I. Packer, *A Quest for Godliness: The Puritan Vision of the Christian Life* (Wheaton, Ill.: Crossway Books, 1990), p. 199.

16. On sacraments as the Word of God sensible, see Thomas Cranmer, "On the True and Catholic Doctrine of the Lord's Supper," in *Writings and Disputations of Thomas Cranmer relative to the Sacrament of the Lord's Supper*, ed. J. E. Cox (Cambridge: Parker Society, 1844), Vol. 1, p. 41.

17. *Summa theologiae*, II, II, 17, 2, obj. 2; cf. II, II, 83, 1 ad 1.

18. See especially the papers by R. U. Smith, "The Prayer Book and Devotional Life," and D. P. Curry, "Doctrinal Instrument of Salvation: The Use of Scripture in the Prayer Book Lectionary," both in *The Prayer Book* (Charlottetown: Theological Conference Report, 1985).

19. On despair (*desperatio*) as most dangerous, see St. Thomas Aquinas, *Summa theologiae*, II–II, Q. 20, a. 3.

20. See E. Mâle, *The Gothic Image: Religious Art in France of the Thirteenth Century*, tr. D. Nussey (New York: Harper Torchbook, 1958), pp. 112–115, with illustrations.

21. H. Bullinger, *Fifty Sermons Divided into Five Decades*, Decade I, no. 4, ed. T. Harding (Cambridge: Parker Society, 1849), Vol. 1, p. 88.

22. Meister Eckhart, *Counsels on Discernment*, no. 11, in E. Colledge and B. McGinn, eds., *Meister Eckhart: The Essential Sermons, Commentaries, Treatises and Defense* (New York: Paulist Press, 1981), p. 259.

24

RENEWAL IN THE FULLNESS
OF THE TRINITY
THE CHARISMATIC PROMISE

TOM MAXWELL

The Holy Spirit may without exaggeration be called the heartbeat of the Christian, the life-blood of the Christian church.
—Doctrine Commission of the Church of England,
We Believe in the Holy Spirit, 1991

There is little to attract the unbeliever in the traditional organized church.... We have neglected our prayer life, we have stopped listening to God ... [yet people are] hungry and thirsty for God or some form of spiritual reality.

—David Watson, 1980

I am not an academic, nor would I regard myself as a theologian. This chapter is, to borrow Jim Packer's words, a "*testimonial* to renewal in life and ministry by the Holy Spirit." It has often been said that the Holy Spirit is, or has been, the neglected member of the Holy Trinity. Therefore, if most of my words are centred around the person and work of the Holy Spirit, it is in an attempt to draw attention to this oversight and does not in any way diminish or overlook the need for a balanced approach in our theology and experience of God as Father, Son, and Holy Spirit.

As a priest of the Anglican Church of Canada for the past thirty-seven years, I have had the privilege of serving in a variety of parishes in both the east and the west. I have sat on executive committees of a number of dioceses and spent considerable time as a regional dean and territorial archdeacon. In recent years I have had the added experience of travelling across much of Canada on behalf of Anglican Renewal Ministries and in this capacity have had the pleasure of interacting with bishops, clergy, and laity in many dioceses. I am a cradle Anglican, born into the Anglican Church, rather than converting at a later age. I was nurtured in the "high church"–Anglo-Catholic side of our tradition but over the years have also become evangelical and charismatic. I firmly believe that spiritual health requires all of these elements of the gospel and that these are not opposing theologies but the necessary ingredients of a healthy theology and Christian lifestyle.

I have managed to survive the fifties and the "God is dead" sixties, and lived through encounter groups, "T-groups," and every other kind of group that the sixties, seventies, and eighties could dream up. In addition, I have been caught up in almost every stewardship programme devised by human hands. None of them had any lasting effect on the life of the church and thus we all faced one special appeal after another. It is a miracle to have survived with one's sanity and faith intact and still be excited about Christian ministry. I can honestly say that this would not be the case without the overwhelming encounter I had with God in the power of the Holy Spirit some thirty years ago. However one might define this experience, I know without doubt that it was the beginning of an "equipping and empowering for ministry" that has continued to sustain me to this day. Throughout the years, I was aware that the church into which I was born and baptized was facing many serious tensions, and that our response to these tensions would be either life-giving or death-dealing.

Today we are being confronted by a number of disturbing realties, none of which is really new. As we look out upon our world we are aware more than ever of the need for vital and effective ministry. Yet the church, particularly the Anglican branch to which we belong, is in crisis. With its resources shrinking, and its sense of identity and purpose in confusion, it is being confronted by predictions of almost total decimation in the next ten to twenty years.[1] The symptoms have been around for almost as many years as I have been in ministry. Back in 1963, the Anglican Congress of Toronto proclaimed boldly that "the church that lives to itself, will die by itself." Even then, statistical predictions indicated that unless things turned around, the Anglican Church of Canada would cease to exist by the end of the century.[2] Here we are in 1994, and unless "things" (whatever that might mean) turn around, the prophets of doom may be close to their target. No longer considered a "mainline" church, we have been marginalized by our society and by other expressions of the Christian faith.

This is not a very uplifting beginning to a chapter whose main purpose is to discuss "renewal" and give a sense of new life and purpose. But unless we fully accept the "reality" of our present situation, we are not likely to respond with any real enthusiasm or energy. It has been my experience as I have moved around the country that many clergy, parishes, and dioceses are so caught up in self-preservation that they seem almost to be living in a state of denial. The idea that the church exists for those who are not yet part of her family appears to be totally foreign. The vision of the mission field beginning at the door steps of each parish church is ignored when a "maintenance mentality" misleads a church to see her mission as that of a chaplain to a list of names on a parish roll.[3] All of this at a time when the "reality" of the good news is needed more than ever in our society and culture, which is itself in crisis. It is as if we ourselves have lost confidence in, or lost touch with, the reconciling love of God in Christ. We no longer know God as *Abba*, "Father," and no longer experience the overwhelming healing and empowering presence of God in the power of the Holy Spirit. It is almost impossible to convince others that the good news of the Christian gospel can be good news for them if we no longer experience good news in our own personal and parish lives. Many years ago a report issued by the World Council of Churches had a statement that went something like this: In a spiritually alive and healthy church, evangelism is spontaneous, continuous and contagious. It is the natural overflow (out flow) of the love of God in the day-to-day life of the congregation.

I fully believe that the gates of hell will not prevail against the church (Matt. 16:18). I also know that God will not be left without witnesses to do his work. And I know that God can and will by-pass an institution that no longer responds to him or seeks to do his will. So it is not my purpose to defend or promote the continuation of the Anglican Church of Canada as such. But I am an Anglican and I sincerely believe that God has entrusted to the Anglican tradition, by accident of history as some might put it, many very important aspects of the Christian faith. As Anglicans we have much to share with other Christians, as they do with us, in our common goal of bringing Jesus Christ to our community and world. We must, above all, retain our biblical understanding of the call to be "a transforming community" for the sake of the world, affirming our special gifts as resources to be shared. Conforming to the world's agenda will not bring new life.

It is time to reaffirm the essentials of our faith and to know the power for Christian life and ministry given to everyone reconciled to God in Christ and willing to live out the commitment of his or her baptism. This does not happen automatically. God most certainly pours out his gifts of the spirit as he wills (1 Cor. 12:11), but there is a need for each of us to make a conscious decision to receive and use the grace given. This is one of the most important issues we face. Legalistic biblical orthodoxy, which only focuses on an intellectual correctness, does not by itself bring about the transforming community in Christ that is good news to the world.[4] On the other hand, the fullness of the Spirit cannot be appropriated through a theology that denies biblical truth.

It is my conviction that the present crisis in our church and other mainline denominations is not of the devil, as some might say (although I am sure he has his hand in it), nor is it sent by God as a form of punishment. Rather, it is a natural by-product of a church losing touch with God and no longer open to the Holy Spirit, either because we have neglected to accept or even expect the gift offered, or because we have drifted theologically from "the truth once delivered to the saints." In the past we have experienced both catholic and evangelical renewals within the life of the church. Now it is time, not to lose the realities and truths of these revivals, but to bring into this mix a renewal in the theology and experience of the Holy Spirit.

At the beginning of this chapter, I quoted a statement from a little book produced by the Doctrine Commission of the Church of England—"the Holy Spirit may without exaggeration be called the heartbeat of the Christian, the life-blood of the Christian church." This being true, it is time for a massive transfusion. I believe that God has been trying to get our attention on this matter for some time. But we in the so-called mainline churches have been slow to open our eyes.

At the turn of the last century, a small group of Bible students in Topeka,

Kansas, began questioning the seeming powerlessness of the church.[5] As they read Acts they were confronted by the amazing witness of the power of the Holy Spirit at work. They were puzzled by the church's powerlessness, and by a doctrine that some of their churches offered as an explanation—that God had not intended the Holy Spirit to work in the same way beyond the Apostolic age (dispensationalism). Was this really true, they asked, or was it merely an attempt to make an excuse for the powerlessness of the church? The group decided to put it to the test. Accepting the account of the Day of Pentecost as recorded in Acts at face value, they decided to wait upon God in prayer. They waited in their upper room for a number of days in expectant prayer as the century changed. Their waiting was not in vain, for they soon were overwhelmed by the presence and manifestations of the Holy Spirit. They excitedly ran out to tell their local clergy about their experience, but their news was rejected. To make a much longer and very interesting story short, out of this "renewal in the spirit" came one of the fastest growing of all Christian denominations, the classic Pentecostal churches. Born in excitement and rejection, they turned their back on mainline Christianity, both to their loss and ours.

Some sixty years went by before the next chapter in this story could be told. This time an Episcopal priest in a fashionable and "successful" California parish asked the questions: Where is the power, excitement, and expectation of Acts to be found in the life of the Anglican Church? This priest, Dennis Bennett, soon found out in discussion with his neighbours over a cup of coffee. His neighbours were members of a Pentecostal church, and they shared their own experience with Dennis. Then they prayed with him. Bennett tells his own story in the book called *Nine O'clock in the Morning*.[6] Needless to say, he had a life-changing experience of God the Holy Spirit. He too experienced rejection at the hands of his church. Moving to Seattle, he was given a small parish that was near death. Through Bennett's faithful witness, testimony, and teaching, and the reality of a ministry empowered by the Holy Spirit, St. Luke's soon became one of the fastest growing Episcopal parishes in the United States.

Thus began the "renewal" movement in the mainline denominations. Sixty years after Topeka, mainline Christians began sharing renewal in the life and work of the Holy Spirit. Within a few years, this would spread to Lutheran, Roman Catholic, and other denominational expressions of Christianity, including the Anglican Church; not just in Canada and the United States, but worldwide. This did not turn Anglicans or Lutherans or Roman Catholics or Baptists into Pentecostals, but did renew the best within each tradition and began opening doors that allowed more open and cooperative relationships between expressions of the Christian church.

My own story begins in Toronto in 1963—the year of the great Anglican Congress, which brought together bishops, clergy and lay men and women from most dioceses in the Anglican Communion. It was a time of tremendous excitement as we were caught up in the great themes of "Mutual Responsibility and Interdependence in the Body of Christ," and "The Parish—A Powerhouse for

World Mission." We heard the inspired warning that the church that lived to itself would die by itself. We listened intently as Bishop Stephen Bayne, then executive officer of the Anglican Communion, gave his impressions of the Anglican world gained from his travels throughout the Communion. He compared the worldwide Anglican Church to a Shakespearian Society whose purpose was to keep alive the works of that greatly honoured, but long-dead author. He said the Anglican Church was much like such a memorial society, dedicated to the task of keeping the name and memory of a long-dead God alive. What he was saying, of course, was that what we were doing in our worship and parish activities no longer seemed to have any relevance to the world outside the church building. There was no longer any sense that God was alive and active. There was little excitement, little challenge, and no expectation or vision. There was no sense of purpose beyond maintaining the local parish structure and tradition.

The congress closed with a now famous blessing. When most Anglicans would have expected to hear about the peace of God, that passes all understanding, what we heard was something like this: May the disturbing power of the Holy Spirit rest upon you. Note that this was in the same period of time that the Holy Spirit was just beginning to move in a new way within North American churches. I firmly believe, with the gift of hindsight, that we, as the church, were being given a choice at that time, a choice which meant either new life or slow death. It was a choice between God's way and the way of the world. I believe we chose the world's way to a great extent.

My experiences at the congress caused me to confront my own struggles and doubts about myself later that same year. I was newly married, functioning as a curate in a prominent Toronto parish. At the same time, I was doing post-graduate studies in an attempt to find the God who was so real in the book of Acts. Finally, having given up hope of ever finding him, I went into the church late one evening to hand in my resignation to God. If he were anywhere, I thought, at least he would be in a church. I knelt down. I don't remember exactly what I said, but I can distinctly remember being told to talk to a certain priest who happened to be leading a quiet day for a group of women and was in the building.

I didn't act upon this immediately. For two more weeks, I wrestled with my pride: how would I tell another priest of the church that I could no longer find any purpose or meaning in Christian ministry? When I finally found the courage, I made the appointment and eventually found myself in a small chapel, with flickering candles and a faint smell of incense. I was warmly welcomed by the priest (adorned in cassock, cape, and biretta), who invited me to sit down. For hours we talked, discussed, and argued, and finally I told him what was going on inside. He smiled, and with one hand on my shoulder, said, "Tom, there is nothing wrong with you, except for the fact that you have never met the God you have been working for. You know all about him, but you have never met him." Kneeling at the altar rail in that small chapel, I offered myself to God in a renewal of my Baptism/Ordination Vows. I opened my life to Jesus Christ in a way I had never done before. I sought a personal relationship—I wanted to know the God who had reached out to me. Nothing dramatic happened at that moment. It was late and I got up to leave. As I was heading for the door, I turned to say thanks to the warm and friendly priest who had been so patient with me. He said, "Tom, please come back in a few days; there is still something more."

During the next few days I began noticing that indeed something had happened. For the first time I was sensing the peace that passes all understanding. In spite of my reservations I returned, partly out of curiosity and partly with a sense of expectation, to find out about this "something more." Having been brought up as a very conservative Anglo-Catholic, I was not inclined to get involved in questionable theology or non-Anglican practices. All my defences were in place, even though I knew for certain that something new was at work in me. I was at a loss to figure out what else to expect. Again hours were spent in theological debate; this time it centred around the person and work of the Holy Spirit. There isn't room here to enter into the breadth of that discussion, except to say that there was nothing I could detect that contradicted what I had been taught: that God through Word and Sacrament empowers his people, including clergy, for the ministries to which they are called.

Again, kneeling at the altar rail, this time with a sense of "expectation," I asked God to release in me the power of the Holy Spirit, already received in my Baptism, Confirmation, and Ordination. Hands were laid upon me as I made this request, and all heaven broke loose. Human language fails when one attempts to describe such events. This would be a new beginning, not only for me, but for hundreds of people to whom I would minister over the years. What I had always accepted intellectually now became an experiential reality in my life and, above all, in my ministry. It was as if God had put his arms around me. For the first time I not only knew with my head that I was a child of God but experienced this reality filling my whole being. There would be many surface storms in my life after this; but this inner sense of God's caring and affirmation has never been lost. Needless to say, a tongue-speaking Anglican priest was not welcomed with open arms in a prominent society parish in 1963.

I think it is important for me to interject at this point that the gift of speaking in tongues in and of itself does not indicate any special status in one's spirituality, nor can it be said to be the confirming sign of spiritual renewal. As Paul said, "If I speak in the tongues of men and of angels, but have not love, I am only a resounding gong or a clanging cymbal" (1 Cor. 13). On the other hand, speaking in tongues is "a gift of the spirit," according to Scripture, and has purpose in God's plan. For me, at this new beginning, it was a means of praising God and expressing the inexpressible joy that overwhelmed me.

In the months that followed, I would experience many "gifts" of the Holy Spirit. The Scriptures came alive in a most profound way. The healing ministry took on new meaning and a new reality.[7] The gifts of inspired speech, discernment, a new excitement in worship, and other gifts soon became a regular part of daily life and ministry. I would like to dispel any impression that somehow, from this moment on, I became an instant "saint" and all problems and difficulties disappeared. As Scripture tells us, Jesus went from his baptism in water and the Spirit to a personal encounter with the devil. Neither can we escape this pattern. Jesus was without sin; not so his disciples. Praise God for his mercy and forgiveness! The good news really is *good news*.

Ministry is the most exciting when I am able to share in the spiritual journeys of my people and see God at work in them, bringing them to new birth in Christ. I have seen the reconciling love of God in Christ working through his people, bringing healing and inspiration. I have seen the gospel, the good news, actually at work in a congregation, turning a maintenance-minded parish into a community with a vision and mission beyond itself. I have been to a Parish Council (Vestry) meeting where there is little need to be concerned about financial matters because the congregation gives thankfully in response to God's blessings. Rather, time is spent on developing the spiritual health of the parish community and guiding its social outreach and evangelism in an atmosphere of prayer and praise. I have worked with laity who give of their time willingly in empowered ministry, the lay members of the congregation becoming what God intended them to be: the front line in pastoral care, in healing ministry, in outreach and evangelism, in social action and concern to the local community. And I have taken part in Eucharist-centred worship where time is no longer a restrictive element, and we are regularly "lost in wonder, joy and praise."

These things did not happen overnight. For we are not reborn as instantly mature Christians. The spiritual journey is just that, a journey with an infancy, childhood, and adolescence, and somewhere along the line, an ever-growing level of maturity is attained. This road is often up and down; it has long plateaus and many foggy stretches. It is a road that requires spiritual guides and companions. It is a road that can be strewn with pot holes and sharp turns. It is a journey only possible in Christ, under the power of the Holy Spirit, and where *Abba*—our Heavenly Father—is both in the beginning and the end.

Every renewal movement in the church's history has been plagued by growing pains. Human beings, suddenly overwhelmed by spiritual experiences, are often tempted to see themselves as an elitist group, judging all others to be in need of exactly what they themselves have experienced. No doubt this has happened and does happen with the renewal of today. Sadly this has often made it easy for others to pass off a new outpouring of God's grace as just another fad. Great discernment is required in order that we not ignore what is of God. Evangelicals, catholics, charismatics, those who have been on Cursillo Retreats or Marriage Encounters, all can form "elitist" communities. Parties in the church and denominationalism on the wider Christian scene often form such mindsets, blinding us to the sovereign work of God in our midst.

Yet somewhere in all of these there is a truth that is worth discovering. The renewing of the Anglican Church cannot take place outside of the context of the whole Christian community. The renewing work of the Holy Spirit is at work in most denominations and there is a strong indication that a major part of his work is to bring the denominational family back into a more open and cooperative relationship. I would suggest that the Holy Spirit is seeking the restoration of "the one holy, catholic and apostolic church," which will be in all its glory catholic, evangelical, and charismatic.

As an institution, the church is not always open to the new actions of God, who is often left to move outside mainline church structures to get his work accomplished. I know many Anglicans, even clergy, who have never heard of John Wimber and the Vineyard movement.[7] Yet many young Anglicans are flocking to worship with them. Why? Maybe we are afraid to learn the answer? Possibly we are being challenged to take a look and see something we have overlooked in our Anglican exclusiveness. There are some strange things happening both inside and outside the church, and not all of them are healthy. This is the main reason we have to rely more than ever on our heritage of Scripture and tradition, supported by sanctified reason, which is a "gift of the Spirit."

At Canterbury in 1978, just a week before the Lambeth Conference of that year, some 380 clergy and lay people, including some thirty bishops and archbishops, gathered from all over the Anglican Communion to share in the first International Conference on Renewal and Evangelism in the Anglican world. At this gathering emerged the amazing story of the outpouring of the Holy Spirit "on every continent and island." We soon discovered that what had happened in California, Toronto, and other North American cities was also happening in the United Kingdom, Africa, Australia, Singapore, in First World and Third World countries. God seemed to be pouring out his Spirit as he willed, across all denominational and geographical lines.[8] He truly was getting our attention. This moving of the Holy Spirit was equipping and empowering the church for the work of ministry and evangelism.

By the time my wife and I returned to Montreal where I was serving, I was seeing with a new set of eyes. I had shared, worshipped, and studied with representatives of every branch of the Anglican Communion, black and brown, oriental and white, male and female, and from every "brand" of Anglicanism. Together we rejoiced in prayer and praise as we gathered around the high altar in Canterbury Cathedral. For me this was an unbelievable experience. In this historic cathedral, the mother church of Anglicanism that represented for me my spiritual roots, I saw God at work in the here and now. I knew without doubt that "the gates of hell would never overcome" the body of Christ. My conviction that renewal in the power of the Holy Spirit was not an option but the sovereign act of God in restoring his church to its apostolic vision, mission, and power was not only confirmed, but became the guiding reality in my life and ministry. We met again in Canterbury in 1988, ten years later, and the amazing story of God's grace continued to be shared and experienced.

If I had the space, I would tell more about the Canadian scene. Believe me, there is a story to tell.[9] But at this point I feel the need to draw attention to the ecumenical dimension of the renewal movement. For me this became a living reality in 1991 in Brighton, England, when representatives of the whole Christian spectrum, from Roman Catholics to Pentecostals, gathered in mutual fellowship, prayer, and study. Together we were called to affirm a common reality—God was calling his family to affirm our common mission, to affirm those things that we shared, and to pray for healing and reconciliation in the areas of our divergence.

And now here we are, four years into the "Decade of Evangelism," in an "institutional" church that spends more time arguing about the meaning of "evangelism" than doing it. Synods, both Diocesan and General, are caught up in the painful dilemma of a financial crunch that is only a symptom of a more serious disease. Without God's empowering, the church cannot begin to fulfil its purpose and mission. As I travel the Canadian scene, my heart often aches as I encounter a church that does not want to accept "the gift" that God so willingly seeks to give. Yet as I look back over the past thirty-five years I do see God's plan unfolding. Renewal comes in many forms and through many different agencies, but it is happening.

It is very important to note that renewal begins and grows only in the atmosphere of prayer, authentic worship, and faithfulness to the scriptural revelation.[10] It happens only in those who are searching for a personal relationship with God in Jesus Christ, who have a deep sense of their own inadequacies, and an awareness of their need for repentance and forgiveness—while accepting in faith the promises of Scripture, and expecting to be empowered by God through the Holy Spirit.

In those Scriptures we encounter God as Father, Son, and Holy Spirit. The work and ministry of the Spirit is not to draw attention to himself but to reveal and make possible a deep personal relationship with Jesus Christ. The Holy Spirit always points or leads to Jesus, as Jesus is the way to the Father. Let us not create God in our own image. Let us not forget that we do not have to fight God's battles for him, but only be obedient and willing to serve him when and where we are called.

I hope that this very brief "testimonial" will serve to inspire others. There is much available in print for those moved to delve more deeply into this subject. (See Suggested Reading below.)

Let me close with a quote from St. Cyprian (AD 246): "I went down into those life-giving waters and was born again, a new man. All my doubts vanished. I could see what had been hidden from me. I could do what had been impossible." This is a personal testimony of a profound experience of personal conversion and redemption and the power of baptism from the third century.[11] The very same thing encourages us today. This renewal is not new. It is the reclaiming of our Christian heritage.

SUGGESTED READING

Charles E. Hummel, *Fire in the Fireplace: Charismatic Renewal in the Nineties* (Downers Grove, Ill.: InterVarsity Press, 1993).

Dennis J. Bennett, *Nine O'clock in the Morning* (Plainfield, N.J.: Logos Publishing, 1970).

Bill Burnett, ed., *By My Spirit: Renewal in the Worldwide Anglican Church* (Toronto: Hodder & Stoughton, 1988).

George Carey, *The Church in the Marketplace* (Harrisburg, Pa.: Morehouse, 1984, 1989).

The Doctrine Commission of the Church of England, *We Believe in the Holy Spirit* (London: Church House Publishing, 1991).

Kilian McDonnell and George Montague, *Christian Initiation and Baptism in the Holy Spirit: Evidence from the First Eight Centuries* (Collegeville, Minn.: The Liturgical Press, 1991).

C. Peter Wagner, *The Third Wave of the Holy Spirit: Encountering the Power of Signs and Wonders* (Ann Arbor: Michigan, Servant Books, 1988).

ENDNOTES

1. Reginald Bibby, *Unknown Gods* (Toronto: Stoddart, 1993).

2. Anglican Congress, *Mutual Responsibility and Interdependence in the Body of Christ* (Toronto: Anglican Book Centre, 1963).

3. Loren Mead, *The Once and Future Church* (Washington: The Alban Institute, 1991).

4. James D. G. Dunn, *Baptism in the Holy Spirit* (London: SCM Press, 1970).

5. Charles Hummel, *Fire in the Fire Place* (Downers Grove, Ill.: InterVarsity Press, 1993).

6. Dennis Bennett, *Nine O'clock in the Morning* (Plainfield, N.J.: Logos, 1970).

7. John Wimber, *Power Evangelism: Signs and Wonders Today* (London: Hodder & Stoughton, 1985).

8. Hummel, *Fire in the Fire Place*.

9. David A. Reed, "From Movement to Institution: A Case Study of Charismatic Renewal in the Anglican Church of Canada" (Toronto: Wycliffe College, 1991).

10. Michael Marshall, *Renewal in Worship* (Wilton, Conn.: Morehouse-Barlow, 1985).

11. Anne Field, *From Darkness to Light: What It Meant to Become a Christian in the Early Church* (Ann Arbor: Servant Books, 1978).

What Is the Church's Task?

The Most Rev. George Carey
Archbishop of Canterbury

The Church of England, declared Bishop Charles Gore, "is an ingeniously devised instrument for defeating the objects which it is supposed to promote." No doubt this could be said of any church around the world. No doubt it is being said by some of the Anglican Church of Canada.

Now, I want to declare at the outset my whole-hearted commitment to the Anglican Church. I dare say that everyone has, like me, on occasion, despaired of our church. No doubt at times we have been frustrated by its structures and, perhaps, been uninspired by its worship. I know that similar criticisms can be made of other churches too. In spite of that, I love our church. I love it because its way of living, its way of "doing theology," its sacraments and worship still draw my allegiance. In spite of all its deficiencies, I am an Anglican committed to the worldwide Anglican family and neither have, nor want, any other ecclesiastical home.

But, though personally committed to this great Communion, I recognize that we, and all Christian churches in the Western world, have to live out the faith in cultures that are materialistic, secularized, and pluralist. In these cultures no church nowadays can claim a monopoly, and some non-Christian faiths and quasi-Christian sects are beginning to grip the imagination of young people in a way that Christianity does not.

Facing such a confused and confusing world, we find ourselves having to address the question: *What is the church's task?* To answer it, I want to concentrate on some of the themes in the letter to the Ephesians. It was written, of course, against a background not dissimilar to ours today. Ephesus, too, was syncretistic, materialistic, and pluralist, though it was far from "secularized." The tiny Christian congregations were in the minority and no doubt they too were wondering: What is the church's task? Where do we go from here? What is our mission and our function today?

In the Epistle the author makes a number of responses to these questions that are, in essence, a call to faithfulness to God in his mission to his world. These responses are the ones we need to be reminded of if we are to take the opportunities God is offering us in our own generation.

It Is Time to Proclaim Afresh the Faithfulness of God and the Breadth of His Vision

Ephesians offers a breathtaking theological panorama. The catholicity of the Christian message is an inspiration. The first chapter reveals the character of God who blesses us with every spiritual blessing, who chooses us before the foundation of the world, who destines us in love to be his children, who lavishes grace upon us and makes known to us his wisdom and insight. The passage focuses on "praise," "thanksgiving," and "wisdom." These are the dynamics in which faithfulness takes up a positive attitude towards the past. *Praise* celebrates the activity of God in salvation; *thanksgiving* focuses the mind on what he has done for us; *wisdom* stretches our minds and imaginations as we build upon the foundation of the apostles and prophets, "Jesus Christ himself being the cornerstone."

The letter to the Ephesians contains a brilliant exposition of the breadth, depth, and height of the Christian faith. There is nothing parochial or limited in its vision. God's salvific action reaches everywhere to redeem, change, energize, and transform. It is God's plan "to unite all things in him, things in heaven and things on earth" (1:10).

I encourage you to think of what that involves for a moment. Such a unity, as we know from experience, can only be achieved through complex, painful, costly, intellectually and emotionally demanding processes. There is nothing easy about bringing unity to the divisions of our world whether they exist between communities or nations, in broken relationships and situations of mistrust, or in the alienation between humanity and the environment.

Yet, central to this vision is the risen and ascended Christ and "the church, which is his body, the fullness of him who fills all in all" (1:22–23). The church is seen in Ephesians as a focus for God's work in creating such a unity. The key to its social identity is the uniting of Jews and Gentiles in "one new humanity," thereby making peace. St. Paul uses the image of the temple's dividing wall crashing down as a result of the crucifixion and resurrection of Christ. Now there is a new reconciled humanity. All things have the potential to be renewed. Here is the theological vision of a truly "catholic" church whose centre is Christ. What does it say to us today?

1. We need to cultivate a broader theological vision.

I have noticed in recent years a shrinking of Christian vision. Our view of God's work and the scope and power of the gospel has too often been narrowed to what we believe we can achieve in our own strength. Our preaching too has become one-dimensional. It often sounds the note of experience but lacks the fullness of a theology founded on the finality of Christ. Perhaps, too, we have lost the sense of hope that a full-blooded eschatological vision excites. The writer to the Ephesians—and there are good reasons for supposing him to be St. Paul—had no doubt that in Christ, God is working his purposes out. There is hope; there is salvation; there is eternal life—because there is Christ! We shall see no fundamental changes in the church, any church, unless we regain a theological vision that is rooted in God's commitment to his world and its future, and to his church.

2. We need a greater commitment to real comprehensiveness within the church.

The later chapters of Ephesians show the writer working from inclusive theology to address the real needs of the church. One major concern of the church was the problem of living with differences. He appeals to them to be "generous one to another, tender hearted, forgiving one another as God in Christ forgave you" (4:32). There is a tremendous emphasis upon the use of language and the use of words. I sometimes wonder what effect we would we see on church and inter-church life if chapter four, verses twenty-nine to thirty-two, were truly obeyed?

One of the great features of Anglicanism is our commitment to comprehensiveness. This does not mean that we as a church cannot make up our minds about anything and are cheerfully content to believe two irreconcilable theologies at the same time. Indeed not. There is an integrity about Anglican theology that, while it draws upon historic Christianity, has its own shape and beauty. I am an Anglican because, more than many churches, we have realized that the catholicity of the church means there is room for disagreement, differences, and variety within the over-arching theology of our church. We have deliberately internalized dispute so that we may "image" a gospel that is inclusive. In encouraging variety of expression, style, and argument, we are "imaging" the generosity of the God who accepts us as we are and seeks to make us more like Christ.

The intolerance that treats other Christians as strangers because they do not come from our theological stable or speak our spiritual language must be resisted. No doubt you are working this out in the Canadian church as we are in England. Ephesians gives us encouragement to speak the truth in love, to work at our unity and to wrestle with our differences. We are bidden to do so because the gospel is catholic in scope. It emanates from a God who calls all things into the unity already achieved by the work of his Son.

IT IS TIME TO REAFFIRM THE CHURCH'S COMMITMENT TO THE FAITH

I have mentioned our church's over-arching theology. Let me expand a little on what I mean by that. It is well nigh impossible to speak of the "catholicity" of the Christian faith and the implications of this for the life of the church without speaking of the need for faithfulness to the faith of the church. Today we are beginning to feel some strains as "single issue" problems call responses from some of our fellow Christians that seem to go far beyond the historic faith of the church. Confronting these difficult problems requires from us all integrity of life, honesty, and candour with respect to other Christians, and a fierce commitment to the body of Christ.

How is Paul true to the truth he has received? I discern three strands of truth on which he draws: first, the Old Testament; second, the revelation that had come to him through Christ; and third, his personal experience of Christ. All three are grafted together to assist the congregations of Asia Minor to face the present and future. Indeed, this marvellous Epistle is a highly sophisticated piece of thinking and writing, skilfully weaving this three-fold cord into a tapestry that depicts the church being built up into a body with Christ as its head. We see St. Paul relating his inherited traditions, his experiences, and the Scriptures to each other and trusting that there is wisdom, through the Spirit and our God-given reason, for appropriate improvisations to be made in new situations.

We, in turn, need to imitate him in this. The three-fold cord we often speak about in the Anglican tradition is that of Scripture, reason, and tradition. In many respects this is a reordering of the Pauline pattern described above. We speak of a "dispersed authority." It is a part of our heritage that helps us to be a comprehensive church. While a dispersed authority may contain the seeds of fragmentation, it need not do so if the primacy of Scripture is affirmed and maintained. Faithfulness to the traditions of the church is excellent—as long as we do not allow it to be the all-determining criterion of truth. The scope of this discussion does not allow me to take the point further, except to point out that the breadth of Anglican comprehensiveness is contained within a doctrinal framework for which the primacy of Scripture and the rock-solid basis of a trinitarian faith remain our foundations. The maxim for scholars, as for all Christians, is that "speaking the truth in love we are to grow up in every way into him who is the head, into Christ" (4:15).

Central to Ephesians is this emphasis upon maturity—a gift much needed by that church, which was probably seeing the second or third generation of converts among its members. It was facing the problems of both living out the faith in a pluralist society and dealing with the severe divisions that were beginning to appear in the church itself. Hence the great emphasis on teaching and on knowledge for "equipping of the saints for the work of ministry for building up the body of Christ" (4:12).

Let me attempt to relate this to our own day. One obvious parallel can be drawn with the relationship between academic theologians and other believers. We still need to work hard at breaking down barriers between what is called "critical scholarship" and the life of the church. Some generations ago it was often thought that the way to commend the gospel was to prune or "demythologize" it. Rudolf Bultmann provided the classic example of this. As a New Testament scholar, he was committed to a radical skepticism that pruned away much of the Synoptic Gospels in order to reach the supposed "Jesus of history." Yet, as a deeply committed Lutheran, he was also committed to a faith he expressed in terms of the Continental philosophy of his day, namely, existentialism. The trouble was, this convinced very few skeptics. They were mystified as to why Bultmann did not prune it all away and join them. Our challenge is to express the gospel to our generation, but to do so in ways that are consistent with our historic faith.

IT IS TIME TO COMMEND THE GOSPEL
BY BOTH LIVING IT AND LIVING WITHIN IT

There is a double edge to the gospel. On the one hand, throughout the Western world churches are becoming aware that, as society becomes more secular, it is more important than ever that Christians live lives consistent with the claims they make. Sadly, it is sometimes those Christians who make the most noise about preaching the gospel who are the ones who display its fruits the least. As someone nurtured in the evangelical wing of the church, I recognize that the world sees as authentically Christian those who, from whatever wing of the church, display the love of Christ in their lives. For instance, Mother Teresa has in our generation proclaimed the gospel very powerfully indeed, simply by living it. The same can be true, too, of all of us if we are prepared to model Christ's patterns of love, forgiveness, and reconciliation both in our personal lives and in our churches.

On the other hand, there is the call to "live within the gospel," with the far-reaching consequences that involves. The letter of the Ephesians, of course, is a remarkable exploration of the wonder of God's love and of the radical gospel that now commands us. This was the way Paul saw it. He was possessed by the good news of Christ. His life was completely changed as he now lived within that good news. If you were to challenge me to portray what it means to "live within the gospel," my unhesitating answer would be to take you to churches and Christians around the globe whose simple commitment to the truth of Christ has transformed their way of looking at life. Our problem and our great opportunity is to grasp the riches and diversity of the gospel—not to demythologize it, not to reduce it, but to explore its radical implications for our day.

Allied to this is yet another challenge to us all. In Ephesians there is a striking stress upon teaching, knowledge, and wisdom. In this context, *epignosis* means more than our "human ways of knowing." It has to do with "knowing God." Such knowledge of God should not, however, be seen as something totally distinct from the other types of knowledge we acquire as human beings. The situation in Asia Minor addressed by St. Paul clearly demanded men and women who knew their Lord and knew their faith.

What was needed then, and now, were first class Christian educators and communicators. What is conspicuously missing in Ephesians is an emphasis upon numerical growth. While the *missio Dei* is clearly the burden of the Epistle, there is nothing in it that talks of numbers. Rather, what is conspicuously present is the writer's commitment to quality—men and women who love the living God, whose hearts have been touched and whose minds have been quickened by the desire to know him better. Without a doubt, among our priorities today must be the teaching and learning of the faith to the highest possible standards. Even so, we have to recognize the limits of our knowledge, limits so clearly expressed by St. Paul in that marvellous paradox, "to know the love of Christ which surpasses knowledge" (3:19).

IT IS TIME TO DEEPEN OUR COMMITMENT TO MISSION

Ephesians has perhaps the most profound theology of mission in the New Testament. Chapter one is a paean of praise. Indeed, all Christian communication should begin, as chapter one does, with praise, for all true theology is doxological. When we understand that we are part of something so glorious that God sent his son into the world for us and all humankind, how can we keep it to ourselves? Mission at its best is the overflow of doxology: first, as it emerges in worship and intercession (two of the most powerful prayers in the New Testament are in chapters one and three); second, in service, as is seen in chapter three, with apostles, prophets, and evangelists topping the list of ministries in the church. Despite the fact that Paul does not mention numbers, Ephesus and the other churches in Asia Minor were growing both spiritually and numerically as they gave themselves to proclaiming the wonders of God.

But how is this not to be triumphalistic and offensive in a pluralist society? Remember, Ephesus was a pluralist city. Paul himself spent more time there than anywhere else on his missionary journeys—debating, listening, arguing, proclaiming, working, and serving. His own pattern of life was, in his eyes, an example for others to follow. He writes to his fellow Christians: "I therefore, a prisoner for the Lord, beg you to lead a life worthy of the calling to which you have been called, with all lowliness and meekness, with patience, forbearing one another in love, eager to maintain the unity of the Spirit in the bond of peace" (4:1–3). Such behaviour within the Christian community should be mirrored in our relationships with those outside it. God invites us into relationship with him. His call comes with generosity and love. If we reflect those characteristics, it is hard to see how there would be anything harsh, manipulative, or coercive about our evangelism.

Since the "Decade of Evangelism" was launched in 1990 we have been rightly warned not to make too sharp a distinction between "evangelism" by proclamation and "mission" as the working out of the message in social care and witness. If we are to deepen our commitment to God's mission, the whole of the church's life should be directed towards living out the faith in our world. We see from Christ's own example that there was a unity about his ministry, whether it involved preaching the kingdom or performing works of healing. A healthy church will inevitably have a concern for the needy. It will equally be keen to proclaim the gospel in season and out of season.

Mission, instead of being one of many things a church might do, must become the heart and soul of all it does. Recently I visited *HMS Victory*, Admiral Nelson's flagship at the battle of Trafalgar. I was shown the ornate furniture in his luxurious quarters. I was told that when battle was imminent, all the furniture was taken out and put in a small vessel that floated behind. Everything on the ship was strapped down so that nothing could impede the battle that lay ahead. Sadly, the Church is not always geared for the battle she needs to fight. She sometimes forgets that she is always just one generation away from extinction. A church that fails to make disciples simply fails. Very few Western churches can now depend on the expectation that their youth will automatically go to church regardless of what the church does. We live in cultures alien to the Christian faith. The church's message must be proclaimed afresh to each generation, fully attuned to all the variety of the societies in which we live.

In deepening our commitment to mission, we must be willing to change our methods. I have already stressed the ethic of gentleness and courtesy that is at the heart of Ephesians. I have never apologized, and never will apologize, for the fact that we are called to present Christ as Saviour and Lord. But I have always insisted that the message comes as an invitation and asks, as Philip did of the Eunuch: "Do you understand what you are reading?" In inviting others to listen to me, I must be prepared to listen to them. Only in that way can a genuine two-way dialogue be established, one which may or may not culminate in a life-changing encounter with the Holy God.

If we commit ourselves to mission, we can, with confidence, expect God to be at work in people's lives. His faithfulness to us more than matches ours to him. What is more, we can take heart that this is actually happening these days. In England it is no longer the case that the Church of England is in numerical decline. Enormous energy is being put into evangelism and many churches are growing—some of them very fast indeed. But there is no room for complacency; much needs to be done if our churches are to be the powerful instruments God longs to use. We must constantly ask ourselves, in the midst of all our busyness, if we are truly doing what God requires.

IT IS TIME TO PROCLAIM THE UNIQUENESS OF JESUS CHRIST

One of the most disturbing trends in the Western church has been a tendency for some to loosen their grip on the singularity of Jesus Christ, who is, of course, the centre of the Christian faith. We have been bullied into this by powerful theological voices that have suggested that Christianity must come to terms with its own "parochiality." It has no right to challenge Islam or any other religion. It is merely a Western face of God. It must therefore surrender its commitment to being accepted in every part of the world and be content to be one face and one voice among many.

This view is to be rejected firmly. Of course, as I have said, I deplore forms of presentation that are insincere, manipulative, or coercive. We do not hear the tones of Christ in such expressions. His ethic of gentleness and love should control our theology of conversion. But to be concerned for these things does not mean we therefore cease to proclaim the uniqueness of Christ. To do so is a denial of both our history and our theology. Nowhere is this more clearly stated than in Ephesians. The commitment to love is basic to the Epistle, culminating in the image of marriage as a metaphor of the relationship of Christ to his bride, the church. Central to this love is the outpouring of the grace of God that finds its tangible manifestation in the death and resurrection of Christ. The so-called scandal of particularity finds its sharpest expression in chapter two, with the powerful retelling of humankind's reconciliation with God through Christ's death on the cross. And yet, despite this emphasis on love, there is no hint of an apology for the stress on the particularity of the Christian message. Rather, it stresses that through the defeat of evil and the establishment of peace by Christ a new space of love has been created, capacious enough for all humanity and leading to a new identity whereby the old enmities are gone forever. As the writer is keen to remind us, the Father, after whom every family in heaven and earth takes its name, wishes all people to know his love (3:14), a love that centres around knowing Christ's love for us.

There are, of course, practical implications that flow from this daring affirmation in Ephesians of the uniqueness of the Lordship of Christ. We are given no encouragement to apologize for this doctrine as central to all we believe. We must relate it to all the truth found in the cosmos. We are called to embody Christ's and Paul's mode of communicating it—by suffering, by peacemaking, and by loving. We need to mature in a community of love and truth that is Christ-centred and faithful to his way of living. We need, sadly, to be prepared for fierce opposition and all sorts of enmity. The faith has to be worked out in practical living, taking the structures of society and church and transforming them in accordance with the gospel. And this brings us back to "living within the gospel."

IT IS TIME TO AFFIRM WHAT GOD IS DOING IN OUR DAY THROUGH HIS SPIRIT

I have spoken of some of the great challenges we face today. But we can overestimate those challenges. Secularism is not as attractive as some have claimed it to be. The materialistic secularism of Russia and Eastern Europe has blighted the lives of many millions of people. While the culture of acquisitiveness has been very successful in the free markets of the Western world, we dare not and must not assume that most people are now happy and contented with their lot. Winston Churchill's statement, spoken in the early days of World War II, rings true today: "Man's control has extended over practically every sphere—except over himself." We have only to look around us to be aware of the truth of that—whether in personal life, in the home, or in the community.

It is not only religious thinkers who recognize that secularism frustrates the deeply grounded aspirations of our hearts. Indeed, the poet Philip Larkin—himself unsympathetic to the church—points out the dilemma for modern people in his evocative poem, "Church Going":

> When churches fall completely out of use
> What shall we turn them into...
> ... superstition like belief must die
> and what remains when disbelief has gone?
> Grass, weedy pavements, brambles, buttress, sky,
> A shape less recognizable every week,
> A purpose more obscure.

Yet even for this humanist the church meant something:

> A serious house on earth it is,
> In whose blent air all our compulsions meet,
> Are recognized, and robed as destinies.
> And that much never can be obsolete,
> Since someone will forever be surprising
> A hunger in himself to be more serious...

It is "a serious house." And around the world, our Communion and, yes, other great churches too, are doing great things through the Holy Spirit. This century has witnessed the rise of what Lesslie Newbigin called the third great wave of Christianity—the Pentecostal or charismatic stream. Many millions of Christians have been transformed through this movement of the Spirit. Whatever stances we take towards certain aspects of this movement, we cannot deny that the Holy Spirit is central to Christian mission and service. He is central too in the Epistle to the Ephesians.

Every Christian has received the seal of the Spirit who "is the pledge of our heritage" (1:14) and empowers us for service in the world (3:16). As for the church, its task is to be built up in Christ "for a dwelling place of God in the Spirit" (2:22). The Spirit is the fountain of worship in prayer and praise; he is the source of wisdom and knowledge. He is the one who empowers Christian community and is the source of holiness in personal and communal life. We see the Spirit's activity in the call to the church to be a temple fit for God and for service in the world.

THE CHURCH'S TASK

So, what is the church's task today? I trust I have given some pointers. I have resisted the language of "reclaiming" because that suggests that the church has somehow departed from its heritage. I have preferred instead to emphasize the fact that now is the right time to remind ourselves of some great truths of our faith and of their relevance to this generation. We are not in the business of keeping the "rumour of God alive" as some have said. I am not interested in rumours but in the reality of faith, enlivening, enriching, and resourcing our people. If we wish to be a church on the move, it is to the living God that we must look—in complete assurance of faith and trust in his resources and not ours.

But the last word belongs to St. Paul. I have shown the parallels between the situation in Asia Minor and the problems and opportunities facing us in Canada, the United States, and Western Europe. The apostle's words (4:1) wing their way to us across the centuries: "I beg you then—I a prisoner for the Lord—as God has called you, live up to your calling."

THE MONTREAL DECLARATION OF ANGLICAN ESSENTIALS

"In essentials, unity; in non-essentials, liberty; in all things, charity."
—Richard Baxter, after St. Augustine

As members of the Anglican Church of Canada from every province and territory, and participants in the Essentials 1994 Conference in Montreal, we unite in praising God for his saving grace and for the fellowship we enjoy with our Lord and with each other. We affirm the following Christian essentials:

1. The Triune God

There is one God, self-revealed as three persons, "of one substance, power and eternity," the Father, the Son, and the Holy Spirit. For the sake of the gospel we decline proposals to modify of marginalize these names and we affirm their rightful place in prayer, liturgy, and hymnody. For the gospel invites us through the Holy Spirit to share eternally in the divine fellowship, as adopted children of the God in whose family Jesus Christ is both our Saviour and our brother. *(Deuteronomy 6:4; Isaiah 45:5; Matthew 28:19; 2 Corinthians 13:14; Galatians 4:4–6; 2 Thessalonians 2:13–14; 1 Peter 1:2; Jude 20–21. Cf. Article I of the 39 Articles, Book of Common Prayer [BCP], p. 699.)*

2. Creator, Redeemer and Sanctifier

The almighty triune God created a universe that was in every way good until creaturely rebellion disrupted it. Sin having intruded, God in love purposed to restore cosmic order through the calling of the covenant people Israel, the coming of Jesus Christ to redeem, the outpouring of the Holy Spirit to sanctify, the building up of the church for worship and witness, and the coming again of Christ in glory to make all things new. Works of miraculous power mark the unfolding of God's plan throughout history. *(Genesis 1–3; Isaiah 40:28; 65:17; Matthew 6:10; John 17:6; Acts 17:24–26, 28; 1 Corinthians 15:28; 2 Corinthians 5:19; Ephesians 1:11; 2 Timothy 3:16; Hebrews 11:3; Revelation 21:5. Cf. Article I.)*

3. The Word Made Flesh

Jesus Christ, the incarnate Son of God, born of the virgin Mary, sinless in life, raised bodily from the dead, and now reigning in glory though still present with his people through the Holy Spirit, is both the Jesus of history and the Christ of Scripture. He is God-with-us, the sole mediator between God and ourselves, the source of saving knowledge of the Godhead, and the giver of eternal life to the church catholic. *(Matthew 1:24–25; Mark 15:20–37; Luke 1:35; John 1:14; 17:20–21; Acts 1:9–11; 4:12; Romans 5:17; Philippians 2:5–6; Colossians 2:9; 1 Timothy 2:5–6; Hebrews 1:2; 9:15. Cf. Articles II–IV, the Nicene Creed, BCP.)*

4. The Only Saviour

Human sin is prideful rebellion against God's authority, expressing itself in our refusing to love both the Creator and his creatures. Sin corrupts our nature and its fruit is injustice, oppression, personal and social disintegration, alienation, and guilt before God; it destroys hope and leads to a future devoid of any enjoyment of either God or good. From the guilt, shame, power, and path of sin, Jesus Christ is the only Saviour; penitent faith in him is the only way of salvation.

By his atoning sacrifice on the cross for our sins, Jesus overcame the powers of darkness and secured our redemption and justification. By his bodily rising he guaranteed the future resurrection and eternal inheritance of all believers. By his regenerating gift of the Spirit, he restores our fallen nature and renews us in his own image. Thus in every generation he is the way, the truth, and the life for sinful individuals, and the architect of restored human community. *(John 14:6; Acts 1:9–11; 2:32–33; 4:12; Romans 3:22–25; 1 Corinthians 15:20–24; 2 Corinthians 5:18–19; Philippians 2:9–11; Colossians 2:13–15; 1 Timothy 2:5–6; 1 Peter 1:3–5; 1 John 4:14; 5:11–12. Cf. Articles II–IV, XI, XV, XVIII, XXXI.)*

5. The Spirit of Life

The Holy Spirit, "the Lord, the Giver of life," sent to the church at Pentecost by the Father and the Son, discloses the glory of Jesus Christ, convicts of sin, renews the sinner's inner being, induces faith, equips for righteousness, creates communion, and empowers for service. Life in the Spirit is a supernaturalizing of our natural existence and a true foretaste of heaven. The loving unity of Spirit-filled Christians and churches is a powerful sign of the truth of Christianity. *(Genesis 1:2; Exodus 31:2–5; Psalm 51:11; John 3:5–6; 14:26; 15:26; 16:7–11; 13–15; 1 Corinthians 2:4; 6:19; 12:4–7; 2 Corinthians 3:18; Galatians 4:4–6; 5:22–26; Ephesians 1:13–14; 5:18; 1 Thessalonians 5:19; 2 Timothy 3:16. Cf. Article V, the Nicene Creed.)*

6. The Authority of the Bible

The canonical Scriptures of the Old and New Testaments are "God's Word written," inspired and authoritative, true and trustworthy, coherent, sufficient for salvation, living and powerful as God's guidance for belief and behaviour.

The trinitarian, Christ-centred, redemption-oriented faith of the Bible is embodied in the historic ecumenical creeds and the Anglican foundational documents. To this basic understanding of Scripture, the Holy Spirit leads God's people and the church's counsels in every age through tradition and reason prayerfully and reverently employed.

The church may not judge the Scriptures, selecting and discarding from among their teachings. But Scripture under Christ judges the church for its faithfulness to his revealed truth. *(Deuteronomy 29:29; Isaiah 40:8; 55:11; Matthew 5:17–18; John 10:35; 14:26; Romans 1:16; Ephesians 1:17–19; 2 Timothy 2:15; 3:14–17; 2 Peter 1:20–21. Cf. Articles VI–VIII, XX.)*

7. The Church of God

The supernatural society called the church is the family of God, the body of Christ, and the temple of the Holy Spirit. It is the community of believers, justified through faith in Christ, incorporated into the risen life of Christ, and set under the authority of Holy Scripture as the word of Christ. The church on earth is united through Christ to the church in heaven in the communion of the saints. Through the church's ministry of the word and sacraments of the gospel, God ministers life in Christ to the faithful, thereby empowering them for worship, witness, and service.

In the life of the church only that which may be proved from Scripture should be held to be essential to the faith and that which is non-essential should not be required of anyone to be believed or be enforced as a matter of doctrine, discipline, or worship. *(Ephesians 3:10–21; 5:23, 27; 1 Timothy 3:15; Hebrews 12:1–2; 2 Timothy 3:14–17. Cf. Articles XIX, XX, and XXI.)*

8. The New Life in Christ

God made human beings in the divine image so that they might glorify and enjoy their creator forever, but since the fall, sin has alienated us all from God and disorders human motivation and action at every point. As atonement and justification restore us to fellowship with God by pardoning sin, so regeneration and sanctification renew us in the likeness of Christ by overcoming sin. The Holy Spirit, who helps us practice the disciplines of the Christian life, increasingly transforms us through them. Sinlessness, however, is not given in this world, and we who believe remain flawed "in thought, word and deed" until we are perfected in heaven. *(Genesis 1:26–28; 3; John 3:5–6; 16:13; Romans 3:23–24; 5:12; 1 Corinthians 12:4–7; 2 Corinthians 3:17–18; Galatians 5:22–24; Ephesians 2:1–5; Philippians 2:13; 2 Peter 3:10–13. Cf. Articles IX–XVI; Book of Alternative Services, p. 191.)*

9. The Church's Ministry

The Holy Spirit bestows distinctive gifts upon all Christians for the purpose of glorifying God and building up his church in truth and love. All Christians are called in their baptism to be ministers, regardless of gender, race, age, or socio-economic status. All God's people must seek to find and fulfil the particular form of service for which God has called and equipped them.

Within the priesthood of all believers we honour the ministry of word and sacrament of which bishops, priests, and deacons are set apart by the Ordinal. *(Romans 12:6–8; 1 Corinthians 3:16; 6:11; 12:4–7, 27; 2 Corinthians 5:20; Galatians 2:16; Ephesians 4:11–13; 1 Timothy 3:1, 12–13; 5:17; Hebrews 2:11; 1 Peter 2:4–5; 9–10. Cf. Articles XIX, XXIII.)*

10. The Church's Worship

The primary calling of the church, as of every Christian, is to offer worship, in the Spirit and according to truth, to the God of creation, providence, and grace. The essential dimensions of worship are praise and thanksgiving for all good things, proclamation and celebration of the glory of God and of Jesus Christ, prayer for human needs and for the advancement of Christ's kingdom, and self-offering for service. All liturgical forms— verbal, musical, and ceremonial—stand under the authority of Scripture.

The Book of Common Prayer provides a biblically grounded doctrinal standard, and should be retained as the norm for all alternative liturgies. It should not be revised in the theologically divided climate of the contemporary church. The Book of Alternative Services meets a widely felt need for contemporary liturgy, and brings life and joy to many Anglican worshippers.

No form of worship can truly exalt Christ or draw forth true devotion to him without the presence and power of the Holy Spirit. Prayer, public and private, is central to the health and renewal of the church. Healing, spiritual and physical, is a welcome aspect of Anglican worship. *(John 4:24; 16:8–15; Acts 1:8; 2:42–47; Romans 12:1; 1 Corinthians 11:23– 26; 12:7; 2 Corinthians 5:18–19; Ephesians 5:18–20; Colossians 3:16; 1 Thessalonians 1:4–5; 5:19. Cf. The Solemn Declaration of 1893, p. viii, BCP; Articles XXV, XXXIV.)*

11. The Priority of Evangelism

Evangelism means proclaiming Jesus Christ as divine Saviour, Lord, and Friend, in a way that invites people to come to God through him, to worship and serve him, and to seek the empowering of the Holy Spirit for their life of discipleship in the community of the church. All Christians are called to witness to Christ, as a sign of love both to him and to their neighbours. The task, which is thus a matter of priority, calls for personal training and a constant search for modes of persuasive outreach. We sow the seed, and look to God for the fruit. (*Matthew 5:13–16; 28:19–20; John 3:16–18; 20:21; Acts 2:37–39; 5:31–32; 1 Corinthians 1:23; 15:2–4; 2 Corinthians 4:5; 5:20; 1 Peter 3:15.*)

12. The Challenge of Global Mission

Cross-cultural evangelism and pastoral care remain necessary responses to the Great Commission of Jesus Christ. His command to preach the gospel worldwide, making disciples and planting churches, still applies. The church's mission requires missions.

Christ and his salvation must be proclaimed sensitively and energetically everywhere, at home and abroad, and cross-cultural mission must be supported by praying, giving, and sending. Global mission involves partnership and interchange, and missionaries sent by younger churches to Canada should be welcomed. (*Matthew 28:19–20; Mark 16:15; Luke 10:2; Romans 15:23–24; 1 Corinthians 2:4–5; 9:22–23; 2 Corinthians 4:5; 8:1–4, 7; Ephesians 6:19–20; Philippians 2:5–7; 1 Thessalonians 1:6–8.*)

13. The Challenge of Social Action

The gospel constrains the church to be "salt" and "light" in the world, working out the implications of biblical teaching for the right ordering of social, economic, and political life, and for humanity's stewardship of creation. Christians must exert themselves in the cause of justice and in acts of compassion. While no social system can be identified with the coming kingdom of God, social action is an integral part of our obedience to the gospel. (*Genesis 1:26–28; Isaiah 30:18; 58:6–10; Amos 5:24; Matthew 5:13–16; 22:37–40; 25:31–46; Luke 4:17–21; John 20:21; 2 Corinthians 1:3–4; James 2:14–26; 1 John 4:16; Revelation 1:5–6; 5:9–10. Cf. Article XXXVIII.*)

14. The Standards of Sexual Conduct

God designed human sexuality not only for procreation but also for the joyful expression of love, honour, and fidelity between wife and husband. These are the only sexual relations that biblical theology deems good and holy.

Adultery, fornication, and homosexual unions are intimacies contrary to God's design. The church must seek to minister healing and wholeness to those who are sexually scarred, or who struggle with ongoing sexual temptations, as most people do. Homophobia and all forms of sexual hypocrisy and abuse are evils against which Christians must ever be on their guard. The church may not lower God's standards of sexual morality for any of its members, but must honour God by upholding these standards tenaciously in face of society's departures from them.

Congregations must seek to meet the particular needs for friendship and community that single persons have. (*Genesis 1:26–28; 2:21–24; Matthew 5:27–32; 19:3–12; Luke 7:36–50; John 8:1–11; Romans 1:21–28; 3:22–24; 1 Corinthians 6:9–11, 13–16; 7:7; Ephesians 5:3; 1 Timothy 1:8–11; 3:2–4, 12.*)

15. The Family and the Call to Singleness

The family is a divinely ordained focus of love, intimacy, personal growth, and stability for women, men, and children. Divorce, child abuse, domestic violence, rape, pornography, parental absenteeism, sexist domination, abortion, common-law relationships, and homosexual partnerships, all reflect weakening of the family ideal. Christians must strengthen family life through teaching, training, and active support, and work for sociopolitical conditions that support the family. Single-parent families and victims of family breakdown have special needs to which congregations must respond with sensitivity and support.

Singleness also is a gift from God and a holy vocation. Single people are called to celibacy and God will give them grace to live in chastity. (Psalm 119:9–11; Proverbs 22:6; Matthew 5:31–32; Mark 10:6–9; 1 Corinthians 6:9–11; Ephesians 5:21–6:4; Colossians 3:18–21; 1 John 3:14–15.)

The New Beginning

Together we reaffirm the Anglican Christianity that finds expression in the historic standards of the ecumenical creeds, the Thirty-Nine Articles, the Solemn Declaration of 1893, and the 1962 Book of Common Prayer. Respect for these standards strengthens our identity and communion. In humility we recognize we have often been ashamed of the gospel we have received and disobedient to the Lord of the church. God helping us, we resolve to maintain our heritage of faith and transmit it intact. This fullness of faith is needed both for Anglican renewal and for the effective proclamation of the good news of Jesus Christ in the power of the Holy Spirit.

We invite all Anglicans to join us in affirming the above as essentials of Christian faith, practice, and nurture today. In this declaration we believe that we are insisting upon only what is genuinely essential. In regard to non-essentials, we should recognize and respect that liberty and that comprehensiveness which have been among the special graces of our Anglican heritage.

Participants in Essentials 94, with the Sponsoring Bodies:
Anglican Renewal Ministries of Canada;
Barnabas Anglican Ministries;
The Prayer Book Society of Canada.

21 June 1994, Montreal, Canada

CONTRIBUTORS

CHARLES ALEXANDER

Born and raised in Liverpool, England, Charles Alexander was ordained in the Diocese of Brandon in 1965 after training in Saskatoon. He served with parishes in Snow Lake and Neepawa, Manitoba, then moved to Calgary, where he lived for seventeen years. Charles has been rector of the Church of St. Mary of the Incarnation, Metchosin, on Vancouver Island, since 1987. He recently established the Timothy Institute of Ministry to promote skills in evangelism and develop leadership for a future church. The founding chairperson of Anglican Renewal Ministries, Charles is the author of *Power to Serve* (1986.)

ANTHONY BURTON

Anthony Burton is the youngest Anglican bishop in the world. Born in Ottawa, he was educated at Trinity College (Toronto), Dalhousie University, and Oxford University. Anthony served in two Nova Scotia parishes before being appointed dean of St. Alban's Cathedral in Prince Albert, Saskatchewan, in 1991. He was consecrated bishop of Saskatchewan in 1993.

FRED CARSON

Fred Carson is a graduate of Huron College, London, Ontario, a holds a Bachelor of Ministry degree. He was ordained as deacon in 1973 and as priest in 1974. Fred has had a special interest in the healing ministry for many years. He studied substance abuse at McMaster University, from which he received a diploma in Addiction Studies. A chaplain with the Order of St. Luke, Fred has served in Ontario, Alberta, and Manitoba, and has spent several years in the north ministering among both native and non-native Canadians in isolated situations. He is the incumbent of St. John's Church in Richmond Hill, Ontario, and in 1992 was appointed national director of Sharing Of Ministries Abroad (SOMA), Canada.

ROBERT CROUSE

Robert Crouse is a priest of the Diocese of Nova Scotia, and since 1963 has taught as professor of Classics at Dalhousie University. Educated at Dalhousie, University of King's College (Halifax), Trinity College (Toronto), Tübingen University, and Harvard University, where he received his Ph.D., he was awarded an honorary Doctor of Divinity degree from Trinity College in 1983. Robert has taught at Trinity, Harvard, Bishop's University, and Dalhousie-King's. He has been appointed as visiting professor of Patrology for 1995 at the Institutum Patristicum Augustinianum, Pontifical Lateran University, Rome, where he also served in 1990–91. The author of many essays and articles on historical and theological subjects, Robert is the examining chaplain to the Bishop of Nova Scotia.

RON DART

Ron Dart teaches in the Political Science department at University College of the Fraser Valley, British Columbia. He is a member of St. Matthew's parish in Abbotsford, and he is the deanery representative on the New Westminster Diocesan Council. In 1992–93, Ron served as facilitator of an eighteen-part lecture series called "A Brief History of Anglicanism." Ron was on staff with Amnesty International for five years, and is currently the national country coordinator of Saudi Arabia and Kuwait.

GEORGE EGERTON

George Egerton is associate professor of History at the University of British Columbia, where he has taught since 1972; prior to this he taught for two years at Memorial University of Newfoundland. A native of Winnipeg, he holds degrees from the Universities of Manitoba, Minnesota, and Toronto, the latter from which he received his doctorate in History in 1970. He is the author of *Great Britain and the Creation of the League of Nations* (1978) and editor of *Political Memoir: Essays in the Politics of Memory* (1994). George teaches and writes in the field of international history and is currently working on the religious history of post-World War II Canada.

CRAIG GAY

Craig M. Gay is associate professor of Interdisciplinary Studies at Regent College in Vancouver. Originally from California, Craig holds an undergraduate degree in Urban Planning from Stanford University and degrees in Theology from Regent College and Boston University. Teaching in the area of "Religion and Society," Craig's research interest focuses on the process of secularization in modern societies and extends more broadly to modern society and culture. He has also published in the area of Christian social and economic ethics.

MICHAEL GREEN

Michael Green holds master's degrees from both Oxford and Cambridge Universities, and in 1992, he received an honorary Doctor of Divinity degree from the University of Toronto. He served as principal of St. John's College, Nottingham, from 1969 to 1975, and then as rector of St. Aldate's Church, Oxford, from 1975 to 1986. In 1987 he joined the faculty of Regent College, Vancouver, as professor of Evangelism, returning to England in 1993 to serve as Adviser in Evangelism to the Archbishops of Canterbury and York. The author of some thirty books, many on evangelism, Michael has recently published *Evangelism and the Local Church* (1991), and *Who Is This Jesus?* (1992).

ROBIN GUINNESS

Robin Guinness was born into a vicarage in Hove, and in 1963, after studies at Cambridge University, was ordained as deacon in Coventry Cathedral. He served as a curate in the parish of Bedworth, then served in association with the Church Missionary Society for two years and with Inter-Varsity Christian Fellowship in Ontario from 1968 to 1970. Before becoming rector of St. Stephen's-Westmount in 1975, Robin served as assistant minister at Little Trinity Church, Toronto, and as rector of Holy Trinity Church, Lakefield, Quebec, from 1972 to 1974. He was made a canon of Christ Church Cathedral, Montreal, in 1992.

REGINALD HOLLIS

Reginald Hollis was ordained in 1956 after graduating from Cambridge and McGill Universities. Before being elected Bishop of Montreal in 1974, he served as university chaplain, seminary lecturer, and parish priest, all within the Diocese of Montreal. He was elected archbishop of the ecclesiastical province of Canada in 1989. When he was appointed as international director of the Anglican Fellowship of Prayer, he resigned from his diocese and became assistant bishop in the Episcopal Diocese of Central Florida. He recently returned to parish ministry as rector of St. Paul, New Smyrna Beach, Florida. Reginald is the author of *Abiding in Christ: A Series of Meditations on The Lord's Prayer and the Ten Commandments* (1987).

EDITH HUMPHREY

Edith Humphrey is a specialist in New Testament and early Christian origins. After completing a degree in Classics at Victoria University, Toronto, she earned her doctorate in the faculty of Religious Studies at McGill University in 1991. Since then she has lectured in Hebrew Bible and New Testament at Carleton University, Bishop's University, Wycliffe College, and McGill, where she is presently instructing. Edith is the author of *The Ladies and the Cities: Transformation and Apocalyptic Identity in Joseph and Aseneth, 4 Ezra, the Apocalypse and the Shepherd of Hermas* (Sheffield: JSOT Press, forthcoming).

GRANT LEMARQUAND

Grant LeMarquand is a priest of the Diocese of Montreal. A graduate of McGill University, Grant is writing a doctoral dissertation in New Testament studies that explores the differences between biblical hermeneutics in Africa and the Western world. Formerly a lecturer in New Testament and Theology at St. Paul's United Theological College, Limuru, Kenya, Grant is currently the director of Extension Studies and lecturer in Homiletics at Wycliffe College, Toronto.

DON LEWIS

Don Lewis holds an undergraduate degree in History from Bishop's University in Quebec, a master's degree from Regent College in Vancouver, and a doctorate in Theology from Oxford University. Since 1981 he has taught at Regent College. A church historian, Don has published several articles and a book on popular Victorian religion. He is also the editor of *Crux*, an academic journal published by Regent College. He has recently completed the editing of *The Blackwell Dictionary of Evangelical Biography, 1730–1860* (1995).

THOMAS MAXWELL

Thomas W. Maxwell holds a Bachelor of Arts degree from the University of Alberta, a Licentiate in Theology from St. Chad's College, Regina, and a Bachelor of Sacred Theology from Trinity College, Toronto. Ordained as a priest in the Anglican Church of Canada in 1957, Tom has served parishes in Toronto, Winnipeg, Montreal, and Edmonton. He was appointed as a canon in the Diocese of Montreal and served as a diocesan archdeacon for nine years in Edmonton. He is currently rector of St. Paul's Anglican Church, Edmonton, and national coordinator of Anglican Renewal Ministries, Canada.

PETER MASON

Peter Mason is bishop of the Diocese of Ontario. He holds degrees from McGill University and Montreal Diocesan Theological College, and a D.Min. from Princeton Theological Seminary. He has served as principal of Wycliffe College (1985–1992), lecturer in Homiletics, Atlantic School of Theology, Halifax, Nova Scotia (1983–1985), and rector of St. Paul's Church, Halifax (1980–1985). Peter is presently a member of the Primate's Commission on Evangelism, the Doctrine and Worship Committee of General Synod, and the National Executive Council Task Force on Homosexuality.

ALISTER E. MCGRATH

Alister E. McGrath is lecturer in Historical and Systematic Theology, Wycliffe Hall, Oxford, and research professor of Theology at Regent College. He is also research lecturer in the faculty of Theology at Oxford University. Author of many popular and academic works of theology, including *Luther's Theology of the Cross* (1985), *The Making of Modern German Christology* (1986), and *The Genesis of Doctrine* (1990), Alister has recently addressed current issues within the international Anglican communion in *The Renewal of Anglicanism* (1993).

PETER C. MOORE

Peter C. Moore holds degrees from Yale (B.A.), Oxford (M.A.), Eastern Theological Seminary (M.Div.), and Fuller (D.Min.) and is the author of several books and articles, including *Disarming the Secular Gods* (1989), *One Lord, One Faith* (1994), and *A Church to Believe In* (1994). After founding a ministry to secondary school students in the United States and helping to establish Trinity Episcopal School for Ministry in Ambridge, Pennsylvania, where he served as board chairman, he became the tenth rector of Little Trinity Anglican Church in Toronto in 1985. Peter also serves as the North American secretary of the Evangelical Fellowship in the Anglican Communion, of which Barnabas Anglican Ministries is the Canadian affiliate.

JAMES I. PACKER

James I. Packer was born in England and educated at Oxford University where he earned degrees in Classics and Theology. He received his Doctor of Philosophy degree in 1954. Ordained in 1952, he served as assistant minister at St. John's Church, Harborne, Birmingham, until 1954, and then as senior tutor at Tyndale Hall, an Anglican Seminary in Bristol, from 1955 to 1961. Then, after nine years as warden of Latimer House, an Anglican evangelical study centre in Oxford, he returned to Bristol to become principal of Tyndale Hall in 1970. In 1979 he was appointed professor of Systematic and Historical Theology at Regent College, Vancouver, where in 1989 he was installed as the first Sangwoo Youtong Chee Professor of Theology. Among his many books are *Fundamentalism and the Word of God* (1958), *Knowing God* (1973), *Beyond the Battle for the Bible* (1980), *A Quest for Godliness* (1990), *Rediscovering Holiness* (1992), and *Concise Theology* (1993). Dr. Packer is a senior editor and visiting scholar for *Christianity Today*.

ARCHIBALD PELL

Archie Pell is a chaplain with the Canadian Forces, currently serving as pastor of Christ Church Anglican parish in Hope, British Columbia. He holds six degrees, including a Master of Social Work degree from the University of Toronto, and a Doctor of Ministry degree from Luther Northwestern Theological Seminary, St. Paul, Minnesota.

BARBARA PELL

Barbara Pell is associate professor of English at Trinity Western University in Langley, British Columbia. She holds a doctorate in Canadian Literature from the University of Toronto. Barbara has taught at Mohawk College and Redeemer College, both in Hamilton, Ontario, and at the University of Toronto.

HAROLD PERCY

A graduate of York University and Wycliffe College, Harold Percy is rector of Trinity Church, Streetsville, in the Diocese of Toronto, and director of the Wycliffe College Institute of Evangelism. He travels widely throughout the Anglican Church of Canada, conducting training events in the areas of congregational vitality and evangelism. Harold is the author of *Following Jesus: First Steps on the Way* (1993), and writes a monthly column on evangelism, "Sharing the Joy," in the *Anglican Journal*.

DONALD POSTERSKI

Don Posterski is vice president of national programmes for World Vision Canada and co-director for Project Teen Canada, which interprets North American cultural trends and their implications to educators, parents, government policy-makers, and church leaders. His past ministry includes seven years of pastoring and fifteen years with Inter-Varsity Christian Fellowship, where he devoted himself to full-time student ministry. He is the author of several studies relating to youth ministry, including *Friendship* (1985) and, with Reginald Bibby, *The Emerging Generation* (1985) and *Teen Trends* (1992). Don's latest book, *"Where's a Good Church?" Canadians Respond from the Pulpit, Podium and Pew* (1993), is based on research that assessed the characteristics of effective churches.

ELAINE POUNTNEY

Elaine Pountney holds a Master of Education degree in Counselling Psychology from McGill University, and a Bachelor of Science degree in Chemistry from the University of Alberta. As well as having a private practice in counselling individuals, couples, and families, Elaine is a frequent speaker at Christian conferences and retreats, addressing pastoral issues related to integrating a Christian understanding of personhood with professional psychological theory. Her special interests include spiritual direction, women's issues, marriage counselling, stress management, and use of the Myers-Briggs Type Inventory.

HARRY ROBINSON

Harry Robinson was born and raised in the parish of St. John's, York Mills, Toronto. He is a graduate of University and Wycliffe Colleges (University of Toronto), and Oak Hill College (University of London), and holds an honorary doctorate from Wycliffe College. He has served as rector of Little Trinity Church in Toronto (1963–1978), and of St. John's Shaughnessy in Vancouver (1978–1992), and is a canon of St. James Cathedral in Toronto. Harry is currently director of Nanton Avenue Ministries, which supports work in teaching, preaching, conferences, and pastoral ministry.

TONY TYNDALE

Tony Tyndale was born and raised in England and was educated at Winchester College and the Royal Military College during World War II. He joined the Royal Dragoon Guards as a career officer, and served in Europe, Palestine, and the Korean War over a period of eleven years. He received a Master of Arts degree in Russian Language and Literature at Oxford University. Retiring in 1954 to accept an invitation from Canadian Inter-Varsity Christian Fellowship, Tony worked with students for twenty-five years. He received a master's and a doctorate degree in Adult Education, and has served on the faculty of Wycliffe College for the past eight years. His cross-cultural experience includes twelve years with the South American Missionary Society (SAMS) Canada, and teaching and training on every continent, including northern Canada, where he taught Inuit ordinands. Tony is currently engaged in a series of teaching visits in Africa.

JOHN PAUL WESTIN

John Paul Westin was born into an Anglican rectory in Montreal, and grew up in Jamaica and the provinces of New Brunswick, Nova Scotia, and Prince Edward Island. He did his undergraduate work at the University of King's College, Halifax, and received a master's degree in Classics from Dalhousie University, Halifax. He continued his graduate studies at the University of Toronto School of Theology, and Uppsala University, Sweden, graduating with a Master of Divinity degree from Wycliffe College, Toronto, in 1986. John Paul has been active in youth ministry, founding the St. Michael Youth Conference, P. E. I., for teenagers in 1987 and serving as director until 1993. He has also been active in promoting classical Christianity through the Prayer Book Society of Canada since its inception in 1985. For seven years he was rector of the parish of Riviere and New Dublin, Nova Scotia, and is currently rector of the Church of St. John the Evangelist in Montreal.

JOHN WEBSTER

John Webster is professor of Systematic Theology at Wycliffe College, University of Toronto. He holds a master's degree and a doctorate from Cambridge University. John is an honorary assistant at the Church of St. Bride, Clarkson, in the Diocese of Toronto. The author of books and articles on contemporary theology, he is also a member of the Anglican Church of Canada's Doctrine and Worship Committee and the Book of Alternative Services Evaluation Commission.

LOREN WILKINSON

Since 1981 Loren Wilkinson has been professor of Inter-Disciplinary Studies and Philosophy at Regent College, Vancouver. He holds degrees from Wheaton College, Johns Hopkins University, Trinity Evangelical Divinity School, and Syracuse University, where he received his doctorate in 1972. The author of many articles on the environmental movement, particularly its religious dimensions and relationship to New Age spirituality, Loren's books include: *Earthkeeping: Christian Stewardship of National Resources* (1980), *Earthkeeping in the 90's: Stewardship of Creation* (1991), *Caring for Creation in Your Own Backyard*, with Mary Ruth Wilkinson (1992), and *Alive to God: Studies in Spirituality, Presented to James Houston*, with J. I. Packer (1992). Loren is active in the environmental movement, bringing Christian advocacy and spirituality to the stewardship of God's creation.